MICROSOFT®
QUICKBASIC
THIRD EDITION

MICROSOFT®
QUICKBASIC

THIRD EDITION

*Developing Structured Programs in
the Microsoft QuickBASIC Environment*

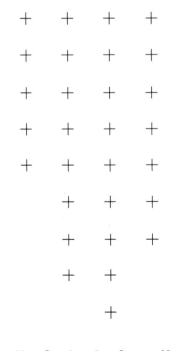

D O U G L A S   H E R G E R T

PUBLISHED BY
Microsoft Press
A Division of Microsoft Corporation
16011 NE 36th Way, Box 97017, Redmond, Washington 98073-9717

Library of Congress Cataloging in Publication Data

Hergert, Douglas.
Microsoft QuickBASIC.
Includes index.
     1. BASIC (Computer program language)   2. Microsoft QuickBASIC (Computer
program)   I. Title.
QA76.73.B3H48   1989   005.13'3   89-35201
ISBN 1-55615-236-1

Printed and bound in the United States of America.

1 2 3 4 5 6 7 8 9   MLML   3 2 1 0 9

Distributed to the book trade in the United States
by Harper & Row.

Distributed to the book trade in Canada by General
Publishing Company, Ltd.

Distributed to the book trade outside the United States
and Canada by Penguin Books Ltd.

Penguin Books Ltd., Harmondsworth, Middlesex, England
Penguin Books Australia Ltd., Ringwood, Victoria, Australia
Penguin Books N.Z. Ltd., 182-190 Wairau Road, Auckland 10, New Zealand

British Cataloging in Publication Data available

IBM®, PC/AT®, and PS/2® are registered trademarks of International Business Machines
Corporation.

Microsoft® and MS-DOS® are registered trademarks of Microsoft Corporation.

CONTENTS

SPECIAL OFFER

Companion Disk for
MICROSOFT® QUICKBASIC, 3rd ed.

Microsoft Press has created a Companion Disk for MICROSOFT QUICKBASIC, 3rd ed. This disk is available in either 5.25-inch or 3.5-inch format and contains QuickBASIC source code for the six major programs and two sample programs listed in the book—more than 4,900 lines of code. This companion disk for MICROSOFT QUICKBASIC is an essential resource for anyone who wants to forego the drudgery of typing code (and the time required to find and correct those inevitable typing errors) and begin to learn structured programming in QuickBASIC immediately.

If you have any questions or comments about the files on the disk, send your written queries to Douglas Hergert, c/o Microsoft Press, 16011 NE 36th Way, Box 97017, Redmond, WA 98073-9717.

The Companion Disk for MICROSOFT QUICKBASIC is available only from Microsoft Press.

Domestic Ordering Information:
To order, use the special reply card bound in the back of the book. If the card has already been used, please send $19.95, plus sales tax if applicable (CA residents 5% plus local option tax, CT 7.5%, FL 6%, KY 5%, MA 5%, MN 6%, MO 4.225%, NY 4% plus local option tax, WA state 7.8%), and $2.50 per disk set for domestic postage and handling charges. Mail your order to: Microsoft Press, Attn: Companion Disk Offer, 21919 20th Ave SE, Box 3011, Bothell, WA 98041-3011. Specify 5.25-inch or 3.5-inch format. Payment must be in U.S. funds. You may pay by check or money order (payable to Microsoft Press) or by American Express, VISA, or MasterCard; please include both your credit card number and the expiration date. Allow 2–3 weeks for delivery.

Foreign Ordering Information (except within the U.K., see below):
Follow procedures for domestic ordering and add $6.00 per disk set for foreign postage and handling.

U.K. Ordering Information:
Send your order in writing along with £17.95 (includes VAT) to: Microsoft Press, 27 Wrights Lane, London W8 5TZ. You may pay by check or money order (payable to Microsoft Press) or by American Express, VISA, MasterCard, or Diners Club; please include both your credit card number and the expiration date. Specify 5.25-inch or 3.5-inch format.

Microsoft Press Companion Disk Guarantee
If this disk proves defective, send the defective disk along with your packing slip (or copy) to: Microsoft Press, Consumer Sales, 16011 NE 36th Way, Box 97017, Redmond, WA 98073-9717.

INTRODUCTION

Microsoft QuickBASIC is a powerful programming environment in which you can create applications for IBM personal computers and compatibles. Whatever your programming background, you will appreciate the outstanding new features of QuickBASIC 4.0 and 4.5, which include:

- The "smart" editor that checks syntax and interprets each line as you enter it, allowing you to run your program instantly at any point in the development process.

- An on-line help facility that gives you fast descriptions of QuickBASIC commands or functions.

- Support for modular programming that enables you to build programs consisting of multiple-module files.

- Powerful debugging tools that give you efficient ways to explore the logic of a program.

- Built-in compiler options that generate fast stand-alone programs that can be performed directly from MS-DOS, and Quick libraries of compiled procedures that you can incorporate into new programming projects.

- A structured BASIC language, offering many important new elements, including subprograms and functions, parameter passing, local and global variables, a wide variety of structured decisions and loops, data types, record structures, an expanded library of built-in functions, and support for interlanguage procedure calls.

This book is for BASIC programmers who are ready to make the transition to a professional programming environment. The aim is to teach structured programming techniques through a collection of useful application examples. Six major programs appear in the book:

- **List,** an MS-DOS–style utility program that illustrates the use of data types and data structures.

- **Twenty-one,** a game program that displays the power of QuickBASIC's control structures—decisions and loops.

- **Survey,** an information-gathering and data-analysis program that shows how to create and use sequential data files.

- **Employee,** a company database management program that demonstrates the techniques of random-access file handling.

- **QuickChart,** a chart-creating and table-creating utility that illustrates many of QuickBASIC's powerful graphics commands.

- **Advanced Menu,** a menu-driven user interface that exploits the power of event trapping.

These programs are presented as exercises—for you to explore, study, use, and revise.

How this book is organized

The book contains two parts. Part I, "Introduction to QuickBASIC," is a concise and informal introduction to the development tools and language elements in Microsoft QuickBASIC.

Chapter 1, "Understanding the QuickBASIC Environment," introduces the important new development tools and language features of QuickBASIC 4.0 and 4.5. The chapter summarizes the features of the environment and surveys the QuickBASIC menus.

Chapter 2, "Using Subprograms and Functions," begins a continuing discussion of structured programming, focusing on QuickBASIC's two procedure structures: subprograms and functions.

Chapter 3, "Building Programs," describes three techniques for introducing tested procedures into a current programming project. You'll learn to merge procedures directly into a program, to create a program from multiple-module files, and to load a Quick library into the QuickBASIC development environment.

The six chapters of Part II, "Language Topics and Sample Programs," present a diverse collection of QuickBASIC programs. These programs serve two purposes. First, as learning exercises, they illustrate specific QuickBASIC commands and structured programming techniques. Second, they are useful applications that you can work with and revise to meet your own programming needs. Each chapter is a self-contained tutorial on the use of a particular language element, in the context of a specific programming application.

Chapter 4, "Data Types and Data Structures: The *List* Program," reviews and illustrates the data types and data structures available in

QuickBASIC, including strings, numeric types, logical values, arrays, and record structures. The *List* program is an enhancement of the MS-DOS directory (dir) command. The program displays directory listings in a variety of sorted orders and allows you to select files by date.

Chapter 5, "Decisions and Loops: The *Twenty-one* Program," focuses on the control structures available in QuickBASIC—the IF and SELECT CASE decision structures and the DO and FOR loop structures. The *Twenty-one* game program contains many examples of these powerful control structures.

Chapter 6, "Sequential Data Files: The *Survey* Program," demonstrates effective techniques for working with sequential data files. The *Survey* program uses sequential data files to generate survey questionnaires and analyze the results. The program is useful for conducting surveys such as opinion polls, customer satisfaction surveys, and consumer attitude surveys.

Chapter 7, "Random-Access Data Files: The *Employee* Program," covers the QuickBASIC commands and functions especially designed for handling random-access files. You'll learn how to use QuickBASIC's new record structure to streamline the tasks of random-access file programming. The chapter presents a database management program, called *Employee,* which works with a database of employee profiles. The program illustrates a variety of database management techniques: adding records to a database, locating and displaying records, modifying records, and printing tables of records.

Chapter 8, "Graphics: The *QuickChart* Program," focuses on QuickBASIC's graphics commands and functions. The *QuickChart* program produces three kinds of charts on the computer's display screen—column charts, line charts, and pie charts—to illustrate QuickBASIC's powerful graphics commands. The program also demonstrates techniques for producing graphics effects on text-only display hardware and for printing charts on printers of varying graphics capabilities.

Chapter 9, "Event Trapping: The *Advanced Menu* Program," describes the techniques of event trapping in QuickBASIC and surveys the programming tools available for responding to specific external events. The *Advanced Menu* program is a menu-driven interface for all the other applications in this book. The program contains interesting illustrations of event trapping.

This book teaches programming techniques through a collection of realistic and useful application examples. As you study and work with each exercise, you'll expand your skills and refine your understanding of structured programming in Microsoft QuickBASIC.

PART

I

Introduction to QuickBASIC

CHAPTER 1

Understanding the QuickBASIC Environment

Microsoft QuickBASIC is a new kind of programming environment that combines the speed and efficiency of Microsoft's latest compiler technology with the immediacy and convenience of an interpreter. In this chapter you'll explore this new environment and discover how it streamlines the steps of program development. You'll also take a brief first look at some major new QuickBASIC language features.

Later in the chapter you'll examine the various menu tools you can use to create, edit, save, run, and debug QuickBASIC programs. You'll see how the menu-driven user interface works, and you'll survey the features it offers. This chapter is no substitute for the detailed introduction in the QuickBASIC documentation, but the summary presented here will give you a broad perspective of the QuickBASIC package.

THE QUICKBASIC PROGRAMMING ENVIRONMENT

You begin a session with QuickBASIC by typing the QB command from the MS-DOS prompt:

```
C>QB
```

When you do so, QuickBASIC's menu line appears at the top of the screen, and the flashing cursor shows you that the editor is ready to accept the first statements of a new program. You are in the QuickBASIC programming environment.

The practical details of this environment—the menu commands, the display screens, the keyboard and mouse operations, and so on—are clear and intuitive. Whether your programming background is in the BASICA interpreter or a previous version of QuickBASIC, you will find these details easy to master. But before you begin to create new programs, you should learn about QuickBASIC's most important design features:

- The "smart" editor
- The QB Advisor
- Windows in the QuickBASIC environment
- Multiple-module programs
- The debugging facility
- Stand-alone compiled programs (EXE files)
- Quick libraries

The following sections briefly describe each of these features.

The "smart" editor

The QuickBASIC "smart" editor is much more than a tool for entering and revising the text of a program. The editor performs several important tasks—instantly and almost invisibly—as you enter each program line from the keyboard:

- First, the editor checks the syntax of the line. If a line of code contains a syntax error, QuickBASIC recognizes the problem and displays a message box on the screen that tells you what is wrong.

- The editor also ensures that each new line of code conforms to QuickBASIC's standard line format. You can enter each line in any convenient way; the editor automatically reformats the line to match the standard format. In QuickBASIC's standard format, reserved words appear in capital letters, and operators and operands are separated by spaces.

- Finally, QuickBASIC stores the line in memory in a translated form. The result is that each new line—and, in fact, the entire program—is ready to run as soon as you enter it into the editor. For all practical purposes, there is no longer a compile step between editing and running; the program runs almost as soon as you give the command.

The smart editor is the entry point into QuickBASIC's instant environment—an environment that offers greater speed of execution along with a streamlined development process. But the editor has other convenient features. A number of the basic keyboard commands are the same as the WordStar control-key commands that many programmers know so well. And an extensive on-line help facility is built into the editor.

The QB Advisor

There are several ways to get help in QuickBASIC, but one of the easiest is through the QB Advisor. Using this language-help feature, you can get immediate help with the syntax of any command or function in two simple steps:

1. Type a QuickBASIC reserved word in the editor.

2. Press the F1 function key while the cursor is still next to the word.

In response, QuickBASIC displays a help window (called a QuickSCREEN) that describes the usage and syntax of the command or function you have entered.

For example, let's say you are typing a statement that includes a call to the built-in INSTR function:

```
spacePos% = INSTR_
```

But before you complete the line, you want to review the syntax of INSTR. With the cursor still located immediately after the reserved word, INSTR, press F1.

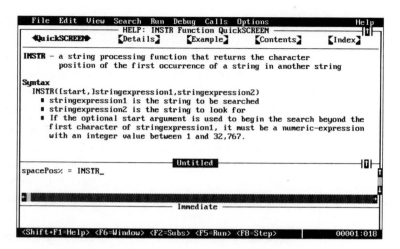

Figure 1-1. *QB Advisor's context-sensitive help for the INSTR function.*

Figure 1-1 shows the resulting display. After reading this concise summary, you will probably be able to continue writing the program line without consulting other documentation.

But the QB Advisor, new in version 4.5, offers you even more information if you want it. Notice the bracketed options at the top of the help window; these options—called *hyperlinks*—can take you to additional screens of information about the INSTR function. The Details hyperlink, for example, gives you more detailed instructions on the syntax and usage of the function. The Example hyperlink gives you a complete program example that illustrates the function. You can even copy this program from the Example help screen into the QuickBASIC editor (using the Copy and Paste commands in the Edit menu) and experiment with it.

To select a hyperlink, press the F6 function key twice to activate the help window, press the Tab key until the cursor appears beneath the option you want to view, and press the Enter key to complete the selection. Alternatively, you can click on any bracketed hyperlink option with the right mouse button. Finally, to close the help window and continue with your work, press Esc.

Windows in the QuickBASIC environment

Windows are an important feature of the QuickBASIC environment. When you first begin a session with QuickBASIC, two windows appear on the screen. The large window in the upper part of the screen is the

View window; this is where you enter or edit the lines of your program. Below the View window is a smaller screen area called the *Immediate window*. In the Immediate window you can experiment with QuickBASIC statements and functions before you enter them into your program. Yet another type of window area that you can open onto the screen is called the *Watch window*. This window displays information about your program during a debugging session. The following sections briefly summarize the use of these three windows.

The View window

A well-structured QuickBASIC program typically contains many small procedures, each one devoted to a particular task. A section at the top of the program—often referred to as the *main program section*—controls the action of the program by calling the procedures below it. To simplify the development of programs that conform to this general structure, QuickBASIC displays procedures one at a time on the screen. While a program resides in memory, you can select any individual procedure and work with it in the View window.

The main program section appears in the View window when you first load a program into the editor from disk. To view any of the program's procedures, you simply pull down the View menu and select the SUBs command. This command presents you with a list of all the procedures in the program, arranged in alphabetic order. Figure 1-2 shows how the list for a program named *Schedule* might appear.

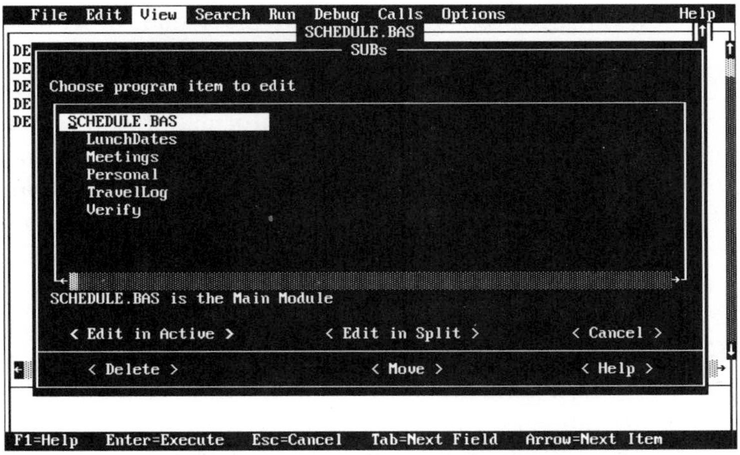

Figure 1-2. *Viewing a procedure list with the SUBs command.*

7

The *Schedule* program has five procedures, any one of which you can select for viewing and editing in a window.

The View menu also has a Split command that gives you a second View window for your program. With two View windows visible, you can look at two different procedures at one time. You can edit in either window; the active window is the one that contains the edit cursor. Press the F6 function key to activate the next window on the screen. Press Shift-F6 to rotate through the windows in reverse.

The Immediate window

The Immediate window is a QuickBASIC feature that brings back one of the conveniences of the BASICA interpreter—the ability to interpret *immediate-mode* statements and instantly display their results on the screen. The Immediate window lets you perform fast experiments with QuickBASIC statements. After you press F6 to activate this window, you can enter almost any executable QuickBASIC statement. In response, QuickBASIC switches to the output screen and shows you the result of the statement. (Press any key to return to the editor.) This is a useful way to find out how a statement works before you include it in your program.

As you will learn later, the Immediate window also has important uses during the process of debugging a QuickBASIC program.

The Watch window

The Watch window appears on the screen only when you initiate a debugging session. It gives you particular information about the performance of your program—specifically, the changing values of selected variables or expressions. You use commands in the Debug menu to specify exactly what information you want to be displayed. By examining the changes that occur in the Watch window while your program is running, you can often find flaws in your program's logic that would otherwise be difficult to detect. You'll learn more about the Watch window and the QuickBASIC debugging commands later in this chapter.

Multiple-module programs

A major innovation in QuickBASIC 4.0 and 4.5 is support for multiple-module programs. As you begin to write application programs in QuickBASIC, you'll almost certainly develop general-purpose procedures that you'll want to use in other programming projects.

QuickBASIC 4.0 and 4.5 encourage you to organize groups of such procedures into individual files stored on disk. Then, when you are ready to write a new program, you can load any number of these files into memory at one time as the *modules* of a program.

A program can contain as many individual module files as will fit in memory. All the procedures of each module are then available for use. When you save the program, each module is still stored in its own file on disk, but QuickBASIC also creates a special file (called a MAK file) that identifies all the modules included in the program.

This feature gives new meaning to the term *modular programming* in QuickBASIC. You can develop and test groups of general-purpose procedures and save their source code on disk in any number of files. Then, when you need those tested routines in a new program, you simply load the files into the program as modules.

For convenience and clarity, the long application programs presented in Part II of this book are all arranged as self-contained, single-module files. But as you work with these programs, you may want to separate several common procedures into module files of their own, to take full advantage of QuickBASIC's support for modules. We'll discuss the use of modules in Chapter 3.

Debugging

A powerful set of debugging tools is built into the QuickBASIC programming environment. Along with the Watch window, QuickBASIC offers a variety of *tracing* modes that step through a program line by line or procedure by procedure. You can use the tracing modes to examine the results of individual statements in a program.

You can also establish predefined stopping points to suspend program execution when a particular statement is reached or when a particular condition is met. While execution is suspended, you can examine the output screen and use the Immediate window to look at the values of variables and expressions. You can even make changes in the program and then continue to run it.

The Debug menu gives you easy access to QuickBASIC's debugging features. After you master the Debug menu and a few special keyboard commands, you'll be able to find and correct errors—much more efficiently than ever before—even in long and complicated programs.

Creating EXE files

An *EXE file* is a compiled program you can run directly from MS-DOS. QuickBASIC provides a simple process for creating such files. After you have developed and tested a program inside the QuickBASIC environment, you use the Make EXE File command in the Run menu to create a compiled version of the program on disk. QuickBASIC performs all the steps necessary for creating the program file. To run the resulting program outside the QuickBASIC programming environment, you simply enter the file's base name from the MS-DOS prompt.

For example, let's say you have used the Make EXE File command to compile a program named *Survey*. QuickBASIC stores the compiled code on disk under the filename *SURVEY.EXE*. To run the program, you enter the name of the program as an MS-DOS command:

```
C>SURVEY
```

We'll examine the steps for creating an EXE file later in this chapter.

Quick libraries

A *Quick library* is a collection of compiled procedures stored in a file on disk. Like an EXE file, a Quick library file can be created directly from the QuickBASIC environment—using the Make Library command in the Run menu. You can form a Quick library from any module or group of modules.

To use procedures from a Quick library, you load the file into memory when you start up QuickBASIC. The /L option of the QB command loads a Quick library along with the QuickBASIC programming environment. For example, the following command loads a library named *TOOLBOX.QLB*:

```
C>QB /L TOOLBOX.QLB
```

The procedures of such a library become, in effect, extensions of the language. Your program can call these procedures even though the source code for the library procedures is not included in the program. You'll learn about Quick libraries in more detail in Chapter 3.

Like the new programming environment, the QuickBASIC language has some major new elements. QuickBASIC 4.0 and 4.5 are generally compatible with other versions of BASIC you may have used—including the BASICA interpreter and previous versions of the compiler. As a result, most existing programs run with little or no revision.

But QuickBASIC versions 4.0 and 4.5 include some important commands and functions that were not available before. In the next section of this chapter, you'll survey some of the features of the QuickBASIC language.

THE QUICKBASIC LANGUAGE

By taking advantage of several QuickBASIC language features, you'll be able to write programs that are efficient, powerful, and well structured. Your programs will be easier to create, debug, and modify than ever before.

We'll preview the following language elements in this chapter:

- Subprograms and functions
- Recursion
- Extended data types and data structures
- Structured decisions and loops
- Calls to procedures written in other languages

We'll return to most of these topics and discuss them in detail as we work with the application examples in Part II.

Subprograms and functions

The design of QuickBASIC encourages you to divide long programming projects into small procedures. QuickBASIC 4.0 and 4.5 support two kinds of procedures: *subprograms* and *functions*. These two organizational units have several important characteristics in common:

1. A call to either kind of procedure can pass *argument values* for the procedure to work with.

2. Variables defined inside a procedure are *local* by default, meaning that their values can be used and modified by only the procedure in which they are defined.

3. Argument variables can be passed to a procedure *by reference* or *by value*. This distinction determines whether a changed value can be returned from the procedure to the calling program.

When you save a program that is divided into subprograms and functions, QuickBASIC 4.0 and 4.5 automatically generate special procedure-declaration statements at the top of your program. These

11

statements, which begin with the reserved word DECLARE, allow QuickBASIC to check the type and number of arguments sent in a call to a procedure.

In Chapter 2, we'll explore all these features and examine the specific syntax of subprograms, functions, and the DECLARE statement.

Recursion

QuickBASIC 4.0 and 4.5 support recursive procedures. A recursive procedure calls itself one or more times in the process of performing a task. A few common algorithms take advantage of this technique; one classic example is a sorting routine called the *quick sort*. We'll study a version of the quick sort in Chapter 4.

Data types and data structures

The following data types and data structures—new in QuickBASIC 4.0 and 4.5—are among the most important and useful features of the QuickBASIC language:

- The *long integer* is a numeric data type that allows a much wider range of values than standard integers do.

- The *fixed-length string variable* is a string data type that represents text values of constant length.

- The *record variable* is a compound data structure that can represent multiple values of different data types. (A record variable belongs to a corresponding *user-defined type*.)

- The *symbolic constant* is a named constant value belonging to any numeric or string data type.

Data types and data structures are the main topics of Chapter 4.

Structured decisions and loops

QuickBASIC supports two powerful decision structures:

- The block-structured IF statement, which expresses a conditional choice among different courses of action

- The SELECT CASE statement, which organizes alternative actions into a series of CASE blocks

The essential difference between these two decision structures is in the method of selecting the action that the program will perform. In an IF statement, the decision is based on one or more conditional expressions. A SELECT CASE statement looks for a match between a target test value and a list of CASE values.

For controlling repetitive actions, QuickBASIC supports the versatile DO loop along with the more traditional FOR...NEXT loop. The DO loop executes a block of code repeatedly, using a conditional expression to determine the scope of the looping. Using this structure, you can create both DO...WHILE loops and DO...UNTIL loops.

We'll concentrate on decision structures and loop structures in Chapter 5.

Calls to procedures written in other languages

QuickBASIC also supports interlanguage calls. This means that you can incorporate procedures from any of several Microsoft languages into a QuickBASIC program. The eligible languages include Microsoft C, Microsoft QuickC, Microsoft Pascal, Microsoft FORTRAN, and Microsoft Macro Assembler (MASM). To introduce a routine from another language into a QuickBASIC program, you first compile and link the routine into a Quick library. Then you can load the library into the QuickBASIC environment. For more information about interlanguage calls, see the QuickBASIC documentation.

USING THE QUICKBASIC MENUS

When you start a session with QuickBASIC, the editor is ready for you to begin your programming work. Here are the steps that you typically follow to create a program from within the editor:

1. Type a new program directly from the keyboard into the QuickBASIC editor, or load an existing program from disk into the editor.

2. Use the various editing features to make any necessary changes to your program.

3. Save the current version of the program on disk. (You may also send a listing of the program to your printer.)

4. Run the program.

5. If the result is not exactly what you want, activate selected debugging features and then go back to step 2.

6. When the program behaves exactly as you want it to, compile the code and store it in a disk file as an executable MS-DOS program.

The QuickBASIC environment supplies the tools you'll need to accomplish all these steps simply and efficiently. You access these development tools by selecting commands from the QuickBASIC menus. To "pull down" a menu and display its command options, you press the Alt key and then the first letter of the menu you want to examine. For example, pressing Alt and then F (Alt-F) pulls down the File menu. To choose a specific command from a menu that is currently displayed, type the character that is highlighted in the command's name. An ellipsis (...) following the name of a menu command means that a dialog box appears on the screen when you select that command.

The QuickBASIC 4.5 menus have two distinct formats called Full Menus and Easy Menus. The Full Menus format gives you the complete set of options available for use in the QuickBASIC environment. The Easy Menus format provides a convenient abbreviated set of commands—including all the commands you are most likely to need as you develop new QuickBASIC programs. You can choose between these two menu formats by selecting the Full Menus command in the Options menu. Full Menus is a toggle: If a bullet appears next to the command, the Full Menus format is active; if the bullet does not appear, you are currently in the Easy Menus format. This chapter describes the Full Menus format, but you may find that the Easy Menus are adequate for most of your work in QuickBASIC.

Some of the QuickBASIC menu commands have special shortcut key combinations. You can use these shortcuts to choose commands directly from the keyboard without taking the extra steps of going through a menu. For example, pressing Shift-F5 has the same effect as choosing the Start command from the Run menu. This command runs the program currently stored in memory.

QuickBASIC also supports using a mouse to control the QuickBASIC menus:

- Pull down menus and select menu options.

- Activate windows and change their sizes.

- Move the cursor to new positions in the editor.

- Select blocks of text in the editor.

The mouse also has special uses in debugging.

For detailed information about all the menus, refer to the QuickBASIC documentation. The documentation gives complete descriptions of all the menu commands and instructions for using them.

The following sections highlight the most important tools that QuickBASIC puts at your disposal in each of the menus.

The File menu

```
 File  Edit  View  Search  Run  Debug  Calls  Options            Help
┌─────────────────────────── Untitled ───────────────────────────┐
│ New Program                                                    ↑│
│ Open Program...                                                 │
│ Merge...                                                        │
│ Save                                                            │
│ Save As...                                                      │
│ Save All                                                        │
│                                                                 │
│ Create File...                                                  │
│ Load File...                                                    │
│ Unload File...                                                  │
│                                                                 │
│ Print...                                                        │
│ DOS Shell                                                       │
│                                                                 │
│ Exit                                                            │
│                                                                ↓│
├─────────────────────────── Immediate ──────────────────────────┤
│                                                                 │
└─────────────────────────────────────────────────────────────────┘
 F1=Help │ Removes currently loaded program from memory │ 00001:001
```

Figure 1-3. *The File menu.*

You use the commands in the File menu, shown in Figure 1-3, to perform the following tasks:

- Clear the current program from memory so that you can type in a *new* program.

- Load a program into the editor from memory.

- Merge a disk file with the current program.

- Save all or part of the program that is currently in the editor with the same or a new name.

- Create, load, or unload individual program modules or other files.

- Print a listing of the program.

- Make a temporary or permanent exit to MS-DOS.

The following sections briefly explore each of the commands in the File menu.

The New Program command

The New Program command clears the current program from
QuickBASIC's memory. If you have made changes to the program since
the last time you saved it, QuickBASIC presents a dialog box on the
screen with the following question:

```
One or more loaded files are not saved. Save them now?
```

The dialog box contains Yes, No, Cancel, and Help options. You can
use either the keyboard or the mouse to respond to a dialog box. For
example, to select an option in the New Program dialog box, you simply press Y or N or click an option with the mouse. Alternatively, you
can use the Tab key to select any element of a dialog box; if you select
an option, you can then press Enter or the spacebar to perform the
corresponding action. The Esc key always cancels an operation, clear-
ing the current dialog box from the screen.

The Open Program command

The Open Program command reads a program from one or more files
on disk and loads the program into the editor. The command's dialog
box includes a File Name text box into which you can type the name
of the file that you want to open. The dialog box also includes a Files
box, which lists the program files from the current directory, and a
Dirs/Drives box from which you can select the current directory or
drive. To open a program, type the name directly into the File Name
box and press Enter. Alternatively, follow these steps to select a program from the Files box:

1. Press the Tab key to activate the Files box.

2. Use the arrow keys to select the name of the program you want
   to open, or type the first letter of the program's filename.

3. Press Enter to load the file.

To view another directory or to open a file from another directory,
type a pathname into the text box or select the directory from the
Dirs/Drives box. Of course, you can also use the mouse to select elements from the Open Program dialog box.

   If a program consists of more than one module, Open Program
loads all the module files at one time. To determine the modules of a
multiple-module program, QuickBASIC reads the program's MAK file.
(You'll recall that this text file contains a list of all the module files
that make up a given program.) Open Program searches for a MAK file

when you enter a filename; if no MAK file exists, QuickBASIC assumes that the program has only one module.

You can also use Open Program to load a BASICA program into the QuickBASIC editor, as long as the program is stored on disk as a text file. To create an ASCII text file from BASICA, use the *A* option of BASICA's SAVE command; for example:

```
SAVE "SURVEY.BAS", A
```

If you omit the *A* option, BASICA saves programs in a form that QuickBASIC cannot use.

The Merge command

The Merge command merges a file of QuickBASIC code into the current program. The Merge command's dialog box includes a File Name text box, a Files box that lists the files in the current directory, and a Dirs/Drives box listing the available directories and drives. If the program in memory contains more than one module, the Merge command loads the file you choose into the current module (that is, the module that is displayed in the View window). We'll discuss uses for the Merge command in Chapter 3.

The Save commands

The File menu has three commands that save files on disk: Save, Save As, and Save All.

The Save command saves the latest version of the current module on disk. You typically use this command after you have saved the file at least once and want to record changes you have made since the last save operation.

The first time you save a program module, use the Save As command. This command displays a dialog box in which you can enter a filename for the current module. (Actually, this dialog box always appears on the screen during the first save operation of a given module, whether you choose Save or Save As.)

Save As gives you a choice between two storage formats for saving your program:

```
( ) QuickBASIC -
      Fast Load and
      Save

( ) Text -
      Readable by
      Other Programs
```

The first of these is QuickBASIC's own format for storing the code of your program. This format results in quicker saves and a fast and efficient loading operation when you later read the program back into QuickBASIC. The second format option creates a simple text file; use this format if you want to transfer the source code of your program to some other editing environment. (You can use the TYPE command from MS-DOS to view the contents of a file that is stored in the text format.)

The Save All command saves all modules of the current program on disk. Each individual module is saved in its own separate file. For a multiple-module program, this command also creates the necessary MAK file, which lists the names of the module files that make up the program. The base name of a MAK file is the name of the main module. For example, let's say you use Save All to save a multiple-module program named *Survey*. If the name of the main module is *SURVEY.BAS*, the module list will be saved under the name *SURVEY.MAK*. QuickBASIC creates no MAK file for a single-module program.

The File commands

You use the Create File, Load File, and Unload File commands to create, load, and unload module files. In addition, you can use these three commands to work with include files and nonprogram document files. (An include file contains lines of code that are read into a program at compile time by the $INCLUDE metacommand. We'll discuss this process in Chapter 3.)

The Create File command creates a new module for the current program. You type the name for the new module in the command's dialog box. You can then use the SUBs command from the View menu to work with this module; for example, you might use the SUBs command to move a procedure from an existing module to the new module.

Load File reads a module file from disk and loads the module into the current program. The Load File dialog box includes the current directory listing and a text box in which you can type the name of the module that you want to load. Again, the SUBs command in the View menu is useful for viewing the procedures in a newly loaded module.

Unload File removes a module from the current program. The Unload File dialog box gives you a list of all the modules in the program. When you unload a module, QuickBASIC removes the module from memory and deletes the module's name from the program's MAK file, but the module file is not erased from disk.

The Print command

The Print command sends a listing of all or part of the current program to the printer. The Print command's dialog box gives you four options: The Selected Text option sends the currently selected block of text to the printer. The Active Window option prints the single procedure that appears in the active window. The Current Module option prints all the procedures of the current program module. Finally, if you want to print your entire program—including all modules—select the All Modules option.

Because the Selected Text option works with a block of selected text, you begin this operation by selecting a portion of your program in the editor. You can use the keyboard or the mouse to select text. To select text with the keyboard, hold down the Shift key while you press any of the direction keys on the numeric keypad. (For example, Shift-Down Arrow selects a line of text.) To select text with the mouse, hold down the left mouse button while you drag the mouse pointer over the text you want to select. The selected text appears in reverse video.

The DOS Shell command

DOS Shell is a useful command that lets you leave QuickBASIC temporarily to perform one or more operations from MS-DOS. You can return to QuickBASIC by using the MS-DOS EXIT command:

```
C>EXIT
```

The Exit command

The Exit command ends the current session of QuickBASIC. If you select Exit and the current program contains any unsaved changes, QuickBASIC displays an Exit dialog box. The options in the Exit dialog box let you save or abandon the changes you've made to a program or cancel the Exit command.

The Edit menu

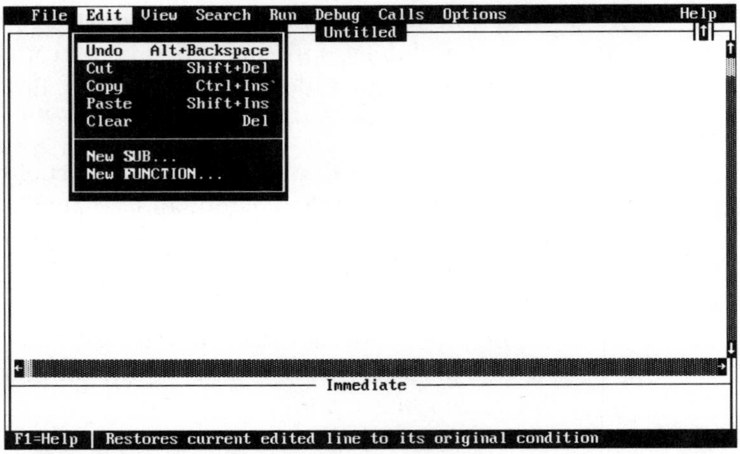

Figure 1-4. *The Edit menu.*

You use commands in the Edit menu, shown in Figure 1-4, to perform any of the following operations:

- Restore the contents of a line
- Move a block of code from one location to another inside the current program (cut and paste)
- Copy a block of code from one location to another (copy and paste)
- Delete a block of code from the program
- Create a new procedure window

Notice that you can use shortcut keys to perform any of the first five commands in the Edit menu.

The Undo command

Undo restores the contents of the current line, undoing any editing changes that you have made in the line. This operation is available only while the cursor is still on the line that you want to restore. When you move the cursor to another line, QuickBASIC records your editing changes, and you can no longer use Undo.

The Cut, Copy, Paste, and Clear commands

The Cut and Paste commands together allow you to move a block of statements from one location to another inside your program. Here are the steps for a cut-and-paste operation:

1. Select the block of code that you want to move. Use either the keyboard (the Shift key plus a direction key on the numeric keypad) or the mouse to make the selection.

2. Choose the Cut command (or press the Shift-Del shortcut key combination). QuickBASIC removes the selected code from the program and stores it in a memory location called the *Clipboard*.

3. Move the cursor to the point in the listing at which you want to paste the selected code.

4. Choose the Paste command (or press Shift-Ins). QuickBASIC copies the selected code from the Clipboard to the target location.

You can use the Copy and Paste commands to copy a block of statements to a new location without deleting the original block of code. Here are the steps for the copy-and-paste operation:

1. Select the block of code that you want to copy.

2. Choose the Copy command (or press Ctrl-Ins). QuickBASIC stores a copy of the selected text in the Clipboard.

3. Move the cursor to the location at which you want to copy the selected code.

4. Choose the Paste command (or press Shift-Ins).

Each new Cut or Copy operation replaces the current contents of the Clipboard with a new block of text. Information remains in the Clipboard until you replace it with another selection or until you exit from QuickBASIC. To delete information without copying it to the Clipboard, select the block of code you want to delete and use the Clear command (or press Del).

The New SUB and New FUNCTION commands

The New SUB command creates a new subprogram in the current module, and the New Function command creates a new function in the current module. These commands display dialog boxes that

21

prompt you to type a name for the new procedure. Then QuickBASIC creates the new procedure and displays it in the View window.

The New SUB command generates SUB and END SUB statements, and the New Function command generates FUNCTION and END FUNCTION statements for the new procedure. Inside the View window, QuickBASIC positions the cursor after the procedure name so that you can begin your work by entering a parameter list.

The View menu

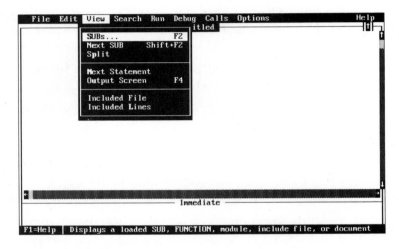

Figure 1-5. *The View menu.*

The View menu, shown in Figure 1-5, gives you quick access to any procedure or module in the current program and displays individual procedures in the View window. The menu also has options for working with include files. We'll discuss the View commands in the following sections.

The SUBs command

For a program that is organized into procedures and modules, SUBs (or F2) is one of the most important of QuickBASIC's menu commands. The SUBs dialog box displays a list of all the modules in the current program and of all the subprogram and function procedures contained in each module. To display a particular part of your program in the View window, you select a module or procedure from this list.

The SUBs dialog box gives you the option of placing the procedure in the active window or in a split window. If you choose the Edit in Active option, the selected procedure replaces the previous contents of the View window. If you choose the Edit in Split option, QuickBASIC creates a second View window on the lower half of the screen and displays the selected procedure in this window. In this case, the upper View window still displays the procedure that was there before you chose the SUBs command.

The SUBs dialog box also provides two important options that you can use to move or delete procedures. The Move option moves a procedure from one module to another. Here are the steps for this operation:

1. Select a procedure in the list box.

2. Press Alt-M to choose the Move option. (You can also move to the option by pressing the Tab key or click on the option with the mouse.)

3. The SUBs command next displays a list of the program's modules. Select the module to which you want to move the procedure and press Enter.

The Delete option deletes a procedure from a module. To perform this operation, you simply select the procedure that you want to delete and press Alt-D to choose the Delete option. Use this option carefully: If you delete a procedure and then save the module on disk, the procedure will be permanently deleted from the module file.

The Next SUB command

The Next SUB command (Shift-F2) displays the current module's next procedure in the active window. (QuickBASIC arranges a module's procedures in alphabetic order.) You can press Ctrl-F2 to move backward through the procedures (that is, in reverse alphabetic order).

The Split command

You can look at two different parts of a program at once by putting two View windows on the screen. The Split command is a toggle: The first time you invoke the command, QuickBASIC divides the View window into two windows; the next time, QuickBASIC restores the single View window.

The active window is the one that contains the cursor. Press the F6 function key to activate the next window on the screen, cycling through the View windows and the Immediate window. (Shift-F6 activates the previous window.) Alternatively, you can activate a window by pointing to it with the mouse and clicking the left mouse button.

Use the Alt-+ key combination to increase the size of the active window by one line, or the Alt-− keys to decrease the size by one line. Ctrl-F10 is a toggle that switches the active window between full-screen and split-screen displays. Ctrl-F5 decreases a full-screen window to its previous size.

Changing the size of a window is even easier with the mouse. Drag a window's top border to increase or decrease the window's size, or double-click on the top border to toggle between full-screen and split-screen displays.

The Next Statement command

If you suspend the execution of a program, you can use the Next Statement command to position the cursor at the next statement that QuickBASIC will perform when you resume program execution. This statement is a convenience during the process of debugging a program; no matter what part of the program you are viewing, you can always return quickly to the point where the execution left off.

The Output Screen command

The Output Screen command (F4) displays the current output screen without resuming the execution of the current program. Press any key to return to the editor when the output screen is displayed.

The Included File and Included Lines commands

The Included File and Included Lines commands both read the lines of an include file from disk and display those lines on the screen.

Included File displays the include file in a View window so that you can actually edit the lines and then save a new version of the file. Use the Unload File command from the File menu to remove the include file after you have finished working with it.

Included Lines simply displays the include file for viewing; in this case, the lines appear just below the $INCLUDE statement. To remove the display, select Included Lines a second time.

The Search menu

```
 File  Edit  View  Search  Run  Debug  Calls  Options                    Help
┌──────────────────────┤Find...              ├──────────────────────────┤↕├─┐
│                       Selected Text  Ctrl+\                               ↑│
│                       Repeat Last Find    F3                              │
│                       Change...                                           │
│                       Label...                                            │
│                                                                           │
│                                                                           │
│                                                                           │
│                                                                           │
│                                                                           │
│█                                                                         ↓│
│█░░░░░░░░░░░░░░░░░░░░░░░░░░░░░░░░░░░░░░░░░░░░░░░░░░░░░░░░░░░░░░░░░░░░░░░░░░░░░│
│─────────────────────────────────┤Immediate├─────────────────────────────│
 F1=Help │ Finds specified text                            │  00001:001
```

Figure 1-6. *The Search menu.*

The Search menu, shown in Figure 1-6, offers an assortment of commands that locate and replace text. For some of these commands you can optionally use the shortcut keys familiar to WordStar users:

Search Command	*WordStar Key Combination*
Find	Ctrl-Q-F
Repeat Last Find	Ctrl-L
Change	Ctrl-Q-A

The notation *Ctrl-Q-F* means that you should first hold down the Ctrl key and press the Q key, then release both keys and press F.

The Find command

The Find command displays a dialog box in which you can enter the text that you want to find and specify how you want the search to be conducted. In response, the editor scrolls forward from the current cursor position to the first occurrence of the text, which is highlighted on the screen. (A *Match not found* message appears if the editor cannot find the text you have specified.)

The default value in the Find dialog box is the word located immediately to the right of the cursor in the edit screen.

You can use options in the Find command's dialog box to specify the scope of the search: the active window only, the current module

25

only, or all modules. Other options determine how QuickBASIC compares the Find Text entry with text inside the program: Match Upper/Lowercase requires matching capitalization; Whole Word compares whole words only, not strings contained inside words.

The Selected Text command

The Selected Text command (Ctrl-\) locates the next occurrence of text that you selected in the program listing. To use this command, select a line of text or a portion of a line, and then choose the Selected Text command.

The Repeat Last Find command

The Repeat Last Find command (F3 or Ctrl-L) searches forward again for the next occurrence of the target text specified in the previous Find operation.

The Change command

The Change command performs a search-and-replace operation. The Change dialog box asks you to specify the target text and the replacement text. Change works in one of two modes: the Find and Verify mode, in which you must confirm each replacement; or the Change All mode, in which all replacements are made without your confirmation.

Like the Find command, Change lets you specify the scope of the search: the active window only, the current module only, or all modules of the entire program. You can also specify whether QuickBASIC will search for whole words only and whether case will be significant in the search.

Use the Change command carefully. Change All mode can result in revisions throughout an entire program that you do not really want. A more cautious approach is to make changes in one procedure at a time, in Find and Verify mode.

The Label command

The Label command adds a colon character (:) to the end of the text you specify in the Label dialog box and then conducts a search for a QuickBASIC alphanumeric line label.

A *line label* is a name that identifies the destination of a GOTO or GOSUB statement. (The name can contain a maximum of 40 characters and must begin with a letter and end with a colon.) In general, the use of GOTO or GOSUB is stylistically contradictory to the spirit of structured programming in QuickBASIC. Nonetheless, you might sometimes use line labels to identify the locations of error-trapping and event-trapping routines. Event-trapping techniques are discussed in Chapter 9.

The Run menu

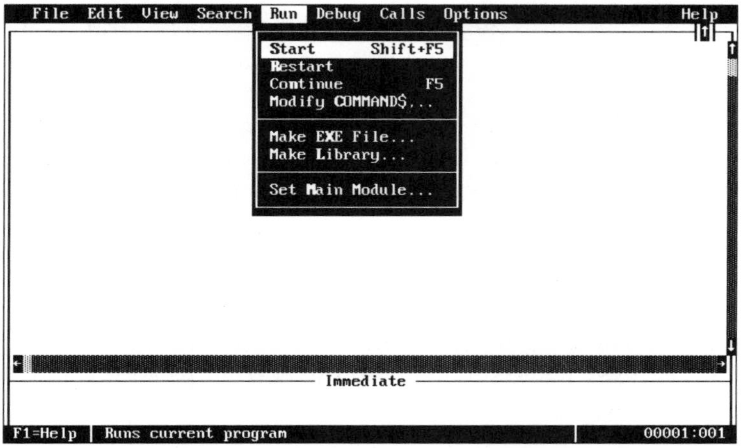

Figure 1-7. *The Run menu.*

You use the Run menu commands, shown in Figure 1-7, to perform a variety of essential operations, including

- Running the current program
- Continuing to run the program after a suspension
- Establishing test values for the COMMAND$ function
- Creating compiled EXE files on disk from the current program
- Creating Quick libraries
- Selecting a main module for controlling a program's execution

The following sections examine the commands in this menu.

The Start command

The Start command runs the program, starting from the first executable statement. If the program consists of more than one module, the program's entry point is the code located at the top of the main module. (The QuickBASIC documentation refers to the top section of any module as the *module-level code*—that is, the code that is not part of any procedure. This book uses the more familiar term *main program section* to refer to the module-level code of a program's main module.)

Because QuickBASIC translates each line of code as you enter it into the editor, you will notice hardly any pause between the moment you select the Start command and the program's beginning to run. In essence, the program is already stored in memory in a nearly compiled form and is ready to run as soon as you give the Start command. QuickBASIC requires no separate compilation step before running a program.

The Restart command

The Restart command reinitializes all variables and highlights the first executable statement in the current program. This command is a convenience for debugging.

The Continue command

The Continue command resumes execution after you have suspended a program. You can use QuickBASIC's debugging features to suspend execution at a predefined point. During the suspension you can study the program, examine the values of variables, and even make changes in the code. To resume execution at the line where the program was suspended, use the Continue command. When you invoke Continue, variables in the program retain the values they had when execution stopped.

The Modify COMMAND$ command

When you are developing and testing a program that relies on the built-in QuickBASIC COMMAND$ function, you can use the Run menu's Modify COMMAND$ command to establish test values for COMMAND$ inside the QuickBASIC environment.

COMMAND$ is a built-in function for use in compiled EXE programs. If the user enters a parameter string when running an EXE program from MS-DOS, the COMMAND$ function makes the string available to the program. You'll find an example of COMMAND$ in the *List* program, presented in Chapter 4; *List* is designed as an MS-DOS–style utility, similar to the DIR command. Once compiled as an EXE file, *List* accepts a number of optional parameters to determine how to display files on the screen. For instance, the following command lists all BAS files in chronological order:

```
C> LIST *.BAS /SC
```

The *List* program uses the COMMAND$ function to gain access to the parameter string. In this example, COMMAND$ returns the string value *.BAS /SC.

During the development of a program such as *List*, the Modify COMMAND$ command allows you to test the program's execution with various parameter strings. In the Modify COMMAND$ dialog box, you type the string value that you want to supply to the COMMAND$ function. Thanks to this command, you are not obliged to compile the program and exit from QuickBASIC in order to test the program's action. Of course, this command has meaning only in a program that uses COMMAND$.

The Make EXE File command

When you have completed the testing and debugging phases of a program's development, you will probably want to create a compiled version of the program that can be run outside the QuickBASIC environment. The Make EXE File command performs this operation.

In versions of QuickBASIC before 4.0 the process of creating a compiled stand-alone EXE file required some detailed steps that had to be performed outside the QuickBASIC environment. In QuickBASIC 4.0 and 4.5, the Make EXE File command takes complete control of the entire process. All you have to do is specify a few options in the command's dialog box.

First, you can enter the filename under which you want to store the executable file. (If you want the EXE file to have the same base name as the current program file, you can simply leave the File Name box alone.)

Next, you have a choice between two kinds of EXE files. The dialog box expresses the options as follows:

```
EXE Requiring BRUN45.EXE
Stand-Alone EXE File
```

The first of these options produces a program file that needs the QuickBASIC runtime module BRUN45.EXE to run. The second option produces a completely independent stand-alone program file that contains all the code required for execution. The first kind of EXE file is usually much smaller than the second variety. On the other hand, a stand-alone file is completely self-contained and therefore more convenient to use.

After you have selected one of these two options, you also must decide whether you want QuickBASIC to generate error-handling code for certain potential runtime errors. If you do, select the Produce Debug Code option.

Finally, you select one of two options to specify what you want to do after the EXE file has been produced. The Make EXE option returns you to the QuickBASIC editor after the compilation process, whereas the Make EXE and Exit option ends the session with QuickBASIC and drops you back into MS-DOS.

To create an EXE file, QuickBASIC must be able to locate the following files on disk:

- BC.EXE

- LINK.EXE

- BRUN45.LIB (for programs that require the runtime module)

- BCOM45.LIB (for stand-alone program files)

The Make Library command

The Make Library command creates a Quick library file. As you have learned, a Quick library is a collection of tested and compiled procedures that you can load into memory when you start QuickBASIC. Creating a Quick library is one of several techniques for introducing procedures into a program in QuickBASIC 4.0 and 4.5. We'll discuss this topic and examine the Make Library command in detail in Chapter 3.

The Set Main Module command

You can use the Set Main Module command to specify a new main module for the current program. The main module contains the entry point (or the ''main program section'') for the program's execution.

The Set Main Module dialog box presents a list of all the modules in the program; you simply select the module that you want to designate as the main module. You may want to choose this command while you are designing or redesigning a multiple-module program.

The Debug menu

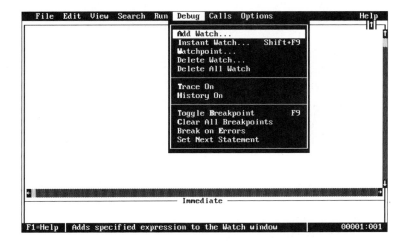

Figure 1-8. *The Debug menu.*

The Debug menu, shown in Figure 1-8, controls the sophisticated and powerful debugging facility built into the QuickBASIC programming environment. This menu gives you several ways to investigate the execution of a program. Using the Debug menu's commands, you can:

- Open the Watch window at the top of the screen. The Watch window displays the changes that occur in specified variables or expressions as the program runs.

- Investigate *instant watches*—that is, view the values of variables or expressions during a suspension of a program performance.

- Establish *watchpoints*. A watchpoint is a logical expression that suspends program execution when the value of the expression becomes true.

- Activate the *animated trace mode.* In this mode, each statement of the program is highlighted as it is executed.

- Activate a *history* mode so that you can later trace through the last 20 lines that were executed.

- Specify the location of a *breakpoint.* A breakpoint is a selected line in your program at which QuickBASIC will suspend execution. During the suspension, you can investigate the current status of the program by looking at the values of certain variables.

- Delete watchpoints and clear breakpoints when you have completed a particular debugging operation.

- Suspend the program performance when an *error-trap routine* is triggered.

- Set a new starting point for continuing the program after a suspension.

As you read about the Debug menu, you may want to load a short program into memory and experiment with the various debugging facilities that the menu's commands represent. After such an exercise, you'll be ready to use the commands when you need them in a real programming situation. You can use the following simple program for this purpose; the program displays a table of ASCII code values on the screen. Save the program on disk with the filename *ASCII.BAS*:

```
CLS
rowPos% = 0
colPos% = 1
FOR i% = 127 TO 254
    rowPos% = rowPos% + 1
    LOCATE rowPos%, colPos%
    PRINT i%; " "; CHR$(i%)
    IF rowPos% = 16 THEN
        rowPos% = 0
        colPos% = colPos% + 10
    END IF
NEXT i%
```

The Add Watch command

The Add Watch command displays a dialog box into which you can enter a watch variable or a watch expression. In response, QuickBASIC opens the Watch window at the top of the screen and displays the current value of the variable or expression. For example, let's say you establish the variable $i\%$ as a watch variable in *ASCII.BAS*. After a performance of the program, the following line appears in the Watch window:

```
ASCII.BAS i%:  255
```

This line gives the *context* of the watch expression—in this case, simply *ASCII.BAS*—along with the variable or expression. Finally, you see the current value of the expression. Depending upon the action of a program, this value may change frequently as the program runs.

You can create multiple watch expressions by choosing the Add Watch command more than once. To see the watch expression change, activate a trace mode so that the program listing stays on the screen. (The watch window does not remain in sight when the output screen appears.)

The Instant Watch command

The Instant Watch command allows you to take a quick look at the value of a variable or expression during a suspension in your program's performance. To view a current value, position the edit cursor at the target variable, or highlight a target expression; then press Shift-F9 to invoke the Instant Watch command. The Instant Watch dialog box displays the expression you have selected along with the expression's current value. If you wish, you can then select the Add Watch option to add the expression to the Watch window.

QuickBASIC provides a mouse shortcut for activating the Instant Watch command: Position the mouse pointer over the target variable, hold down the Shift key at the keyboard, and press the right mouse button.

The Watchpoint command

You use the Watchpoint command to establish a logical expression as a watchpoint. When you then run your program, QuickBASIC monitors the value of this expression and suspends execution when the expression becomes true.

You enter the watchpoint expression into the Watchpoint dialog box. Enter any expression that QuickBASIC can evaluate to be either true or false. For example, in *ASCII.BAS* you might enter an expression such as $i\% > 150$. QuickBASIC suspends execution when the variable $i\%$ contains a value that is greater than 150. While the program runs, the watchpoint expression appears in the Watch window.

The Delete Watch and Delete All Watch commands

Two commands delete watch and watchpoint expressions that you have established for debugging the current program. The Delete Watch dialog box contains a list of all current watch and watchpoint expressions. You select the expression that you wish to delete.

The Delete All Watch command closes the Watch window and deactivates all watch and watchpoint expressions. Use this command when you have finished working with the Watch window during a debugging session.

The Trace On command

The Trace On command is a toggle that turns the animated trace mode on and off. To activate this feature, pull down the Debug menu and select Trace On. The next time you look at the menu, you will see a bullet at the left of the Trace On command. To turn the feature off, pull down the menu and select Trace On again.

During an animated trace you can watch the execution of your program in one-line steps. QuickBASIC moves slowly through the program, highlighting each line as it is executed. You can examine the flow that results from your program's logical structure.

The trace mode is useful when the program you are developing is not producing exactly the results that you want. In a long or complex program, finding the program location responsible for the problem can be difficult. In trace mode you step line by line through the program and examine the behavior of each line of code. While running your program in trace mode, you can suspend the action, examine variables, and continue again, by following steps such as these:

1. Before running the program, set a breakpoint or a watchpoint to suspend the action at a predefined location or condition. (Alternatively, you can press Ctrl-Break to suspend execution while the program is running.)

2. While execution is suspended, press F4 (the shortcut key for the View menu's Output Screen command) to examine the output screen at the point of suspension.

3. Press F6 to move to the Immediate window; use PRINT statements to examine the values of variables or expressions, or assignment statements to change the values of program variables.

4. Use the Set Next Statement command (from the Debug menu) to specify the next statement to be executed when the program continues.

5. Set new watchpoints or breakpoints for the next part of the program to be executed.

6. Press F5 (the shortcut key for the Run menu's Continue command) to continue execution. Alternatively, move the cursor to a stopping point and press the F7 key; in response,

QuickBASIC runs the program from the current line to the line at which the cursor is located. (Optionally, you can use the mouse pointer to specify the stopping point. To do so, you must first select the Right Mouse command from the Options menu and activate the option called *Execute up to this line.* Then, when you press the right mouse button, execution will continue in the View window up to the program line at which the mouse pointer is located.)

After you have found the source of the problem in the program, you can revise the appropriate line or lines, turn the trace mode off, and try to run the program normally.

In addition to the animated trace mode, you can use two function keys to run the program one statement at a time:

- Press F8 to execute the next statement. F8 steps line by line through each part of your program, including procedures.

- Press F10 to execute the next statement. If the statement is a procedure call, F10 executes the entire procedure at once rather than moving line by line through the procedure.

The History On command

The History On command is a toggle. You select it once to turn it on and again to turn it off. When the toggle is on, QuickBASIC records the last 20 statements that were executed in the current program. When execution stops or is suspended, you can use the following keys to step backward or forward through the 20 statements:

- Press Shift-F8 to step backward. With each keypress, QuickBASIC moves the cursor to each statement that was executed.

- Press Shift-F10 to step forward.

When you reach the beginning or the end of the 20-line history record, QuickBASIC beeps in response to Shift-F8 or Shift-F10.

The Trace On command also produces a 20-line history record. You can use the History On command to produce the same record outside the trace mode. History On slows the program considerably.

The Toggle Breakpoint command

The Toggle Breakpoint command (F9) establishes a breakpoint at the line at which the cursor is currently located. QuickBASIC highlights the breakpoint line. When you next run the program, execution will be suspended when the breakpoint would be executed. (If the breakpoint is not within the flow of control, no suspension occurs.) To clear the breakpoint, invoke the command a second time at the same line. You can set multiple breakpoints throughout a program.

The Clear All Breakpoints command

The Clear All Breakpoints command deactivates all breakpoints that you have set.

The Break on Errors command

The Break on Errors command is another toggle, for use in programs that perform error trapping. When the command is toggled on and an error occurs, QuickBASIC suspends the program at the beginning of the most recently called error-handling routine. You can then press Shift-F8 to back up to the program statement that triggered the error.

The Set Next Statement command

Use the Set Next Statement command to establish a new starting point for resuming the program.

When you select Continue (F5) after suspending execution, QuickBASIC normally continues the program at the point where execution stopped. Sometimes you may want to skip one or more lines in the path of control and begin execution at some new point in the program. To do so, follow these steps:

1. Move the cursor to the desired line.

2. Pull down the Debug menu and select the Set Next Statement command.

3. Select Continue (F5) to continue the program.

The Calls menu

An additional debugging tool included in QuickBASIC 4.0 and 4.5 is the Calls menu. Unlike other menus, Calls does not contain commands. Rather, it lists the current procedure calls that are in operation during execution of a program and allows you to investigate those calls.

For example, suppose you have suspended a program called *Survey* at a point when one of the program's procedures is being executed. If you pull down the Calls menu, you might see a list such as the one shown in Figure 1-9.

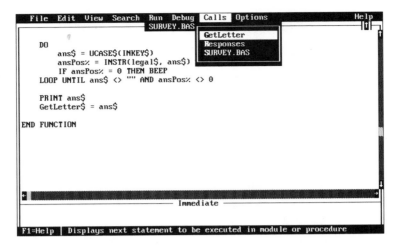

Figure 1-9. *A typical Calls menu.*

This list shows you that the *GetLetter* procedure was in control at the time of the suspension. *GetLetter* was called by the *Responses* procedure, which was in turn called at the main program level.

To examine a procedure listed in the Calls menu, simply select the name and press Enter. QuickBASIC displays the procedure in the active View window and positions the cursor immediately after the line that resulted in the next procedure call up the Calls list. (You can then press the F7 key to execute the program up to the cursor position.)

The Options menu

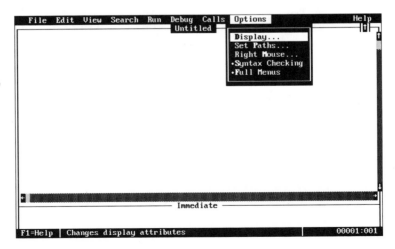

Figure 1-10. *The Options menu.*

The Options menu (Figure 1-10) gives you control over several characteristics of the QuickBASIC environment. These include

- Screen colors and the appearance of other screen elements

- Default paths for QuickBASIC files

- The use of the right button on the mouse

- Syntax checking performed by the smart editor

- The choice between Full Menus and Easy Menus

The following paragraphs provide brief descriptions of these options.

The Display command

The Display command's dialog box contains options for controlling various elements of the display screen. If you are working on a color display device, you can select your own color preferences for the screen. The dialog box also includes a toggle that turns the scroll bar displays on and off and an entry in which you can change the number of characters between tabs in the QuickBASIC editor. The default tab value is eight characters.

The Set Paths command

The dialog box for the Set Paths command allows you to specify directory locations for four kinds of files used in the QuickBASIC environment: EXE files, include files, library files, and help files.

The Right Mouse command

The Right Mouse dialog box gives you two options for the use of the right button on the mouse. The default option, *Context-sensitive Help*, allows you to use the right button to call up a help screen from the QB Advisor. When this option is active, you can position the mouse pointer over a QuickBASIC command or function in the View window and press the right mouse button to get help.

The second option, *Execute up to this line*, transforms the right mouse button into a debugging tool. As described earlier in this chapter, this option suspends a program performance at the line where the mouse pointer is currently located.

The Syntax Checking command

The Syntax Checking command activates or deactivates the smart editor's syntax-checking operation.

The smart editor is on by default when you begin to create a program. As we have discussed, the editor instantly performs three important operations when you press Enter at the end of a new program line—syntax checking, automatic format conversion, and code translation. The Syntax Checking command is a toggle that turns the first of these operations on or off. A bullet appears to the left of the command in the Edit menu when syntax checking is on. This command has no effect on the other operations of the smart editor.

The Full Menus command

As you have already learned, this toggle command switches between the two menu formats—Full and Easy—available in QuickBASIC.

The Help menu

Figure 1-11. *The Help menu.*

The Help menu, shown in Figure 1-11, provides access to QuickBASIC's extensive on-line help facility.

The Index command

The Index command gives you an alphabetic list of all the reserved words in the QuickBASIC language. Select one of the keywords, and QuickBASIC displays a brief summary of the command's usage and syntax.

The Contents command

The Contents command gives a topical outline of the entire help system, from which you can select any subject you want to read about.

The Topic command

The Topic command displays the name of the current QB Advisor topic, selected by the current position of the cursor in the View window.

The Help on Help command

The Help on Help command provides a screen of information explaining how to use the help system itself.

Conclusion

In QuickBASIC you can develop structured programs containing one or more modules. The features of the QuickBASIC programming environment are designed to simplify each step you perform during the development process:

- Entering code into the smart editor
- Editing individual lines of the program
- Combining multiple source code files
- Debugging the program
- Running the program
- Producing stand-alone EXE files

The remaining two chapters of Part I focus on two important subjects: Chapter 2 discusses the two kinds of procedures available in QuickBASIC, and Chapter 3 surveys the techniques you can use to build a program from multiple source files.

CHAPTER 2

Using Subprograms and Functions

QuickBASIC offers two structures for dividing long programming tasks into manageable, self-contained procedures. They are called *subprograms* and *functions*. By using these structures appropriately, you can create well-organized QuickBASIC programs that are easy to understand and modify. Furthermore, you can incorporate tested procedures into other programming projects, thereby reducing the development time required for new programs.

As we saw in Chapter 1, the QuickBASIC development environment encourages the use of subprograms and functions in several interesting ways:

- The editor displays subprograms and functions individually in the View window.

- The View menu's SUBs command provides convenient access to the subroutines and functions included in the program.

- The editor generates DECLARE statements for a program saved on disk. These statements list each procedure's name and parameters, and allow QuickBASIC to check the type and number of arguments in a call to a procedure.

All six of the major application programs presented in Part II of this book are carefully structured into many short subprograms and functions. In this chapter we'll examine the syntax and characteristics of these two procedure structures, and look at examples of each.

SUBPROGRAMS IN QUICKBASIC

QuickBASIC subprograms have several important advantages over the traditional BASICA-style subroutine:

- A call to a subprogram can pass specific argument values for the procedure to work with.

- Arguments can be passed to a subprogram by *reference* or by *value*. An argument variable sent by reference serves as a medium for sending information back to the calling procedure. In contrast, an argument sent by value is local to the subprogram; changes in the value are not returned to the calling procedure.

- Variables used inside a subprogram are *local* by default. Local variables never interfere with variables used elsewhere in the program, even if two variables have the same name.

QuickBASIC 4.0 and 4.5 also support some additional refinements in the use of subprograms:

- The name of a subprogram serves as a call to the procedure; the CALL statement is no longer required as in previous versions of QuickBASIC.

- A subprogram can make calls to itself, a process called *recursion*.

We'll discuss all of these characteristics in detail later in this chapter. Let's begin by examining the syntax of a subprogram.

Defining a subprogram

A subprogram always begins with a SUB statement and ends with an END SUB statement. Between these two lines are located any number of QuickBASIC commands, which together accomplish the particular task of the subprogram:

```
SUB SubprogramName (parameterList) STATIC
    [the statements of the subprogram]
END SUB
```

The reserved word *SUB* is followed by the subprogram's name. This name can contain up to 40 characters, and must not be used as the name for any other procedure in the same program. The optional reserved word STATIC specifies that all local variables will retain their values between calls to the subprogram. Depending upon the design of a particular subprogram, this feature can be advantageous or not. Omitting STATIC may result in slightly slower execution.

The parameter list, enclosed in parentheses, gives the names of variables that will receive argument values sent to the subprogram. Note the distinction between the two terms *parameter* and *argument*: A parameter is a variable that is listed in the SUB statement; as a result of a call to the subprogram, the parameter variable receives a value. An argument, on the other hand, is a value that is sent to the procedure in a call statement. Let's discuss the format of a parameter list.

Identifying parameters

The parameter list in the SUB statement contains one name for each value or data structure that the subprogram is to receive. The names in the list are separated by commas. Actually, the list is optional; you can write a subprogram that takes no arguments.

Each element in the parameter list specifies the type of value that must be sent to the routine; for example, consider the following SUB statement for a hypothetical subprogram named *Sample*:

```
SUB Sample (strVal$, intVal%) STATIC
```

Looking at this particular parameter list, you know that the *Sample* subprogram expects to receive two argument values, a string (*strVal$*) and an integer (*intVal%*). In a call to the subprogram, the values must be sent in the same order.

In QuickBASIC 4.0 and 4.5, a subprogram can receive any of the following as arguments:

- A single string or numeric value
- An array of values
- A record
- An array of records

An *array* is a variable that represents a list or table of values, and a *record* is a compound data structure containing multiple values of various types. All of the programs in this book use arrays and records as convenient structures for organizing and storing data values. We'll discuss these structures in detail in Chapter 4. For now, let's preview the special notations that identify these structures in a parameter list.

The name of an array must be followed by empty parentheses in a parameter list. For example, imagine a subprogram named *CalcStats* that is designed to accept an array of numbers as an argument. The SUB statement for this subprogram might appear as follows:

```
SUB CalcStats (baseValues()) STATIC
```

In this example, *baseValues()* is an array parameter of unspecified dimensions. When a call to *CalcStats* sends an array to the procedure, *baseValues()* takes on the same dimensions as this array.

In versions of QuickBASIC before Version 4.0, the correct notation for an array parameter included the number of dimensions in the array. For example, a two-dimensional array would be designated as in the following SUB statement:

```
SUB CalcStats (baseValues(2)) STATIC
```

This is no longer part of the notation in QuickBASIC 4.0 and 4.5. A pair of empty parentheses now designates an array parameter of any dimensions.

A record parameter is identified by the name of its user-defined type. As we will see in Chapter 4, the TYPE statement defines the name and structure of a record variable. In a parameter list, the following notation defines a record parameter:

```
recordName AS recordType
```

The *recordType* is the structure's name, as defined in a corresponding TYPE statement.

For example, let's say a program has defined a record structure named *employeeType* for storing employee records. The following procedure expects to receive a record variable conforming to the *employeeType* structure:

```
SUB PrintEmployee (employee AS employeeType) STATIC
```

Likewise, the following procedure receives an array of employee records:

```
SUB ListEmployees (empList() AS employeeType) STATIC
```

You will become familiar with these various notations as you study the program examples in Part II of this book.

Next let's look at the statements that call subprograms in QuickBASIC.

Calling a subprogram

In QuickBASIC 4.0 and 4.5 you can express a subprogram call as a CALL statement, or, more simply, as a reference to the name of the subprogram.

The CALL command is compatible with previous versions of QuickBASIC. The command takes the following syntax:

```
CALL SubprogramName (argumentList)
```

The argument list in the CALL statement can contain literal string or numeric values, variable names, or expressions. Each element in the list corresponds, in the order given, to a name in the parameter list of the subprogram that is being called.

Alternatively, QuickBASIC 4.0 and 4.5 allow the following simpler syntax for calling a subprogram:

```
SubprogramName argumentList
```

In this syntax, you omit the word CALL, and you do not enclose the argument list in parentheses. In this second format, a subprogram call resembles a call to a built-in QuickBASIC command.

A call to a subprogram can appear anywhere in the program that contains the subprogram itself, including in a different module. In this sense, we might say that a subprogram is available *globally*. Furthermore, since subprograms can now be recursive, a subprogram can even call itself.

Let's look again at the hypothetical subprogram named *Sample*. A call to this subprogram sends two arguments: a string value and an integer value. The subprogram's SUB statement establishes the parameter variables *strVal$* and *intVal%* for receiving these two values:

```
SUB Sample (strVal$, intVal%) STATIC
```

We'll look at sample calls to this procedure in both legal formats—with and without the reserved word CALL. The application examples presented throughout this book use the simpler format, without CALL.

The following example sends a literal string value (enclosed in quotation marks) and a literal integer value:

```
CALL Sample ("Hello", 19)
```

The equivalent command without CALL is:

```
Sample "Hello", 19
```

As a result of this call, *Hello* will be stored in the parameter variable *strVal$*, and *19* will be stored in *intVal%*.

The next example sends the results of two expressions—a combination (or "concatenation") of two strings and a sum of two numbers:

```
CALL Sample (string1$ + " Wednesday", number1% + 2)
```

The alternative format is:

```
Sample string1$ + " Wednesday", number1% + 2
```

In this case, QuickBASIC first evaluates the expressions and then sends the result to the subprogram.

The last example sends the values currently stored in two variables, *mainStr$* and *mainInt%*:

```
CALL Sample (mainStr$, mainInt%)
```

Without CALL, this command appears as:

```
Sample mainStr$, mainInt%
```

This final example—in which both arguments are expressed as simple variables—is a special case. We'll use this example to discuss the difference between passing arguments by reference and passing arguments by value.

Passing arguments by reference or by value

Variable arguments are normally passed to a subprogram by reference. This means that any new values that the subprogram subsequently assigns to the corresponding parameter variables will in turn be passed back to the calling program.

To see how this works, let's say that the argument variable *mainInt%* contains a value of *6* at the time of the call to the *Sample* subprogram:

```
mainInt% = 6
Sample mainStr$, mainInt%
```

As we have seen, *Sample* receives this value in the parameter variable *intVal%*. Imagine that *Sample* doubles the value of *intVal%* before relinquishing control back to the calling program:

```
SUB Sample (strVal$, intVal%) STATIC
    [other program lines]
    intVal% = 2 * intVal%
    [other program lines]
END SUB
```

When the action of *Sample* is complete, the new value of *intVal%* will be passed back to the original argument variable, *mainInt%*. In other words, after the call to *Sample, mainInt%* will contain a new value of *12*. This feature can prove extremely useful. In many programs you might establish parameter and argument variables (such as *intVal%* and *mainInt%*) expressly to pass a particular value from the subprogram to the calling routine.

On other occasions, however, you may not want a variable argument to be passed by reference. Rather, you may want a variable to retain its original value, even after a subprogram call. In this case, you can use a special notation to pass the variable argument by *value* rather than by reference. The notation is simply to enclose the variable name in parentheses. For example, consider the following revised call to *Sample*:

```
CALL Sample (mainStr$, (mainInt%))
```

Without CALL, the same statement appears as:

```
Sample mainStr$, (mainInt%)
```

In both of these forms, notice the parentheses around the variable *mainInt%*. These extra parentheses specify that the variable will be sent to *Sample* by value. Now, no matter what new value *Sample* might assign to the corresponding parameter variable, *mainInt%* is guaranteed to retain its original value after *Sample* runs.

Keep in mind that arguments that appear in the form of expressions or literal values are always passed by value. You have the choice between passing by value and passing by reference only when the argument is expressed as a simple variable name.

Passing arrays as arguments requires yet another special notation, as we'll see in the next section.

Passing arrays as arguments

Let's look again at the hypothetical *CalcStats* subprogram, which takes an array argument:

```
SUB CalcStats (baseValues()) STATIC
```

The name of an array sent as an argument to a procedure such as this one must be followed by empty parentheses. Here are examples of the two possible formats, with and without CALL:

```
CALL CalcStats (valueList())
CalcStats valueList()
```

Array arguments are always passed by reference in QuickBASIC. If the called subprogram makes any changes in the values stored in the array, these changes will be passed back to the calling program.

You can also send an array *element* as an argument to a subprogram. For example, the following call sends one value from the two-dimensional integer array *numArray%()* to the *Sample* subprogram:

```
Sample string1$, numArray%(7, 2)
```

Sample receives this value in its parameter variable *intVal%*:

```
SUB Sample (strVal$, intVal%) STATIC
```

In this case, the array element is passed by reference. If *Sample* makes a change in the value stored in *intVal%*, that new value will be passed back to the element *numArray%(7, 2)*. To prevent this, you can pass the array element by value:

```
Sample string1$, (numArray%(7, 2))
```

Notice the parentheses around the array reference, specifying that the element should be passed by value rather than by reference.

In the next section we'll look at a sample subprogram called *Frame*, and we'll compare this routine with an equivalent BASICA subroutine.

The *Frame* subprogram

Thoughtful programmers always devote careful attention to the way output information appears on the display screen. The *Frame* subprogram, shown in Figure 2-1, is a tool that we'll use in the programming projects in this book to help present screen information usefully and attractively.

```
SUB Frame (left%, right%, top%, bottom%) STATIC

'     The Frame subprogram draws a rectangular double-line frame on
'          the screen, using "text-graphics" characters from the
'          IBM Extended ASCII character set.

'     ---- Draw the four corners.

      LOCATE top%, left%: PRINT CHR$(201)
      LOCATE top%, right%: PRINT CHR$(187)
      LOCATE bottom%, left%: PRINT CHR$(200);
      LOCATE bottom%, right%: PRINT CHR$(188);

'     ---- Draw the vertical lines.

      FOR vert% = top% + 1 TO bottom% - 1
          LOCATE vert%, left%: PRINT CHR$(186);
          LOCATE vert%, right%: PRINT CHR$(186);
      NEXT vert%

'     ---- Draw the horizontal lines.

      horiz% = right% - left% - 1
      hline$ = STRING$(horiz%, 205)
      LOCATE top%, left% + 1: PRINT hline$
      LOCATE bottom%, left% + 1: PRINT hline$;

END SUB
```

Figure 2-1. *The* Frame *subprogram.*

Frame simply creates a rectangular frame on the screen. This frame can serve a variety of purposes; for example, to separate sections of information that appear together on the same output screen, or to draw the user's attention to certain display features.

The subprogram has four parameters, all integers. It uses the values passed to these four variables to locate the four corner screen addresses of the resulting frame. A call to the routine should send integer values that are within the dimensions of the text screen: The values for *left%* and *right%* should be screen column locations from *1* to *80*, where the value of *left%* is smaller than the value of *right%*. Likewise, the values for *top%* and *bottom%* should be line numbers from *1* to *25*, where *top%* is smaller than *bottom%*. For example, the following call to the program draws a frame from column *15* over to column *65*, and from line *5* down to line *20*:

```
Frame 15, 65, 5, 20
```

Figure 2-2 shows the result.

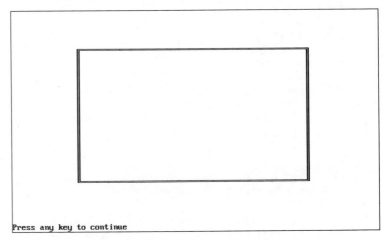

```
Press any key to continue
```

Figure 2-2. *A frame drawn by the* Frame *subprogram.*

Let's look briefly at how the procedure works. The four parameter values become the addresses in a series of LOCATE statements. These statements move the cursor to a particular screen location in advance of a PRINT command; for example:

```
LOCATE top%, left%: PRINT CHR$(201)
```

The subprogram uses six "text-graphics" characters from the IBM Extended ASCII character set to create the frame, as shown in the following table:

Extended ASCII Code	Character
201	Upper-left corner
187	Upper-right corner
200	Lower-left corner
188	Lower-right corner
186	Vertical character
205	Horizontal character

The CHR$ function supplies the actual characters corresponding to these six ASCII code numbers.

After the four corners are displayed, a FOR...NEXT loop draws the two vertical lines from the top of the frame to the bottom:

```
FOR vert% = top% + 1 TO bottom% - 1
```

The STRING function creates the horizontal lines after the appropriate length of each line, *horiz%*, has been computed:

```
horiz% = right% - left% - 1
hline$ = STRING(horiz%, 205)
```

The listing of the *Frame* subprogram contains comments that briefly explain its actions. A few comment lines at the top of the listing give the procedure's purpose. Then, inside the routine, occasional short comments serve to identify the tasks performed by distinct blocks of code. A single quote character, rather than the reserved word REM, is the comment delimiter. This is the general pattern we'll follow for commenting programs throughout this book.

In the next section we'll compare the *Frame* subprogram with an equivalent BASICA-style subroutine. This comparison will demonstrate some of the advantages of subprograms.

QuickBASIC subprograms and BASICA subroutines

Figure 2-3 on the next page contains a BASICA version of *Frame*, implemented as a subroutine that starts at line 100 of the program.

Unlike subprograms, subroutines do not allow parameter passing. For this reason, the BASICA program requires some other technique for sending the four screen addresses to the subroutine.

Before calling the subroutine with a GOSUB statement, the program must assign values to the variables *LEFT%, RIGHT%, TOP%,* and *BOTTOM%*:

```
40 LEFT% = 15: RIGHT% = 65
50 TOP% = 5: BOTTOM% = 20
60 GOSUB 100
```

In BASICA programs, all variables are global: Any section of the program can gain access to variables established in any other section of the program. So, assigning values to these four variables is the program's means of communicating the values to the subroutine.

Since BASICA does not have parameter passing, global variables are needed to share information among the parts of a program. But global variables can often turn out to be a distinct disadvantage, particularly in long and complex programming projects. The programmer has to keep track of all variable names in a program and guard against using the same name for two different purposes. If a subroutine assigns a new value to a variable that is important elsewhere in the program, unexpected and often undesirable effects may result.

```
100 REM The Frame subroutine draws a rectangular double-line frame
110 REM     on the screen, using "text-graphics" characters from
120 REM     the IBM Extended ASCII character set.
130 REM
140 REM ---- Draw the four corners.
150 LOCATE TOP%, LEFT%: PRINT CHR$(201)
160 LOCATE TOP%, RIGHT%: PRINT CHR$(187)
170 LOCATE BOTTOM%, LEFT%: PRINT CHR$(200);
180 LOCATE BOTTOM%, RIGHT%: PRINT CHR$(188);
190 REM
200 REM ---- Draw the vertical lines.
210 FOR VERT% = TOP% + 1 TO BOTTOM% - 1
220     LOCATE VERT%, LEFT%: PRINT CHR$(186);
230     LOCATE VERT%, RIGHT%: PRINT CHR$(186);
240 NEXT VERT%
250 REM
260 REM ---- Draw the horizontal lines.
270 HORIZ% = RIGHT% - LEFT% - 1
280 HLINE$ = STRING$(HORIZ%, 205)
290 LOCATE TOP%, LEFT% + 1: PRINT HLINE$
300 LOCATE BOTTOM%, LEFT% + 1: PRINT HLINE$;
310 RETURN
```

Figure 2-3. *A BASICA version of the* Frame *subprogram in Figure 2-1.*

Fortunately, the variables in a QuickBASIC subprogram are local by default. Local variables that happen to have the same name but are located in different subprograms cannot interfere with each other because QuickBASIC treats them as completely different variables. Thanks to this characteristic, you can spend less time worrying about duplicate variable names in a long program. To send information from one procedure to another, you generally use parameter passing rather than global variables.

Let's look at an example that illustrates the significance of local variables. Notice that the *Frame* subprogram contains a FOR...NEXT loop that uses a variable named *vert%* as a counter:

```
FOR vert% = top% + 1 TO bottom% - 1
```

What happens if another procedure in the program uses the same variable for a FOR...NEXT loop that makes repeated calls to *Frame*? For example, here is a loop that displays a series of twelve progressively smaller frames enclosed one inside another:

```
FOR vert% = 1 TO 12
    Frame (3 * vert%), 81 - (3 * vert%), vert%, 25 - vert%
NEXT vert%
```

In QuickBASIC, this loop will execute successfully, producing the pattern of frames shown in Figure 2-4. QuickBASIC treats the two variables named *vert%*—located in two different procedures—as two distinct variables. Neither interferes with the value stored in the other.

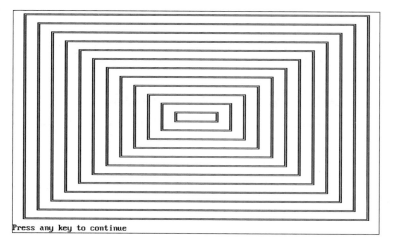

Figure 2-4. *An experiment with local variables.*

However, the result of the same loop in a BASICA program is not so predictable. Like all other BASICA variables, *vert%* is global; each call to the subroutine will change the value of the counter in the main program. In order for the program to behave as planned, you have to change the name of one of the loop variables.

Establishing global variables

Despite the clear advantages of local variables in QuickBASIC subprograms, you may sometimes want to establish a few key variables as global in a program. If specific variables are required by most or all of the routines in a program, declaring those variables global may turn out to be more convenient than passing the variables as arguments to each routine that needs them.

QuickBASIC offers several statements for declaring global variables. One is the COMMON SHARED statement. For example, the following statement declares three variables as global:

```
COMMON SHARED okData%, files$, tableRows%
```

The values stored in these three variables will be available to any routine in the program, and any routine can also change the value stored in any of these variables. The COMMON SHARED statement appears in the top section of a program, above any executable commands.

The DIM statement, used for establishing the dimensions of arrays, can also include a SHARED clause in QuickBASIC; for example:

```
DIM SHARED intArr%(5), strArr$(50)
```

The SHARED clause specifies that these two arrays are global.

Next we'll look at functions, the second kind of procedure available in QuickBASIC.

FUNCTIONS IN QUICKBASIC 4.0 AND 4.5

Functions have many characteristics in common with subprograms:

- A function definition includes an optional parameter list, consisting of string or numeric variables, records, or arrays.

- A call to a function can pass arguments either by reference or by value.

- Variables defined inside a function are local by default.

- Recursive functions are legal in Versions 4.0 and later.

However, functions differ from subprograms in one crucial respect: A function returns a single value of a specified type. Unlike a subprogram call, a function call never stands alone as a statement. Rather, a function call appears as part of a statement or expression that performs some further operation on the returned value.

Here is the general form of a function:

```
FUNCTION FunctionName (ParameterList) STATIC
    [the statements of the function]
    FunctionName = expression
END FUNCTION
```

Notice the various elements of this structure:

- The FUNCTION statement supplies the name of the function and the list of parameter variables. The function's name indicates the type of value that the function will return. For example, a function name that ends in $ returns a string value, and one that ends in % supplies an integer value.

- The optional reserved word STATIC specifies that the local variables inside the function will retain their values from one call to another.

- Inside the function, usually near the end, a special statement assigns a value to the function's name, thus specifying the value that the function itself will return.

- The END FUNCTION statement marks the end of the function definition.

A call to a function takes the following form:

```
FunctionName (argumentList)
```

A function call always appears as part of a larger statement that uses the value returned by the function.

Functions are new in QuickBASIC Versions 4.0 and 4.5. Previous versions of the language offered the DEF FN statement for creating routines known as *user-defined functions*. QuickBASIC still supports the DEF FN statement, but the characteristics of such a user-defined function are somewhat different from those of a function:

- The variables inside a DEF FN function are global by default. In contrast, function variables are local by default.

- A DEF FN function cannot accept arrays or records as arguments, whereas a function can accept any type of value or structure as an argument.

- The QuickBASIC 4.0 and 4.5 development environments do not treat DEF FN functions as separate procedures in a program. As we have seen, functions are displayed individually in the View windows and are included in the View menu's SUBs list; DEF FN functions are not.

For all of these reasons, we will use only functions in this book, never DEF FN functions. Let's look at an example of a function.

The *HeadlineStyle$* Function

The *HeadlineStyle$* function, shown in Figure 2-5, receives a string argument and returns a string as its result. The purpose of the *HeadlineStyle$* function is to convert each word in the string argument to a consistent alphabetic case—an initial capital letter followed by all lowercase letters. For example, the following PRINT statement contains a call to the function:

```
PRINT HeadlineStyle$("the SAN FRANCISCO opera house")
```

The result of this PRINT statement is:

```
The San Francisco Opera House
```

Given an appropriate text argument, *HeadlineStyle$* loops through the string one word at a time, recognizing embedded space characters as the markers between one word and the next. The function stores a given word in the string variable *oneWord$* and then uses several of QuickBASIC's built-in string functions to perform the case conversion:

```
oneWord$ = UCASE$(LEFT$(oneWord$, 1)) + LCASE$(MID$(oneWord$, 2))
```

In this statement, the LEFT$ function isolates the first letter of the word, and UCASE$ provides the uppercase equivalent of the letter. Likewise, MID$ isolates the remaining letters in the word, and LCASE$ supplies the lowercase equivalent of those letters. The procedure concatenates the result of each one-word conversion to the variable *outString$*:

```
outString$ = outString$ + oneWord$
```

When the looping is finished, the new string stored in *outString$*
is returned as the value of the function:

```
HeadlineStyle$ = outString$
```

```
FUNCTION HeadlineStyle$ (inString$)

'   The HeadlineStyle$ function removes leading and trailing
'       blanks from its string argument and then converts the
'       case of each word in the string to an initial uppercase
'       letter followed by all lowercase letters.

    inString$ = LTRIM$(RTRIM$(inString$))

    IF inString$ = "" THEN
        outString$ = ""
    ELSE

'   ---- Search for words inside the string.

        nextSearch% = 1
        DO
            spacePos% = INSTR(nextSearch%, inString$, " ")
            IF spacePos% <> 0 THEN
                oneWord$ = MID$(inString$, nextSearch%, spacePos% - nextSearch%)
                nextSearch% = spacePos% + 1
            ELSE
                oneWord$ = MID$(inString$, nextSearch%)
            END IF

'   ---- Capitalize the first letter and convert the rest
'       of the word to lowercase.

            oneWord$ = UCASE$(LEFT$(oneWord$, 1)) + LCASE$(MID$(oneWord$, 2))
            IF spacePos% <> 0 THEN oneWord$ = oneWord$ + " "
            outString$ = outString$ + oneWord$
        LOOP UNTIL spacePos% = 0
    END IF

    HeadlineStyle$ = outString$

END FUNCTION
```

Figure 2-5. *The* HeadlineStyle$ *function.*

The *HeadlineStyle$* function is similar to several functions that we'll discuss in Part II of this book—functions that perform equally detailed conversion tasks on string arguments.

To tie together everything we have learned about subprograms and functions, we'll next look briefly at a complete demonstration, listed in Figure 2-6. This program, which we'll simply call *Demo*, calls both the *HeadlineStyle$* function and the *Frame* subprogram.

A DEMONSTRATION PROGRAM

```
'   DEMO.BAS
'   Demonstrates a function call and subprogram calls.

'   ---- Definitions and declarations section.

DECLARE FUNCTION HeadlineStyle$ (inString$)
DECLARE SUB Frame (left%, right%, top%, bottom%)
DECLARE SUB GetMessage ()
DECLARE SUB Pause ()
DECLARE SUB ShowMessage ()

COMMON SHARED message$

'   ---- Main program section.

CLS
GetMessage
ShowMessage

Frame 1, 80, 1, 25
Pause

END

SUB Frame (left%, right%, top%, bottom%) STATIC

'   The Frame subprogram draws a rectangular double-line frame on
'       the screen, using "text-graphics" characters from the IBM
'       Extended ASCII character set.

'   ---- Draw the four corners.
```

Figure 2-6. *The* Demo *program.* *(continued)*

Figure 2-6. *continued*

```
      LOCATE top%, left%: PRINT CHR$(201)
      LOCATE top%, right%: PRINT CHR$(187)
      LOCATE bottom%, left%: PRINT CHR$(200);
      LOCATE bottom%, right%: PRINT CHR$(188);

   '   ---- Draw the vertical lines.

      FOR vert% = top% + 1 TO bottom% - 1
          LOCATE vert%, left%: PRINT CHR$(186);
          LOCATE vert%, right%: PRINT CHR$(186);
      NEXT vert%

   '   ---- Draw the horizontal lines.

      horiz% = right% - left% - 1
      hline$ = STRING$(horiz%, 205)
      LOCATE top%, left% + 1: PRINT hline$
      LOCATE bottom%, left% + 1: PRINT hline$;

END SUB

SUB GetMessage STATIC

   '   The GetMessage subprogram elicits a message string from
   '       the keyboard and converts the string to headline style.

   '   ---- Get a message string.

      INPUT "Enter your message here: ", message$

   '   ---- Convert the string to headline style.

      message$ = "*** " + HeadlineStyle$(message$) + " ***"

END SUB

FUNCTION HeadlineStyle$ (inString$)

   '   The HeadlineStyle$ function removes leading and trailing
   '       blanks from its string argument and then converts the
   '       case of each word in the string to an initial uppercase
   '       letter followed by all lowercase letters.

      inString$ = LTRIM$(RTRIM$(inString$))
```

(continued)

Figure 2-6. *continued*

```
    IF inString$ = "" THEN
        outString$ = ""
    ELSE

'   ---- Search for words inside the string.

        nextSearch% = 1
        DO
            spacePos% = INSTR(nextSearch%, inString$, " ")
            IF spacePos% <> 0 THEN
                oneWord$ = MID$(inString$, nextSearch%, spacePos% - nextSearch%)
                nextSearch% = spacePos% + 1
            ELSE
                oneWord$ = MID$(inString$, nextSearch%)
            END IF

'   ---- Capitalize the first letter and convert the rest
'        of the word to lowercase.

            oneWord$ = UCASE$(LEFT$(oneWord$, 1)) + LCASE$(MID$(oneWord$, 2))
            IF spacePos% <> 0 THEN oneWord$ = oneWord$ + " "
            outString$ = outString$ + oneWord$
        LOOP UNTIL spacePos% = 0
    END IF

    HeadlineStyle$ = outString$

END FUNCTION

SUB Pause STATIC

'   The Pause subprogram simply creates a pause in the action
'       until the user presses a key at the keyboard.

    DO
        inChar$ = INKEY$
    LOOP UNTIL inChar$ <> ""

END SUB

SUB ShowMessage STATIC

'   The ShowMessage subprogram displays the message on
'       the screen, inside a frame.
```

(continued)

Figure 2-6. *continued*

```
'    ---- Determine frame coordinates.

     leftColumn% = (80 - LEN(message$)) \ 2 - 3
     rightColumn% = 80 - leftColumn%
     topRow% = 10:  bottomRow% = 14

'    ---- Draw the frame and print the message.

     CLS
     Frame leftColumn%, rightColumn%, topRow%, bottomRow%
     LOCATE topRow% + 2, leftColumn% + 4:   PRINT message$

END SUB
```

Demo conducts a very simple sequence of activities, but nonetheless represents the general structure of programs presented in this book. The program begins by asking you to enter a message string. After you type the message, the program redisplays your message in the center of the screen, enclosed in a pair of frames. Figure 2-7 shows a sample of the program's output. This sample screen is the result of the following input dialog:

```
Enter your message here: the microsoft q u i c k b a s i c compiler
```

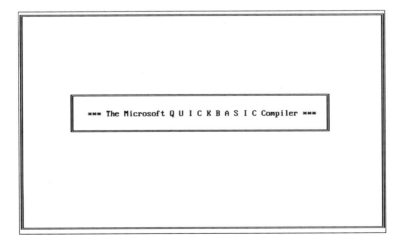

Figure 2-7. *Sample output from the* Demo *program.*

As you can see, the output message is displayed in "headline" style, with the first letter of each word capitalized.

The various tasks performed by the program are divided into several sections. First, a series of definition and declaration statements appears at the top of the listing. Every program in this book begins with a section such as this one; let's discuss its general role in a program.

The definitions and declarations section

Here are the various elements that can be included in a program's definitions and declarations section:

- CONST statements, defining symbolic constants
- TYPE statements, establishing user-defined data types
- DECLARE statements, for subprograms and functions
- COMMON SHARED statements, listing global variables
- DIM statements, creating array variables
- DATA statements, supplying lines of READ data

We will discuss these statements in Chapter 4, and we'll encounter each of them again and again in examples throughout the book.

The short *Demo* program contains only an abbreviated selection of definition and declaration statements: A group of DECLARE statements lists the names and parameters of the program's procedures, and a COMMON SHARED statement establishes one global variable. The DECLARE statements actually have three purposes in a QuickBASIC 4.0 or 4.5 program:

- To allow the program to call subprograms without using the reserved word CALL
- To allow the program to call functions that are defined in modules other than the main module
- To activate argument checking for all call statements that you write inside the QuickBASIC development environment

The syntax of the DECLARE statement for a subprogram is:

```
DECLARE SUB SubprogramName (parameterList)
```

Likewise, the syntax for a function is:

```
DECLARE FUNCTION FunctionName (parameterList)
```

Fortunately, you almost never have to write a DECLARE statement yourself. QuickBASIC automatically generates a statement for each subprogram and function when you first save a program on disk.

The section that controls the action of the program is located immediately after the definitions and declarations section.

Controlling the program

In this book we'll use the term *main program* to refer to the controlling section of any QuickBASIC program. (In a program that contains more than one module, the main program is the controlling section, or *module-level code*, at the top of the main module.) The main program section is usually short and consists primarily of calls to the procedures that the program contains. For example, here is the complete main program section of the *Demo* program:

```
'    ---- Main program section.

CLS
GetMessage
ShowMessage

Frame 1, 80, 1, 25
Pause

END
```

The main program section outlines the program's activities: The *GetMessage* procedure conducts the input dialog; *ShowMessage* displays the message on the screen; a call to *Frame* produces the outer frame around the message; and *Pause* halts the action so you can examine the screen.

Of these four subprograms, only *Frame* takes arguments. The global variable *message$* is the medium for communicating the message string to each subprogram that needs it. For example, *GetMessage* uses an INPUT statement to place a prompt on the screen and to store the input in the *message$* variable. A call to the *HeadlineStyle$* function then prepares the string for display:

```
message$ = "*** " + HeadlineStyle$(message$) + " ***"
```

The *ShowMessage* subprogram calls *Frame* to produce the small frame around the message, and then it displays the string value:

```
Frame leftColumn%, rightColumn%, topRow%, bottomRow%
LOCATE topRow% + 2, leftColumn + 4:   PRINT message$
```

The four variables in this passage are the coordinates of the inner frame. The program calculates the values of the horizontal coordinates (*leftColumn%* and *rightColumn%*) from the length of the message.

Simple though this program is, it illustrates a structured approach to organizing QuickBASIC programs. Each program task is isolated in an individual subprogram or function. If you want to change any task, you can easily locate the appropriate procedure to revise.

Conclusion

QuickBASIC 4.0 and 4.5 provide two kinds of procedures: subprograms and functions. Both kinds of procedures support the following important features:

- Local variables
- Parameters (including record structures and arrays)
- Arguments passed by reference or by value
- Recursion

Furthermore, the QuickBASIC development environment makes using procedures easier than ever before.

In Chapter 3 we'll examine several techniques for building a QuickBASIC program: merging procedure files, using modules, and creating Quick libraries.

Building Programs

Most QuickBASIC programming projects require a combination of application-specific procedures and general-purpose procedures. The latter category, general-purpose procedures, can prove useful in any number of different contexts. Over time, you'll probably build a significant collection of general-purpose procedures that perform common programming tasks. After developing and testing such procedures, you'll want to be able to use them over and over, without having to reinvent them for each new project.

Finding effective ways to introduce general-purpose procedures into a current project is one of the recurring problems in the process of building a program. This chapter discusses this important issue and presents three practical techniques for incorporating tested procedures into a QuickBASIC program. The techniques are:

- Merging a procedure file directly into the current program
- Combining multiple modules in a single program

- Developing Quick libraries of compiled procedures and using such libraries in the QuickBASIC environment

These techniques involve options and features new to QuickBASIC in Versions 4.0 and 4.5. Previous versions of QuickBASIC have also supported various approaches for combining procedures in a program, but no previous version has offered solutions that are as simple and elegant as those now available.

To illustrate these techniques, we'll work with two general-purpose procedures in this chapter. The first is the *Frame* subprogram, which we discussed in Chapter 2. This simple but important routine draws a rectangular frame on the screen. The second procedure is a function named *Menu%*, which displays a menu of program options on the screen and accepts the user's menu selections from the keyboard.

For convenience, the major applications in this book are all presented as self-contained, single-module programs, even when they include general-purpose tools such as *Frame* and *Menu%*. As you work with the applications and develop your own version of each program, you can use any of the techniques outlined in this chapter to incorporate procedures into a project. Once you have developed and tested subprograms and functions such as *Frame* and *Menu%* for one program, you can transform the routines into ready-to-use tools for any new programming project that you undertake.

Let's begin by examining the *Menu%* function.

PRESENTING MENUS ON THE SCREEN — THE *MENU%* FUNCTION

Several of the application programs in this book are menu driven. To operate such a program, the user makes choices from a recurring menu—that is, a list of program options that appears repeatedly on the screen. The *Menu%* function performs two tasks in this scheme:

1. It displays the program's menu attractively and clearly on the screen.

2. It elicits a response from the user and ensures that the response is appropriate in the context of the program's options.

Figure 3-1 shows an example of a menu screen presented by the *Menu%* function. The function lists the menu choices on the screen inside a frame. The first letter of each choice is a capital letter, and a parenthesis character separates this first letter from the rest of the string. Below the choices, *Menu%* also displays the following input prompt:

```
G  A  D  P  Q ->  _
```

This presentation tells the user how to respond to the menu. To choose one of the five options, press the key that corresponds to the first letter of the option.

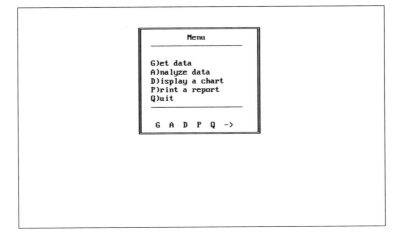

Figure 3-1. *A sample menu presented by the* Menu% *function.*

For example, to choose the Get data option, press the letter G. In response, *Menu%* displays the following message on the screen beneath the menu box:

```
<Enter> to confirm; <Esc> to redo.
```

To confirm the menu choice, the user presses the Enter key. To undo the menu choice and start again, the user presses the Esc key.

The *Menu%* subprogram exerts careful control over the input process. If the user presses a key that does not represent a menu choice, *Menu%* causes the computer's speaker to beep. On the other hand, the *Menu%* routine conveniently allows either uppercase or lowercase input responses.

Menu% consists of three different routines:

- The *Menu%* function (Figure 3-2), which controls the major action of the procedure
- The *DisplayMenuBox* subprogram (Figure 3-3), which takes care of the rather detailed screen-display tasks that the procedure performs
- The *Frame* subprogram (Figure 3-4 on page 72), which displays a frame around the menu options

We discussed the *Frame* routine in Chapter 2; let's now look briefly at the *Menu%* function, shown in Figure 3-2, and the *DisplayMenuBox* subprogram, shown in Figure 3-3.

```
FUNCTION Menu% (choices$()) STATIC

'   The Menu% function displays a menu on the screen and
'       elicits a menu choice from the user. Menu% receives a
'       string array (choices$) containing the menu choices
'       and returns an integer indicating the user's
'       selection from among those choices.

    listLength% = UBOUND(choices$)
    DisplayMenuBox choices$(), leftMargin%, promptStr$, okStr$

'   ---- Get a menu choice. Validate and verify the choice.

    controlKeys$ = CHR$(13) + CHR$(27)
    DO
        LOCATE , , 1
        charPos% = 0
        DO
            answer$ = UCASE$(INKEY$)
            IF answer$ <> "" THEN
                charPos% = INSTR(okStr$, answer$)
                IF charPos% = 0 THEN BEEP
            END IF
        LOOP UNTIL charPos% > 0

        PRINT answer$
        LOCATE 11 + listLength%, 23, 0
        PRINT "<Enter> to confirm; <Esc> to redo."
        inChoice% = charPos%
```

Figure 3-2. *The* Menu% *function.*

(continued)

Figure 3-2. *continued*

```
        charPos% = 0
        DO
            answer$ = INKEY$
            IF answer$ <> "" THEN
                charPos% = INSTR(controlKeys$, answer$)
                IF charPos% = 0 THEN BEEP
            END IF
        LOOP UNTIL charPos% > 0

        IF charPos% = 1 THEN
            done% = true%
            CLS
        ELSE
            done% = false%
            LOCATE 11 + listLength%, 23: PRINT SPACE$(35)
            LOCATE 9 + listLength%, leftMargin% + 3 + LEN(promptStr$): PRINT " ";
            LOCATE , POS(0) - 1
        END IF
    LOOP UNTIL done%

    Menu% = inChoice%

END FUNCTION
```

```
SUB DisplayMenuBox (choiceList$(), leftCoord%, prompt$, ok$)

'   The DisplayMenuBox subprogram displays the menu choices on the
'       screen and prepares the prompt string and validation string.
'       This routine is called from the Menu% function.

'   ---- Find the number of choices (numChoices%) and initialize variables.

    numChoices% = UBOUND(choiceList$)
    prompt$ = " "
    ok$ = ""
    longChoice% = 0

'   ---- Prepare the prompt string (prompt$) and the string of
'       legal input characters (ok$). Also, find the length of
'       the longest choice string (longChoice%).
```

Figure 3-3. *The* DisplayMenuBox *subprogram.*   *(continued)*

Figure 3-3. *continued*

```
    FOR i% = 1 TO numChoices%
        first$ = UCASE$(LEFT$(choiceList$(i%), 1))
        ok$ = ok$ + first$
        prompt$ = prompt$ + first$ + "  "
        longTemp% = LEN(choiceList$(i%))
        IF longTemp% > longChoice% THEN longChoice% = longTemp%
    NEXT i%

    longChoice% = longChoice% + 1
    prompt$ = prompt$ + "-> "

'   ---- Test to see if the prompt string is longer than longChoice%.

    IF LEN(prompt$) >= longChoice% THEN longChoice% = LEN(prompt$) + 1

'   ---- Given longChoice% and numChoices%, determine the dimensions
'        of the menu frame. Draw the frame, calling on the Frame
'        subprogram.

    leftCoord% = 37 - longChoice% \ 2
    rightCoord% = 80 - leftCoord%
    topCoord% = 3
    bottomCoord% = 10 + numChoices%
    Frame leftCoord%, rightCoord%, topCoord%, bottomCoord%

'   ---- Display the menu choices. The first letter of each choice is
'        displayed in uppercase, followed by a parenthesis character.

    FOR i% = 1 TO numChoices%
        LOCATE 6 + i%, leftCoord% + 3
        PRINT UCASE$(LEFT$(choiceList$(i%), 1)) + ")" + MID$(choiceList$(i%), 2)
    NEXT i%

    LOCATE 4, 38: PRINT "Menu"
    line$ = STRING$(longChoice%, 196)
    LOCATE 5, leftCoord% + 3: PRINT line$
    LOCATE 7 + numChoices%, leftCoord% + 3: PRINT line$

'   ---- Print the input prompt.

    LOCATE 9 + numChoices%, leftCoord% + 3: PRINT prompt$;

END SUB
```

The *Menu%* function contains one parameter, a string array containing the menu choices:

```
FUNCTION Menu% (choices$()) STATIC
```

The function begins by using the built-in UBOUND function to determine the length of this array:

```
listLength% = UBOUND(choices$)
```

Then *Menu%* calls the *DisplayMenuBox* subprogram to display the menu on the screen:

```
DisplayMenuBox choices$(), leftMargin%, promptStr$, okStr$
```

DisplayMenuBox lists the menu choices and then calls *Frame*, shown in Figure 3-4, to display the box around the menu. The procedure also builds two string values and returns them to *Menu%* via the arguments *promptStr$* and *okStr$*. The first of these, *promptStr$*, is the prompt that appears at the bottom of the menu. The second, *okStr$*, serves as an input validation string; it contains an uppercase letter representing each of the actual menu choices. *DisplayMenuBox* also passes back an integer value, *leftMargin%*, which is the screen coordinate for the left side of the menu display.

Back in the *Menu%* routine, a series of nested DO...UNTIL loops control the input process for the user's menu selection. The first of two inner loops accepts a single-character menu choice, and beeps if the user enters an invalid choice. The second inner loop reads either the Enter key (ASCII 13) to confirm the choice, or the Esc key (ASCII 27) to cancel the choice. The outer loop repeats the process until the user has entered and confirmed a valid menu choice.

The whole process relies on two of QuickBASIC's built-in functions: INKEY$, which reads a single character from the keyboard; and INSTR, which searches for the input character in one of the two strings of valid choices, *okStr$* or *controlKeys$*.

Figure 3-5 on page 73 shows the controlling section of a demonstration program called *MenuTest*, which illustrates the use of the *Menu%* function. (This program creates the menu shown in Figure 3-1.) *MenuTest* begins by creating an array named *menuOptions$()* that will contain the program's five menu options. The program reads these strings into *menuOptions$()* from a series of DATA lines, as shown on the next page.

```
                        DATA get data
                        DATA analyze data
                        DATA display a chart
                        DATA print a report
                        DATA quit

                        '   ---- Main program section.
                        FOR i% = 1 TO 5
                            READ menuOptions$(i%)
                        NEXT i%
```

```
SUB Frame (left%, right%, top%, bottom%) STATIC

'   The Frame subprogram draws a rectangular double-line frame on
'       the screen, using "text-graphics" characters from the
'       IBM Extended ASCII character set.

'   ---- Draw the four corners.

    LOCATE top%, left%: PRINT CHR$(201)
    LOCATE top%, right%: PRINT CHR$(187)
    LOCATE bottom%, left%: PRINT CHR$(200);
    LOCATE bottom%, right%: PRINT CHR$(188);

'   ---- Draw the vertical lines.

    FOR vert% = top% + 1 TO bottom% - 1
        LOCATE vert%, left%: PRINT CHR$(186);
        LOCATE vert%, right%: PRINT CHR$(186);
    NEXT vert%

'   ---- Draw the horizontal lines.

    horiz% = right% - left% - 1
    hline$ = STRING$(horiz%, 205)
    LOCATE top%, left% + 1: PRINT hline$
    LOCATE bottom%, left% + 1: PRINT hline$;

END SUB
```

Figure 3-4. *The* Frame *subprogram.*

```
'    MenuTest
'    Demonstrates the Menu% function.

'    ---- Definitions and declarations section.

CONST false% = 0, true% = NOT false%

DECLARE FUNCTION Menu% (choices$())
DECLARE SUB DisplayMenuBox (choiceList$(), leftCoord%, prompt$, ok$)
DECLARE SUB Frame (left%, right%, top%, bottom%)

DIM menuOptions$(5)

DATA get data
DATA analyze data
DATA display a chart
DATA print a report
DATA quit

'    ---- Main program section.

FOR i% = 1 TO 5
    READ menuOptions$(i%)
NEXT i%

CLS

'    ---- Display the menu and react to the user's choices.

DO
    SELECT CASE Menu%(menuOptions$())
    CASE 1
        CLS : PRINT "The Get data option."
    CASE 2
        CLS : PRINT "The Analyze data option."
    CASE 3
        CLS : PRINT "The Display a chart option."
    CASE 4
        CLS : PRINT "The Print a report option."
    CASE ELSE
        done% = true%
    END SELECT
```

Figure 3-5. *The main program section of the* MenuTest *program.*   *(continued)*

Figure 3-5. *continued*

```
    IF NOT done% THEN
        PRINT
        PRINT "Press the spacebar to continue."

        DO
            ch$ = INKEY$
        LOOP UNTIL ch$ = " "

        CLS
    END IF

LOOP UNTIL done%

END
```

To avoid ambiguity, each string in the array of options must begin with a different letter or digit. If two options were to begin with the same character, the *Menu%* function would always select the first of the two options, never the second.

After creating the *menuOptions$* string, the *MenuTest* program calls the *Menu%* function at the top of a SELECT CASE structure:

```
SELECT CASE Menu%(menuOptions$())
```

In this demonstration program, the controlling decision structure simply displays messages on the screen in response to each menu selection. A DO...UNTIL loop in *MenuTest* repeats the call to *Menu%* until the user selects the last option, Quit. This is a typical way to produce a recurring menu.

In a real program—such as the *Survey, Employee,* and *QuickChart* programs presented in Part II—each block of the decision structure calls procedures that actually conduct the activities corresponding to a given menu choice.

Now we return to the problem outlined at the beginning of this chapter: How do we incorporate *Menu%* and *Frame* into a program that uses these general-purpose procedures as tools? Perhaps the simplest and most direct technique is to merge the files containing these procedures directly into the program. We'll discuss this approach in the next section.

MERGING PROCEDURE FILES INTO A PROGRAM

The Merge command in QuickBASIC's File menu merges code from a disk file into the current program. To use this command, pull down the File menu and select Merge. When the Merge dialog box appears on the screen, enter the name of the file that you want to merge into the current program.

If the disk file contains subprograms or functions, QuickBASIC displays these procedures individually in View windows. To examine the newly merged procedures, pull down the View menu and select the SUBs command, or simply press the F2 function key.

For example, let's say you have saved the *Menu%* and *Frame* procedures in two disk files, as follows:

- *MENU.BAS* contains both the *Menu%* function and the *DisplayMenuBox* subprogram.

- *FRAME.BAS* contains the *Frame* subprogram.

Imagine that you have written the main program section of *MenuTest* (Figure 3-5), and you are now ready to incorporate *Menu%* and *Frame* into the program. To do so, choose the Merge command twice, once to merge the *MENU.BAS* file and again to merge the *FRAME.BAS* file. The SUBs command dialog box will subsequently show you the following outline of your program:

```
MENUTEST.BAS
   DisplayMenuBox
   Frame
   Menu
```

If you have not written DECLARE statements for the newly merged procedures, QuickBASIC generates the statements for you when you first save the complete program. With the three general-purpose procedures installed in *MenuTest*, you can now try running the program (by selecting Start from the Run menu) to see if everything works correctly.

In versions of QuickBASIC before Version 4.0, the $INCLUDE metacommand was a common tool for incorporating procedures into a larger program. This technique is not allowed in QuickBASIC 4.0 and 4.5. For this reason, you might have to use the Merge command to load $INCLUDE files before you can run a program that you developed in a previous version of QuickBASIC. Let's discuss this situation.

Working with $INCLUDE files

$INCLUDE is a *metacommand,* a specific instruction to the QuickBASIC compiler. A metacommand always appears in a REM statement, and the command is preceded by a dollar-sign character ($). $INCLUDE statements appear in the following format:

```
REM $INCLUDE : 'filename'
```

The name of the disk file is enclosed in single quotation marks, and a colon separates the $INCLUDE command from the filename. This command instructs the compiler to incorporate the named file into the current program.

Although QuickBASIC still supports the $INCLUDE command, the environment can no longer handle include files that contain subprograms or functions. But a program developed in a previous version of QuickBASIC might contain $INCLUDE commands designed to read procedures into the program.

For example, the following commands would have successfully loaded the *Menu%* and *Frame* procedures into a program developed before QuickBASIC 4.0:

```
REM $INCLUDE : 'MENU.BAS'
REM $INCLUDE : 'FRAME.BAS'
```

Since these $INCLUDE operations are no longer legal, you should perform the following steps before trying to run a program that contains $INCLUDE commands:

1. Use the File menu's Merge command to merge the include files directly into the program you are developing.

2. Delete the $INCLUDE statements.

3. Perform a save operation so that QuickBASIC will generate DECLARE statements for the newly included procedures.

In general, the advantages of the Merge operation are convenience and simplicity. The operation is easy to use, and allows you to incorporate any source code file directly into the program you are developing.

However, a long and complicated program might require the use of several different collections of general-purpose procedures. In this case, you might prefer a more sophisticated approach for incorporating procedures into a current programming project: using multiple program modules, or developing a Quick library. We'll examine these two approaches in the following sections.

USING MULTIPLE PROGRAM MODULES

As we discussed in Chapter 1, programs in QuickBASIC 4.0 and 4.5 can contain multiple modules. Each different module can in turn consist of a collection of subprograms and functions. When two or more modules are loaded into the QuickBASIC environment at once, the resulting program has access to all of the subprograms and functions in all of the multiple modules.

Each module is stored as an individual file on disk. A convenient way to incorporate a group of related general-purpose procedures into a program is to load them all at once from a module file. For example, you might store the *Menu%*, *DisplayMenuBox*, and *Frame* procedures together in a single disk file called *MENUPROC.BAS*. When you are developing a program that requires these procedures, you can simply load *MENUPROC* into memory as a separate program module.

Once again, let's say you have written the main program section of the *MenuTest* program, and you are now ready to incorporate the menu procedures into the current program. Perform the following steps to load the *MENUPROC* module:

1. Pull down the File menu and select the Load File command.

2. In the Load File dialog box, enter the name of the file that you want to open as a module, *MENUPROC.BAS*. (You can either type the filename directly into the text box or select the filename from the list box.) Make sure the Load as Module option remains selected for this operation.

3. Press Enter to complete the operation.

Now, if you pull down the View menu and select the SUBs command, you will find that your program contains two modules:

```
MENUTEST.BAS
MENUPROC.BAS
  DisplayMenuBox
  Frame
  Menu
```

As a result of the Load File operation, QuickBASIC keeps any current modules in memory, and loads a new module to combine with the current ones. In this case the *MENUTEST* file is the main module, but the program can also call the procedures stored in the second module, *MENUPROC*.

To save *MenuTest* on disk after loading the second module, choose the Save All command from the File menu. QuickBASIC retains each module as a separate file on disk. Furthermore, QuickBASIC creates a special disk file that supplies the names of all the modules in the program. The extension name of this special file is always MAK. For the *MenuTest* program, the file's name is *MENUTEST.MAK*. The MAK file is a text file, so you can examine its contents by using the TYPE command from MS-DOS. The *MENUTEST.MAK* file contains a list of the two module files that now make up the *MenuTest* program:

```
MENUTEST.BAS
MENUPROC.BAS
```

Whenever you load a multiple-module program into memory, QuickBASIC searches for the program's MAK file and opens all the module files listed the MAK file.

In a program that contains multiple modules, several techniques are available for sharing information between modules. Variables declared global in one module are not automatically accessible to another module. You use COMMON statements to share global variables between modules.

Furthermore, a module must be a self-contained unit of code. Consider, for example, the CONST statement located at the top of the *MenuTest* program:

```
CONST false% = 0, true% = NOT false%
```

We'll discuss the CONST statement in detail in Chapter 4. This statement establishes the two logical values *true%* and *false%* as *symbolic constants*. But symbolic constants are available only within the module that defines them. Since the *Menu%* function requires the use of these constants to work properly, you must include the same CONST statement in the controlling section of the *MENUPROC* module.

Keep in mind the role of the DECLARE statements located in the main program section. DECLARE is particularly important for defining functions that are located in another module. Without a DECLARE statement, the main program will not be able to locate the procedure.

Finally, let's discuss the use of Quick libraries in QuickBASIC 4.0 and 4.5.

CREATING A QUICK LIBRARY

A Quick library is a file that contains one or more compiled program modules. In QuickBASIC 4.0 and 4.5 you can create a Quick library directly from the QuickBASIC environment in one simple operation. Then, whenever you start QuickBASIC, you can load the Quick library into memory, making all of the procedures in the library available to your current program.

You use the Make Library command from QuickBASIC's Run menu to create a Quick library. Here are the steps of the operation:

1. Load into memory the module or modules that you want to include in the Quick library. (Use the Load File command from the File menu to load module files. Alternatively, you can use the Unload File command to remove any modules that you do not want to include in your Quick library.)

2. Pull down the Run menu and choose the Make Library command.

3. Enter the filename under which you want to store your Quick library. If you do not supply an explicit extension name, QuickBASIC gives the Quick library file an extension of QLB. If you do not supply a drivename or pathname, QuickBASIC stores the Quick library file in the current drive and directory.

4. Select the Make Library option to create the library and stay in the QuickBASIC environment, or the Make Library and Exit option to create the library and return to MS-DOS.

For example, consider the process of creating a Quick library for the menu procedures. Begin by loading the *MENUPROC.BAS* module into memory and choosing the Make Library command from the Run menu. Enter the name *MENUPROC* for your Quick library, and press Enter to complete the operation. In response, QuickBASIC creates the Quick library named *MENUPROC.QLB* on disk.

To create a Quick library, QuickBASIC requires access to several files that are included on the QuickBASIC program disks. These files are:

```
QB.EXE
BC.EXE
LINK.EXE
LIB.EXE
BQLB45.LIB
```

If you are working with QuickBASIC on a hard disk, you should be sure that all of these files are included in the current directory or in the established search path. On a floppy-disk system, QuickBASIC displays messages on the screen when it needs a particular file that it cannot find. You'll swap disks several times during the operation.

After you create a Quick library, you can load the library into memory any time you start up QuickBASIC. For example, if you are developing a program that uses the procedures stored in the *MENUPROC* library, you should enter the following command at the MS-DOS prompt to begin your session with QuickBASIC:

```
C>QB /L MENUPROC
```

In this case, the /L option of the QB command instructs QuickBASIC to load the procedures of the *MENUPROC.QLB* Quick library into memory. Any program that you write during the subsequent session can make calls to the *Menu%* function, the *DisplayMenuBox* subprogram, and the *Frame* subprogram. You can create as many Quick library files as you wish, but only one library can be loaded into memory for a given session with QuickBASIC.

Actually, QuickBASIC creates two different files when you choose the Make Library command. The QLB library is the file that is loaded into memory when you start up QuickBASIC with the /L option. The second file, with an extension name of LIB, is the library format that QuickBASIC uses if you later decide to create a compiled EXE file from a program that relies on a Quick library.

QuickBASIC cannot generate automatic DECLARE statements for procedures stored in a Quick library; this is one case in which you have to write the declaration statements yourself. For this and other reasons, employing a Quick library may result in inadequately documented programs. A Quick library creates no automatic record of the subprograms that it makes available to a program. A person examining the listing of such a program may not be aware that a successful execution relies on the presence of the Quick library. To help solve this problem, you should write a comment in the program listing that supplies the name and location of the required library file.

A Quick library can prove to be a useful medium for managing a collection of subprograms that you use frequently. For instance, if you have written several general-purpose routines that you find yourself using in almost every program you write, you might want to put those routines into a Quick library. The advantages are clear. Whenever you load the procedures of a Quick library into memory for a particular session with QuickBASIC, the procedures are automatically available for use in your current programming project.

Conclusion

We have discussed three useful techniques that QuickBASIC offers for introducing procedures into a program. The simplest technique is to use the Merge command from the File menu. The second technique, organizing a program into multiple modules, is the quintessential approach for the QuickBASIC 4.0 and 4.5 development environment.

The third technique uses the Make Library command from the Run menu to create a Quick library from one or more program modules. QuickBASIC 4.0 and 4.5 perform this operation simply and efficiently within the development environment itself.

Part I of this book has concentrated on the QuickBASIC environment, and on the characteristics of procedures and modules in QuickBASIC 4.0 and 4.5. The goal of these three chapters has been to prepare you for studying the application programs that follow in Part II. However, QuickBASIC is a complex product, and there are many more details to master. You should consult frequently with the QuickBASIC documentation as you work with the chapters ahead.

PART

II

Language Topics and Sample Programs

C H A P T E R 4

Data Types and Data Structures: The *List* Program

A QuickBASIC program requires effective techniques for organizing, storing, and handling data values. Specifically, in planning a program you need to give careful attention to several related tasks:

- Creating appropriate types of variables to represent the data used in your program

- Performing the variety of steps necessary to assign values to those variables

- Designing efficient schemes for passing data from one routine to another in your program

In this context, one of the most important new features of the QuickBASIC language in Versions 4.0 and 4.5 is the expanded collection of data types and data structures available for you to use. These data types and structures are the main subject of this chapter.

If you've written programs in BASIC, you are already familiar with the data types that are traditionally available in the language. There have always been three standard numeric types: integers, single-precision floating-point values, and double-precision values. In addition, BASIC supplies the *string* data type for working with text values. We can refer to these as *elementary* data types.

QuickBASIC now adds two important new elementary types to the language: *long integers* and *fixed-length strings*. These new types give you additional options for working with numeric and string values in your programs. We'll explore both of these types in this chapter. Briefly, the long integer type supports very large whole numbers with perfect accuracy, and is useful whenever the range of standard integers is too small to be practical. With the fixed-length string type, you can establish string variables that accommodate a fixed number of characters.

You can refer to a value belonging to any of the elementary types in two general ways:

- Literally, by entering an actual constant value into the code of your program

- Symbolically, by creating a named variable to represent a data value

A variable in one of the elementary types stores a single data value at a time.

In contrast, QuickBASIC's *data structures* give you ways to represent multiple data values by a single variable name. Previous versions of QuickBASIC supported one kind of data structure—the *array*. Arrays are subscripted variables that represent lists or tables of data values. Each array has a specified type, and every individual data value in the array must conform to that type. We'll review the characteristics of arrays in this chapter, and we'll discuss the DIM statement, which you use to define arrays. We'll see that QuickBASIC now allows new flexibility for specifying the range of subscripts in an array.

In addition, QuickBASIC now supports an important *user-defined* type, which you can use to create compound data structures called *records*. Unlike an array, a record structure can store any combination of different numeric and string data types. You define this compound type with QuickBASIC's new TYPE statement, and then you choose from a variety of statements to create the corresponding record variable.

You can create any number of individual record variables for a program. Each single record variable stores one complete record of values at a time. The data values stored in such a variable are called the *elements* of the record. Significantly, you can also define arrays of records to store lists or tables of record values. Used appropriately, this versatile new data structure can vastly simplify programs that process whole records or groups of records at a time.

As we examine these new language elements in this chapter, we'll also discuss general techniques for storing and handling data in QuickBASIC 4.0 and 4.5. Specifically, we'll review the following topics:

- The range and precision of the various numeric data types now available in QuickBASIC and the arithmetic operations that a program can perform on numbers

- The differences between variable-length and fixed-length strings and the expanded library of built-in functions that QuickBASIC offers for working with string values

- The use of *logical values* (that is, the values *true* and *false*) in QuickBASIC programs and the operations that you can perform on these values

- The CONST statement, a new QuickBASIC feature you can use to name the numeric, string, and logical constants in a program

- The important new user-defined type and the variety of uses for record variables

- New features of arrays in QuickBASIC 4.0 and 4.5; specifically, the expanded notations available for defining subscript ranges and QuickBASIC's new support for arrays of records

To illustrate all these topics, this chapter presents a complete QuickBASIC program called *List*. This program helps you select, arrange, and examine lists of MS-DOS disk files. Its operation is in many ways similar to the MS-DOS directory command, DIR, but *List* offers many features and operations that are not available with DIR. In the next section we'll preview the program briefly, and then we'll look more closely at it later in the chapter.

A FIRST LOOK AT THE *LIST* PROGRAM

The *List* program is designed to be compiled as a stand-alone EXE file and then used as a command-style MS-DOS utility. Like DIR, *List* allows you to examine an entire directory or a selected portion of a directory. You can use the "wildcard" characters * and *?* to specify the pattern of filenames that you want to search for. In addition, *List* offers the following unique features:

- You can sort the directory in three ways: alphabetically by filename, numerically by the size of files, or chronologically by date and time. The program allows both ascending and descending sorts.

- You can select files by date, specifying a single target date or a range of dates. The resulting directory listing will include only those files that are stamped with the date or dates that you indicate.

- You can use the program to determine the total number of bytes contained in a selected group of files; this information is included at the bottom of each *List* directory.

When you run *List* from the MS-DOS prompt, the program allows a variety of switch-style options. Like the options available with several MS-DOS commands, each *List* option begins with a slash character (/). For example, the following command displays EXE files in the current directory:

```
C>LIST *.EXE /SCD /P
```

The /SCD option performs a descending chronological sort (listing files from the most recently created file to the oldest file), and the /P option displays the filenames one screenful at a time.

We'll discuss all *List* options in detail, and see examples of their results, later in this chapter. Figure 4-1 shows a help screen that the *List* program produces to summarize its features. This screen appears as the result of the program's /H option:

```
C>LIST /H
```

```
The List Program:

List is a command-style program that is similar to the DIR
command in MS-DOS. You can supply a drive name, a path name,
and a filename (optionally including the wildcard characters
? and *) to specify the files that you wish to list. In addition,
each of the following options results in a sorted list of files:
    /SN or /SND         Sorts alphabetically by the filenames.
    /SS or /SSD         Sorts numerically by file size (in bytes).
    /SC or /SCD         Sorts chronologically by date and time.
(The letter D in a sort option results in a descending sort.)

The /D option allows you to specify a date or a range of dates
for selecting files:
    /D mm-dd-yy              Selects files that match the date.
    /D mm-dd-yy TO mm-dd-yy  Selects files in the range of dates.
    /D TO mm-dd-yy           Selects files up to the given date.
    /D mm-dd-yy TO           Selects files from the date forward.

/P lists files one screenful at a time. /H displays this screen.
At the bottom of the file list, the LIST command displays the
total number of bytes in the selected files.

C>
```

Figure 4-1. *The* List *help screen.*

Along with a variety of data types and data structures, *List* illustrates other important programming topics, including:

- The COMMAND$ function, which returns user-supplied parameters from the execution of a compiled EXE program.

- A set of techniques designed for working with date and time values in QuickBASIC.

- Recursion, the process by which a procedure calls itself. To illustrate this technique, *List* includes a specially designed version of the recursive *quick sort* algorithm.

Before we turn to the *List* program, let's review the characteristics of QuickBASIC's data types and data structures.

THE ELEMENTARY DATA TYPES

We will begin this discussion by examining the elementary numeric and string types and the operations that QuickBASIC supports for these types.

We'll also discuss the use of the logical values, true and false. These values, sometimes called *Boolean values,* are not represented formally by a distinct type in QuickBASIC. Nonetheless, the language includes important sets of operations that result in logical values, which we'll examine in this section.

Finally, we'll explore QuickBASIC's new support for *symbolic constants.*

Numeric data types in QuickBASIC

As we have seen, the four numeric data types now available in QuickBASIC are integers, long integers, single-precision numbers, and double-precision numbers. To create a variable name that will represent a value in one of these numeric types, you can use a special suffix symbol that declares the variable's type. The following table summarizes these type-declaration symbols and provides examples of variable names:

Numeric Data Types	Suffix Symbols	Examples
Integers	%	month%
Long integers	&	targetBytes&
Single-precision numbers	!	income! or income
Double-precision numbers	#	dateValue#

The *!* suffix is always optional for single-precision variables. A simple variable name that includes no type suffix—and has not otherwise been declared to belong to a particular type—is normally a single-precision numeric variable. However, QuickBASIC offers other techniques for declaring variable types, which we will discuss as we continue in this chapter.

Two important characteristics of numeric types are *precision* and *range*. Precision refers to the number of accurate digits or decimal places in a number, and range refers to the largest and smallest positive and negative numbers you can work with in a numeric type. In the following sections we will look at the features of each numeric type in turn.

Standard integers

Integers are positive or negative whole numbers. The advantage of integers is that they are always represented with perfect precision. The disadvantage is that their legal range is only from –32,768 to +32,767. QuickBASIC stores each integer value in two bytes of memory. As we have seen, the *%* symbol at the end of a variable name declares that the variable stores an integer. For example, the following are integer variable names: *i%, hyphen1%, day%, temp%*.

You can also use the DEFINT statement at the beginning of a program to declare a range of initial letters that will subsequently represent integer variables. For example, the following statement means that variable names beginning with the letters *i, j,* and *k* will designate integer variables:

```
DEFINT i-k
```

In a program that contains this statement, the variables *i, jump,* and *keypress* all represent integers, even though they do not end in the % suffix.

You can always override the effect of the DEFINT statement by supplying a different type suffix at the end of a variable name. For example, the variable name *interest!* represents a single-precision number, regardless of any previous DEFINT statement.

The range of standard integers is clearly inadequate in applications that work with very large whole numbers. For example, the *List* program keeps track of the total number of bytes contained in a group of files. On a hard disk, this value can reach many hundreds of thousands—or even millions—of bytes. Since *List* needs to store this total with complete precision, the application calls for the use of QuickBASIC's new long integer type.

Long integers

The long integer type provides precise representation for a large range of whole numbers—from about –2 billion to +2 billion. To be exact, the range of long integers is –2,147,483,648 to +2,147,483,647. QuickBASIC requires four bytes of memory to store a long integer value.

The & suffix identifies a long integer variable, as in these names: *memoryAmount&, bytes&, population&, annualIncome&.* The DEFLNG statement designates initial letters that will subsequently represent long integer variables.

Single-precision numbers

QuickBASIC stores single-precision numbers with an accuracy of up to seven digits. You can write single-precision numbers in various forms, the most common of which is simply a number with a decimal point; for example:

```
123.4567
```

You can also use the exponential form, in which the number is separated into a decimal value and an exponent of 10. The exponent is preceded by the letter *E*:

```
1.234567E2
```

The actual value of this number is 1.234567 times 100. (The notation *E2* signifies 10 to the second power, or 100.) A negative exponent means that the value should be divided by a power of 10; for example, the following number is equal to *0.0001234567:*

```
1.234567E-04
```

As we have seen, single-precision variable names require no special suffix character. For example, QuickBASIC will treat all of the following as single-precision values: *rate, num, totalIncome.* However, you can include the *!* symbol for clarity, or you can use the DEFSNG statement to declare single-precision variables.

The approximate range of positive single-precision values is from 1.4E–45 up to and including 3.4E+38. For negative numbers, the range is from –1.4E–45 down to and including –3.4E+38. A single-precision value requires four bytes of memory.

For internal storage of floating-point numbers—that is, for both single-precision and double-precision values—QuickBASIC now follows a standard known as the *IEEE format.* IEEE stands for Institute of Electrical and Electronics Engineers. Previous versions of QuickBASIC used an internal storage format devised by Microsoft. The use of the IEEE format means that QuickBASIC can take full advantage of an 8087 or 80287 numeric coprocessor chip, thus performing faster and more precise calculations.

The main instance in which this new format can affect your programming techniques is when you work with random-access data files. We'll discuss this topic in Chapter 7.

Double-precision numbers

Double-precision numbers have an accuracy of up to 15 or 16 digits. The suffix for declaring double-precision variables is the pound (#) symbol; for example, *dateValue#* and *scalarTime#.* You can also use the DEFDBL statement to declare double-precision variable names.

Double-precision values take up eight bytes of memory. Their use can prove essential in any application that requires greater precision than is offered in other numeric data types. For example, let's say you are working on a financial application in which you want to store dollar-and-cent values such as $1,234,567.89. If you were to assign this value to a single-precision variable, QuickBASIC would provide only seven digits. In this case, the value would be rounded to the nearest dollar, as shown on the following page.

```
principal = 1234567.89
PRINT principal
```

The result of this PRINT statement is *1234568*. Notice that this value actually contains only six accurate digits; the seventh digit is rounded up from the value of the now-missing eighth digit. The final two digits are lost. To retain full accuracy, you must instead store the number in a double-precision variable:

```
principal# = 1234567.89
PRINT principal#
```

Here the PRINT statement displays the full value of *1234567.89*.

A double-precision constant is any numeric value that has more than seven digits. (QuickBASIC appends a # suffix to the end of such values.) The double-precision exponential format uses a *D* (rather than an *E*) to designate the exponent; for example:

```
1.23456789D6
```

In the next section we'll discuss the arithmetic operations that you can perform on numeric values in QuickBASIC programs.

ARITHMETIC OPERATIONS IN QUICKBASIC

The four most familiar operations are, of course, multiplication (*), division (/), addition (+), and subtraction (−). But other important operations are also available. Exponentiation, which is represented by the caret symbol (^), yields a base number to the power of an exponent. Exponents can be positive or negative integers or decimal values, as you can see in the following examples:

Statement	*Result*
PRINT 5 ^ 2	25
PRINT 5 ^ -2	.04
PRINT 2 ^ .5	1.414214

A fractional exponent finds a root of a number. For example, notice that the third statement in the table gives the square root of *2*.

In this context, it is important to understand how QuickBASIC treats arithmetic expressions that contain values of mixed numeric types. In general, the result will conform in precision to the most precise value type in the expression. For example, consider the following statement:

```
PRINT 2# ^ .5
```

This statement displays the number *1.414213562373095*. Since the first operand in the expression is a double-precision number, the result is also double precision.

QuickBASIC has two integer operations. Integer division, symbolized by the backslash character (\), yields the integer portion of a quotient. For example, the following statement displays a result of *2*:

```
PRINT 7 \ 3
```

Before performing integer division, QuickBASIC always truncates the fractional portion of both the dividend and the divisor. (After truncation, both numbers must be within the legal range of long integers, −2,147,483,648 to +2,147,483,647.)

Finally, the MOD operation gives the remainder from the division of two integers. (This operation, sometimes called *modulo arithmetic,* is available for both standard integers and long integers in QuickBASIC 4.0 and 4.5.) For example, the following statement displays a value of *1*:

```
PRINT 7 MOD 3
```

We'll find some interesting examples of the MOD operation in the *List* program, particularly in routines that deal with chronological values. For instance, consider the following statement:

```
day% = dayNumber% MOD 7
```

As we'll discuss later in this chapter, *List* converts each file's date string to a numeric form called a *scalar date.* The assignment statement shown above is part of a routine that finds the day of the week corresponding to a scalar date. The expression *dayNumber% MOD 7* yields an integer from 0 through 6, representing a day from Monday through Sunday.

ORDER OF OPERATIONS

When an expression contains more than one operation, QuickBASIC performs the operations in the following standard order:

1. Exponentiation
2. Negation (that is, a minus sign before a value)

3. Multiplication and division

4. Integer division

5. The MOD operation

6. Addition and subtraction

If there is a tie, expressions are evaluated left to right. To force a different order of operations, you can supply parentheses in an expression. For example, note the different results from the following expressions:

```
PRINT 2 * 3 + 4
PRINT 2 * (3 + 4)
```

The first of these statements displays the value *10*, while the second displays *14*.

You can also use parentheses simply to improve the readability of an expression, even if the parentheses do not change the order in which QuickBASIC would normally perform the operations; for example:

```
PRINT (2 * 3) + 4
```

BUILT-IN NUMERIC FUNCTIONS

In addition to the arithmetic operations, QuickBASIC has a diverse collection of *built-in functions* that work with or supply numeric values. A call to a built-in function typically requires one or more predefined *arguments* enclosed in parentheses after the function name. Each built-in function returns a single elementary value as its result.

For example, we'll find an illustration of the INT function in the *List* program. INT supplies the integer portion of a single-precision or double-precision number, as in the following lines:

```
tempVal# = 1375.82911#
PRINT INT(tempVal#)
```

This PRINT statement displays the integer value *1375*.

We'll encounter many other numeric functions in coming chapters. In the next section, we'll discuss QuickBASIC's string data types, along with string operations and functions.

STRING DATA TYPES

A *string* is a text value that consists of letters of the alphabet, digits, punctuation marks, and other special characters. QuickBASIC now supports two types of string values: *variable-length strings* and *fixed-length strings*. We will discuss each type in turn.

Variable-length strings

A variable-length string is a familiar string data type available in all versions of QuickBASIC. A variable-length string can contain from 0 to 32,767 characters. A string constant is enclosed in double quotation marks, and a string variable can be designated by a dollar-sign ($) suffix. For example:

```
title$ = "Microsoft QuickBASIC"
```

A string variable like *title$* can store a string of varying length. For example, you might append a second string to the end of an original string and store the result in the *title$* variable. The process of combining strings is called *concatenation* and is executed with the plus sign (+), as in the following statement:

```
title$ = title$ + " Version 4.5"
```

After this concatenation, the string variable *title$* contains the string "Microsoft QuickBASIC Version 4.5."

You can clear all characters from a string variable by assigning an empty string to the variable.

```
title$ = ""
```

Notice that no character—not even a space—appears between the two quotation marks in this statement.

Any newly referenced string variable of the variable-length type is empty until a program assigns a string value to it. A string containing no characters is sometimes called a *null string*. However, we have to use this term cautiously; it has a rather different meaning in the context of fixed-length strings, as we will see in the next section.

Fixed-length strings

A fixed-length string has a declared length that remains constant throughout the execution of a program. You must explicitly declare a fixed-length string variable before its first use. The variable name cannot include the familiar dollar-sign ($) suffix.

You can use any of several familiar declaration statements to create a fixed-length string variable, including DIM, REDIM, COMMON, SHARED, and STATIC. In other words, the usage of these statements has been extended to allow specific variable declarations. For example, the following DIM statement declares a fixed-length string variable named *productCode* that is six characters long:

```
DIM productCode AS STRING * 6
```

After declaring a fixed-length string variable, you can use a normal assignment statement to store a value in a fixed-length string variable, for example:

```
productCode = "pencil"
```

However, if you try to assign a string value that contains more characters than the declared length of the variable, the extra characters will be lost. For example, the assignment statement

```
productCode = "printer"
```

stores the string "printe" in the variable because the length of *productCode* is fixed at six characters.

If you assign a string that is shorter than the declared length of the variable, QuickBASIC fills the remainder of the fixed-length string with spaces. For example, the following statement assigns a three-character string to *productCode*:

```
productCode = "pen"
```

After the statement, the variable contains the string "pen   ", consisting of three letters followed by three space characters.

Before you assign a string value to a fixed-length string variable, the variable's default value is a string of null characters (ASCII 0). Even at this initial point the variable contains a string of the declared length. Consequently, it is now wise to distinguish between the terms *empty string* and *null string:*

- An empty string is a string with no characters. This is the default value of a variable-length string variable.

- A null string is a string that contains only null characters (ASCII 0). This is the default value of a fixed-length string variable.

Probably the most important context for using QuickBASIC's fixed-length strings is in user-defined types and their corresponding record variables. As we will see later in this chapter, a record variable can contain fixed-length string elements but not variable-length strings.

Incidentally, the DIM, REDIM, COMMON, SHARED, and STATIC statements can be used to declare variables of any type, not just fixed-length strings. For example, this statement declares the variable *annualIncome* as a long integer:

```
DIM annualIncome AS LONG
```

You cannot include a type suffix in a variable name that is declared in this manner.

QuickBASIC 4.0 and 4.5 have an extended library of built-in functions that work with string values. You can use these functions with both variable-length and fixed-length strings. The *List* program illustrates many of these functions; we'll survey them briefly in the next section.

STRING FUNCTIONS

The following list summarizes the functions that we'll review:

- The LEFT$, RIGHT$, and MID$ functions extract specified characters from string arguments.

- The VAL function provides the numeric equivalent of a string of digits. Conversely, the STR$ function converts a number to a string of digits.

- The INSTR function finds the location of a group of characters inside a string.

- The new UCASE$ and LCASE$ functions perform alphabetic case conversions.

- The new LTRIM$ and RTRIM$ functions eliminate leading or trailing blanks from a variable-length string.

- The CHR$ and ASC functions supply information about the ASCII code.

LEFT$, RIGHT$, and MID$

The LEFT$ and RIGHT$ functions extract characters from the beginning or the end of a string argument. Each function takes two arguments: a string and an integer representing the number of characters to be extracted from the beginning or the end of the string. (The string argument is not changed by either of these functions.) Here are samples of these two functions:

```
title$ = "QuickBASIC"
PRINT LEFT$(title$, 5)
PRINT RIGHT$(title$, 5)
```

The first PRINT statement displays the string *Quick* and the second displays *BASIC*.

The MID$ function extracts characters from within a string argument. MID$ takes three arguments: the target string, an integer representing the starting character position inside the string, and a second integer representing the number of characters to be extracted. For example, the following statement displays the word *stand*:

```
PRINT MID$("understanding", 6, 5)
```

If you omit the third argument of MID$, the function extracts all characters from the specified position to the end of the string. For example, this statement displays *standing*:

```
PRINT MID$("understanding", 6)
```

We'll see that the *List* program uses LEFT$, RIGHT$, and MID$ extensively for two major purposes: to isolate portions of the date and time strings and to analyze the contents of the user-supplied string of parameter options.

VAL and STR$

The VAL function also plays an important role in the *List* program. VAL attempts to convert a string value to a number. For example, let's say the variable *value$* contains this string of digits:

```
"23456"
```

The following statement converts this string into a number and stores the result in *num%*:

```
num% = VAL(value$)
```

Note the difference between the string value and the numeric value. The string *"23456"* is stored in the computer's memory as a sequence of ASCII characters, all of which happen to be digits; the value is not a number and cannot be treated as one. On the other hand, the number 23456 is stored in memory in QuickBASIC's integer format and therefore is available for use in any numeric operation.

VAL ignores characters that cannot be converted to a number. If the first character in the argument string is not a numeric character, as in this example:

```
PRINT VAL("hello")
```

VAL returns a value of *0*.

If the string begins with digits followed by non-numeric characters, VAL converts only to the first non-numeric character. For example, the following statement displays a value of *3*:

```
PRINT VAL("3 o'clock")
```

As we will see, the *List* program uses VAL to convert the components of date strings and time strings into numbers.

The STR$ function performs the opposite operation: It converts a numeric value into a string of digits. For example, the expression *STR$(123)* supplies the string value *"123"*.

INSTR

The INSTR function returns an integer representing the position of one string inside another. The function takes two string arguments: The first is the string to be searched through, and the second is the string to be searched for. For example, the following statement displays a value of *2*, the position of the first hyphen in the date string:

```
PRINT INSTR("6-10-89", "-")
```

You can also supply an optional integer argument before the two string arguments; this integer tells INSTR where to begin searching inside the first string for the second string. The following statement returns a value of *5*, the position of the second hyphen:

```
PRINT INSTR(3, "6-10-89", "-")
```

The *List* program uses INSTR to search for strings inside date and time strings and inside the user's parameter option string. INSTR returns a value of *0* if the search is not successful—that is, if the second string argument is not located inside the first string. We'll see that the *List* program frequently relies on this information to determine the validity of a string.

UCASE$ and LCASE$

UCASE$ and LCASE$ are useful functions new in QuickBASIC 4.0 and 4.5. UCASE$ provides an uppercase version of its string argument, and LCASE$ provides a lowercase version. For example, these PRINT statements display the words *QUICKBASIC* and *quickbasic*, respectively:

```
title$ = "QuickBASIC"
PRINT UCASE$(title$)
PRINT LCASE$(title$)
```

Obviously, these two functions operate only on letters of the alphabet; they have no effect on any nonalphabetic characters.

Either function can be useful in normalizing keyboard input to simplify comparisons between strings. For example, consider the following statements:

```
INPUT "Y)es or N)o"; answer$
IF UCASE$(LEFT$(answer$, 1)) = "Y" THEN DoNext
```

The test contained inside the IF statement results in a value of true if the input string begins with an uppercase or lowercase *Y*.

LTRIM$ and RTRIM$

LTRIM$ and RTRIM$ are new functions that supply "trimmed" versions of a string argument. LTRIM$ eliminates spaces from the beginning of the string, and RTRIM$ eliminates spaces from the end. These functions can prove particularly useful when you want to display combinations of fixed-length strings without the extra spaces that QuickBASIC includes in such strings. Consider this example:

```
DIM firstName AS STRING * 10, lastName AS STRING * 10
firstName = "John"
lastName = "Doe"
PRINT RTRIM$(firstName) + " " + RTRIM$(lastName) + " ";
PRINT "was hired on "; DATE$; "."
```

The PRINT statements in this example display the following sentence:

```
John Doe was hired on 06/11/1988.
```

Without the RTRIM$ function, the sentence would include undesirable spaces after the first name and the last name:

```
John        Doe        was hired on 06/11/1988.
```

We'll find more examples of these two functions in the *List* program.

CHR$ and ASC

A string can contain any sequence of characters from the standard ASCII character set or the IBM Extended Character Set. These codes assign decimal integers from *0* to *255* to all the characters that are available on IBM personal computers and compatibles. The standard ASCII character set (*0* to *127*) contains lowercase and uppercase letters, digits, punctuation marks, and a group of *control characters* that have various special functions. The IBM Extended Character Set (*128* to *255*) contains letters from foreign-language alphabets and a collection of graphics characters that you can use to build shapes and designs on the screen.

Sometimes you may want to build strings of characters that have no single-key equivalents on your keyboard. In this case, you can use the built-in CHR$ function to convert an ASCII or IBM Extended code number into its equivalent character. For example, the following statements display the corner characters that are part of the frame displayed around the *List* program's help screen:

```
LOCATE top%, left%: PRINT CHR$(201)
LOCATE top%, right%: PRINT CHR$(187)
LOCATE bottom%, left%: PRINT CHR$(200);
LOCATE bottom%, right%: PRINT CHR$(188);
```

The ASC function supplies the code number of a character argument. For example, the expression ASC("a") yields a value of 97, the ASCII code of the letter *a*. We'll see specific uses of the ASC function in programs presented later in this book.

This concludes our discussion of string types, string operations, and string functions. Next we'll turn to the subject of logical values and the logical operations available in QuickBASIC.

LOGICAL VALUES

A logical expression contains values and operations that QuickBASIC can evaluate to one of two logical values: true or false. (We also sometimes refer to these as *Boolean values*, named after George Boole, the nineteenth-century English mathematician). A program uses such values to make decisions about the course of its execution. For example, logical values are essential in determining the results of decision structures and loops.

Logical expressions typically contain *relational operations* or *logical operations*, or a combination of both. In the following sections we'll review these operations and explore QuickBASIC's internal representation for logical values.

Relational operations

The six relational operators compare values. The comparison always results in a value of true or false. Here are the operators and their meanings:

=	Equal to
<>	Not equal to
<	Less than
>	Greater than
<=	Less than or equal to
>=	Greater than or equal to

You can use these operators to compare numbers or strings. Consider the following numeric example:

```
value1% = 1234
value2% = 3456
IF value1% >= value2% THEN
    PRINT "same size or larger"
ELSE
    PRINT "smaller"
```

In this case, the expression *value1% >= value2%* results in a value of false, since the integer *value1%* is smaller than *value2%*. The IF statement performs the ELSE clause, displaying the word *smaller*.

In string comparisons, QuickBASIC actually compares the ASCII code equivalents of the strings, character by character. For example, look at the following sequence:

```
job1$ = "Tinker"
job2$ = "Tailor"
IF job1$ > job2$ THEN SWAP job1$, job2$
```

The comparison *job1$ > job2$* results in a value of true. The first characters in both strings are equal, but the second characters are not: The ASCII equivalent of *i* is greater than the ASCII equivalent of *a*. The IF statement consequently performs the SWAP command. As we'll see in the *List* program, this decision structure and the resulting SWAP are the essential elements in a sort operation.

Logical operations

QuickBASIC also has five logical operators that you can use to combine two or more logical expressions (AND, OR, XOR, EQV, IMP), and one logical operator that reverses the value of a logical expression (NOT).

The most commonly used operators are AND, OR, and NOT. In the following descriptions, assume that *L1* and *L2* represent logical expressions:

- *NOT L1* reverses the value of *L1*. The expression is true if *L1* is false, or false if *L1* is true.

- *L1 AND L2* is true only if both *L1* and *L2* are true. (If either *L1* or *L2* is false or if both are false, the AND expression is also false.)

- *L1 OR L2* is true if either *L1* or *L2* is true or if both are true. (If both *L1* and *L2* are false, the OR expression is also false.)

The remaining three logical operators stand for *exclusive or* (XOR), *equivalence* (EQV), and *implication* (IMP). For example:

- *L1 XOR L2* is true if either *L1* or *L2* is true. (If both are true or if both are false, the XOR expression is false.)

- *L1 IMP L2* is true if both *L1* and *L2* are true, or if *L1* is false. (If *L1* is true and *L2* is false, the IMP expression is false.)

- *L1 EQV L2* is true if *L1* and *L2* have the same logical values—that is, if both are true or if both are false. (If they have different logical values, the EQV expression is false.)

The *List* program contains several interesting illustrations of logical operations. Here is a simple example:

```
IF date2% <> 0 AND date1% > date2% THEN SWAP date1%, date2%
```

In this statement, the SWAP command arranges two integer values (*date1%* and *date2%*) in ascending order. However, the swap is only performed if the two conditions expressed in the IF statement are both true: The second integer is not equal to *0* (*date2% <> 0*), and the two integers are initially in the wrong order (*date1% > date2%*).

INTERNAL REPRESENTATION OF LOGICAL VALUES

Unlike some other programming languages, QuickBASIC does not possess an explicit logical type. Internally, QuickBASIC represents the results of logical expressions as numbers. Given a logical expression consisting of some combination of relational and logical operations, QuickBASIC evaluates the expression to one of two numeric values:

- A false expression evaluates to *0*.

- A true expression evaluates to *-1*.

In most cases, you don't really need to know that this is the nature of the evaluation; you simply write a logical expression and rely on QuickBASIC to act according to the result.

But in some special circumstances you might want to use the numeric equivalents of true and false. You can, in effect, create *logical variables* for a program to keep track of true-or-false, yes-or-no conditions that are important to the program's execution. Such variables, containing integer values, can appear in any contexts that normally call for logical expressions. QuickBASIC reads the values as follows:

- A value of zero represents false.

- Any nonzero value represents true.

We typically use *-1* to represent true; however, QuickBASIC actually reads any nonzero value as true.

For example, let's say a program uses the logical variable *ready%* to keep track of a certain condition. The condition must be true before certain key routines in the program can be executed successfully. The following statement initializes the variable to a value of false:

```
ready% = 0
```

When the proper conditions are met, this statement sets the variable to true:

```
ready% = -1
```

The following statement switches the value of *ready%* to the opposite of its current value:

```
ready% = NOT ready%
```

The program can use *ready%* as a logical expression. For example, the variable can appear in IF statements:

```
IF ready% THEN CALL Sample
```

You can also use the variable as the condition in a DO...WHILE loop:

```
DO WHILE ready%
```

In this case, a statement inside the loop should eventually switch *ready%* to false to stop the looping.

All programs in this book use QuickBASIC's new CONST statement to establish logical values as *symbolic constants*. This technique fosters clarity and readability in a program. We'll discuss symbolic constants and the CONST statement in the next section.

SYMBOLIC CONSTANTS

A symbolic constant is a name you devise to represent an unchanging data value. You can create as many symbolic constants as you want for a program, to represent any string or numeric values.

Each symbolic constant is assigned its value only once in the program, in a CONST statement. The form of a CONST statement is:

```
CONST constantName = value
```

A program can contain multiple CONST statements. For example, the following statements declare the symbolic constants *true%* and false %:

```
CONST false% = 0
CONST true% = NOT false%
```

Multiple constants can be declared in a single CONST statement, as in the following line from the *List* program:

```
CONST false% = 0, true% = NOT false%
```

In the CONST statement you can express a constant's value as a literal string or number, or as an expression. A CONST assignment can contain literal values along with references to previously defined constants; however, the expression cannot contain variables. You can use operations—except exponentiation and concatenation—in a CONST expression.

Constant names are much like variable names. You can declare the type of a constant by including one of the explicit type suffixes

(*%, &, !,* or *#*) in the name. However, this suffix is optional in subsequent references to the constant. If you omit the type suffix in the CONST statement, QuickBASIC determines the most appropriate type for the value that you assign to the constant.

CONST statements in the main program section of your program establish "global" constants, available in any procedure in the program. (However, if a program consists of more than one module, symbolic constants are available only within the module in which they are actually defined.) CONST statements inside a procedure create constants that are local to that procedure.

We'll see several examples of symbolic constants in the *List* program and in programs presented in later chapters.

Now that we have discussed all QuickBASIC elementary data types, we are ready to explore the data structures supported by the language. This is the topic of the next section.

DATA STRUCTURES IN QUICKBASIC

Each of the variables illustrated up to now in this chapter stored a single data value at a time. When you assign a new value to a simple numeric or string variable, any value contained in the variable is erased from memory. These simple variables are fine for applications that process data values one at a time. However, some programs are created to work with entire groups of data values; such programs clearly have more complex data storage requirements. QuickBASIC's data structures meet these requirements, giving you convenient ways to store multiple data values under a single variable name.

We'll begin this section by briefly reviewing the familiar characteristics of arrays. Then we'll examine QuickBASIC's new user-defined type, and we'll see how to create record variables to represent multiple data values of different types. We'll also discuss an even more complex and versatile category of data structures—arrays of records. This discussion will lead us to an understanding of the major data structure employed in this chapter's *List* program.

Arrays

An *array* is a variable that represents one of the following arrangements of data:

- A list of values (a one-dimensional array)
- A table of values (a two-dimensional array)

- Some other multidimensional arrangement of values (QuickBASIC allows up to 63 dimensions)

Each value in an array is called an *element* of the array. A program accesses elements via numeric subscripts that identify the position of a value in the array. You use the DIM statement to define an array.

The DIM statement

The DIM statement declares the name, size, and type of an array. The general form of the DIM statement is:

```
DIM arrayName(subscripts)
```

Array names can include the same type-declaration suffixes that are used for simple variable names: $ for strings; % for integers; & for long integers; ! (or no suffix) for single-precision floating-point numbers; and # for double-precision floating-point numbers.

A program can contain multiple DIM statements. For example, the following statements define a one-dimensional array of integers named *intList%()* and a two-dimensional array of strings named *strTable$()*, respectively:

```
DIM intList%(10)
DIM strTable$(2, 3)
```

Multiple arrays can also be declared in a single DIM statement, as in the following line:

```
DIM intList%(10), strTable$(2, 3)
```

The DIM statement also allows an optional SHARED clause for declaring arrays as global. For example, here is a DIM statement from the top section of the *List* program:

```
DIM SHARED daysInMonth%(12)
```

This statement defines the integer array *daysInMonth%()* and makes it available to any procedure in the program. (In a program consisting of multiple modules, global arrays are explicitly available only in the module that actually defines them.)

Array subscripts

In previous examples we expressed dimension lengths as single integer values in the DIM statement:

```
DIM intList%(10), strTable$(2, 3)
```

By default, the subscripts for these two arrays range from *0* up to the maximum value indicated in the statement. We can thus think of *intList%()* as a list of 11 values with subscripts ranging from *0* to 11. Likewise, we can think of *strTable$()* as a three-column-by-four-row arrangement of values where the column subscripts range from *0* to *2* and the row subscripts from *0* to *3*. Each individual value in *strTable$()* is represented by a pair of subscripts; for example, *strTable$(1,2)* is the element located in the third row of the second column.

Sometimes a program has no practical use for the array elements represented by the subscripts of *0*. In this case, you can conserve memory space by including an OPTION BASE statement at the beginning of your program to start all subscripts at *1*:

```
OPTION BASE 1
```

This means that all arrays defined in the program will have subscripts that begin with *1*. For example, the *intList%()* array would have subscripts ranging from *1* to *10*. The *strTable$()* array would have column subscripts from *1* to *2* and row subscripts from *1* to *3*.

In QuickBASIC 4.0 and 4.5, the syntax of the DIM statement has been extended to give you even greater flexibility over defining the range of subscripts for an array. An array's subscripts can now be expressed in the following compound format:

```
lowSubscript TO highSubscript
```

This means that the lower end of the subscript range is no longer restricted to values of *0* or *1*. Instead, you can design the range to match the characteristics of a particular application.

For example, let's say you are setting up a double-precision array to store annual income amounts for the years 1975 through 1987. You might write a DIM statement such as the following:

```
DIM annualIncome#(75 TO 87)
```

In this array the subscripts identify the individual years of the period. For example, the element *annualIncome#(85)* will contain the income figure for 1985.

You can also represent the subscript range with negative integers. For example, let's say you are writing a program that analyzes daily temperature statistics for a city. You want to create an array in which you can tally the number of days on which a temperature was recorded in the range from –20 to 40 degrees centigrade. You might set up your array as follows:

```
DIM tempDays%(-20 TO 40)
```

In this array, elements with negative subscripts will record the number of below-freezing temperature readings, and elements with positive subscripts will record above-freezing readings.

In QuickBASIC, you can define either *static* or *dynamic* arrays. We'll investigate these categories in the next section.

Static and dynamic arrays

The size of a static array is fixed at the time you compile your program and remains unchanged throughout the subsequent execution. The size of a dynamic array, however, is not defined until you run your program. Furthermore, the dimensions of a dynamic array can change one or more times during execution.

When you know in advance the number of elements that are required in an array—that is, when a fixed array size is predefined by the nature of the task at hand—you should use a static array. However, when the size is determined by events that occur during execution of the program or when the required size can change during execution, you should use a dynamic array.

The simplest way to declare an array as static is to supply the dimensions as constants in the DIM statement. For example, the *strTable$()* array, as we originally defined it, is static:

```
DIM strTable$(2, 3)
```

On the other hand, an array declared with variables as dimensions is dynamic by default. Consider the following statements in which a program elicits values from the keyboard for the dimensions *i%* and *j%*:

```
INPUT i%
INPUT j%
DIM newTable$(i%,j%)
```

The size of the dynamic *newTable$()* array is determined by the user's input.

The REDIM statement allows you to change the size of a dynamic array during a program's execution. REDIM has the same syntax as the DIM command; for example:

```
REDIM newTable$(i%,j%)
```

Actually, you can use REDIM to declare both the initial dimensions of an array and subsequent new dimensions. Any values previously stored in the array are lost when REDIM is executed.

QuickBASIC also has the metacommands $STATIC and $DYNAMIC, which you can use to declare the status of arrays. Either of these metacommands, placed in a comment at the top of a program, controls the status of all arrays defined in subsequent DIM statements.

Now let's turn to QuickBASIC's important new data structure, the user-defined type.

User-defined types

Suppose you are writing a program that works with collections of related data values—values that belong to various data types but are nonetheless grouped together by the nature of the application at hand. QuickBASIC's user-defined type allows you to create a structure that will conveniently store an entire collection of such data values under one variable name. This type of structure is called a *record variable*.

Creating a record variable is a two-step process in QuickBASIC:

1. Write a TYPE…END TYPE statement to declare the name and the elements of a user-defined type.

2. Use one of the following statements to create a record variable belonging to the user-defined type: DIM, REDIM, COMMON, STATIC, or SHARED.

Let's examine this process, starting with the TYPE statement.

The TYPE statement

You use the TYPE statement to establish the list of elements contained in a user-defined type. Here is the general form of the TYPE statement:

```
TYPE userTypeName
    elementName1 AS type
    elementName2 AS type
    elementName3 AS type
    [additional type declarations]
END TYPE
```

The *userTypeName* is the name you assign to the type you are creating, and the *elementNames* are the names you give to the individual elements of the type. These are similar to variable names, except that they cannot include type-declaration suffixes.

Each element defined in the TYPE statement includes a *type* specification. For numeric or string elements, *type* must be one of the following QuickBASIC reserved words:

- INTEGER for an integer-type element
- LONG for a long integer element
- SINGLE for a single-precision numeric element
- DOUBLE for a double-precision numeric element
- STRING * *length* for a fixed-length string element

For example, the following TYPE statement creates a user-defined type named *sampleType*, which contains four elements:

```
TYPE sampleType
    strElement AS STRING * 5
    intElement AS INTEGER
    longElement AS LONG
    doubleElement AS DOUBLE
END TYPE
```

Note that any of the four QuickBASIC elementary numeric types can appear as elements. However, only fixed-length strings are allowed, not variable-length strings. This is because a record variable must have a fixed length.

An element type can also be declared as another user-defined type that was previously created in the program. In this case, the syntax for the element declaration is:

```
elementName AS userTypeName
```

For example, the following statement creates a user-defined type containing two elements; the first element is an integer, and the second is a record of *sampleType*:

```
TYPE newType
    newIntElement AS INTEGER
    recordElement AS sampleType
END TYPE
```

When you have written a TYPE statement to outline the elements of a user-defined type, you can create any number of record variables belonging to the type.

Record variables

The DIM, REDIM, COMMON, STATIC, and SHARED statements are available for creating record variables. For example, here is the general format for the DIM statement:

```
DIM recordName AS userTypeName
```

In this syntax, *recordName* is the name you devise for the new record variable, and *userTypeName* is the name of a previously established user-defined type.

A record variable stores one data value for each of the elements in the corresponding user-defined type. Once you have declared a record variable, you use a special notation to refer to individual record elements. The notation is:

```
recordName.elementName
```

The first part of the notation gives the name of the record variable, and the second part gives the name of an individual element in the structure. The two parts of the name are separated by a period.

Let's look at an example. Imagine a program that processes information about residential real-estate sales. The program keeps track of several items of information about individual home sales:

- The address of the home

- The size of the home in square feet

- The number of bedrooms

- The seller's name

- The buyer's name

- The sale price

The program might create a user-defined type for this information as follows:

```
TYPE saleType
    address AS STRING * 20
    squareFootage AS INTEGER
    bedRooms AS INTEGER
    sellerName AS STRING * 15
    buyerName AS STRING * 15
    salePrice AS LONG
END TYPE
```

Subsequently the following DIM statement declares a record variable named *homeRecord*, corresponding to the *saleType* structure:

```
DIM homeRecord AS saleType
```

Once *homeRecord* has been created as a record variable, the program uses the *recordName.elementName* notation to refer to individual record elements. Here are the full names of the six elements of the *homeRecord* variable:

```
homeRecord.address
homeRecord.squareFootage
homeRecord.bedRooms
homeRecord.sellerName
homeRecord.buyerName
homeRecord.salePrice
```

You can use these names just as you would use any simple variable name. For example, the following input statements accept data from the keyboard for the first three elements of the record:

```
INPUT "Address of property"; homeRecord.address
INPUT "Size of property"; homeRecord.squareFootage
INPUT "Number of bedrooms"; homeRecord.bedRooms
```

The *homeRecord* variable stores one complete sale record at a time. If we want the real-estate program to be able to store an entire list of records in one data structure, we would create an array of *saleType* records. We'll see how to do that in the next section.

Arrays of records

Here is the general format of a DIM statement that creates an array of records:

```
DIM recordArrayName(subscripts) AS userTypeName
```

For example, the following DIM statement declares a one-dimensional array named *homeArray()*:

```
DIM homeArray(100) AS saleType
```

This array allows the real-estate program to store up to 100 sales records under one variable name. The notation for referring to one individual record in this array is the same as for any array value; for example, *homeArray(5)* is record number 5 in the array.

However, the notation becomes a bit more complex when you want to refer to a single element in one of the records of this array. The general form of this notation is:

```
recordArrayName(index).elementName
```

For example, here is how we would refer to the *address* element of record number *5*:

```
homeArray(5).address
```

Notice that the array name is followed by an index enclosed in parentheses. A period separates the array name from the element.

As we examine the *List* program—and other programs presented later in this book—we'll discover several important advantages in the use of QuickBASIC's new record structure. Here are a few of these advantages:

1. Record structures tend to simplify passing data from one routine to another or making data available globally.

2. Records can be used to define the structure of a random-access file, resulting in simpler and more versatile file-handling techniques. (We'll discuss this topic in Chapter 8.)

3. Arrays of records are very easy to use in data-processing operations like sorting and searching. (We'll see an example of sorting in this chapter's sample program.)

Now that we have the background information about data types and data structures in QuickBASIC, let's begin exploring the *List* program. First we'll see exactly how the program behaves and what kinds of directory listings it can supply; then we'll examine the program listing and focus on the data types, data structures, and operations.

RUNNING THE *LIST* PROGRAM

Keep in mind that the *List* program is designed to run directly from MS-DOS, rather than from the QuickBASIC environment. For this reason, you should compile *List* as a stand-alone program file, creating a file called LIST.EXE. When you have taken this step, you can run *List* with any of the options described on the help screen shown in Figure 4-1 on page 89.

As we discussed earlier in this chapter, *List* has three basic advantages over the built-in MS-DOS directory command, DIR. First, you can use *List* to arrange directories by any of three sorting keys. Second, *List* allows you to select files by dates or date ranges. Finally, the *List* program supplies an item of information that is missing from the DIR-style directory listings: the total number of bytes contained in the files in the listing.

You could achieve some of these effects using tools that are already available in MS-DOS. Specifically, the DIR command, along with the SORT utility, can provide directories that are arranged alphabetically by filenames, or even numerically by file sizes. In addition, you can use the MORE utility to display listings one screenful at a time. However, *List* gives you these features in one stand-alone package.

Furthermore, the *List* program allows you to select and sort files chronologically. For a chronological sort, *List* uses file dates as the primary key and times as the secondary key.

It is interesting to note that the CHKDSK program, a utility supplied with MS-DOS, supplies the total number of bytes used by all files on a disk. However, you cannot use CHKDSK to find out the number of bytes contained in a selection of files. *List* gives you this information with every directory listing. Furthermore, the number of bytes reported by CHKDSK can be larger than the actual combined size of all the files on the disk, because CHKDSK includes unused portions of disk space that MS-DOS reserves for individual files. *List,* on the other hand, simply adds up the actual sizes of the files and reports the total.

Let's look at some sample directories produced by the *List* program. First we'll examine the results of the various /S options, which sort directory listings. /SN sorts by names, /SS by size, and /SC by the date-and-time stamps. For example, the following command displays all the EXE files in a subdirectory named \DOS and sorts the file listing by name:

```
C>LIST \DOS\*.EXE /SN
```

This command produces a directory listing similar to the following example.

```
Volume in drive C has no label
Directory of  C:\DOS

ATTRIB    EXE    15091     Tue.,   5-14-85   12:02a
CHKDSK    EXE     9296     Wed.,   5-15-85   12:00a
DEBUG     EXE    15364     Wed.,   5-15-85   12:00a
EDLIN     EXE     7122     Wed.,   5-15-85   12:00a
FIND      EXE     6403     Wed.,   5-15-85   12:00a
FORMAT    EXE    10351     Tue.,   2-04-86   12:19p
JOIN      EXE     8956     Wed.,   5-15-85   12:00a
PRINT     EXE     7832     Thu.,   5-30-85   11:14a
RECOVER   EXE     3895     Wed.,   5-15-85   12:00a
SHARE     EXE     7856     Wed.,   5-15-85   12:00a
SORT      EXE     1664     Thu.,   5-30-85   11:23a
SUBST     EXE     9910     Wed.,   5-15-85   12:00a

    Total of   103740 bytes in 12 files.
```

Adding the letter *D* to the end of any /S option results in a descending sort. For example, consider the following command, which works with the same directory as the previous example but sorts the directory in descending order by file size:

```
C>LIST \DOS\*.EXE /SSD
```

Here is the listing produced by this command:

```
Volume in drive C has no label
Directory of  C:\DOS

DEBUG     EXE    15364     Wed.,   5-15-85 12:00a
ATTRIB    EXE    15091     Tue.,   5-14-85 12:02a
FORMAT    EXE    10351     Tue.,   2-04-86 12:19p
SUBST     EXE     9910     Wed.,   5-15-85 12:00a
CHKDSK    EXE     9296     Wed.,   5-15-85 12:00a
JOIN      EXE     8956     Wed.,   5-15-85 12:00a
SHARE     EXE     7856     Wed.,   5-15-85 12:00a
PRINT     EXE     7832     Thu.,   5-30-85 11:14a
EDLIN     EXE     7122     Wed.,   5-15-85 12:00a
FIND      EXE     6403     Wed.,   5-15-85 12:00a
RECOVER   EXE     3895     Wed.,   5-15-85 12:00a
SORT      EXE     1664     Thu.,   5-30-85 11:23a

    Total of   103740 bytes in 12 files.
```

The /D option allows you to select files with a specified date. The date must be expressed in the format *mm-dd-yy*, and only hyphens can be used as the separator characters inside the date. For example, the following command lists all files from the current directory that have BAS extensions and are stamped with the date 7-29-86:

```
C>LIST *.BAS /SN /D 7-29-86
```

Notice that the /SN option is included to sort the files by name. Here is how the listing might appear:

```
Volume in drive C has no label
Directory of  C:\QB45

AFRAME   BAS      893    Tue., 7-29-86  2:47p
COLFRTST BAS      996    Tue., 7-29-86  2:54p
DEMOCOL  BAS     2413    Tue., 7-29-86  1:50p
FRAME    BAS      798    Tue., 7-29-86  2:04p
FRAMETST BAS      914    Tue., 7-29-86  2:52p
MENUTSTC BAS     2441    Tue., 7-29-86  4:13p
MORT     BAS     9532    Tue., 7-29-86 10:48a

   Total of    17987 bytes in 7 files.
```

The /D option also allows you to supply a range of dates in the following format:

```
/D mm-dd-yy TO mm-dd-yy
```

The resulting directory listing will contain only those files that have dates within the specified range. For example, this command:

```
C>LIST *.BAS /SC /D 9-20-87 TO 9-30-87
```

would produce a listing similar to this:

```
Volume in drive C has no label
Directory of  C:\QB45

QC4      BAS    28422    Thu., 9-24-87  2:49p
QCTEST   BAS    28878    Thu., 9-24-87  3:48p
ASCII    BAS      233    Fri., 9-25-87  9:50a
DECTEMP  BAS      640    Tue., 9-29-87  1:38p
DECLSORT BAS      512    Wed., 9-30-87 10:21a
21       BAS    15780    Wed., 9-30-87 12:05p

   Total of    74465 bytes in 6 files.
```

Notice that the /SC option results in a chronological sort. When the listing contains more than one file stamped with the same date, *List* uses the time stamp as the secondary sorting key.

The /D option offers two additional formats. You can use the following option to list files that are dated up to a specified date:

```
/D TO mm-dd-yy
```

In this case, *List* uses 1-1-80 as the starting date. (This is the earliest system date that MS-DOS accepts.) Another format of the /D option selects all files dated from a specified date up to today's date:

```
/D mm-dd-yy TO
```

For example, the following command lists all BAS files that have dates between 10-1-87 and today's date:

```
C>LIST *.BAS /SCD /D 10-1-87 TO
```

The resulting listing might appear as follows:

```
Volume in drive C has no label
Directory of  C:\QB45

LIST      BAS    22769    Fri., 11-13-87    9:40a
QUIKTEST  BAS     1142    Tue., 11-10-87    4:22p
PRLIST    BAS    22415    Fri., 10-23-87    2:22p
ADVMENU   BAS     8851    Wed., 10-21-87    9:08a
BOOKMENU  BAS     5099    Tue., 10-20-87    2:11p
PRQC      BAS    34682    Mon., 10-19-87    4:27p
QC        BAS    34706    Mon., 10-19-87   12:24p
DECLTEMP  BAS      963    Thu., 10-15-87    4:16p
SURVEY    BAS    21720    Thu., 10-15-87    3:45p
TOOLBOX   BAS     5143    Thu., 10-15-87    3:23p
EMPFIX    BAS    22950    Wed., 10-14-87   12:40p
YESNO     BAS      768    Tue., 10-13-87    4:36p
DISPMENU  BAS     1920    Tue., 10-13-87    4:36p
MENUFUN   BAS     1536    Tue., 10-13-87    4:34p
EMPLOYEE  BAS    22362    Tue., 10-13-87    5:17a
NEWMENU   BAS     2934    Wed., 10-07-87    4:04p
TEMP      BAS     5094    Wed., 10-07-87    5:51a

    Total of   215054 bytes in 17 files.
```

Notice that the files in this listing are sorted in descending chronological order (/SCD) from the newest to the oldest file.

The *List* program allows two additional options. If a directory listing is longer than one screen, the /P option displays the listing one screenful at a time. The /H option displays the program's help screen; if you include this option, the program ignores any other options.

You can use MS-DOS to redirect the result of the *List* program to a printer or to a text file. In MS-DOS, the *greater-than* (>) symbol represents a redirect operation. Consider these two examples:

```
C>LIST *.COM /SN >PRN:
C>LIST /SCD >BYDATE.TXT
```

The first of these commands sends the listing to the printer, and the second stores the listing in the file *BYDATE.TXT*.

Now that we have seen some examples of *List*, let's examine the program. The complete listing appears in Figure 4-2, beginning on page 139. The various declarations and definitions required by the program appear at the top of the program listing, followed by the main program section and then by the functions and subprograms in alphabetic order. Throughout the program discussion you'll see references to functions and subprograms—these are labeled along the right and left margins of the listing with tabs bearing the function or subprogram name. We'll begin our discussion with a broad look at the program's major activities, and then we'll return to the beginning to focus on specific data types and structures used in the program.

INSIDE THE *LIST* PROGRAM

As we have seen, the action of the *List* program depends upon the specific parameters supplied when running the program from the MS-DOS command line. The program gains access to the parameter line through a string value supplied by the COMMAND$ function. Let's take a look at this function.

Using the COMMAND$ function

The behavior of the COMMAND$ function is quite simple. It returns all information entered on the MS-DOS command line after the program name. COMMAND$ eliminates any spaces entered between the program name and the first parameter. The function also converts alphabetic characters in the command line to uppercase. For example, let's say a user enters the following command to run the *List* program from MS-DOS:

```
C>list *.bas /scd /d 10-1-87 to
```

In this case, COMMAND$ returns the following string of parameters:

```
*.BAS /SCD /D 10-1-87 TO
```

Individual routines in the program must respond appropriately to the options in this string. Various procedures in *List* search directly for specific parameters that are relevant to particular tasks.

An alternative approach would be to design a single routine that reads and analyzes the entire command line at once and then passes the relevant information to other routines. This approach is discussed briefly at the end of this chapter as a suggestion for an additional programming exercise that you might want to try after you have studied the current version of the *List* program. By the way, when you are developing a program like *List* inside the QuickBASIC environment, you can use the Modify Command$ option—located in the Run menu— to supply test parameter strings for the program to work with. The COMMAND$ function returns any string that you supply in this option.

The main program section takes the first look at the command line to see if the user supplied the /H option, the request for the program's help screen:

```
IF INSTR(COMMAND$, "/H") THEN
    Help
```

Notice the use of the INSTR function to test for the presence of a particular sequence of characters in the string supplied by the COMMAND$ function. Normally a program uses INSTR to find the position of a group of characters inside a larger string; but in this case, the program only needs to know if the /H option is present. If INSTR gives a nonzero value, this value is read as a value of true, and the program calls the Help procedure to display the help screen. The program then ends without any further action.

However, if the /H option is not present in the command line, INSTR returns a value of 0, or false. The next step is to create an initial directory listing that the program can work with. The program accomplishes this by running DIR as a SHELL operation, as we'll see in the next section.

Using the SHELL command

The SHELL command temporarily exits to MS-DOS, executes an MS-DOS command, and then returns control to the current QuickBASIC program. The following statement executes the DIR command from the *List* program and stores the resulting directory in the file named *FILETEMP.TXT*:

```
SHELL "DIR " + Skeleton$ + " > FILETEMP.TXT"
```

Notice that this SHELL command contains a call to the function named *Skeleton$. Skeleton$* examines the command line and returns any file-pattern string that the user supplied. This file pattern—which some programmers refer to as a *file skeleton*—can contain the wildcard characters *?* and ***, which select specified filenames from the directory. *List* expects the skeleton at the beginning of the command line, before any of the optional switch parameters. The program incorporates this string into the DIR command during the SHELL operation:

```
"DIR " + Skeleton$
```

So, for example, if the COMMAND$ string is

```
*.BAS /SCD /D 10-1-87 TO
```

then the complete DIR command issued by the SHELL operation becomes:

```
DIR *.BAS > FILETEMP.TXT
```

When the program saves the selected listing on disk in the file *FILETEMP.TXT,* the next task is to read the file line by line and organize the data conveniently for the activities that follow.

Reading the directory

The *ReadFile* procedure reads *FILETEMP.TXT* as a sequential file and stores the directory information as an array of records named *dirFile()*. Each record in the *dirFile()* array contains one complete file description.

Several additional procedures contribute to the reading process:

- The *GetInDates* subprogram reads the optional /D parameter if the user supplied it and reports back the date or range of dates that should be used to select files from the directory.

- The *SkipLine%* function determines whether or not a line of text in *FILETEMP.TXT* should be selected as a target file description. In effect, this function instructs the program to skip any irrelevant lines of text included in the directory and to skip file descriptions that do not match the user-supplied dates in the /D parameter.

- The *ConvertDate%* function converts a date string (such as "*10/11/87*") into an integer scalar date, representing a number of days forward in time from a fixed starting point. This conversion simplifies the process of selecting and sorting files chronologically.

- The *ConvertTime#* function converts a time string (such as "*11:29a*") into a double-precision decimal value, representing a fractional portion of a 24-hour day. Thanks to this conversion, the program can use the time stamp as a secondary key in chronological sorts.

As we'll see, the program combines the results of *ConvertDate%* and *ConvertTime#* and saves the sum as one of the elements in each file-description record. Together, these two functions introduce an important programming topic that we'll discuss peripherally in this chapter: How to work effectively with chronological values in a QuickBASIC program. In some programming environments—such as spreadsheets and database management programs—date and time values are handled as distinct data types, and entire libraries of functions and operations are sometimes available to work with such values. QuickBASIC, however, has no such built-in facilities, so we have to supply our own library of procedures to perform chronological operations. *ConvertDate%* and *ConvertTime#* are the beginning elements of such a library.

After creating the array of file-description records, the program next turns to the task of sorting the array.

Sorting and displaying the directory

A function named *WhichSort%* searches the COMMAND$ string for the user's sorting instructions. A call to *WhichSort%* actually supplies two items of information, as shown in the following statement from the main program section:

```
sortCommand% = WhichSort%(sortingOrder%)
```

The function returns an integer code representing the sort key that the user requests: *1* for an alphabetic sort by filenames; *2* for a numeric sort by file sizes; and *3* for a chronological sort. (If the user does not include a /S option, *WhichSort%* returns a value of *0*.) In addition, the function returns a logical value to the argument variable *sortingOrder%*—true if the user requests an ascending sort or false if the user requests a descending sort.

Both of these items of information are sent to the *RecursiveSort* procedure, which actually performs the sort operation. This procedure is organized so that the array of file descriptions can be sorted in any of the ways described on the program's help screen. Depending on the sort that was requested, the sorting procedure makes use of one of three subsidiary procedures to complete the operation: *SortByNames, SortByMemory,* or *SortByDates.* We'll take a look at these procedures later in this chapter.

The program's last task is to display the directory listing on the screen. This is done by the *DisplayDir* procedure. The procedure takes one final look at the COMMAND$ string to see if the user supplied a /P parameter. If so, the directory is displayed one screen at a time. In addition, this routine calls on the *DayOfWeek$* function to display the day of the week corresponding to each file's date stamp.

With this overview of the program in mind, let's now return to the beginning to examine the data structures used in the program.

DATA TYPES AND STRUCTURES IN THE *LIST* PROGRAM

The program's central data structure is the array of records named *dirFile()*. This array stores the directory listing in a format that is convenient both for the sorting process and for the subsequent display procedure. Let's see exactly how this array is structured.

Defining the *fileLine* type

The records in the *dirFile()* array conform to a user-defined type named *fileLine*. The TYPE statement for this structure, located in the declarations section, includes a variety of numeric and string elements:

```
TYPE fileLine
    baseName AS STRING * 8
    extName AS STRING * 3
    fullName AS STRING * 12
    memBytes AS LONG
    dateString AS STRING * 8
    dateScalar AS DOUBLE
    timeString AS STRING * 6
END TYPE
```

Five of the seven record elements are strings. The *baseName* and *extName* elements store the two parts of a filename—the base name and the extension—respectively. The *fullName* element is for the full name of the file, used in an alphabetic sort. The *dateString* and *timeString* elements store a file's date and time stamps. As we discussed earlier in this chapter, all string elements in a user-defined type must be fixed-length strings. This requirement suits this application perfectly because each part of a file-description string has a predictable length.

The *fileLine* type also contains two numeric elements. The *memBytes* element is a long integer that stores the size of each file. As we discussed earlier, QuickBASIC's new long integer is thus the ideal type for storing this particular value.

The *dateScalar* element stores a calculated "scalar" value representing a file's date and time stamps. This scalar value is a number containing two parts: an integer scalar date supplied by the *ConvertDate%* function and a decimal scalar time value supplied by the *ConvertTime#* function. Let's pause briefly here to discuss these scalar values.

For a date-string argument, the *ConvertDate%* function supplies an integer representing a number of days forward in time from the date 1-1-80, the earliest date that MS-DOS accepts as the system date. For example, the date 11-9-87 would be converted to a scalar date value of 2870. This simply means that 11-9-87 is the 2870th day since 1-1-80.

The *ConvertTime#* function represents a time-string argument as a fractional portion of a day. For example, the function converts the string *"6:00a"* to the value .25, since one-fourth of the day has gone by at 6 o'clock in the morning. Likewise, 12 o'clock noon is represented as .5, and 6 o'clock in the evening is represented as .75. To provide minute-by-minute accuracy in this conversion, *ConvertTime#* uses a double-precision number.

The sum of these two values accurately represents date and time values for chronological sort operations. For example, let's say a file is stamped with the date string *"11-09-87"* and with the time string *"6:00p"*. The *List* program computes a value of 2870.75 as the scalar equivalent for these two chronological values. An array of such numbers will be easy for the program to sort—much easier than trying to rearrange records by date-string and time-string keys. Later in this chapter we'll see how the program calculates these scalar values: For now, just keep in mind that the *dateScalar* record element is a reasonably precise numeric conversion of a file's date and time stamps.

Once the elements of the *fileLine* type are defined, the program sets up the array of records required for storing the directory information.

Creating the directory array

The following DIM statement defines the *dirFile()* array:

```
DIM SHARED dirFile(max%) AS fileLine
```

As you can see, *dirFile()* is a global array available to any procedure in the program. The value *max%* is one of several constants established at the beginning of the program:

```
CONST max% = 200
```

This constant dictates the maximum number of file descriptions that the program can handle during execution. (If you find that you examine directories containing more than 200 files, you should adjust the value of *max%* accordingly, and then recompile the *List* program.)

Here are the other symbolic constants the program uses:

```
CONST minute# = 1 / 1440#
CONST false% = 0, true% = NOT false%
```

The *minute#* constant is a decimal fractional value representing a minute as a portion of a 24-hour day. We'll see that this value is used in the process of converting time strings to scalar values. The constants *false%* and *true%* represent the two logical values.

Now that we have examined the program's main data structure, the *dirFile()* array, let's see how data records are assigned to the array. The *ReadFile* procedure provides important insights into the use of record structures; we'll examine it in the next section.

Working with record structures

The *ReadFile* procedure has a number of central tasks to perform. After opening the *FILETEMP.TXT* file for sequential reading, the routine must read each line of the file and determine whether a line represents a filename that should be selected for the directory listing. If so, the routine breaks the line into individual record elements and stores these elements in the *dirFile()* array.

Finally, the procedure counts the number of selected files and the total number of bytes contained in those files. These two totals are returned to the main program via the variables *num%* and *bytes&*, respectively. The first two lines of the procedure initialize these two variables to *0:*

```
num% = 0
bytes& = 0
```

Notice that the first of these variables is a standard integer, and the second is a long integer.

After these initializations, the routine opens the directory file:

```
OPEN "FILETEMP.TXT" FOR INPUT AS #1
```

Several LINE INPUT# commands then read the file one line at a time. (LINE INPUT# reads an entire line from a sequential file, regardless of punctuation marks that might otherwise be considered as field delimiters. We'll study sequential file operations in detail in Chapter 6.) The routine saves the first four lines of the DIR directory in the string array named *titles$():*

```
FOR i% = 1 TO 4
    LINE INPUT #1, titles$(i%)
NEXT i%
```

These four lines contain general information about the directory, which will be displayed without revision as part of the *List* program's output.

The rest of the file is read in a DO...WHILE loop that continues reading lines until the program reaches either the end of the file or the maximum number of filenames that the *dirFile()* array can handle:

```
DO WHILE NOT EOF(1) OR num% >= max%
```

Recall that *max%* is the symbolic constant that determines the size of the *dirFile()* array.

Inside this loop, the program reads each line from the file and initially sends the line to the *SkipLine%* function to determine whether the line should be selected as a file description:

```
LINE INPUT #1, inLine$
IF NOT SkipLine%(inLine$, fileDate$, scalarDate%) THEN
```

SkipLine% returns a value of true if the line does not represent a selected directory file (that is, if the line should be skipped).

The function performs a number of different tests on each line. Perhaps most significantly, it filters out file descriptions that do not match the user's target date range as specified in the /D option. *SkipLine%* also returns two elements of the file description to *ReadFile*: the date string and its scalar date equivalent.

If *SkipLine%* results in a value of false (telling the program not to skip the current line), the *ReadFile%* routine continues to extract the remaining record elements from the current file-description string and to store the elements in the *dirFile()* array. The counter variable *num%* keeps track of the current file number and serves as an index into the array. This value is incremented before each individual record is processed:

```
num% = num% + 1
```

The following lines provide good examples of several of the string-related functions that we discussed earlier in this chapter—including LEFT$, MID$, RIGHT$, RTRIM$, LEN, and VAL. In using these functions, the program relies on the fixed lengths and starting positions of each element in the original file-description line, as produced by the DIR command. A file-description line is 39 characters long; for example:

```
TOOLBOX  BAS     5143  10-15-87   3:23p
```

The following table summarizes the contents of a file-description line:

Item	Starting Position	Characters
Base name	1	8
Extension	10	3
File size	13	10
Date	24	8
Time	34	6

This table helps you see how the program extracts record elements from a file-description line.

First, the LEFT$ and MID$ functions extract the base name and the extension name, respectively:

```
name1$ = LEFT$(inLine$, 8)
name2$ = MID$(inLine$, 10, 3)
```

These values are stored as the *baseName* and *extName* elements of the current record:

```
dirFile(num%).baseName = name1$
dirFile(num%).extName = name2$
```

The *fullName* element is a concatenation of the base name and the extension name:

```
dirFile(num%).fullName = RTRIM$(name1$) + "." + name2$
```

Notice once again the correct notation for referring to an individual record element in an array of records:

```
dirFile(num%).fullName
```

The indexed array name is followed by a period and then by the name of the record element.

The next step is to extract the integer representing the size of the file—the *memBytes* element. The program uses VAL to convert the string of digits to a long integer, *fileSize&* :

```
fileSize& = VAL(MID$(inLine$, 13, 10))
dirFile(num%).memBytes = fileSize&
```

Then the following line accumulates the total size of all the selected files in the variable *bytes&* :

```
bytes& = bytes& + fileSize&
```

The final record elements that the *ReadFile* routine must deal with are the date and time strings and the calculated scalar date value. Recall that the *SkipLine%* function already supplied the *fileDate$* string and the integer *scalarDate%* value.

The time string can be missing in some file-description lines. To find out whether or not the time is included, the program simply looks at the length of the line. Its full length, with the time stamp, should be 39 characters. If this is the actual length of a line, the routine extracts the last six characters as the time string and calls the *ConvertTime#* function to produce a scalar time value:

```
IF LEN(inLine$) = 39 THEN
    fileTime$ = RIGHT$(inLine$, 6)
    scalarTime# = ConvertTime#(fileTime$)
```

However, if the *inLine$* string falls short of the full length, the routine must assume that no time stamp is available in the current file-description line:

```
ELSE
    fileTime$ = ""
    scalarTime# = 0
END IF
```

Accordingly, the *ReadFile* procedure stores the three chronological values in their respective record elements:

```
dirFile(num%).dateString = fileDate$
dirFile(num%).dateScalar = scalarDate% + scalarTime#
dirFile(num%).timeString = fileTime$
```

Notice that the *dateScalar* element is calculated as the sum of the scalar date and the scalar time values. In the next section of this chapter, we'll look more closely at these two values, finding out exactly how they are calculated and how the program uses them.

CHRONOLOGICAL VALUES IN THE *LIST* PROGRAM

Six procedures in the *List* program deal explicitly with chronological values:

1. The *ConvertDate%* function supplies the scalar date equivalent of a date string.

2. The *ConvertTime#* function supplies the scalar time equivalent of a time string.

3. The *DayOfWeek$* function supplies a three-character day-of-the-week abbreviation corresponding to a scalar date value.

4. The *GetInDates* subprogram reads the /D option and extracts the user's target date or dates for selecting directory files.

5. The *SkipLine%* function selects files by dates according to the instructions in the user-supplied /D option.

6. The *SortByDates* subprogram, called by the *RecursiveSort* routine, sorts the directory listing chronologically.

In the following sections we'll examine the first five procedures in this list. Then, to complete our discussion of the *List* program, we'll take a brief look at the *RecursiveSort* procedure.

The *ConvertDate%* function

The *ConvertDate%* function takes one argument, a string representing a date:

```
FUNCTION ConvertDate% (strDate$) STATIC
```

As we have seen, *ConvertDate%* expects this date string to appear in the format *mm-dd-yy*. Only hyphens are acceptable as delimiters inside the date string.

The *List* program uses *ConvertDate%* to produce scalar dates from two input sources: the date strings from file-description lines and the user-supplied date or dates appearing in the /D option.

Dates from a directory listing can be expected to conform reliably to the expected date-string format. However, the /D option dates may not be so reliable; a user might inadvertently supply an invalid or unusable date string. For this reason, *ConvertDate%* must be sure a date string is valid before performing the scalar date conversion. For an invalid date string, the function simply returns a value of *0*.

The first task is to isolate the three elements of a date—the month, the day, and the year. To do this, the routine uses the INSTR function to find the location of the two expected hyphen delimiters:

```
hyphen1% = INSTR(strDate$, "-")
hyphen2% = INSTR(hyphen1% + 1, strDate$, "-")
```

Assuming both hyphens are present in the date string, *ConvertDate%* next uses the LEFT$ and MID$ functions to extract the three date elements and then uses the VAL function to convert these elements to integers:

```
IF hyphen1% <> 0 AND hyphen2% <> 0 THEN
    month% = VAL(LEFT$(strDate$, hyphen1% - 1))
    day% = VAL(MID$(strDate$, hyphen1% + 1, hyphen2% - hyphen1% - 1))
    year% = VAL(MID$(strDate$, hyphen2% + 1)) MOD 1900
```

Next, the routine begins a series of validation tests. The month must be an integer from *1* to *12*, and the year must be within the range of the scalar date system—1980 to 1999:

```
ok% = month% >= 1 AND month% <= 12
ok% = ok% AND year% >= 80 AND year% <= 99
```

Furthermore, the day must be a value from *1* up to the actual number of days in the month. The declarations section of the *List* program previously set up a global array called *daysInMonth%()*, which contains the correct total number of days in each month of the year. *Convert-Date%* uses this array to validate the day element:

```
IF ok% THEN ok% = day% >= 1 AND day% <= daysInMonth%(month%)
```

Assuming the date string is valid, the routine can now begin calculating the scalar date equivalent. The integer value is accumulated in the variable *temp%*. First the function adds 365 days for each whole year that elapsed since 1980:

```
FOR i% = 80 TO year% - 1
    temp% = temp% + 365
    IF i% MOD 4 = 0 THEN temp% = temp% + 1
NEXT i%
```

For leap years the function includes an extra day. In the context of this program, a leap year is identified as a year that is evenly divisible by *4*. Notice the use of the MOD operation to test for this condition.

The next step is to add up the days of the whole months that have elapsed in the current year. The *daysInMonth%()* array again serves to supply the appropriate number of days for each month:

```
FOR i% = 1 TO month% - 1
    temp% = temp% + daysInMonth%(i%)
NEXT i%
```

Finally, the routine adds the number of days that have elapsed in the current month:

```
temp% = temp% + day%
```

In the end, the value of *temp%* is returned as the value of the *ConvertDate%* function:

```
ConvertDate% = temp%
```

The *ConvertTime#* function

ConvertTime# also takes a single string argument, a time string in the format *"hh:mma"* or *"hh:mmp"*:

```
FUNCTION ConvertTime# (strTime$)
```

Unlike *ConvertDate%*, the *ConvertTime#* function is used only for converting the time strings extracted from the directory listing; for this reason, the function does not need to perform validation checks on the time string.

The function's first task is to locate the colon position in the time string and to use this information to separate the hour value from the minute value:

```
colon% = INSTR(strTime$, ":")
hours% = VAL(LEFT$(strTime$, colon% - 1)) MOD 12
mins% = VAL(MID$(strTime$, colon% + 1))
```

Notice the use of the LEFT$, MID$, and VAL functions to extract the time components and to convert them to integers. Also note that the routine performs a MOD 12 operation on the hours value. For the subsequent calculations to work properly, time strings from ''12:00'' to ''12:59'' must be assigned hour values of *0*.

The scalar time calculation requires several steps. The function stores the intermediate scalar time values in the double-precision variable *temp#*. If the time argument is after 12:00 noon, the *temp#* variable is initialized to the scalar equivalent of noon, *.5;* otherwise, *temp#* starts out with a value of *0:*

```
IF UCASE$(RIGHT$(strTime$, 1)) = "P" THEN
    temp# = .5
ELSE
    temp# = 0
END IF
```

In either case, the procedure's next task is to add up the number of whole hours that have elapsed since 12:00. An hour is calculated as *minute# * 60*:

```
FOR i% = 1 TO hours%
    temp# = temp# + (minute# * 60)
NEXT i%
```

Recall that the *List* program previously defined a symbolic constant named *minute#* to store the fractional value of a minute.

Finally, *ConvertTime#* adds up the minutes that have elapsed in the current hour:

```
FOR i% = 1 TO mins%
    temp# = temp# + minute#
NEXT i%
```

After all these calculations, *temp#* is returned as the value of *ConvertTime#*:

```
ConvertTime# = temp#
```

The *DayOfWeek$* function

DayOfWeek$ is a very short function that returns a three-character string representing the day of the week. The function receives an integer scalar date value as its single argument.

To find the correct weekday string for a date, the routine first performs a MOD 7 operation on the scalar date argument:

```
day% = dateNumber% MOD 7
```

This operation produces an integer from *0* to *6*.

The day abbreviations are all stored together in a single string variable, *days$*:

```
days$ = "MonTueWedThuFriSatSun"
```

To extract the correct day from this string, the function uses the integer *day%* to calculate the starting point for a subsequent MID$ function:

```
startPos% = day% * 3 + 1
DayOfWeek$ = MID$(days$, startPos%, 3)
```

Note that if the MOD 7 operation produces a value of *1*, the MID$ function extracts "TUE" from the *days$* string. The first day in the program's scalar date system—1-1-80—is, in fact, a Tuesday.

The *DisplayDir* procedure calls *DayOfWeek$* once for each file in the directory listing. The argument it sends to the function is the integer portion of the *dateScalar* record element:

```
PRINT "    "; DayOfWeek$(INT(dirFile(i%).dateScalar));
```

The *GetInDates* subprogram

If the /D option is included in the COMMAND$ string, *GetInDates* reads it and converts the date strings to scalar date values. The procedure then passes these scalar dates back to the calling routine via the parameter variables *date1%* and *date2%*:

```
SUB GetInDates (date1%, date2%)
```

If the user did not supply a /D option or if the dates supplied in the /D option are not valid, both of the date values are passed back as *0*. On the other hand, if the user supplies only one target date, *GetInDates* supplies the scalar date value in the parameter *date1%*. In this case, *date2%* is returned with a value of *0*.

The first step is to locate the /D option in the COMMAND$ string.

```
commPos% = INSTR(COMMAND$, "/D")
```

If the /D option is present, the routine determines the starting and ending positions of the /D option dates (*startPos%* and *endPos%*, respectively) and the position of the word TO if it was included (*toPos%*). These values are essential in string operations that follow.

If TO is present, the function assumes that the user supplied a range of dates rather than a single date. The following lines extract the first date and find its scalar equivalent:

```
IF toPos% THEN
    date1$ = MID$(COMMAND$, startPos%, toPos% - startPos%)
    date1% = ConvertDate%(date1$)
```

If *date1%* is *0*, the routine assumes that the user wants to use the date 1-1-80 as the beginning of the range. The scalar equivalent for this date is, of course, *1:*

```
IF date1% = 0 THEN date1% = 1
```

The second date is located after the word TO:

```
date2$ = MID$(COMMAND$, toPos% + 2, endPos% - toPos% - 1)
date2% = ConvertDate%(date2$)
```

If this date is *0, GetInDates* uses today's date (supplied by the DATE$ function) as the second date in the range:

```
IF date2% = 0 THEN date2% = ConvertDate%(DATE$)
```

If the word TO is not included in the /D option, the procedure extracts a single date and returns its value in the variable *date1%*:

```
date1$ = MID$(COMMAND$, startPos%, endPos% - startPos% + 1)
date1% = ConvertDate%(date1$)
```

The *SkipLine%* function calls *GetInDates* and uses the resulting scalar date values to determine whether or not a file should be included in the directory listing. In the next section, we'll look at the process of selecting file descriptions by date.

The *SkipLine%* function

SkipLine% makes the following call to *GetInDates* and receives the target scalar date values in the variables *d1%* and *d2%*:

```
GetInDates d1%, d2%
```

The function then extracts the date string from the current file-description line and calls *ConvertDate%* to find the scalar date equivalent:

```
dateString$ = MID$(lineString$, 24, 8)
dateNumber% = ConvertDate%(dateString$)
```

Given these scalar date values—*d1%*, *d2%*, and *dateNumber%*—the selection process is quite simple. If both *d1%* and *d2%* are greater than *0*, the user supplied a valid range of dates in the /D option. The current file description should be skipped if the file's date falls outside the range:

```
IF d1% > 0 AND d2% > 0 THEN
    skip% = dateNumber% < d1% OR dateNumber% > d2%
```

On the other hand, if only *d1%* contains a valid scalar date value, then the current file description should be skipped unless its date is equal to *d1%*:

```
ELSEIF d1% > 0 THEN
    skip% = dateNumber% <> d1%
END IF
```

As we have seen, *SkipLine%* returns the value of *skip%* as its logical result. If the value is true, the program excludes the current file from the directory listing; if false, the file is included.

Let's turn to the subject of recursion, as illustrated by the *List* program's *RecursiveSort* subprogram. This procedure shows why the *dirFile()* array is such a convenient structure for the program's data. Because the directory is organized as an array of records, the routine can perform its sort by exchanging the positions of entire records rather than swapping individual record elements one at a time.

The *RecursiveSort* subprogram

The *RecursiveSort* subprogram can sort the directory alphabetically, numerically, or chronologically, in ascending or descending order. The procedure takes four arguments:

```
SUB RecursiveSort (sortKey%, startPos%, endPos%, ascendSort%)
```

The *sortKey%* argument is a code number representing the target sorting key. The *startPos%* and *endPos%* arguments are pointers marking the beginning and ending points of the current sort operation. Finally, *ascendSort%* is a logical value indicating whether the sort should be performed in ascending order (true) or descending order (false).

To support the various sorting options, the program includes three associated procedures— *SortByNames, SortByMemory,* and *SortByDates.* Each of these three procedures performs either an ascending or a descending sort, using a particular record element as the key to the sort.

The sorting algorithm implemented in these routines is commonly called the quick sort. The idea of the quick sort algorithm is to subdivide the list of records continually into smaller and smaller pairs of partitions. At each level of subdivision, the routine exchanges pairs of individual records that are located in the wrong partition. This process continues until each partition contains only one record, at which point the list is correctly sorted.

The first call to the *RecursiveSort* routine begins by selecting a target record from the middle of the array:

```
middleElement% = (startPos% + endPos%) \ 2
```

Then, through repeated calls to one of the three subsidiary sorting routines, this target record is compared to records located both above and below it. These comparisons determine whether two records should be swapped to place them in the correct partition. When two records are found to be out of order, the subsidiary sorting routines use the SWAP command to exchange them:

```
SWAP dirFile(record1%), dirFile(record2%)
```

Note that this single SWAP command is actually exchanging several data values at once—specifically, all seven elements contained in a file-description record.

By the end of the first round of swapping, the original target record from the middle of the array will have migrated to a point at or near its final location in the array. Furthermore, each of the two partitions—located above and below the target record—will contain records that are all greater than or all less than the target record. The next step is to repeat the entire process on each of the two partitions.

This is accomplished via two recursive calls to the sorting routine:

```
RecursiveSort sortKey%, (startPos%), (tempEnd%), ascendSort%
RecursiveSort sortKey%, (tempStart%), (endPos%), ascendSort%
```

The values *tempStart%* and *tempEnd%* are pointers that the routine uses to mark the beginning of one partition and the end of another. The partitioning and exchanging continues via repeated recursive calls until partitions contain single records and the sorting is complete.

True to its name, the recursive quick sort algorithm is a fast and efficient way of rearranging an array of records. However, the technique is perhaps more complicated and difficult to understand than other familiar sorting routines. The *RecursiveSort* procedure and its associated subsidiary routines are definitely worth a second look if you are interested in understanding how sorting algorithms work.

Conclusion

Here are a few suggestions for further programming exercises you might want to try to improve the performance of the *List* program:

1. Allow an option that selects files within a range of sizes. For example, in the following hypothetical command, the /B option would select files that are from 1,000 to 2,000 bytes long:

   ```
   C>LIST *.TXT /B 1000 TO 2000
   ```

2. Allow the user to supply more than one filename pattern (or "skeleton") for selecting files to appear in the output list. For example, the following command would select all files that have extensions of either *TXT* or *WS* and sort the directory list chronologically in descending order:

   ```
   C>LIST *.TXT, *.WS /SCD
   ```

   This option could also be used to select files from more than one directory path.

3. Supply error messages in response to illegal or incorrect options that the user supplies. Consider reorganizing the program so that the entire command line is analyzed by a single routine at the beginning of the program. If anything is wrong with a parameter, the program should supply the appropriate error messages and terminate without attempting to prepare a directory listing.

```
'    LIST.BAS
'    This program is an alternative to the DIR command in MS-DOS.
'        When performed as a command-style program from MS-DOS, the
'        program allows several options that are not available with
'        DIR: /SN, /SS, and /SC allow you to sort the directory listing
'        by name, size, and date/time, respectively. (Adding a D to the
'        end of a sort option results in a descending sort.) The /D
'        option allows you to select files by date. /P lists files one
'        screenful at a time, and /H displays a help screen.
'        (The List program is written for QuickBASIC 4.0 and 4.5.)


'    ---- Definitions and declarations section.

CONST max% = 200
CONST minute# = 1 / 1440#
CONST false% = 0, true% = NOT false%


'    ---- The user-defined data type fileLine defines the elements
'        of a single file description for this program.

TYPE fileLine
    baseName AS STRING * 8
    extName AS STRING * 3
    fullName AS STRING * 12
    memBytes AS LONG
    dateString AS STRING * 8
    dateScalar AS DOUBLE
    timeString AS STRING * 6
END TYPE

DECLARE FUNCTION ConvertDate% (strDate$)
DECLARE FUNCTION ConvertTime# (strTime$)
DECLARE FUNCTION DayOfWeek$ (dateNumber%)
DECLARE FUNCTION SkipLine% (lineString$, dateString$, dateNumber%)
DECLARE FUNCTION Skeleton$ ()
DECLARE FUNCTION WhichSort% (direction%)
DECLARE SUB DisplayDir (n%, bytes&)
DECLARE SUB Frame (left%, right%, top%, bottom%)
DECLARE SUB GetInDates (date1%, date2%)
DECLARE SUB Help ()
DECLARE SUB ReadFile (num%, bytes&)
DECLARE SUB RecursiveSort (sortKey%, startPos%, endPos%, ascendSort%)
DECLARE SUB SortByDates (dateValue#, record1%, record2%, ascending%)
```

Declarations

Figure 4-2. *The* List *program.* *(continued)*

Figure 4-2. *continued*

```
DECLARE SUB SortByMemory (memoryAmount&, record1%, record2%, ascending%)
DECLARE SUB SortByNames (nameString$, record1%, record2%, ascending%)

OPTION BASE 1

'    ---- The daysInMonth%() array stores the number of days in
'         each month of the year. The dirFile() array stores a list
'         of fileLine records. The titles$() array stores the first
'         four lines of the DIR display. All of these arrays are
'         used globally.

DIM SHARED daysInMonth%(12)
DIM SHARED dirFile(max%) AS fileLine
DIM SHARED titles$(4)

'    ---- Days in each month, from January to December.

DATA 31, 28, 31, 30, 31, 30
DATA 31, 31, 30, 31, 30, 31

'    ---- Main program section.

FOR mo% = 1 TO 12
    READ daysInMonth%(mo%)
NEXT mo%

'    ---- If the COMMAND$ string contains the /H option, simply display
'         the help screen.

IF INSTR(COMMAND$, "/H") THEN
    Help

'    ---- Otherwise, create a directory file, read it into the
'         dirFile() array, sort it (if appropriate), and display it.

ELSE
    SHELL "DIR " + Skeleton$ + " > FILETEMP.TXT"

    ReadFile numFiles%, totBytes&

    sortCommand% = WhichSort%(sortingOrder%)
    IF sortCommand% <> 0 THEN
        RecursiveSort sortCommand%, 1, numFiles%, sortingOrder%
    END IF
```

Main program

(continued)

Figure 4-2. *continued*

```
    DisplayDir numFiles%, totBytes&
END IF

END

FUNCTION ConvertDate% (strDate$) STATIC                          ConvertDate%

'   The ConvertDate% function receives a string date argument in the
'       form mm-dd-yy and converts the date into an integer "scalar
'       date" value. The function expects dates between 1-1-80 and
'       12-31-99. For any date outside this range, or for a string
'       that is not readable as a date in the required format, the
'       function returns a value of 0. The date 1-1-80 is day 1 in
'       the scalar date system established by this routine.

    temp% = 0
    ok% = false%

'   ---- Look for the two required hyphens in the string argument.

    hyphen1% = INSTR(strDate$, "-")
    hyphen2% = INSTR(hyphen1% + 1, strDate$, "-")

'   ---- If both hyphens are there, begin analyzing the string.

    IF hyphen1% <> 0 AND hyphen2% <> 0 THEN

'   ---- Find the three date elements, and then validate the date.

        month% = VAL(LEFT$(strDate$, hyphen1% - 1))
        day% = VAL(MID$(strDate$, hyphen1% + 1, hyphen2% - hyphen1% - 1))
        year% = VAL(MID$(strDate$, hyphen2% + 1)) MOD 1900

        ok% = month% >= 1 AND month% <= 12
        ok% = ok% AND year% >= 80 AND year% <= 99

        IF year% MOD 4 = 0 THEN
            daysInMonth%(2) = 29
        ELSE
            daysInMonth%(2) = 28
        END IF

        IF ok% THEN ok% = day% >= 1 AND day% <= daysInMonth%(month%)
    END IF
```

(continued)

Figure 4-2. *continued*

```
'    ---- If the date is valid, determine the scalar equivalent.

     IF ok% THEN

'    ---- Add up the days in all the years up to the current year.
'         (Add an extra day for all leap years.)

         FOR i% = 80 TO year% - 1
             temp% = temp% + 365
             IF i% MOD 4 = 0 THEN temp% = temp% + 1
         NEXT i%

'    ---- Add the days in the months up to the current month; then add
'         the days. (The array daysInMonth%() is a global data structure,
'         initialized in the main program section.)

         FOR i% = 1 TO month% - 1
             temp% = temp% + daysInMonth%(i%)
         NEXT i%
         temp% = temp% + day%
     END IF

     ConvertDate% = temp%

END FUNCTION


FUNCTION ConvertTime# (strTime$)

'    The ConvertTime# function receives a time string in the format
'         hh:mma or hh:mmp, and converts the argument into a "scalar
'         time" value between 0 and 1, where .5 is equivalent to noon.

'    ---- Find the colon and determine the hour and minute values.

     colon% = INSTR(strTime$, ":")
     hours% = VAL(LEFT$(strTime$, colon% - 1)) MOD 12
     mins% = VAL(MID$(strTime$, colon% + 1))

'    ---- Determine whether the time value is am or pm.

     IF UCASE$(RIGHT$(strTime$, 1)) = "P" THEN
         temp# = .5
```

`ConvertTime#`

(continued)

Figure 4-2. *continued*

```
    ELSE
        temp# = 0
    END IF

'   ---- Add up the minutes in the hours that have elapsed. (The
'        value minute# is a named constant, initialized in the
'        declarations section as 1 / 1440.)

    FOR i% = 1 TO hours%
        temp# = temp# + (minute# * 60)
    NEXT i%

'   ---- Add the elapsed minutes in the current hour.

    FOR i% = 1 TO mins%
        temp# = temp# + minute#
    NEXT i%

    ConvertTime# = temp#

END FUNCTION

FUNCTION DayOfWeek$ (dateNumber%)                                    DayOfWeek$

'   The DayOfWeek$ function returns a three-character string
'        indicating the day of the week corresponding to a
'        given scalar date value, dateNumber%.

    days$ = "MonTueWedThuFriSatSun"
    day% = dateNumber% MOD 7
    startPos% = day% * 3 + 1

    DayOfWeek$ = MID$(days$, startPos%, 3)

END FUNCTION

SUB DisplayDir (n%, bytes&)                                          DisplayDir

'   The DisplayDir subprogram displays the directory listing
'        after it has been selected and sorted.

'   ---- The titles$() array contains the first four lines of
'        text in the original DIR directory.
```

(continued)

Figure 4-2. *continued*

```
    FOR i% = 1 TO 4
        PRINT titles$(i%)
    NEXT i%
    PRINT


    ' ---- The dirFile() structure is an array of fileLine records.

    FOR i% = 1 TO n%
        PRINT dirFile(i%).baseName; " ";
        PRINT dirFile(i%).extName;
        PRINT USING "#########"; dirFile(i%).memBytes;
        PRINT "    "; DayOfWeek$(INT(dirFile(i%).dateScalar));
        PRINT "., "; dirFile(i%).dateString; "   ";
        PRINT dirFile(i%).timeString

    ' ---- If the command line contains the /P option, pause
    '       after each screenful of information.

        IF INSTR(COMMAND$, "/P") AND i% MOD 18 = 0 THEN
            PRINT
            INPUT "Press <Enter> to continue.", cont$
            PRINT
        END IF

    NEXT i%

    ' ---- Display the total number of bytes in the files
    '       selected for this directory listing.

    PRINT
    totFormat$ = "    Total of ######## bytes in"
    PRINT USING totFormat$; bytes&;
    PRINT n%;

    ' ---- Construct a grammatically correct sentence.

    IF n% = 1 THEN
        PRINT "file."
    ELSE
        PRINT "files."
    END IF

END SUB
```

(continued)

Figure 4-2. *continued*

```
SUB Frame (left%, right%, top%, bottom%) STATIC                    Frame

'   The Frame subprogram draws a rectangular double-line frame on the
'       screen, using "text-graphics" characters from the IBM Extended
'       ASCII character set.

'   ---- Draw the four corners.

    LOCATE top%, left%: PRINT CHR$(201)
    LOCATE top%, right%: PRINT CHR$(187)
    LOCATE bottom%, left%: PRINT CHR$(200);
    LOCATE bottom%, right%: PRINT CHR$(188);

'   ---- Draw the vertical lines.

    FOR vert% = top% + 1 TO bottom% - 1
        LOCATE vert%, left%: PRINT CHR$(186);
        LOCATE vert%, right%: PRINT CHR$(186);
    NEXT vert%

'   ---- Draw the horizontal lines.

    horiz% = right% - left% - 1
    hline$ = STRING$(horiz%, 205)
    LOCATE top%, left% + 1: PRINT hline$
    LOCATE bottom%, left% + 1: PRINT hline$;

END SUB

SUB GetInDates (date1%, date2%)                                 GetInDates

'   The GetInDates subprogram reads one or two dates from the
'       /D option in the command line and returns the dates
'       as scalars in the parameter variables date1% and date2%.

    date1% = 0
    date2% = 0

'   ---- Find the location of the /D option, and begin analyzing
'       the subsequent command string.
```

(continued)

Figure 4-2. *continued*

```
commPos% = INSTR(COMMAND$, "/D")
IF commPos% THEN

'    ---- Find the location of the next command in the command line.

    nextCom% = INSTR(commPos% + 1, COMMAND$, "/")
    com$ = MID$(COMMAND$, nextCom% + 1, 1)
    IF NOT (com$ = "P" OR com$ = "S") THEN nextCom% = 0

'    ---- Find the location of the word TO in the command line.

    toPos% = INSTR(commPos% + 1, COMMAND$, "TO")

'    ---- Find the starting and ending points in the /D string.

    startPos% = commPos% + 2
    IF nextCom% THEN
        endPos% = nextCom% - 1
    ELSE
        endPos% = LEN(COMMAND$)
    END IF

'    ---- If TO is in the command line, look for two dates.

    IF toPos% THEN
        date1$ = MID$(COMMAND$, startPos%, toPos% - startPos%)
        date1% = ConvertDate%(date1$)

'    ---- If date1% is 0 (i.e., missing), assume that the user actually
'         wants all files that have dates up to date2%.

        IF date1% = 0 THEN date1% = 1
        date2$ = MID$(COMMAND$, toPos% + 2, endPos% - toPos% - 1)
        date2% = ConvertDate%(date2$)

'    ---- If the second date is 0, assume that the user wants all
'         files from date1% up to today's date.

        IF date2% = 0 THEN date2% = ConvertDate%(DATE$)
    ELSE
```

(continued)

Figure 4-2. *continued*

```
'    ---- If TO is missing, look for the one target date.

            date1$ = MID$(COMMAND$, startPos%, endPos% - startPos% + 1)
            date1% = ConvertDate%(date1$)
        END IF
    END IF


'    ---- If the two dates are out of order, swap them.

    IF date2% <> 0 AND date1% > date2% THEN SWAP date1%, date2%

END SUB

SUB Help                                                                Help

'    The Help subprogram is called if the /H option is included in
'        the command line. The routine simply displays a description
'        of the program on the screen.

    CLS

    PRINT
    PRINT "    The List Program:"
    PRINT
    PRINT "    List is a command-style program that is similar to the DIR"
    PRINT "    command in MS-DOS. You can supply a drive name, a path name,"
    PRINT "    and a filename (optionally including the wildcard characters"
    PRINT "    ? and *) to specify the files that you wish to list. In addition,"
    PRINT "    each of the following options results in a sorted list of files:"
    PRINT "        /SN or /SND      Sorts alphabetically by the filenames."
    PRINT "        /SS or /SSD      Sorts numerically by file size (in bytes)."
    PRINT "        /SC or /SCD      Sorts chronologically by date and time."
    PRINT "    (The letter D in a sort option results in a descending sort.)"
    PRINT
    PRINT "    The /D option allows you to specify a date or a range of dates"
    PRINT "    for selecting files:"
    PRINT "        /D mm-dd-yy               Selects files that match the date."
    PRINT "        /D mm-dd-yy TO mm-dd-yy   Selects files in the range of dates."
    PRINT "        /D TO mm-dd-yy            Selects files up to the given date."
    PRINT "        /D mm-dd-yy TO            Selects files from the date forward."
    PRINT
    PRINT "    /P lists files one screenful at a time. /H displays this screen."
```

(continued)

Figure 4-2. *continued*

```
      PRINT "   At the bottom of the file list, the LIST command displays the"
      PRINT "   total number of bytes in the selected files."

   '   ---- Draw a frame around the help screen.

      Frame 1, 71, 1, 24

   END SUB

   SUB ReadFile (num%, bytes&)

   '   The ReadFile subprogram reads the directory file "filetemp.txt" and
   '       stores the file lines in an array of records, dirFile(). In the
   '       parameter variables num% and bytes&, the routine returns the
   '       number of selected files in the directory and the total size
   '       of all the files, respectively.

      num% = 0
      bytes& = 0
      OPEN "FILETEMP.TXT" FOR INPUT AS #1

   '   ---- Read the first four lines of text in the DIR listing.

      FOR i% = 1 TO 4
          LINE INPUT #1, titles$(i%)
      NEXT i%

   '    ---- Read file description lines, one at a time.

      DO WHILE NOT EOF(1) OR num% >= max%
          LINE INPUT #1, inLine$

   '   ---- The SkipLine% function returns a value of true if a given
   '        file line should not be included in the directory.

          IF NOT SkipLine%(inLine$, fileDate$, scalarDate%) THEN
              num% = num% + 1
              name1$ = LEFT$(inLine$, 8)
              name2$ = MID$(inLine$, 10, 3)
              dirFile(num%).baseName = name1$
              dirFile(num%).extName = name2$
```

ReadFile

(continued)

Figure 4-2. *continued*

```
'    ---- Store the full filename for the purpose of sorting.

            dirFile(num%).fullName = RTRIM$(name1$) + "." + name2$
            fileSize& = VAL(MID$(inLine$, 13, 10))
            dirFile(num%).memBytes = fileSize&
            bytes& = bytes& + fileSize&

            IF LEN(inLine$) = 39 THEN
                fileTime$ = RIGHT$(inLine$, 6)
                scalarTime# = ConvertTime#(fileTime$)
            ELSE
                fileTime$ = ""
                scalarTime# = 0
            END IF

            dirFile(num%).dateString = fileDate$

'    ---- The dateScalar element is a double-precision number
'         representing the date and time for sorting purposes.

            dirFile(num%).dateScalar = scalarDate% + scalarTime#
            dirFile(num%).timeString = fileTime$

        END IF
    LOOP

    CLOSE #1

'    ---- Delete the "filetemp.txt" file from disk, now that the
'         directory has been stored in the dirFile() array.

    KILL "filetemp.txt"
END SUB

SUB RecursiveSort (sortKey%, startPos%, endPos%, ascendSort%)

'    The RecursiveSort subprogram uses a version of the recursive QuickSort
'         algorithm to sort the dirFile() array. The sortKey% argument
'         indicates the sorting key (1 = file names; 2 = file sizes;
'         3 = file dates and times). The ascendSort% argument is a
'         logical value indicating the direction of the sort
'         (true = ascending; false = descending).
```

RecursiveSort

(continued)

Figure 4-2. *continued*

```
    IF startPos% < endPos% THEN

        tempStart% = startPos%
        tempEnd% = endPos%
        middleElement% = (startPos% + endPos%) \ 2

'   ---- Call the appropriate sorting routine, depending on the
'        the value of sortKey%.

        SELECT CASE sortKey%

        CASE 1
            targetName$ = dirFile(middleElement%).fullName
            DO
                SortByNames targetName$, tempStart%, tempEnd%, ascendSort%
            LOOP UNTIL tempStart% >= tempEnd%

        CASE 2
            targetBytes& = dirFile(middleElement%).memBytes
            DO
                SortByMemory targetBytes&, tempStart%, tempEnd%, ascendSort%
            LOOP UNTIL tempStart% >= tempEnd%

        CASE 3
            targetDate# = dirFile(middleElement%).dateScalar
            DO
                SortByDates targetDate#, tempStart%, tempEnd%, ascendSort%
            LOOP UNTIL tempStart% >= tempEnd%

        CASE ELSE

        END SELECT

'   ---- Recursive calls to this routine continue until the
'        array is sorted.

        RecursiveSort sortKey%, (startPos%), (tempEnd%), ascendSort%
        RecursiveSort sortKey%, (tempStart%), (endPos%), ascendSort%

    END IF

END SUB
```

(continued)

Figure 4-2. *continued*

```
FUNCTION Skeleton$                                                    Skeleton$

'   The Skeleton$ function returns the portion of the command line
'       that represents the filename "skeleton" (possibly including
'       wildcard characters * and ?). This skeleton must appear
'       before any of the "/" options included in the command line.

'   ---- Find the position of the first command-line "/" option.

    slashPos% = INSTR(COMMAND$, "/")

'   ---- Depending on its position, determine the nature of the
'       skeleton string.

    SELECT CASE slashPos%

    CASE 0
'   ---- If there is no "/" option, the entire command line is the
'       skeleton string.
        temp$ = COMMAND$

    CASE 1
'   ---- If the first "/" option appears at the beginning of the
'       command line, there is no skeleton string.
        temp$ = ""

    CASE IS > 1
'   ---- Otherwise, if the first "/" option appears somewhere after
'       the beginning of the command line, the skeleton string consists
'       of all the text that appears before this first option.
        temp$ = LEFT$(COMMAND$, slashPos% - 1)

    END SELECT

    Skeleton$ = temp$

END FUNCTION

FUNCTION SkipLine% (lineString$, dateString$, dateNumber%)            SkipLine%

'   The SkipLine% function returns a Boolean value, indicating whether
'       a given file-description line (lineString$) read from the
'       "filetemp.txt" file should be skipped (true) or selected (false).
```

(continued)

Figure 4-2. *continued*

```
'    ---- Skip subdirectory files.

     skip% = INSTR(lineString$, "<DIR>") > 0
     skip% = skip% OR LEN(lineString$) = 0


'    ---- Skip the "filetemp.txt" file.

     skip% = skip% OR LEFT$(lineString$, 8) = "FILETEMP"


'    ---- Skip the last line of the DIR listing.

     skip% = skip% OR INSTR(lineString$, "bytes free") > 0


'    ---- If none of the previous "skip" tests resulted in a true
'         value, the next test is for the user-supplied date or
'         dates in the command line's /D option.

     IF NOT skip% THEN

'    ---- The GetInDates routine supplies the two /D dates.

         GetInDates d1%, d2%


'    ---- Find the date string in the command line, and call the
'         ConvertDate% function to determine the scalar equivalent
'         of this date. (By the way, these two values will be
'         returned to the calling routine via the parameter variables
'         dateString$ and dateNumber%, respectively.)

         dateString$ = MID$(lineString$, 24, 8)
         dateNumber% = ConvertDate%(dateString$)


'    ---- Compare a file's scalar date with the user-supplied dates
'         d1% and d2%. If both /D dates were supplied, skip any file
'         that does not fall within the range. If only one date was
'         supplied, skip any file that does not match the date.

         IF d1% > 0 AND d2% > 0 THEN
             skip% = dateNumber% < d1% OR dateNumber% > d2%
         ELSEIF d1% > 0 THEN
             skip% = dateNumber% <> d1%
         END IF
     END IF
```

(continued)

Figure 4-2. *continued*

```
    SkipLine% = skip%

END FUNCTION

SUB SortByDates (dateValue#, record1%, record2%, ascending%)

'   The SortByDates subprogram (called by the RecursiveSort subprogram)
'       sorts the dirFile() array chronologically, in either an
'       ascending or a descending order.

    IF ascending% THEN
        DO WHILE dirFile(record1%).dateScalar < dateValue#
            record1% = record1% + 1
        LOOP

        DO WHILE dateValue# < dirFile(record2%).dateScalar
            record2% = record2% - 1
        LOOP
    ELSE
        DO WHILE dirFile(record1%).dateScalar > dateValue#
            record1% = record1% + 1
        LOOP

        DO WHILE dateValue# > dirFile(record2%).dateScalar
            record2% = record2% - 1
        LOOP
    END IF

    IF record1% <= record2% THEN
        SWAP dirFile(record1%), dirFile(record2%)
        record1% = record1% + 1
        record2% = record2% - 1
    END IF

END SUB

SUB SortByMemory (memoryAmount&, record1%, record2%, ascending%)

'   The SortByMemory subprogram (called by the RecursiveSort subprogram)
'       sorts the dirFile() array numerically by file sizes, in either
'       an ascending or a descending order.
```

`SortByDates`

`SortByMemory`

(continued)

153

Figure 4-2. *continued*

```
    IF ascending% THEN
        DO WHILE dirFile(record1%).memBytes < memoryAmount&
            record1% = record1% + 1
        LOOP

        DO WHILE memoryAmount& < dirFile(record2%).memBytes
            record2% = record2% - 1
        LOOP
    ELSE
        DO WHILE dirFile(record1%).memBytes > memoryAmount&
            record1% = record1% + 1
        LOOP

        DO WHILE memoryAmount& > dirFile(record2%).memBytes
            record2% = record2% - 1
        LOOP
    END IF

    IF record1% <= record2% THEN
        SWAP dirFile(record1%), dirFile(record2%)
        record1% = record1% + 1
        record2% = record2% - 1
    END IF

END SUB

SUB SortByNames (nameString$, record1%, record2%, ascending%)

'   The SortByNames subprogram (called by the RecursiveSort subprogram)
'       sorts the dirFile() array alphabetically by filenames, in either
'       an ascending or a descending order.

    IF ascending% THEN
        DO WHILE dirFile(record1%).fullName < nameString$
            record1% = record1% + 1
        LOOP

        DO WHILE nameString$ < dirFile(record2%).fullName
            record2% = record2% - 1
        LOOP
    ELSE
```

SortByNames

(continued)

Figure 4-2. *continued*

```
        DO WHILE dirFile(record1%).fullName > nameString$
            record1% = record1% + 1
        LOOP

        DO WHILE nameString$ > dirFile(record2%).fullName
            record2% = record2% - 1
        LOOP
    END IF

    IF record1% <= record2% THEN
        SWAP dirFile(record1%), dirFile(record2%)
        record1% = record1% + 1
        record2% = record2% - 1
    END IF

END SUB

FUNCTION WhichSort% (direction%)
```
WhichSort%
```
'   The WhichSort% function examines the /S option in the
'       command line. This function returns an integer value
'       indicating which sort has been requested: 1 for a
'       name sort, 2 for a memory-size sort, or 3 for a
'       chronological sort. A return value of 0 means that
'       no valid sort was requested. The direction% argument
'       is returned as a logical value indicating the direction
'       of the sort: true = ascending; false = descending.


'   ---- Find the /S option.

    sortInstr% = INSTR(COMMAND$, "/S")

'   ---- If the option is present, examine the next nonspace
'       character in the command line to determine which sort
'       has been requested.

    IF sortInstr% <> 0 THEN
        sorttype$ = LTRIM$(MID$(COMMAND$, sortInstr% + 2))

'   ---- Use the INSTR function to convert the sort option ("N",
'       "S", or "C") to an integer (1, 2, or 3). INSTR returns
'       a value of 0 if the sort option is not one of these three.
```

(continued)

Figure 4-2. *continued*

```
        temp% = INSTR("NSC", LEFT$(sorttype$, 1))

'   ---- If the user has entered a "D" immediately after the sort
'        option, the file should be sorted in descending order.
'        Send back a value of false in the direction% argument.

        direction% = MID$(sorttype$, 2, 1) <> "D"

    ELSE

'   ---- The return value is 0 if the sort option is missing.

        temp% = 0
    END IF

    WhichSort% = temp%

END FUNCTION
```

CHAPTER 5

Decisions and Loops: The *Twenty-one* Program

In Chapter 4 we examined QuickBASIC's enhanced collection of data structures, which offer a variety of techniques for organizing and storing data values in a program. Now we'll turn to another category of language structures—specifically, a group of statements that control the logical flow of program activity. We refer to these statements as *control structures*.

We'll discuss two kinds of control structures in this chapter: *decisions* and *loops*. Briefly, these structures behave as follows:

- Decision statements choose among different courses of action available during a program's execution.

- Loop statements mark off specific blocks of code for controlled repetition during a program's execution.

If your previous programming experience has been with the BASICA interpreter or with one of the early versions of QuickBASIC, you may be surprised to discover the variety of options that QuickBASIC 4.0 and 4.5 now offer for expressing these two kinds of control structures. Here are the decision statements that we'll explore in this chapter:

- The IF...THEN...ELSE statement, a standard decision structure that allows you to organize complex patterns of activities for a program to choose among

- The SELECT CASE statement, an alternative decision structure that often simplifies the expression of complex decisions

The loop statements that we'll examine are:

- The FOR statement, a familiar loop structure that performs counted repetitions

- The DO statement, a versatile structure that represents a whole family of repetition loops

These four statements may take on a variety of simple and complex forms. In particular, their action is always dependent upon conditions, which may appear as constants, variables, or expressions. A decision statement uses a condition to choose or reject a particular course of action. In a loop, a condition determines how long the looping will continue, or when it will stop.

Each of these structures may be nested inside another controlling structure. Nesting means that one structured activity occurs completely within the control of an outer structure. Additional levels of nesting can increase the complexity and the power of a routine. We'll discuss nesting in this chapter as we examine the syntax of the control structures.

Every program in this book contains interesting examples of decisions and loops. For this introduction to the subject of control structures, we'll examine a game program called *Twenty-one,* an application that illustrates decisions and loops in a variety of formats. Before we begin examining the language structures themselves, let's take a short look at this program.

A FIRST LOOK AT THE *TWENTY-ONE* PROGRAM

Most of the QuickBASIC applications collected in this book perform various useful tasks; for example, the programs include business tools, database programs, and utilities. In this chapter we'll take a short break from all this seriousness and have some fun with a program that plays the popular card game known as Twenty-one or Blackjack.

Twenty-one is a simple gambling game that uses a full deck of 52 cards. In the version of the game conducted by the *Twenty-one* program, the computer acts as the dealer, and you—sitting at the keyboard—are the player. You begin each round of the game by placing a bet, an amount that you ultimately either win or lose unless the round ends in a draw.

When you have placed your bet, the program deals two cards to you and two to the dealer. Figure 5-1 shows how the program turns the computer's display screen into the playing table. Your hand is displayed on the left side of the screen, and the dealer's hand is on the right. After the initial deal, you can request additional cards, or you can stay with your current hand. Your goal in a round is to accumulate a hand with a count that is as close as possible to 21, but not over 21. You win a round when your hand has a higher count than the dealer's, up to a maximum count of 21.

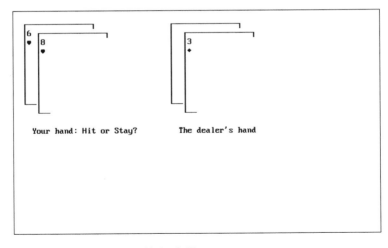

Figure 5-1. *The playing table in the* Twenty-one *program.*

The action is fast and seductive, and you can continue playing rounds as long as you want. By design, the odds of the game are always in the dealer's favor. Happily, this computer-based game offers a striking advantage over real-life gambling: If you find yourself losing too dramatically, you can simply wander away from the table. When you end the game, the computer conveniently forgets about your losses.

The outcome of the game is dependent on three sorts of events and conditions: first, the random shuffle of the deck; second, the decisions that you make as you play your own hand; and third, the fixed rules that govern the dealer's subsequent play. The program must handle a variety of events resulting from these activities. We'll look in more detail at the rules of the game later in this chapter.

Although the game is simple, you may be surprised to discover that the *Twenty-one* program is rich in complex and challenging algorithms. During each round, the program has to deal the cards, display them on the screen, and keep a count of the two hands—yours and the dealer's. Depending on the particular sequences of cards contained in the two hands, the program must also determine the playing options that are available for any turn of the game and control the action accordingly. The *Twenty-one* program is an excellent medium for exploring QuickBASIC's decision and loop structures. Let's begin our survey of these structures.

DECISION STRUCTURES IN QUICKBASIC

You can use either IF...THEN...ELSE or SELECT CASE to divide a complex decision into individual *blocks* of code. A block consists of one or more QuickBASIC statements. Each block in a decision structure expresses one of the alternative courses of action available to the program. In one form or another, a condition always appears at the beginning of each block in a decision structure. When the program evaluates a particular condition as true, the corresponding block of code is executed. During execution of a decision, the program selects only one block, at most, for action.

The practical difference between the IF...THEN...ELSE and SELECT CASE structures lies in the way you express the various conditions. In an IF...THEN...ELSE statement, each condition is a constant, variable, or logical expression that QuickBASIC can evaluate as true or false. (See Chapter 4 for a review of logical expressions.) These expressions need not be related to each other in any way; each can deal with different operands and can perform different logical and relational operations. In contrast, all the conditions of a SELECT CASE statement are related to a single operand. This target operand always appears as an expression at the beginning of the SELECT CASE structure.

Let's examine the syntax of these two structures.

The IF...THEN...ELSE structure

Here is the general format of the IF...THEN...ELSE structure:

```
IF condition1 THEN
      [block of statements that will be
      executed if condition1 is true]
ELSEIF condition2 THEN
      [block of statements that will be
      executed if condition2 is true
      (you may add additional ELSEIF
      blocks in the structure)]
ELSE
      [block of statements that will be
      executed if none of the above
      conditions is true]
END IF
```

As you can see, the major elements of this structure are an IF clause, optional ELSEIF and ELSE clauses, and an END IF statement. As you examine this syntax, keep in mind the following characteristics:

- The conditions in the IF and ELSEIF clauses can be any expressions that QuickBASIC can evaluate as true or false.

- The IF, ELSEIF, and ELSE clauses are each followed by a block of program statements. QuickBASIC evaluates the conditions of the IF and ELSEIF clauses in the order in which they appear and executes the block of statements corresponding to the first condition that results in a true value.

- The ELSE block will be executed if none of the IF or ELSEIF condition expressions evaluates to true. The ELSE clause is optional; if you do not include it and if all of the previous conditions are false, the decision structure will result in no action at all.

- You can include multiple ELSEIF clauses in a decision structure, each with its own condition expression and corresponding block of statements.

- Only one block of statements in the structure will be executed, even if more than one of the IF or ELSEIF conditions evaluates to true. As soon as QuickBASIC encounters one true condition, it ignores the remaining clauses of the structure.

- IF...THEN...ELSE structures can be nested within other structures, creating the potential for complex patterns of decision-making.

- To build conditional expressions, you can use the six relational operators (=, <>, >, <, >=, <=) and the six logical operators, which were discussed in Chapter 4. The most commonly used of the logical operators are AND, OR, and NOT; the other three are XOR (exclusive OR), EQV (equivalence), and IMP (implication).

- QuickBASIC evaluates conditional expressions to one of two numeric values: *-1* for true, *0* for false. Knowing this, you can create special numeric variables that always contain one of these two values; you can use such logical variables to keep track of important conditions that change as a program runs. These variables, once established, can take the place of other forms of conditional expressions in IF and ELSEIF clauses.

Let's look briefly at some examples of IF...THEN...ELSE structures from the *Twenty-one* program. First, here is a simple statement that contains neither ELSEIF nor ELSE blocks:

```
IF NOT busted% THEN
    DealerPlay
END IF
```

In this case, since the block contains only a single statement, a reasonable alternative would be to use the one-line format of the IF statement. The general format of the one-line statement is:

```
IF expression THEN statement1 ELSE statement2
```

But because the example contains no ELSE clause, the one-line equivalent would be:

```
IF NOT busted% THEN DealerPlay
```

These two formats behave identically: The *DealerPlay* procedure is called if the expression *NOT busted%* results in a value of true.

For a slightly more complex example, consider the following code, which announces the current count of the dealer's hand in the *Twenty-one* program:

```
IF dealerVal% > 21 THEN
    PRINT "Count is"; dealerVal%; "==> Busted!" + SPACE$(8)
ELSE
    PRINT "Count is"; dealerVal%; "==> Dealer stays."
END IF
```

Depending upon the logical result of the expression *dealerVal% > 21*, this code displays one of two messages on the screen. Again, with some slight reorganization, we could instead use a one-line IF statement as an alternative approach to producing this message. However, the block structure is probably a bit easier to read.

Here is an example that contains an ELSEIF block:

```
IF playerVal% > 21 THEN
    over21% = true%
    LOCATE playerCards% + 12, 5
    PRINT "Count is"; playerVal%; "==> Busted!"
    BEEP
ELSEIF playerVal% = 21 THEN
    done% = true%
END IF
```

This decision reacts to the current value of the player's hand. The structure results in action only if one of the two conditions—located in the IF statement or the ELSEIF statement—gives a value of true. If both conditions are false, neither block is selected for performance.

Later we'll see IF...THEN...ELSE structures that contain ELSE blocks along with several ELSEIF blocks, offering multiple alternative courses of action to choose among.

Now let's look at the syntax of the SELECT CASE structure.

The SELECT CASE structure

The outcome of the SELECT CASE structure depends upon a sequence of tests performed on a comparison value that appears at the top of the structure. The following lines show the general form of the SELECT CASE statement.

```
SELECT CASE targetExpression
CASE test1
```
   [block of statements that will be executed
   if test1 *matches* targetExpression*]*
```
CASE test2
```
   [block of statements that will be executed
   if test2 *matches* targetExpression
   (you may include additional test *blocks*
   in a CASE structure)]
```
CASE ELSE
```
   [block of statements that will be executed if none
   of the above tests matches targetExpression*]*
```
END SELECT
```

In response to this structure, QuickBASIC begins by evaluating *targetExpression* in the SELECT CASE clause. The resulting value is then compared with the *test* values in each of the subsequent CASE clauses. When one of these tests results in a match, QuickBASIC executes the block of statements corresponding to the selected CASE clause. Any remaining blocks are ignored.

If none of the CASE clauses results in a positive comparison test, QuickBASIC executes the CASE ELSE block, if it exists. A SELECT CASE structure that has no CASE ELSE block will produce a run-time error if none of the comparison tests is positive.

The *test* expressions in the CASE clauses can include any combination of one or more of the following elements:

- A single value or a single variable or expression that results in a value of the same type as *targetExpression*

- A list of values or a list of variables or expressions; again, the type of these values must match *targetExpression*

- A range of values, in the form:

  `lowValue TO highValue`

  You can express these values as constants, variables, or expressions.

- A relational comparison, in the form

  `IS operator expression`

The *operator* can be any one of QuickBASIC's six relational operators, including =, <>, <, <=, >, and >=.

An implied OR connects the elements of a *test* list. If any element matches *targetExpression*, the CASE block is selected. Keep in mind that all elements of each CASE test must relate directly to *targetExpression*.

The following whimsical example illustrates the various forms of *test* expressions:

```
PRINT "Suggestions for birthday gifts."
PRINT
PRINT "How old is the person for whom"
INPUT "you are buying this gift"; age%
PRINT
SELECT CASE age%
CASE IS < 3
    PRINT "Picture books."
    PRINT "Baby clothes."
    PRINT "Toys."
CASE 3 TO 12
    PRINT "Children's video tapes."
    PRINT "Story books."
    PRINT "Clothes."
CASE 13 TO 20
    PRINT "Records."
    PRINT "Recreational computer software."
    PRINT "Magazine subscriptions."
CASE 21
    PRINT "Champagne."
    PRINT "Solid advice."
    PRINT "Cash."
CASE 35, 40, 50
    PRINT "*** Sensitive year!"
    PRINT "Red wine is appropriate."
CASE ELSE
    PRINT "Flowers."
    PRINT "Liquor."
    PRINT "Candy."
END SELECT
```

These program lines print a list of suggestions for birthday gifts, given the user's input for the age of the recipient. Any value of *age%* results in the execution of one of the CASE blocks. If a particular value does not match one of the explicit *test* expressions, the CASE ELSE block is executed instead.

We'll see additional examples of the SELECT CASE statement when we turn our attention to the *Twenty-one* program. But first, let's examine QuickBASIC's loop statements.

STRUCTURED LOOPS IN QUICKBASIC

QuickBASIC supplies two main repetition structures, called FOR…NEXT loops and DO loops. Both result in the repeated execution of a delimited block of statements; the most important difference between FOR…NEXT and DO is the mechanism that determines the number of repetitions (or iterations) that will occur before the looping stops. We'll examine each of these structures in turn.

FOR…NEXT loops

Here is the syntax of the FOR…NEXT loop:

```
FOR countVar = startValue TO endValue STEP stepValue
    [block of statements that will be executed
        once for each iteration of the loop]
NEXT countVar
```

In a FOR…NEXT loop, you must establish a counter variable (*countVar*) and specify the range of values (*startValue TO endValue*) that the variable will take on during execution of the loop. At the beginning of each iteration the counter receives a new value. If the counter is in the range of values specified by *startValue TO endValue* the block of statements is executed once. The looping ends when the counter has gone through the entire range of values. Keep in mind the following characteristics of FOR…NEXT loops:

- The block of statements is delimited by a FOR statement at the top of the structure and a NEXT statement at the bottom of the structure.

- The FOR statement names the counter variable and specifies the beginning and ending values in the range that the counter will go through. You can express these two values as constants, variables that receive values before the start of the loop, or arithmetic expressions that compute a range of values for the counter variable.

- The optional STEP clause specifies the amount (*stepValue*) by which the counter variable will be increased or decreased after each iteration. If this value is a positive number, the value of the counter will increase with each iteration. If *stepValue* is negative, the counter will decrease. (You can supply a constant, a variable, or an expression for *startValue*; the value can be an integer or a decimal number.) If the STEP clause is missing, the default increment amount is *1*.

- A FOR...NEXT loop results in no iterations at all in either of the following situations:
  — *startValue* is less than *endValue*, and *stepValue* is negative; or
  — *startValue* is greater than *endValue*, and *stepValue* is positive.

Here is a simple example of a FOR...NEXT loop that prints multiples of the constant *pi*:

```
pi = 3.14159
FOR i% = 1 TO 10
    PRINT USING "##.#####"; pi * i%
NEXT i%
```

This is the output from the loop:

```
3.14159
6.28318
9.42477
12.56636
15.70795
18.84954
21.99113
25.13272
28.27431
31.41590
```

Significantly, the following loop produces the same list of values:

```
pi = 3.14159
FOR i = pi TO 10 * pi STEP pi
    PRINT USING "##.#####"; i
NEXT i
```

This second FOR...NEXT loop illustrates the use of the STEP clause and the use of expressions rather than constants for *startValue* and *endValue*.

Next let's examine the various forms of QuickBASIC's DO loop structure.

DO loops

A DO loop normally includes a conditional expression that controls the duration of the looping. Depending upon the loop format, QuickBASIC evaluates the condition either before or after each iteration. You can express this condition inside a WHILE clause or inside an UNTIL clause. We'll examine each of these options in turn.

167

DO...WHILE loops

In a DO...WHILE loop, the iterations continue as long as the condition is true. When some event switches the value of the condition to false, looping stops. Traditionally, the WHILE clause is located at the top of a loop in the DO statement, as in the following format:

```
DO WHILE condition
    [block of statements that will be executed
      once for each iteration of the loop]
LOOP
```

However, QuickBASIC also allows the WHILE clause to appear at the bottom of the loop, as part of the LOOP statement:

```
DO
    [block of statements that will be executed
      once for each iteration of the loop]
LOOP WHILE condition
```

The location of the WHILE clause is a very important feature of the loop. With the clause at the top, the loop will perform no iterations if the initial value of the condition is false. In contrast, the block will always be executed at least once if the WHILE clause is located at the bottom of the loop—regardless of the condition's initial value.

Here is a simple DO...WHILE loop from the *Twenty-one* program:

```
DO WHILE tot% > 21 AND aces% > 0
    tot% = tot% - 10
    aces% = aces% - 1
LOOP
```

The role of this loop is to adjust the value of a hand that contains one or more ace cards. An ace can have a value of either *1* or *11*, depending upon the current value of the hand. This loop executes the two assignment statements repeatedly as long as the value of the hand (*tot%*) is greater than 21 and at least one ace remains that has not yet been devalued to *1* (*aces%*). We'll take another look at this code later in the chapter.

You might be familiar with the WHILE...WEND loop from previous versions of BASIC. This loop structure is available in QuickBASIC 4.0 and 4.5, primarily to maintain compatibility with older versions of the language. The following lines show the general format of the WHILE...WEND loop.

```
WHILE condition
```
[block of statements that will be executed
once for each iteration of the loop]
```
WEND
```

This loop's behavior is the same as the following form of the DO...WHILE loop:

```
DO WHILE condition
```
[block of statements that will be executed
once for each iteration of the loop]
```
LOOP
```

In this book we'll always use the more versatile DO loop rather than the WHILE...WEND loop.

DO...UNTIL loops

In a DO...UNTIL loop, the iterations continue as long as the condition is false. When an event switches the value of the condition to true, looping stops. The UNTIL clause is traditionally located at the bottom of a loop, as in the following format:

```
DO
```
[block of statements that will be executed
once for each iteration of the loop]
```
LOOP UNTIL condition
```

If the UNTIL clause is at the bottom of the loop, at least one iteration will always be executed, regardless of the initial value of the condition. QuickBASIC also allows the UNTIL clause to appear at the top of the loop, as part of the DO statement:

```
DO UNTIL condition
```
[block of statements that will be executed
once for each iteration of the loop]
```
LOOP
```

In this case, no iteration occurs if the condition is true at the outset.

In the *Twenty-one* program we'll find a DO...UNTIL loop that controls the entire action of the program:

```
DO
```
[procedure calls that conduct the game]
```
LOOP UNTIL gameOver%
```

Each iteration of the loop conducts one round of the game. In this case, *gameOver%* is a logical variable that indicates whether the user has quit the game. The program ends when this variable receives a value of true. Because the UNTIL clause is located at the bottom of the loop, every performance of the program consists of at least one round.

In summary, here are the important characteristics of the DO loop structure:

- The block of statements is delimited by a DO statement at the top of the structure and a LOOP statement at the bottom.

- The condition in a DO loop can be any logical value, variable, or expression that QuickBASIC can evaluate to true or false. A DO...WHILE loop continues its performance as long as the condition is true, whereas a DO...UNTIL structure continues looping as long as the condition is false.

- If the WHILE or UNTIL clause is located at the bottom of the loop, the first iteration is automatic. In contrast, if the clause is at the top of the loop, the performance of any iteration depends upon the initial value of the condition.

Interestingly enough, you can write a DO loop without a condition, as in the following format:

```
DO
     [block of statements]
LOOP
```

This is formally an "endless" loop, because the structure contains no mechanism for terminating the performance. In practice a statement located inside the loop should be designed to stop the iterations eventually. Occasionally you might find this unusual structure to be the most convenient form for a particular loop.

Keep in mind that the block of statements located inside a loop can include one or more nested loop structures. We'll discover several examples of nested loops in the *Twenty-one* program. Before turning to the program listing, however, let's see how the game is played.

PLAYING THE TWENTY-ONE GAME

The *Twenty-one* program begins by announcing the betting rules and requesting that you place your bet for the first round of the game, as shown in Figure 5-2.

```
Twenty-one
==========

    The computer is the dealer.
    You currently have:    $250

Place your bet.
----------------
    The house betting limits are:
       ->  minimum bet --   $10
       ->  maximum bet --   $100
    (Just press <Enter> for maximum bet.)

        ==>
```

Figure 5-2. *The opening screen of the* Twenty-one *program.*

Notice that the program gives you $250 at the beginning of the game. For each round you can bet any amount from $10 to $100.

When you have placed your bet, the program transforms the display screen into a playing table. (This "table" and the initial betting screen are the only two displays that the program produces. Simplicity is always an important element in the design of game programs.) The program deals two cards each to you and the dealer. The dealer's first card is dealt face down on the table, and the second card is placed face up so that you can see it. Both of your cards are dealt face up; you examine them and compute the count of your hand. Meanwhile, the program also determines the count of the dealer's hand.

You count the cards as follows:

- Face cards (Jack, Queen, King) of any suit are worth *10*.

- Aces are worth either *11* or *1*, whichever count works better to your advantage in reaching but not exceeding *21*.

- The number cards (*2* through *10*) are worth their face value.

If either two-card hand contains a "natural" 21—that is, an ace plus a face card or a 10—the round ends immediately. If the natural is yours, you win twice your bet; if the natural is the dealer's, you lose your bet. Occasionally, both hands come up as naturals, in which case the round is a draw.

Assuming neither hand is a natural, you are the first to play in the round. You must decide whether or not you want to "hit" (take another card) or "stay" (play with your current hand). The program displays the following message below your hand:

```
Your hand: Hit or Stay?
```

A flashing cursor at the end of the question indicates that the program is waiting for you to respond. You simply press *H* to hit or *S* to stay. (Pressing a key other than *H* or *S* produces no response.)

You base your decision on the current count of your hand. (You may also want to base your hit-or-stay strategy partly on what you can deduce from the dealer's up card.) If you indicate that you want to hit, the program gives you another card from the top of the deck. You can continue hitting (receiving additional cards for your hand) until your count either reaches or exceeds 21.

If you go over 21—a "bust"—you lose the round. In this case, the dealer does not play or expose the face-down card. You lose your bet immediately. If, however, you elect to stay at a point where your hand has a count of 21 or less, the dealer plays next. A fixed set of rules determine when the dealer will hit or stay:

- The dealer hits at a count of *16* or less and stays at a count of *17* or more.

- In a "soft" count worth *17* or more—that is, in a hand that contains an ace plus a card worth *6* or more—the dealer does not have the option of counting the ace as *1* and hitting again. The ace counts as *11*, and the dealer must stay.

If the dealer busts, you win the round and your bet. Otherwise, the count of your hand is compared with the count of the dealer's hand. You win if your count is higher. The program displays a message announcing your winnings; for example:

```
You win  $100.
```

You lose if the dealer's count is higher, and the message appears in the following form:

```
You lose  $100.
```

Equal counts in the two hands result in a draw for the round. The program displays this message:

```
A draw...
```

You will also see this message in the lower-right corner:

```
Press any key to continue.
```

When you have finished examining the two hands, you can simply press a key to begin a new round. The program clears the screen and tells you how much money you now have:

```
Twenty-one
==========


    The computer is the dealer.
    You currently have: $350
```

Over the course of several rounds, you might find yourself running out of money. In this case, the program allows you to go into debt to the dealer. If your dollar holdings go below zero, you will see a message like the following:

```
You owe the house:  $1,250.
(The house extends credit.)
```

There is no limit to your credit with the house.

Following this message is the prompt that asks whether or not you want to continue the game:

```
Continue the game?  (Y or N) ->
```

Press *Y* for another round or *N* to quit.

If you press *Y* to continue, the program displays the house betting limits and asks you for your next bet. You can press the Enter key if you want to bet the maximum amount, $100:

```
(Just press <Enter> for maximum bet.)
    ==>
```

If you enter a non-numeric value or a number that is outside the allowable betting range, the program displays this arrow prompt again, eliciting another input value.

When you have placed your new bet, the program once again transforms the screen into a playing table and deals the first cards of the new round. Let's look at some sample rounds of the game.

Sample rounds of the *Twenty-one* program

Figures 5-3 through 5-10 show a selection of screens produced by the *Twenty-one* program. As you examine them, imagine that you are the player, and keep in mind the following two basic goals of the program.

- The keyboard input that the program requires from you should be fast, easy, and obvious. Placing a bet, specifying a hit or a stay, and requesting an additional round should require as few keystrokes as possible, so that the input process does not interfere with the pace of the game.

- The presentation of the game on the screen should be visual, not verbal. You should be allowed to concentrate on your cards. To make this possible, the display of the two hands must be simple but clear, so that the player can make quick decisions based on the cards shown. Furthermore, the program should avoid distracting the player with excessive written instructions or messages.

The user-interface issues of screen design and keyboard input are of course essential in any programming project. In a game program, these issues determine whether the game will be attractive, enjoyable, appropriately paced, and successful.

Figure 5-3 shows the card table at the beginning of a round. Assuming neither starting hand is a natural 21, you must indicate whether you want to hit or stay at this point. Your playing strategy will probably be based primarily on the count of your own hand. If the count is 11 or less, you should certainly hit; no single card that you could receive would put your count over 21. If the count is 17 or over,

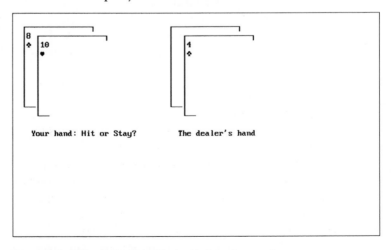

Figure 5-3. *The card table at the beginning of a round.*

you should give serious thought to staying with your current hand: The chances of a bust are high if you take another card, and you know that the dealer stays on a count of 17 or more.

If your count is 12, 13, 14, 15, or 16, you face a more difficult decision. Depending upon how serious a player you are, you might base your strategy on a number of factors, including: the value of the dealer's up card (that is, the card that is displayed), your mental record of the cards that have already been dealt since the last shuffle, and your instinct for percentages. A lot of literature is available on the strategy and the mathematics of the Twenty-one game. But playing strategy is not our main concern in this chapter, so let's look quickly at some additional sample screens from the program.

Figure 5-4 shows a round that has ended in a draw: The two hands have equal counts. You neither win nor lose your bet.

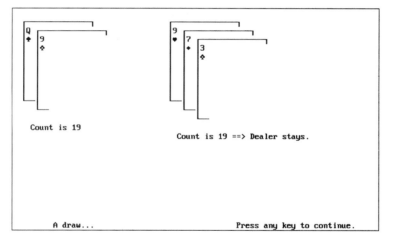

Figure 5-4. *A round ending in a draw.*

Figures 5-5, 5-6, and 5-7 on the following pages show various ways in which you can win a round. In Figure 5-5 your initial deal is a natural 21, and you therefore win twice your bet. In Figure 5-6 you have taken additional cards, and your count is again equal to 21. According to the rules, the dealer has been forced to stay on a count that is less than yours, so you win your bet. (Notice that your winnings are not doubled for just any count of 21—only for a natural.) Figure 5-7 shows a round in which the dealer has busted; again, you win your bet, no matter what your count is.

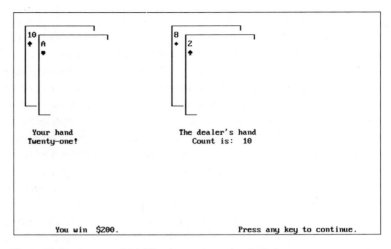

Figure 5-5. *A natural 21 (the player wins twice the bet).*

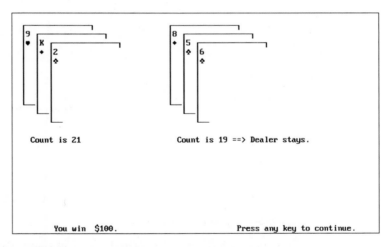

Figure 5-6. *A 21 with additional cards (the player wins the bet).*

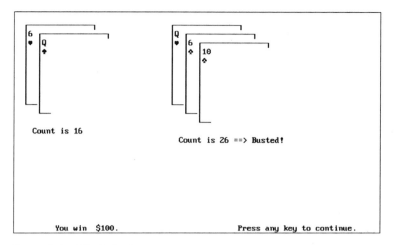

Figure 5-7. *The dealer busts.*

Figures 5-8 and 5-9 show two rounds in which you have lost your bet. In Figure 5-8, the dealer has simply accumulated a higher count than you. In Figure 5-9 on the next page, you have busted on the third card. Notice the message displayed below your hand:

```
Count is 23 ==> Busted!
```

(To rub it in a little, the computer also beeps at you when you bust.)

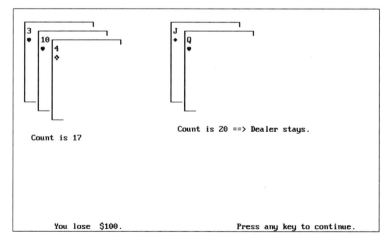

Figure 5-8. *The dealer wins with a higher count than the player.*

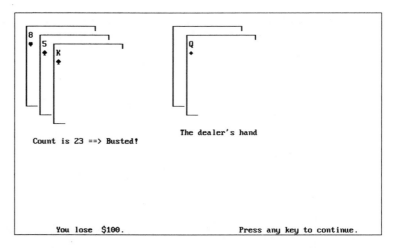

Figure 5-9. *The player busts on the third card.*

The dealer does not take a turn when you bust, but automatically collects your bet. This is the dealer's most important advantage in the design of the game: If he were to play after your bust, he might well bust also, perhaps with a count identical to yours. But by ending the round on your bust, he avoids this risk of ending in a draw.

Figure 5-10, the last of our sample screens, shows the message that appears when the program is reshuffling the cards. The cards currently on the table are not included in the shuffle.

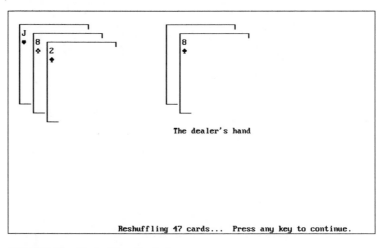

Figure 5-10. *Reshuffling the deck.*

In this example, five cards are on the table, so the reshuffling message appears as:

```
Reshuffling 47 cards...
```

The program intentionally interrupts the game briefly when the reshuffling occurs, so you know that you will subsequently be working with a newly shuffled deck. If you are keeping track of cards that have been dealt, this fact will enter into your playing strategy. (Reshuffling takes less than a second. After you have noted the message, you simply press any key to continue the current round.)

Decisions in the *Twenty-one* program

During play, the first important decisions occur as soon as the two initial hands have been dealt. The program determines the counts of both hands, then proceeds as follows:

- If one of the hands is a natural, the round is over, and the program displays the player's win or loss.

- If both hands are naturals, the round is also over, ending in a draw, and the program displays the *A draw...* message.

- If neither hand is a natural, the program displays the *Hit or Stay?* prompt below the player's cards.

Assuming neither hand is a natural, the next decisions involve the player's decisions to hit or stay. The program proceeds as follows:

- If the player presses *H,* requesting a hit, the program draws a card from the top of the deck, redisplays the player's hand along with the new card, and then determines the player's new count.
    - If the new count is over 21, the player has busted, the round is over, and the program displays the player's loss at the bottom of the screen.
    - If the player's count is less than 21, the program displays the *Hit or Stay?* prompt again and waits for the player's next instruction.
    - If the player's count is exactly 21, the program displays the message *Twenty-one!* and begins the dealer's play.

- If the player presses *S* to request a stay, the program displays the player's final count on the screen and then begins the dealer's play.

Unless the player has busted, the dealer's turn comes next. The program "turns over" the dealer's hidden card, displaying both cards along with the current count of the dealer's hand. The ensuing decision process goes as follows:

- If the dealer's count is less than 16, the program displays the messages *Dealer hits* and *Press any key to continue* at the bottom of the screen. (To carry out each turn in the dealer's play, the program requires you, the player, to press a key. This allows you to examine each new card that the dealer draws. It also prevents the action of the game from moving too quickly.) When the player presses a key, the program deals another card into the dealer's hand and displays the new hand and new count.
  - If the new count is still less than 17, the program displays *Dealer hits* again.
  - If the new count is 17 or over, the program displays the message *Dealer stays.* (If the hand is soft—that is, if it contains an ace—the program counts the ace as 11 as long as the total count is between 17 and 21. However, if a soft hand would become a bust if the ace were counted as 11, the program counts the card as 1 instead; the dealer thus hits again if the total count is still less than 17.)

When the player's and dealer's hands have both been played, the program determines the winner and displays the result of the round:

- If the player's count and the dealer's count are equal, the program displays the message *A draw...* at the bottom of the screen. (The player's current assets do not change.)

- If the player has busted, or if the dealer's hand is greater than the player's hand (so long as the dealer has not busted), the program displays a message like *You lose $100* and deducts the amount from the player's current assets.

- If the player's hand has only two cards and a count of 21 (hence a natural), the program displays a message like *You win $200* and adds twice the amount of the bet to the player's current assets. (However, if the dealer's hand is also a natural, the program ends the game as a draw.)

- If the dealer has busted, or if the player's count is larger than the dealer's count, the program displays a message like *You win $100* and adds the amount to the player's current assets.

These are the major decisions that determine the course of the program. In addition, many less obvious but often quite essential decisions take place as the program executes its carefully designed input and output processes: preparing the two display screens and accepting keyboard instructions from the player.

The program must also keep track of the status of the deck. A "pointer" variable identifies the location of the current "top" of the deck. When the entire 52-card deck has been dealt, the program must reshuffle all the cards that are not currently displayed on the table. These duties require some rather careful planning, which we will see as we study the listing of the program.

INSIDE THE *TWENTY-ONE* PROGRAM

Now that we know what the *Twenty-one* program does, let's begin exploring in detail the decisions and loops that it executes throughout the game. The complete listing of the program appears in Figure 5-11 at the end of the chapter, beginning on page 206. The various declarations and definitions required by the program appear at the top of the program listing, followed by the main program section, and the functions and subprograms in alphabetic order. Throughout the program discussion you'll see references to functions and subprograms—these are labeled along the left and right margins of the listing with tabs bearing the function or subprogram name. We'll begin by examining the declarations and definitions section and the main program section to get a broad look at the action of the program. Then we'll examine the procedures one by one.

Declarations and definitions in the *Twenty-one* program

To represent the playing cards, the *Twenty-one* program creates special record structures that belong to a user-defined type named *cardPicture*. This compound type has two one-character string elements:

```
TYPE cardPicture
    rank AS STRING * 1
    suit AS STRING * 1
END TYPE
```

The *rank* and *suit* elements store the rank and suit characters that appear on the screen for a card.

Given this user-defined type, the program defines three global arrays of records as its central data structures. First, the array *fullDeck()* stores records representing all 52 cards:

```
DIM SHARED fullDeck(52) AS cardPicture
```

In addition, the program creates the arrays *playerHand()* and *dealerHand()* to store the cards in the player's hand and the dealer's hand at any round of the program:

```
DIM SHARED playerHand(11) AS cardPicture, dealerHand(11) AS cardPicture
```

These arrays have dimensions of 11—the largest possible hand that could yield a count of 21—but the odds against accumulating so large a hand are enormous. A hand will very rarely contain more than *5* or *6* cards at a time.

Because none of these arrays require the "zeroth" element, the OPTION BASE statement starts them all out at an element of *1:*

```
OPTION BASE 1
```

Along with these three global arrays, the program establishes a small group of global variables. Using the COMMON SHARED statement to declare a carefully selected group of variables as global can turn out to be a great advantage in a large program. Accordingly, the *Twenty-one* program uses the following variables to store global information about the deck, the two hands, and the status of the game:

nextCard%	A pointer variable that always contains the position of the current "top" card in the *fullDeck()* array.
curWorth%	An integer representing the player's current dollar assets.
betAmount%	The amount of the bet for the current round.
playerCards% *dealerCards%*	The number of cards currently held in the player's hand and the dealer's hand, respectively.
firstRound%	A logical variable that indicates whether the current round is the first round in the game.

Most of these variables are used throughout the program. By declaring them global we avoid having to pass them back and forth as arguments to the various procedures.

Finally, the program creates a set of symbolic constants that also play important roles in execution. You'll find the following three CONST statements at the very top of the listing:

```
CONST false% = 0, true% = NOT false%
CONST lowBet% = 10, highBet% = 100
CONST ranks$ = "23456789TJQKA"
```

The constants *true%* and *false%* represent the two logical values, the integers *lowBet%* and *highBet%* are the minimum and maximum bet amounts that the program allows, and *ranks$* is a string that contains characters representing each of the 13 card ranks. We'll encounter each of these symbolic constants as we discuss the various routines of the program.

The main program section

The main program section of the *Twenty-one* program begins by assigning initial values to some important variables. First, the player's initial betting allowance is set at $250:

```
curWorth% = 250
```

The program then calls the subprogram named *InitDeck* to initialize the *fullDeck()* array and calls another procedure named *Shuffle* to rearrange the entire deck in a random order. These two routines contain some excellent illustrations of FOR...NEXT loops. Let's look at them briefly before we continue with the main program section.

Initializing and shuffling the deck: *InitDeck* and *Shuffle*

The *InitDeck* procedure uses a pair of nested FOR...NEXT loops to assign values to all the *suit* and *rank* elements of the *fullDeck()* array. The outer loop moves through the four suits, and the inner loop deals with the 13 ranks of each suit:

```
FOR suit% = 3 TO 6
    FOR rank% = 1 TO 13
```

Inside the inner loop, a counter variable named *card%* keeps track of the current card number:

```
card% = card% + 1
```

The routine takes the suit characters directly from the ASCII code. Conveniently, the version of the ASCII code for the IBM PC contains four card-suit characters:

- CHR$(3) is the heart.
- CHR$(4) is the diamond.
- CHR$(5) is the club.
- CHR$(6) is the spade.

The outer FOR...NEXT loop in the *InitDeck* procedure increments its counter variable *suit%* through a range of values from *3* to *6*. As a result, the following statement can use the CHR$ function to assign one of these four ASCII characters to the current *suit* element of the *fullDeck()* array:

```
fullDeck(card%).suit = CHR$(suit%)
```

The program then extracts the rank characters from the string stored in the symbolic constant *ranks$*. The MID$ function takes one character from the *rank%* position of the *ranks$* string:

```
fullDeck(card%).rank = MID$(ranks$, rank%, 1)
```

Again, *rank%* is the counter variable for the inner FOR...NEXT loop; during the iterations, the variable takes on values from *1* to *13*.

When *InitDeck* has completed its task, the main program section sets the deck pointer, *nextCard%*, at the top of the deck:

```
nextcard% = 1
```

Then the program shuffles the entire deck for the first time:

```
Shuffle fullDeck()
```

The *Shuffle* routine rearranges the elements of the array into a random order. The routine receives an array of records in the *arr()* parameter:

```
SUB Shuffle (arr() AS cardPicture) STATIC
```

Notice that the SUB statement must explicitly declare the user-defined type of this array parameter. This declaration is always a requirement for any record variable or record array that appears in the parameter list of a SUB or FUNCTION statement. (By the way, the *Twenty-one* program later calls *Shuffle* to rearrange another array. This is why the routine is designed to receive the array as an argument rather than to simply access the global *fullDeck()* array.)

The *Shuffle* routine begins by resetting the "seed" of Quick-BASIC's random-number generator. The routine supplies the value of TIMER as the argument of the RANDOMIZE statement:

```
RANDOMIZE TIMER
```

TIMER yields an integer representing the number of seconds that have elapsed since midnight. This value ensures a random starting point for the random-number generator.

Shuffle next uses the built-in UBOUND function to determine the length of the array it has received:

```
length% = UBOUND(arr)
```

Finally, the shuffling takes place inside a simple FOR...NEXT loop. From the top to the bottom of the array, each element is exchanged with a randomly selected element elsewhere in the array:

```
FOR i% = 1 TO length%
    temp% = INT(RND * length%) + 1
    SWAP arr(i%), arr(temp%)
NEXT i%
```

Notice how the random selection occurs. The RND function supplies a random number between *0* and *1*, and the following expression converts this number to an integer from *1* to *length%*:

```
INT(RND * length%) + 1
```

The subsequent SWAP statement exchanges the values of the array elements numbered *i%* and *temp%*. Keep in mind that each execution of the SWAP statement exchanges the positions of two entire card records in the array.

When the deck has been created and shuffled, the game can begin. Let's return to the main program section to see how the action is controlled.

Conducting rounds of the game

A single DO loop, with a sequence of nested IF statements, conducts the broad action of the game by repeatedly calling on the following five main subprograms:

- *GetBet* finds out if the player wants to play another round, and if so, elicits the player's bet.

- *StartGame* deals two cards to each hand and checks for naturals.

- *PlayerPlay* controls the player's turn at hitting or staying and monitors the count of the player's hand.

- *DealerPlay* conducts the dealer's turn.

- *Winner* determines who has won and adjusts the player's money accordingly.

Three of these subprograms, *GetBet, StartGame,* and *PlayerPlay,* pass logical values back to the main program to indicate various conditions of the game. The program uses these values to decide exactly how each round should proceed. These are the first big decisions of the program, so let's examine them carefully.

First, before any round begins, *GetBet* must find out if the player wants to continue the game. *GetBet* elicits a yes-or-no answer from the player, and, in effect, passes the answer back to the main program as the logical value *gameOver%*:

```
GetBet gameOver%
```

If *gameOver%* is true, the player has chosen to end the game. No further action takes place, and the controlling DO...UNTIL structure ultimately terminates its looping:

```
LOOP UNTIL gameOver%
```

On the other hand, if the player has asked for another round, the program immediately calls on *StartGame* to deal the initial hands:

```
IF NOT gameOver% THEN
    StartGame roundOver%
```

StartGame duly counts the value of each hand, checking for naturals. If either hand has a natural 21, the round ends without any further action. In this case, *StartGame* passes a value of true back to the main program in the variable *roundOver%*. The value true means that neither *PlayerPlay* nor *DealerPlay* needs to be executed this round, because no more cards are dealt when a round begins with a natural.

But if *roundOver%* is false, the program must begin offering additional cards to the player. This is *PlayerPlay*'s job:

```
IF NOT roundOver% THEN
    PlayerPlay busted%
```

PlayerPlay repeatedly gives the player the choice between hitting or staying until one of three events occurs: The player decides to stay with the current cards; the player's hand reaches a count of exactly 21; or the player busts. In the last case, *PlayerPlay* passes a value of true to the variable *busted%*, and the program skips the dealer's play.

On the other hand, if *busted%* is false, meaning that the player has stayed with a count of 21 or less, the dealer must play:

```
IF NOT busted% THEN
    DealerPlay
```

These three decisions are carefully organized to ensure that just the right sequence of subprograms will be called to meet the requirements of a round. The key to this solution is progressive nesting of the IF statements. Let's review the entire sequence:

```
DO
    GetBet gameOver%
    firstRound% = false%

    IF NOT gameOver% THEN
        StartGame roundOver%
        IF NOT roundOver% THEN
            PlayerPlay busted%
            IF NOT busted% THEN
                DealerPlay
            END IF
        END IF
        Winner
    END IF
LOOP UNTIL gameOver%
```

ELSE and ELSEIF clauses would not have worked successfully for this decision sequence, nor would a SELECT CASE statement. In contrast with decision structures we'll look at later, the program here is not attempting to choose one of several alternative courses of action, but rather is deciding at each turn whether or not to take the next step. Each decision is based on the result of the previous step.

In all well-structured programs the main program section stands as a kind of outline of the entire action. Master the logic of the main program, and you will have no trouble understanding how the program flows. Of course, there are many more details to explore; in the sections that follow we'll examine the highlights of the subprograms, starting with *GetBet*.

Place your bet: The *GetBet* subprogram

The *GetBet* subprogram contains a sequence of IF...THEN...ELSE decision blocks. The routine's main tasks are to announce the player's current cash balance, to find out if the player wants to play another round of the game, to elicit the player's bet amount, and to validate the bet, making sure that it is within the established betting limits.

The first decision structure, located near the top of the procedure, looks to see if the value stored in the global variable *curWorth%* is positive or negative. For a positive value, the routine reports the amount of cash that the player currently has; or for a negative value, the routine displays the amount that the player owes:

```
IF curWorth% >= 0 THEN
    PRINT USING "You currently have: $$#,###"; curWorth%
ELSE
    PRINT USING "You owe the house: $$#,###"; ABS(curWorth%)
    PRINT "        (The house extends credit.)"
END IF
```

Notice the use of the ABS function to produce the absolute value of *curWorth%* in the ELSE block.

The job of the next decision statement is to assign a logical value to the variable *continue%*—true if the game is to continue for another round; false if the game should stop. Here is the form that the decision takes:

```
IF NOT firstRound% THEN
    PRINT: PRINT "        ";
    continue% = YesNo%("Continue the game? ")
ELSE
    continue% = true%
END IF
```

If the global variable *firstRound%* is true, the program continues for at least one round. Otherwise, the decision to continue or not is based on the user's input. To elicit this yes-or-no input, *GetBet* calls the *YesNo%* function. *YesNo%* places the prompt on the screen and waits for the user to press *Y* or *N*. The function returns a logical value: true for an affirmative response or false for a negative response. *GetBet* stores this response in the variable *continue%*.

Finally, if *continue%* is true, *GetBet* displays the house betting limits and elicits the player's bet. The routine ultimately stores the player's input in the global variable *betAmount%*. The process of accepting and validating this value is executed inside a rather detailed DO…UNTIL loop:

```
DO
    PRINT"                  ";
    INPUT "==> ", betStr$;
    IF betStr$ = "" THEN
        betAmount% = highBet%
        ok% = true%
    ELSE
        betAmount% = VAL(betStr$)
        ok% = betAmount% >= lowBet% AND betAmount% <= highBet%
    END IF
LOOP UNTIL ok%
```

We have seen that the program allows the player to press Enter to bet the maximum amount. To make this possible, the *GetBet* subprogram initially accepts the bet input as a string value, *betStr$,* rather than as a number. If the player presses Enter in response to the prompt displayed by this INPUT statement, QuickBASIC assigns an empty string to *betStr$;* in this case, *GetBet* assigns the maximum allowable bet to *betAmount%:*

```
IF betStr$ = "" THEN
    betAmount% = highBet%
```

(Recall that *highBet%* and *lowBet%* are symbolic constants, established globally at the beginning of the program.)

Otherwise, if the player enters an actual amount from the keyboard, the routine uses the VAL function to convert *betStr$* into its numeric equivalent:

```
ELSE
    betAmount% = VAL(betStr$)
```

If *betStr$* is a string value that cannot be converted into a number, VAL returns a value of *0.* To make sure that *betAmount%* is within the established range for the house betting limits, the routine evaluates the following compound conditional expression:

```
ok% = betAmount% >= lowBet% AND betAmount% <= highBet%
```

The controlling DO…UNTIL structure continues looping until this variable, *ok%,* contains a value of true.

When *GetBet* has accepted a valid bet, the *StartGame* subprogram takes over and sets up the playing table with two initial hands. We'll look at that routine next.

Dealing the cards: The *StartGame* subprogram

StartGame introduces us to the program's card-dealing procedure, variations of which occur in two other major subprograms: *PlayerPlay* and *DealerPlay*. The procedure goes through several steps each time a card is dealt either to the player or to the dealer. Here is an outline of the steps:

1. Assign the current top card in the deck to the next available element of the appropriate hand array (*playerHand()* or *dealerHand()*).

2. Display the newly dealt card on the screen. (This step is executed by the *DisplayCard* subprogram.)

3. Increase the number of cards in the hand by *1*. (This value is stored in *playerCards%* or *dealerCards%*, which are both global variables.)

4. Move the deck pointer, *nextCard%*, forward by one card. (This step is executed by the *MovePointer* subprogram, which also reshuffles the deck whenever it is necessary to do so.)

5. Compute the new count of the hand that has just received a card. (This step is executed by the *CountHand* subprogram.)

As you can see, the process is complex enough to require the assistance of three different subprograms, *DisplayCard, MovePointer,* and *CountHand.* We'll look at each one of these routines a little later; but first let's see exactly how *StartGame* uses them.

A FOR...NEXT loop deals out the first two cards to each hand. Each iteration of the loop deals one card to the player and one card to the dealer:

```
FOR i% = 1 TO 2
```

The player's hand gets the first card. Because *nextCard%* points to the current top of the deck, the expression *fullDeck(nextCard%)* always supplies the next card to be dealt:

```
playerHand(i%) = fullDeck(nextCard%)
```

Keep in mind that *fullDeck(), playerHand(),* and *dealerHand()* are all arrays of records belonging to the user-defined type *cardPicture*. The card dealt to *playerHand()* in this assignment statement is thus a complete card record, containing both *rank* and *suit* elements. Thanks to the *Shuffle* subprogram, we know that all 52 card records are arranged in a random order inside *fullDeck()*.

Displaying the hands

The *DisplayCard* subprogram has the rather complex task of displaying a single card on the screen. A call to this subprogram requires four arguments, as represented in the procedure's SUB statement:

```
SUB DisplayCard (vPos%, hPos%, card AS cardPicture, show%) STATIC
```

The first two values, *vPos%* and *hPos%*, indicate the location on the screen where *DisplayCard* will place the upper-left corner of the card. The third parameter, *card*, is a record variable representing the card to be displayed. The final parameter, *show*, is a logical value that indicates whether the card is to be displayed face up (true) or face down (false). If *DisplayCard* receives a value of false for *show%*, the routine draws only the outline of the card without displaying the card's rank and suit.

Here is how *StartGame* calls *DisplayCard* to display the cards dealt to the player's hand and the dealer's hand:

```
DisplayCard i% + 1, i% * 3, playerHand(i%), true%
    [other program lines]
DisplayCard i% + 1, 32 + i% * 3, dealerHand(i%), 1 - i%
```

Notice that the *vPos%* and *hPos%* arguments are computed from the loop index, *i%*. Single records from the two hand arrays—*playerHand()* and *dealerHand()*—are sent as the *card* arguments. For the player's hand the *show%* argument is always *true%*, because both of the player's cards are displayed face up. For the dealer's hand, however, the expression *1 − i%* produces a value of false for the first card and true for the second card, resulting in one card face down and one face up.

After a card is displayed, the variable that keeps a count of the number of cards in a hand (*playerCards%* or *dealerCards%*) must be increased by *1;* for example:

```
playerCards% = playerCards% + 1
```

Likewise, the deck pointer, *nextCard%*, must be incremented by *1* so that the next card dealt will come from the top of the deck. The *Move-Pointer* subprogram, which takes no arguments, performs this task:

```
MovePointer
```

Counting the values of the hands

Each newly dealt card results in a new count for the hand that receives it, so the final step in dealing a card is to recount the value of the hand. The *StartGame* subprogram only needs to count the hands once each, after each hand has received two cards. The *CountHand* subprogram, which counts the hands, takes three arguments, as shown in the procedure's SUB statement:

```
SUB CountHand (hand() AS cardPicture, num%, tot%) STATIC
```

The first parameter is an array of records containing the hand to be counted, and the second is the number of cards in the hand. The third parameter, *tot%*, is the variable in which *CountHand* passes the computed count back to the calling subprogram.

Consider the two calls that *StartGame* makes to *CountHand*:

```
CountHand playerHand(), 2, playerVal%
CountHand dealerHand(), 2, dealerVal%
```

After these calls are executed, the variables *playerVal%* and *dealerVal%* will contain the correct counts for the player's hand and the dealer's hand, respectively.

Looking for naturals in the hands

With the initial two hands duly dealt and counted, *StartGame* can analyze the situation and decide whether or not the round should continue. The important question at this point is: Does one or both of the hands have a natural count of 21? This question is answered and acted upon by an IF...THEN...ELSE structure:

```
IF dealerVal% = 21 OR playerVal% = 21 THEN
```

One task of this decision structure is to assign an appropriate value to the logical variable *win%*: true if a natural has occurred, false if not. This value is then passed back to the main program to indicate the status of the round.

If either hand contains a natural, another call to *DisplayCard* shows the dealer's hidden card:

```
DisplayCard 2, 35, dealerHand(1), true%
```

And then a pair of nested IF...THEN...ELSE structures decides which message to display beneath each hand—*Twenty one!* for the natural hand or the count for the losing hand. For example, the following lines determine the decision for the dealer's hand.

```
IF dealerVal% = 21 THEN
    PRINT "Twenty-one!"
ELSE
    PRINT "Count is: "; dealerVal%
END IF
```

After these decisions are made, *StartGame* relinquishes control to the main program section, potentially for calls to the *PlayerPlay* and *DealerPlay* subprograms. But before we move on to study those routines, we should look in greater detail at the three important subprograms that are responsible for displaying a card (*DisplayCard*), incrementing the deck pointer (*MovePointer*), and counting a hand (*CountHand*).

Displaying a card on the screen: The *DisplayCard* subprogram

You'll recall that *DisplayCard* receives four parameter values: *vPos%* and *hPos%* represent the screen coordinates where the card will be displayed; *card* is a record variable that represents the suit and rank of a particular card; and *show%* is a logical value that indicates whether or not the card's suit and rank should be displayed.

The first task of the subprogram is to draw the outline of the card at the correct position. To do this, the subprogram uses the CHR$ function to gain access to five graphics characters available in the IBM Extended Character Set:

- CHR$(218) — upper-left corner character

- CHR$(191) — upper-right corner character

- CHR$(192) — lower-left corner character

- CHR$(196) — horizontal line character

- CHR$(179) — vertical line character

The technique for drawing the card outlines is the same as in the *Frame* procedure, which is discussed in Chapter 2. The LOCATE statement places the cursor at the correct position for a character, and PRINT displays the character supplied by the CHR$ function.

For a horizontal line, we can also take advantage of the STRING$ function to produce a line of identical characters; for example, the expression STRING$(14, 196) produces a string that will become the horizontal outline of the card.

A vertical line, however, has to be built character by character within a FOR...NEXT loop:

```
FOR i% = vPos% + 1 TO vPos% + 8
    LOCATE i%, hPos%: PRINT CHR$(179)
NEXT i%
```

Notice that every element of the display is calculated from the starting-point coordinates of *vPos%* and *hPos%*.

When the outline is on the screen, *DisplayCard* sets about displaying the card's suit and rank, but only if the *show%* parameter received a value of true:

```
IF show% THEN
```

The *suit* element of the *card* record contains one of the four ASCII characters that depict card suits. The procedure displays this character inside the card:

```
LOCATE vPos% + 2, hPos% + 1: PRINT card.suit
```

The program would have been able to use a similar pair of statements to display the rank symbol, except for two problems. In order to assign each rank a single-character symbol, the *ranks$* constant uses the symbol *T* to represent the 10 card. But the *DisplayCard* subprogram needs to display 10 rather than *T*. Furthermore, because new cards are often displayed over the previous positions of other cards, *DisplayCard* needs a way to completely erase the two-character 10 symbol from the screen before placing a one-character rank symbol in its place. The following IF...THEN...ELSE sequence takes care of these two troublesome details:

```
IF card.rank = "T" THEN
    PRINT "10"
ELSE
    PRINT card.rank + " "
END IF
```

A space character is displayed just to the right of any single-character rank symbol in case the previously displayed rank was the two-character string, 10.

As always, planning a complex screen display seems to require more attention to detail than almost any other programming task. But the careful effort produces satisfying results.

Next let's look at the *MovePointer* routine.

Keeping track of the deck: The *MovePointer* subprogram

The *MovePointer* subprogram always begins by performing the essential task of incrementing the deck pointer:

```
nextCard% = nextCard% + 1
```

Only the pointer's value is changed. The *nextCard%* variable simply keeps track of the next card that should be dealt from the array. In other words, no changes are actually made in the *fullDeck()* array between one shuffle and the next. Using this pointer variable is much more efficient than rearranging the deck after each card is dealt.

As long as *nextCard%* contains a value of 52 or less—actually pointing to a card in the deck—the *MovePointer* subprogram does not need to take further action. However, each time *nextCard%* goes past 52, the deck has to be reshuffled. This is the important decision that *MovePointer* makes:

```
IF nextCard% > 52 THEN
    [reshuffle all the cards that are
        not currently on the table]
END IF
```

Unlike the initial shuffle of the entire deck, which takes place once at the beginning of the program, the reshuffling requires careful manipulation of the deck. Cards that are currently displayed on the table must be left out of the shuffle. Furthermore, a record of the same cards must be kept at an appropriate position in the deck so that they will be included in the next shuffle.

If a reshuffling is required, the first step is to count the number of cards on the table for the current round (*tableCards%*—the player's cards plus the dealer's cards) and the number that have been used for previous rounds since the last shuffle (*usedCards%*):

```
tableCards% = playerCards% + dealerCards%
usedCards% = 52 - tableCards%
```

MovePointer displays a message at the bottom of the screen, announcing the reshuffle and showing the number of cards being shuffled:

```
LOCATE 25,25: PRINT "Reshuffling" usedCards%; "cards...";
```

The next step is to create a temporary deck array (*tempDeck()*) to store the card records to be shuffled. Because this dynamic array of

195

records can have a different size each time the deck is shuffled, a REDIM statement is required for specifying the array's dimension:

```
REDIM tempDeck(usedCards%) AS cardPicture
```

Cards that are displayed on the table are located at the bottom of the *fullDeck()* array. For example, if four cards are on the table, they are stored in the array elements *fullDeck(49)* to *fullDeck(52)*. It then follows that the used cards, which need to be reshuffled, are from *fullDeck(1)* to *deck(48)*; the routine assigns these cards to *tempDeck()*:

```
FOR i% = 1 TO usedCards%
    tempDeck(i%) = fullDeck(i%)
NEXT i%
```

Then *MovePointer* calls the *Shuffle* subprogram to reshuffle the cards in *tempDeck()*:

```
Shuffle tempDeck()
```

When *tempDeck()* has been shuffled, *MovePointer* has to reassemble the *fullDeck()* array. First, the cards on the table are placed at the top of the array, where they will be shuffled next time around:

```
FOR i% = 1 TO tableCards%
    fullDeck(i%) = fullDeck(usedCards% + i%)
NEXT i%
```

Then the newly shuffled cards are copied from *tempDeck()* to *fullDeck()*:

```
FOR i% = 1 TO usedCards%
    fullDeck(tableCards% + i%) = tempDeck(i%)
NEXT i%
```

The new effective position for the "top of the deck" will start at the first of the newly shuffled cards:

```
nextCard% = tableCards% + 1
```

With this, the reshuffling process is complete. *MovePointer* calls on a simple routine named *Pause* to create a pause in the action:

```
Pause
```

The *Pause* subprogram is responsible for placing the *Press any key to continue* message on the screen. After displaying the message, the routine simply waits for a key press before sending control back to the calling subprogram. We will encounter calls to this routine several more times before the end of the program.

Next we'll look at the *CountHand* subprogram, which determines the current value of a hand.

Computing the value of a hand: The *CountHand* subprogram

As we have seen, *CountHand* has a list of three parameters:

```
SUB CountHand(hand() AS cardPicture, num%, tot%) STATIC
```

The *hand()* array receives the hand to be counted; *num%* is the number of cards in *hand()*; and *tot%* is the variable that *CountHand* uses to pass the computed total count back to the calling program.

CountHand has two tasks: first, to count the cards according to the prescribed value of each rank; and second, to adjust the count if the hand contains aces that should be valued at *1* instead of *11*.

The routine begins by initializing two counting variables—*tot%* (the total count) and *aces%* (the number of aces in the hand)—to *0:*

```
tot% = 0
aces% = 0
```

Then, in a FOR...NEXT loop that moves card by card through the entire hand, the routine accumulates the total count into the variable *tot%*. Inside this loop is a good example of the SELECT CASE statement:

```
FOR i% = 1 TO num%
    SELECT CASE hand(i%).rank

    CASE "T", "J", "Q", "K"
        cardValue% = 10

    CASE "A"
        cardValue% = 11
        aces% = aces% + 1

    CASE ELSE
        cardValue% = VAL(hand(i%).rank)

    END SELECT
    tot% = tot% + cardValue%
NEXT i%
```

The target comparison value in the SELECT CASE statement is the *rank* element of a card record: *hand(i%).rank*. There are three different cases expressed in the decision structure.

1. If the rank is *T, J, Q,* or *K,* the card's value is *10.*

2. If the rank is *A*—representing an ace—the card's value is set at *11* (at least initially) and the number of aces in the hand is increased by *1.*

3. Otherwise, the rank must be a digit from *2* to *9,* and the card's value is simply *VAL(hand(i%).rank).*

When the value is thus determined for a card, the routine adds *cardValue%* to the value of *tot%* before moving on to the next card:

```
tot% = tot% + cardValue%
```

When all the cards have been counted, *CountHand* may need to devalue aces in the hand. Here is the rule: If the hand contains one or more aces and the current count of the hand is greater than *21,* aces should be devalued one at a time, from *11* down to *1,* until the total count is *21* or less, or until the hand runs out of aces. This rather complex algorithm translates into the simple DO…WHILE loop that we examined earlier in this chapter:

```
DO WHILE tot% > 21 AND aces% > 0
    tot% = tot% - 10
    aces% = aces% - 1
LOOP
```

The *CountHand, MovePointer,* and *DisplayCard* subprograms are the game's real workhorse routines. All three are called upon virtually every time a card is dealt. Now that we have seen what they do and how they are organized, we can continue following through the main activities of the program. *PlayerPlay* is the next subprogram to be executed, then *DealerPlay,* and finally *Winner.* We'll look at each of these routines in turn.

Conducting the player's turn: The *PlayerPlay* subprogram

During the player's turn the *PlayerPlay* subprogram must constantly monitor three conditions; if any of these conditions becomes true, the player's turn is over:

- The count of the player's hand goes over 21.

- The player's hand reaches a count of exactly 21.

- The player indicates that he or she wants to stay with the count of the current hand.

To keep track of the status of these conditions, the subprogram creates two logical variables, *over21%* and *done%,* which are both assigned initial values of false:

```
over21% = false%
done% = false%
```

The main action of the player's turn takes place within a controlling DO…WHILE loop, which repeatedly offers the player the chance to hit or stay. The looping stops when either of the logical variables contains a value of true:

```
DO WHILE NOT (over21% OR done%)
```

Notice the importance of the parentheses in this condition. Another way to write the same condition is:

```
DO WHILE (NOT over21%) AND (NOT done%)
```

The first statement inside the loop makes a call to a user-defined function named *HitorStay%* and assigns the resulting logical value to the variable *done%:*

```
done% = HitorStay%
```

The *HitorStay%* function accepts the player's input in response to the hand currently displayed on the screen. Let's look briefly at this function before we continue with the *PlayerPlay* routine.

Getting the player's directions: The *HitorStay%* function

The *HitorStay%* function has much in common with the *YesNo%* function. Both functions display a prompt on the screen, accept one of two possible single-keystroke responses, and then return a value of true or false to indicate which response was received.

HitorStay% elicits the player's choice between hitting (taking another card) or staying (stopping with the cards currently in hand). The function places the hit-or-stay prompt below the player's hand:

```
PRINT "Your hand: Hit or Stay? ";
```

The INKEY$ function is then used (from inside a DO…WHILE loop) to get the player's keystroke, and the built-in function UCASE$ (discussed in Chapter 4) converts the letter response to uppercase:

```
answer$ = UCASE$(INKEY$)
```

The looping ends when *answer$* contains either an *H* or an *S*:

```
DO WHILE answer$ = "" OR INSTR("HS", answer$) = 0
```

The *HitorStay%* function returns a value of true to indicate a stay or a value of false to indicate a hit:

```
HitorStay% = (answer$ = "S")
```

This statement may seem unusual in format; in performing it, QuickBASIC first evaluates the logical expression *(answer$ = "S")* to true or false and returns that value as the result of *HitorStay%*.

Responding to the player's input

The next action of the *PlayerPlay* subprogram depends directly on the value that *HitorStay%* returns:

```
IF NOT done% THEN
        [deal the player another card, display the hand
          with the new card, and analyze the new count]
ELSE
        [count the current hand]
END IF
```

If *done%* is false, the player gets another card. The routine increments the value of *playerCards%* by *1* and deals the top card in the deck to the player's hand:

```
playerCards% = playerCards% + 1
playerHand%(playerCards%) = fullDeck(nextCard%)
```

PlayerPlay next takes the extra step of sorting the hand before displaying the cards. As a result, the hand that subsequently appears on the screen will be arranged by suits (hearts, diamonds, clubs, spades), and within each suit the cards will appear in order of rank (*2* up to ace). The *Twenty-one* program contains its own sorting routine, *Bsort*, written specifically for the task of rearranging the hands.

Sorting a hand: The *Bsort* subprogram

The *Bsort* subprogram implements a simple algorithm called a bubble sort. This is one of the three sorting routines discussed in this book; the other two are the recursive quick sort (discussed in Chapter 4) and the Shell sort (discussed in Chapter 7). The bubble sort is by far the easiest of the three to write and to understand; on the other hand, it is also a much slower technique for sorting long lists of items.

However, we know that an array representing a hand of cards in *Twenty-one* will seldom have more than five or six elements in it. For this size array, the bubble sort works just as well as the more sophisticated sorting algorithms.

The idea of the bubble sort is to compare each array element with every element below it; any time two elements are found to be out of order, they are swapped. The comparisons occur within a pair of nested FOR...NEXT loops. Inside the loops, an IF...THEN statement performs a swap whenever necessary:

```
FOR i% = 1 to num% -1
    FOR j% = i% + 1 TO num%
    IF CardConvert%(arr(i%)) > CardConvert%(arr(j%)) THEN
        SWAP arr%(i%), arr%(j%)
    END IF
    NEXT j%
NEXT i%
```

Notice the format of the nested loops. The FOR and NEXT statements of the inner loop are both located inside the block defined by the outer loop. Likewise, the nested decision structure is completely enclosed inside the block of the inner loop.

The data structure in this sort procedure is *arr()*, an array of card records. To perform the sort successfully, the routine needs a simple way to compare one record with another. The solution to this problem is to convert each record to an integer from *1* to *52*. Individual calls to the *CardConvert%* function accomplish the conversion, using the built-in ASC and INSTR functions to supply integer equivalents for the *suit* and *rank* elements.

The effect of the bubble sort on a hand is to restore the cards to their original order (as they appeared in the *fullDeck()* array before the first shuffle). A call to *Bsort* takes two arguments: an array representing a hand and an integer representing the number of cards in the hand. Here is how *PlayerPlay* sorts the player's hand:

```
Bsort playerHand(), playerCards%
```

Displaying the hand and counting the cards

After the sort, *PlayerPlay* makes calls to three familiar subprograms to display the cards on the screen (*DisplayCard*), to increment the deck pointer (*MovePointer*), and to count the current value of the hand

(*CountHand*). Given the new count, *playerVal%,* the following IF…THEN structure checks for a bust or a value of exactly 21:

```
IF playerVal% > 21 THEN
    over21% = true%
    LOCATE playerCards% + 12, 5
    PRINT "Count is"; playerVal%; "==> Busted!"
    BEEP
ELSEIF playerVal% = 21 THEN
    done% = true%
END IF
```

Notice that this structure works with the two logical variables, *over21%* and *done%.* If the count is greater than 21, *over21%* is assigned a value of true. If the count is exactly 21, *done%* is assigned a value of true. Because there is no ELSE clause in this structure, a count less than 21 results in no action.

When one of these variables finally becomes true, the large DO…WHILE loop in *PlayerPlay* stops. The final step of the subprogram is to display the player's final count if *done%* is true (meaning either that the player has stayed or that the count of the hand is exactly 21):

```
IF done% THEN
    LOCATE playerCards% + 12, 5
    PRINT "Count is"; playerVal%
END IF
```

PlayerPlay passes the value of *over21%* back to the main program to indicate whether or not the player has busted. If a bust has not occurred (*over21%* is false), the program next calls the *DealerPlay* subprogram to give the dealer a turn. We'll look briefly at that routine in the next section.

Conducting the dealer's turn: The *DealerPlay* subprogram

The *DealerPlay* subprogram starts out by turning up the dealer's hidden card and computing the value of the two-card hand:

```
DisplayCard 2, 35, dealerHand(), true%
CountHand dealerHand(), dealerCards%, dealerVal%
```

Recall the rule that determines the subsequent action: The dealer stays with a count of 17 or higher and hits with a count below 17. Given the calculated count, *dealerVal%,* a DO…WHILE loop takes control of the action.

```
DO WHILE dealerVal% < 17
    [deal another card to the dealer's hand]
LOOP
```

The statements executed inside this DO...WHILE loop are similar to the card-dealing sequence in the *PlayerPlay* subprogram. The *Pause* subprogram waits for the player's keystroke before continuing the action. When a key is pressed, *DealerPlay* increases the number of cards in the dealer's hand (*dealerCards%*) by *1* and assigns the top card in the deck to the *dealerHand%()* array. The *Bsort* subprogram sorts the hand. *DisplayCard* shows each card on the screen. *MovePointer* increments *nextCard%*, the deck pointer. And finally, *CountHand* computes a new count of the hand, adding on the newly dealt card.

The DO...WHILE loop continues as long as the count is below *17*. Recall that the *CountHand* subprogram follows the rules for handling aces in the dealer's hand: If the count would otherwise go over *21*, aces in the hand are devalued to *1;* otherwise aces are worth *11.*

At the end of the subprogram, the following IF...THEN...ELSE structure chooses one of two messages to display on the screen:

```
IF dealerVal% > 21 THEN
    PRINT "Count is"; dealerVal%; "==> Busted!" + SPACE(8)
ELSE
    PRINT "Count is"; dealerVal%; "==> Dealer stays."
END IF
```

After both the player and the dealer have taken their turns, the action of the round is over, except for determining who has won. This final task belongs to the *Winner* subprogram, which we'll look at next.

Declaring the winner: The *Winner* subprogram

The *Winner* procedure actually has two things to do: first, find out how much money the player has won or lost; and second, display an appropriate message on the screen. These activities are carried out within a series of IF...THEN...ELSE decisions.

To start out, the subprogram makes two calls to *CountHand* to compute the final counts of the player's and dealer's hands. These two values are stored in *playerVal%* and *dealerVal%*. The first decision structure then looks to see if the game has ended in a draw:

```
IF playerVal% = dealerVal% THEN
    diff% = 0
```

The variable *diff%* stores the amount of money the player has won or lost during this round; in the case of a draw, there is no change in the player's cash balance.

On the other hand, if the player has busted, or if the dealer's count is greater than the player's count, then the player loses the bet. Recall that the bet is stored in the global variable *betAmount%*:

```
ELSEIF playerVal% > 21 OR (playerVal% < dealerVal%
AND dealerVal% < 22) THEN
    diff% = -1 * betAmount%
```

Notice the compound conditional expression in this ELSEIF clause. If the following expression is true, the player has busted:

```
playerVal% > 21
```

Or, if the following is true, the dealer's hand is better than the player's hand:

```
playerVal% < dealerVal% AND dealerVal% < 22
```

Notice that this expression also checks to make sure that the dealer has not busted.

The player wins twice the bet for a natural (exactly *2* cards, with a count of *21*), or just the bet for a hand that is superior to the dealer's. Another ELSEIF clause and the final ELSE clause check for these possibilities:

```
ELSEIF playerVal% = 21 AND playerCards% = 2 THEN
    diff% = 2 * betAmount%
ELSE
    diff% = betAmount%
END IF
```

Restructuring this particular IF...THEN...ELSE statement into a SELECT CASE statement is not an option here, because the various conditions work with several different values as operands.

A final decision structure in the *Winner* subprogram uses the value of *diff%* to select one of three possible concluding messages. This selection process is executed by the following SELECT CASE statement.

```
SELECT CASE diff%

CASE 0
    PRINT "A draw...";

CASE IS < 0
    PRINT USING "You lose $$###."; ABS(diff%);

CASE ELSE
    PRINT USING "You win $$###."; diff%;

END SELECT
```

Winner next calls on *Pause* to wait for a keystroke that will end the round. After this the screen is cleared with the CLS statement and control returns to the main program, possibly for another round of the game.

Conclusion

In the process of designing and writing almost any game program, two general issues preoccupy the programmer:

1. Creating carefully structured decisions that successfully monitor—and act upon—all of the controlling conditions in the game

2. Designing a good user interface (that is, attractive screen displays and efficient keyboard input techniques) that creates an appropriate atmosphere and pace for the game

The *Twenty-one* program presented in this chapter illustrates both of these issues and presents individual approaches to resolving them. If you are interested in working on a game program of your own, you may prefer to start out by revising this one. Here is an opportunity for a programming exercise: Two playing options traditionally offered in the game of Twenty-one are not permitted in the simplified version played by this program. The options are called *splitting pairs* and *doubling down*.

In the splitting pairs option, a player who receives (in the initial deal) a pair of cards with the same rank may elect to split the pair into two hands and then play each hand out separately. The player's previously specified bet applies twice, once to each hand.

In the doubling down option, after examining the initial hand of
two cards, a player can elect to double the bet. In exchange for this
privilege, the player must take one—and only one—more card, for a
total of three cards in the hand.

Now that you are familiar with the *Twenty-one* program, and with
the game it conducts, you might want to try incorporating one or both
of these optional features into the game. Like all the QuickBASIC programs in this book, the *Twenty-one* program is structured into a
hierarchy of many small and self-contained subprograms. If you decide
to try to expand the program, this structure will clearly work to your
advantage.

THE *TWENTY-ONE* PROGRAM

```
'    21.BAS
'    Plays the game of 21 (or Blackjack). The computer is always
'        the dealer, and the person at the keyboard is the player.
'        No "splitting" of pairs is allowed, nor is "doubling down" of
'        bets allowed. The player begins with $250 and may place bets
'        that range from $10 to $100.  (The 21 program is written for
'        QuickBASIC 4.0 and 4.5.)

'    ---- Definitions and declarations section.

CONST false% = 0, true% = NOT false%
CONST lowBet% = 10, highBet% = 100
CONST ranks$ = "23456789TJQKA"

TYPE cardPicture
    rank AS STRING * 1
    suit AS STRING * 1
END TYPE

DECLARE FUNCTION CardConvert% (card AS cardPicture)
DECLARE FUNCTION HitorStay% ()
DECLARE FUNCTION YesNo% (prompt$)
DECLARE SUB Bsort (arr() AS cardPicture, num%)
DECLARE SUB CountHand (hand() AS cardPicture, num%, tot%)
DECLARE SUB DealerPlay ()
DECLARE SUB DisplayCard (vPos%, hPos%, card AS cardPicture, show%)
DECLARE SUB GetBet (quit%)
DECLARE SUB InitDeck ()
```

Declarations

Figure 5-11. *The* Twenty-one *program.*   *(continued)*

Figure 5-11. *continued*

```
DECLARE SUB MovePointer ()
DECLARE SUB Pause ()
DECLARE SUB PlayerPlay (over21%)
DECLARE SUB Shuffle (arr() AS cardPicture)
DECLARE SUB StartGame (win%)
DECLARE SUB Winner ()

OPTION BASE 1

DIM SHARED fullDeck(52) AS cardPicture
DIM SHARED playerHand(11) AS cardPicture, dealerHand(11) AS cardPicture

COMMON SHARED nextCard%, curWorth%, betAmount%, playerCards%, dealerCards%
COMMON SHARED firstRound%

'   ---- Main program section.

curWorth% = 250
CLS
LOCATE , , 1

'   ---- Initialize the deck and shuffle it.

InitDeck
nextCard% = 1
Shuffle fullDeck()
firstRound% = true%

'   ---- The play: For each round, get a bet, deal two cards
'        each to the player and the dealer, and draw more cards
'        if appropriate. Display the result of the round.

DO
    GetBet gameOver%
    firstRound% = false%

    IF NOT gameOver% THEN
        StartGame roundOver%
        IF NOT roundOver% THEN
            PlayerPlay busted%
            IF NOT busted% THEN
                DealerPlay
            END IF
```

Main program

(continued)

Figure 5-11. *continued*

```
            END IF
            Winner
        END IF
   LOOP UNTIL gameOver%

   END
```

Bsort

```
   SUB Bsort (arr() AS cardPicture, num%) STATIC

   '   The Bsort subprogram is a bubble sort routine used to rearrange
   '       the cards in a hand before the hand is displayed on the screen.
   '       Since a hand seldom has more than four or five cards, a bubble
   '       sort is just as efficient as any of the more sophisticated
   '       sorting algorithms.

       FOR i% = 1 TO num% - 1
           FOR j% = i% + 1 TO num%
               IF CardConvert%(arr(i%)) > CardConvert%(arr(j%)) THEN
                   SWAP arr(i%), arr(j%)
               END IF
           NEXT j%
       NEXT i%

   END SUB
```

CardConvert%

```
   FUNCTION CardConvert% (card AS cardPicture)

   '   The CardConvert% function reads the suit and rank of a card,
   '       and converts the card to an integer from 1 to 52.

       temp% = (ASC(card.suit) - 3) * 13
       temp% = temp% + INSTR(ranks$, card.rank)

       CardConvert% = temp%

   END FUNCTION
```

CountHand

```
   SUB CountHand (hand() AS cardPicture, num%, tot%) STATIC

   '   The CountHand subprogram counts the value of a hand and
   '       returns the value of the count in the tot% parameter.
   '       The other parameters are hand%(), an array of card
   '       records, and num%, the number of cards in the hand.
```

(continued)

Figure 5-11. *continued*

```
     tot% = 0
     aces% = 0

'    ---- Tens, Jacks, Queens, and Kings are worth 10. The ace is worth 11.
'         Other cards are worth their face value.

     FOR i% = 1 TO num%
         SELECT CASE hand(i%).rank

         CASE "T", "J", "Q", "K"
             cardValue% = 10

         CASE "A"
             cardValue% = 11
             aces% = aces% + 1

         CASE ELSE
             cardValue% = VAL(hand(i%).rank)

         END SELECT
         tot% = tot% + cardValue%
     NEXT i%

'    ---- If tot% is over 21, and if the hand contains aces,
'         count one or more aces as 1 rather than 11.

     DO WHILE tot% > 21 AND aces% > 0
         tot% = tot% - 10
         aces% = aces% - 1
     LOOP

END SUB

SUB DealerPlay STATIC
```

DealerPlay

```
'    The DealerPlay subprogram draws more cards for the dealer's
'         hand until the count is 17 or over.

'    ---- Begin by displaying the dealer's hidden card.

     DisplayCard 2, 35, dealerHand(1), true%
```

(continued)

Figure 5-11. *continued*

```
'    ---- Count the hand.

     CountHand dealerHand(), dealerCards%, dealerVal%

'    ---- The dealer must stay at 17 or greater, no matter what the
'         player's count is.

     DO WHILE dealerVal% < 17
         LOCATE 11 + dealerCards%, 37: PRINT SPACE$(30)
         LOCATE 12 + dealerCards%, 37
         PRINT "Count is"; dealerVal%; "==> Dealer hits."
         Pause
         dealerCards% = dealerCards% + 1
         dealerHand(dealerCards%) = fullDeck(nextCard%)
         Bsort dealerHand(), dealerCards%

         FOR i% = 1 TO dealerCards%
             vloc% = i% + 1
             hloc% = 32 + i% * 3
             DisplayCard vloc%, hloc%, dealerHand(i%), true%
         NEXT i%

         MovePointer
         CountHand dealerHand(), dealerCards%, dealerVal%
     LOOP

     LOCATE 11 + dealerCards%, 37: PRINT SPACE$(30)
     LOCATE 12 + dealerCards%, 37

     IF dealerVal% > 21 THEN
         PRINT "Count is"; dealerVal%; "==> Busted!" + SPACE$(8)
     ELSE
         PRINT "Count is"; dealerVal%; "==> Dealer stays."
     END IF

END SUB

SUB DisplayCard (vPos%, hPos%, card AS cardPicture, show%) STATIC

'    The DisplayCard subprogram displays one card on the screen.
'        The subprogram has four parameters: vpos% and hpos%
'        are the line and column locations of the upper-left
'        corner of the card display; card is a record representing
```

`DisplayCard`

(continued)

Figure 5-11. *continued*

```
'        the target card; and show% is a Boolean value (-1 for
'        true, 0 for false) that indicates whether the card
'        is to be displayed face up or face down.

'    ---- Begin by drawing the outline of the card.

     hStr$ = CHR$(218) + STRING$(14, 196) + CHR$(191)
     LOCATE vPos%, hPos%: PRINT hStr$

     FOR i% = vPos% + 1 TO vPos% + 8
         LOCATE i%, hPos%: PRINT CHR$(179)
     NEXT i%

     LOCATE vPos% + 9, hPos%: PRINT CHR$(192) + STRING$(2, 196)

'    ---- If the card is face up (show% is true), display the
'         card's suit and value.

     IF show% THEN
         LOCATE vPos% + 2, hPos% + 1: PRINT card.suit
         LOCATE vPos% + 1, hPos% + 1

'        ---- If the card's rank is "T", print "10"; otherwise, print
'             the card.rank element.

         IF card.rank = "T" THEN
             PRINT "10"
         ELSE
             PRINT card.rank + " "
         END IF
     END IF

END SUB

SUB GetBet (quit%) STATIC

'    The GetBet subprogram announces the player's current holdings
'        (or indebtedness) and invites the player to place a bet.

     CLS
     PRINT : PRINT : PRINT
     PRINT "       Twenty-one"
     PRINT "       ========="
```

GetBet

(continued)

Figure 5-11. *continued*

```
PRINT
PRINT "        The computer is the dealer."
PRINT "           ";

IF curWorth% >= 0 THEN
    PRINT USING "You currently have: $$#,###"; curWorth%
ELSE
    PRINT USING "You owe the house: $$#,###"; ABS(curWorth%)
    PRINT "           (The house extends credit.)"
END IF

IF NOT firstRound% THEN
    PRINT : PRINT "           ";
    continue% = YesNo%("Continue the game? ")
ELSE
    continue% = true%
END IF

IF continue% THEN
    PRINT
    PRINT "      Place your bet."
    PRINT "      ---------------"
    PRINT "         The house betting limits are:"
    PRINT USING "             ->   minimum bet -- $$###"; lowBet%
    PRINT USING "             ->   maximum bet -- $$###"; highBet%
    PRINT "           (Just press <Enter> for maximum bet.)"
    PRINT

'   ---- Read the bet amount as a string value, betStr$. If betStr$ is
'        empty, assume that the player wants to bet the maximum amount.

    DO
        PRINT "              ";
        INPUT "==> ", betStr$
        IF betStr$ = "" THEN
            betAmount% = highBet%
            ok% = true%
        ELSE
            betAmount% = VAL(betStr$)
            ok% = betAmount% >= lowBet% AND betAmount% <= highBet%
        END IF
    LOOP UNTIL ok%
```

(continued)

Figure 5-11. *continued*

```
        quit% = false%
        CLS
    ELSE

'   ---- If YesNo% returns a value of false, set quit% to true.

        quit% = true%
    END IF

END SUB

FUNCTION HitorStay%

'   The HitorStay% function asks the user if he or she wants
'       to hit (i.e., take another card), or stay (i.e., play
'       with the current hand). HitorStay% returns a value of
'       true if the player wants to stay.

    LOCATE playerCards% + 12, 5
    answer$ = ""
    PRINT "Your hand: Hit or Stay? ";

    DO WHILE answer$ = "" OR INSTR("HS", answer$) = 0
        answer$ = UCASE$(INKEY$)
    LOOP

    LOCATE playerCards% + 12, 5: PRINT SPACE$(25);
    HitorStay% = (answer$ = "S")

END FUNCTION

SUB InitDeck STATIC

'   The InitDeck subprogram initializes the fullDeck() array.

    card% = 0
    FOR suit% = 3 TO 6
        FOR rank% = 1 TO 13
            card% = card% + 1

'   ---- CHR$ gives the ASCII value of the suit symbol (3,4,5, or 6).
'        MID$ gives the position of the rank symbol in the ranks$ string
'        constant.
```

HitorStay%

InitDeck

(continued)

Figure 5-11. *continued*

```
                fullDeck(card%).suit = CHR$(suit%)
                fullDeck(card%).rank = MID$(ranks$, rank%, 1)
        NEXT rank%
    NEXT suit%

END SUB

SUB MovePointer STATIC

'   The MovePointer subprogram increments the nextCard% variable.
'       When nextCard% goes past 52, this routine shuffles all the
'       cards that aren't currently on the table.

    nextCard% = nextCard% + 1

    IF nextCard% > 52 THEN
        tableCards% = playerCards% + dealerCards%
        usedCards% = 52 - tableCards%
        LOCATE 25, 25: PRINT "Reshuffling"; usedCards%; "cards...";

'   ---- The tempDeck() array will contain all those cards
'           that are not in a current hand.

        REDIM tempDeck(usedCards%) AS cardPicture

        FOR i% = 1 TO usedCards%
            tempDeck(i%) = fullDeck(i%)
        NEXT i%

'   ---- Shuffle the temporary deck.

        Shuffle tempDeck()

'   ---- Anticipating the next shuffle, keep a convenient record
'           of the cards that are currently on the table.

        FOR i% = 1 TO tableCards%
            fullDeck(i%) = fullDeck(usedCards% + i%)
        NEXT i%

'   ---- Fill up the rest of the deck with the newly shuffled cards.
```

(continued)

Figure 5-11. *continued*

```
        FOR i% = 1 TO usedCards%
            fullDeck(tableCards% + i%) = tempDeck(i%)
        NEXT i%

'   ---- The nextCard% variable should point to the top of
'        the newly shuffled cards.

        nextCard% = tableCards% + 1
        Pause
        LOCATE 25, 25: PRINT SPACE$(54);
    END IF

END SUB

SUB Pause STATIC

'   The Pause subprogram allows the player to examine the
'        playing table until he or she is ready to continue.
'        Pause places a message in the lower-right corner
'        of the screen and waits for the player to press any key.

    LOCATE 25, 50: PRINT "Press any key to continue.";

    DO WHILE INKEY$ = ""
    LOOP

END SUB

SUB PlayerPlay (over21%) STATIC

'   The PlayerPlay subprogram gives the player a chance to take
'        more cards. If the player's hand goes over 21, PlayerPlay
'        returns a value of true in the variable over21%.

    over21% = false%
    done% = false%

'   ---- Continue until the player is done or the hand goes over 21.

    DO WHILE NOT (over21% OR done%)
        done% = HitorStay
```

Pause

PlayerPlay

(continued)

Figure 5-11. *continued*

```
        IF NOT done% THEN
            playerCards% = playerCards% + 1
            playerHand(playerCards%) = fullDeck(nextCard%)
            Bsort playerHand(), playerCards%
            FOR i% = 1 TO playerCards%
                DisplayCard i% + 1, i% * 3, playerHand(i%), true%
            NEXT i%
            MovePointer
            CountHand playerHand(), playerCards%, playerVal%

            IF playerVal% > 21 THEN
                over21% = true%
                LOCATE playerCards% + 12, 5
                PRINT "Count is"; playerVal%; "==> Busted!"
                BEEP
            ELSEIF playerVal% = 21 THEN
                done% = true%
            END IF

        ELSE
            CountHand playerHand(), playerCards%, playerVal%
        END IF
    LOOP

    IF done% THEN
        LOCATE playerCards% + 12, 5
        PRINT "Count is"; playerVal%
    END IF

END SUB

SUB Shuffle (arr() AS cardPicture) STATIC

'   The Shuffle subprogram rearranges an array of cards,
'       resulting in a random order.

'   ---- Set the seed of the random-number generator and
'        find the length of the array.

    RANDOMIZE TIMER
    length% = UBOUND(arr)
```

Shuffle

(continued)

Figure 5-11. *continued*

```
'    ---- Swap each element of the array with a randomly selected element.

     FOR i% = 1 TO length%
         temp% = INT(RND * length%) + 1
         SWAP arr(i%), arr(temp%)
     NEXT i%

END SUB

SUB StartGame (win%) STATIC
```

StartGame

```
'    The StartGame subprogram deals the first two cards to the player
'        and the dealer, and looks to see if anyone has 21 at the outset.
'        If so, StartGame sends a Boolean value of true back to the main
'        program in the win% variable.

     playerCards% = 0: dealerCards% = 0

     FOR i% = 1 TO 2
         playerHand(i%) = fullDeck(nextCard%)
         DisplayCard i% + 1, i% * 3, playerHand(i%), true%
         playerCards% = playerCards% + 1
         MovePointer
         dealerHand(i%) = fullDeck(nextCard%)
         DisplayCard i% + 1, 32 + i% * 3, dealerHand(i%), 1 - i%
         dealerCards% = dealerCards% + 1
         MovePointer
     NEXT i%

     LOCATE 14, 5: PRINT "Your hand"
     LOCATE 14, 37: PRINT "The dealer's hand"

'    ---- Count the hands.

     CountHand playerHand(), 2, playerVal%
     CountHand dealerHand(), 2, dealerVal%

'    ---- Analyze the situation and display the value of each hand.

     IF dealerVal% = 21 OR playerVal% = 21 THEN
         win% = true%
         DisplayCard 2, 35, dealerHand(1), true%
```

(continued)

Figure 5-11. *continued*

```
        LOCATE 15, 40
        IF dealerVal% = 21 THEN
            PRINT "Twenty-one!"
        ELSE
            PRINT "Count is: "; dealerVal%
        END IF

        LOCATE 15, 4
        IF playerVal% = 21 THEN
            PRINT "Twenty-one!"
        ELSE
            PRINT "Count is: "; playerVal%
        END IF

    ELSE
        win% = false%
    END IF

END SUB

SUB Winner STATIC

'   The Winner subprogram announces whether the player has won or lost,
'       and adds the bet amount to--or subtracts it from--the player's
'       current holdings.

    CountHand playerHand(), playerCards%, playerVal%
    CountHand dealerHand(), dealerCards%, dealerVal%

'   ---- If the counts of the two hands are equal, the round is a draw.

    IF playerVal% = dealerVal% THEN
        diff% = 0

'   ---- If the player has busted, or has a lower count than the dealer,
'       the player loses.

    ELSEIF playerVal% > 21 OR (playerVal% < dealerVal% AND dealerVal% < 22) THEN
        diff% = -1 * betAmount%

'   ---- If the player had 21 after the initial deal (of 2 cards)
'       then the player earns twice the bet.
```

Winner

(continued)

Figure 5-11. *continued*

```
    ELSEIF playerVal% = 21 AND playerCards% = 2 THEN
        diff% = 2 * betAmount%

'   ---- Otherwise, the player simply earns the bet itself.

    ELSE
        diff% = betAmount%
    END IF

'   ---- Add diff% (a negative or positive amount) to the player's
'        current worth, curWorth%.

    curWorth% = curWorth% + diff%

'   ---- Announce the result of the round.

    LOCATE 25, 10
    SELECT CASE diff%

    CASE 0
        PRINT "A draw... ";

    CASE IS < 0
        PRINT USING "You lose $$###."; ABS(diff%);

    CASE ELSE
        PRINT USING "You win $$###."; diff%;

    END SELECT

    Pause
    CLS

END SUB

FUNCTION YesNo% (prompt$)                                          YesNo%

'   The YesNo% function asks a yes-or-no question, and returns a logical
'        value indicating the user's response: true means yes; false means no.

'   ---- Display the question prompt.

    PRINT prompt$; " (Y or N) -> ";
```

(continued)

Figure 5-11. *continued*

```
'    ---- Get a single-letter response.

     inOk% = false%

     DO
         answer$ = UCASE$(INKEY$)
         IF answer$ <> "" THEN
             IF INSTR("YN", answer$) <> 0 THEN
                 inOk% = true%
             ELSE
                 BEEP
             END IF
         END IF
     LOOP UNTIL inOk%

     PRINT answer$

'    ---- Convert the response into a logical value.

     YesNo% = (answer$ = "Y")

END FUNCTION
```

C H A P T E R **6**

Sequential Data Files: The *Survey* Program

Creating and reading disk-based data files are essential activities in many personal computer applications, including most of the programs presented in this book. As these programs illustrate, a data file on disk is a reliable medium for saving information between one execution and the next of a program, or for exchanging data efficiently between different applications.

The QuickBASIC language provides an important set of built-in procedures for data-file programming, with a variety of techniques for creating and reading files. In this chapter we'll begin our discussion of this important topic by examining the simplest kind of data file, the *sequential file*. Then in Chapter 7 we'll explore the somewhat more elaborate techniques required for using another kind of file, the *random-access file*.

A sequential file is designed for processing an entire collection of data as a unit. Sequential files possess no special structure enabling a program to go directly to a particular record of information located at some random place within the file. Rather, the data values stored in a sequential file are meant to be read item by item, from the beginning of the file to the end. Nonetheless, the sequential file is a perfectly suitable medium for any application that does not require direct access to individual records in the file.

In this chapter we'll concentrate on the QuickBASIC language elements that work with sequential files. Specifically, we'll review the commands and functions that perform these tasks:

- Opening a sequential file for reading (OPEN...FOR INPUT)

- Reading items of information from the open file (INPUT#)

- Determining when the reading process has reached the end of the file (EOF)

- Opening a new sequential file for writing (OPEN...FOR OUTPUT), or opening an existing file to append information to the end of the file (OPEN...FOR APPEND)

- Writing information to the open file (PRINT# or WRITE#)

- Closing a sequential file when the write operation is complete (CLOSE)

To illustrate the use of sequential files, this chapter presents an unusual application called the *Survey* program. Let's look at this program before resuming our discussion of data-file programming.

THE *SURVEY* PROGRAM

The *Survey* program generates questionnaires of all kinds and analyzes the responses received from them. You might use this program to work with any of the following projects:

- A customer-satisfaction survey

- A voter-attitude survey

- An opinion poll

- A market study for a particular product

In general, the *Survey* program aids in gathering and analyzing information about large groups of people who have some trait or activity in common—for example, customers, employees, voters, TV viewers, newspaper readers, students, consumers, churchgoers, computer owners, cat lovers, club members, sports fans, parents, commuters, business owners, joggers, and so on.

Survey does not maintain specific information about individuals, such as names, addresses, and phone numbers. Rather, the program aims to generalize the opinions, attitudes, and characteristics of a whole group of people. For this reason, the *Survey* program is an ideal application for sequential files.

Using *Survey,* you will be able to:

- Generate and save the text of surveys that contain any number of multiple-choice questions.

- Print questionnaire forms to distribute to survey participants.

- Record responses received from these participants.

- Tally the responses and report the percentage of participants who answered each question in a certain way.

To accomplish all these tasks, the program creates and maintains several data files on disk for each questionnaire. When we examine the program listing, we'll find that these data files store different kinds of information, including the text of the questionnaire, the individual responses received from participants, and a collection of important information about the survey.

We'll explore this program in detail and examine a complete sample survey after we review QuickBASIC's commands and functions devoted to sequential-file handling.

SEQUENTIAL-FILE HANDLING IN QUICKBASIC

A program opens a sequential file for one of three operations: reading a file, writing information to a new file, or appending information to an existing file. A sequential file can only be used for one of these operations at a time. For example, imagine a program that creates a file and subsequently needs to read information from the same file. The program would perform the following sequence of steps.

1. Open the file for writing.

2. Write items of information to the file.

3. Close the file.

4. Open the file for reading.

5. Read items of information from the file.

6. Close the file.

The OPEN command opens a sequential file for one of the three possible operations. In simple form, here are the three commands that open sequential files for reading, writing, and appending, respectively:

```
OPEN "fileName" FOR INPUT AS #fileNumber
OPEN "fileName" FOR OUTPUT AS #fileNumber
OPEN "fileName" FOR APPEND AS #fileNumber
```

In all three of these statements, the FOR clause specifies the particular operation that the program will subsequently execute with the open file. The filename that identifies the file on disk must be a legal MS-DOS name containing up to eight characters, plus an optional three-character extension. The filename can also include path and drive specifications.

The AS clause supplies a file number for each open file. This number is an integer from *1* to *255*, the maximum number of files that can be open at one time. When a file is open, it is identified by its file number in subsequent commands that work with the file. For example, the INPUT#, PRINT#, and WRITE# commands all refer to a specific file by number.

We'll see examples of the OPEN command as we examine the reading and writing operations. Let's begin with the process of reading a file.

Reading data from a sequential file

The following statement opens an existing file named SAMPLE.NUM, located on the disk in drive *B*, and prepares to start reading information from the beginning of the file:

```
OPEN "B:SAMPLE.NUM" FOR INPUT AS #1
```

Notice that the statement gives *SAMPLE.NUM* a file number of *1*. As long as the file is open, any commands that deal with the file will refer to it by this number.

The INPUT# command reads items of information from the file. Here is the general format of INPUT#:

```
INPUT #fileNumber, variableList
```

For example, the following INPUT# command reads a string and an integer value from file #1:

```
INPUT #1, title$, number%
```

Notice the punctuation of the statement: A comma follows the file number, and the variables in the subsequent list are also separated by commas. If this is the first INPUT# command that has been issued after the corresponding OPEN statement, the command reads the first and second data values stored in the file, and assigns the values to the variables *title$* and *number%* respectively. These same values could also have been read by two individual INPUT# commands:

```
INPUT#1, title$
INPUT#1, number%
```

The next INPUT# command after these will read the third value in the file, and then the fourth, and so on until the reading process reaches the end of the file.

Typically the INPUT# statements that read a sequential file are located within a FOR...NEXT or a DO...LOOP structure. Each iteration of the loop reads one or more values from the file. A common error occurs when a program attempts to read more data values than the file contains. When an INPUT# command reads the last value in a file, QuickBASIC records an end-of-file condition for that file. If a subsequent INPUT# statement tries to read another value from the file, the resulting runtime error (*Input past end of file*) will terminate the program.

Fortunately, the built-in EOF function is available to help you avoid this problem. EOF takes a file number as its argument. As long as additional data values are still available to be read from the file, EOF returns a value of false. But when the end-of-file condition occurs for the file, EOF returns a value of true. Using this function as the condition of a DO...LOOP structure, you can loop safely through the file, reading each value down to the end.

Consider the following hypothetical program lines:

```
DO WHILE NOT EOF(1)
    INPUT#1, strValue$
    StringProcess strValue$
LOOP
```

As long as the expression NOT EOF(1) is true, this DO...WHILE loop continues reading individual values from file #1 into the variable *strValue$*. A call to the subprogram named *StringProcess* performs an operation on each value before the loop reads the next value in the file. The looping stops after the last value has been read and processed.

Another reasonable way to handle a sequential file is to maintain a record of the exact number of data values stored in the file. Then your program can employ a FOR...NEXT loop to read the correct number of data values from the file. In the *Survey* program we will see examples of both these approaches: a DO loop that relies on the EOF function, and a FOR...NEXT loop that requires specific information about the length of the file.

To plan successfully for reading a sequential file, you also have to know what types of values are stored in the file. The variable types in the INPUT# statement should correspond correctly to the values read from the file. If they do not correspond, QuickBASIC makes data type conversions where possible, but unexpected results can occur. For example, if an INPUT# function reads a string value from a sequential file and mistakenly attempts to assign the value to a numeric variable, the variable will receive a value of *0*.

A final problem arises when QuickBASIC cannot find the disk file referred to in the OPEN statement. This problem is particularly common in programs that elicit a filename from the user and then open the file for reading. The following sequence illustrates these steps:

```
INPUT "What file do you want to read"; fileName$
OPEN fileName$ FOR INPUT AS #1
```

In this case, the name of the file is stored in the *fileName$* string variable. The OPEN statement looks on disk for the filename stored in the variable. The danger is that the user will enter a filename that does not exist on disk, or that exists in a different directory. If this happens, the OPEN statement produces the runtime error (*File not found*) that normally terminates the program.

You can guard against this problem in two ways. The first is to show the user a list of the files that are available on disk. The FILES command conveniently produces such a directory display on the screen. Here is the general form of the command:

```
FILES "fileSpecifier"
```

This command's optional string parameter, *fileSpecifier,* can include a disk or path specification, and a filename with wildcard characters. For example, the following command uses the * wildcard character to display files that have extension names of *SUR*:

```
FILES "*.SUR"
```

If the current default disk is in drive *B*, the resulting display might look something like this:

```
B:\
CUSTOMER.SUR     SAMPLE  .SUR     EMPLOYEE.SUR
 288768 Bytes free
```

By examining this display, the user should be able to avoid requesting a file that does not exist.

But even with this directory display, errors can occur. The user might simply mistype the filename, for example. For this reason, the ultimate safeguard against a bad filename in an OPEN statement is to create an error trap using the ON ERROR GOTO statement. We'll see an example of this technique in the *Survey* program.

After completing the reading process, a program should close a file using the CLOSE statement. The general form of the CLOSE statement is:

```
CLOSE #fileNumber(s)
```

For example, the following statement closes file #1:

```
CLOSE #1
```

If two or more files are open, they can be closed explicitly in a single CLOSE statement. For example, this statement closes files #1 and #3:

```
CLOSE #1, #3
```

A CLOSE statement without any file numbers closes all open files:

```
CLOSE
```

When you close a file, the file number becomes available again for opening another file. A number is only associated with a file while the file is open.

If you want to read the same sequential file more than once in a program, you must close the file after the first reading, then open it again for a subsequent reading. Each time you open a file for reading, QuickBASIC prepares to read values at the beginning of the file.

Next let's look at the various ways to write information to a sequential file.

Writing data to a sequential file

As we have seen, the OPEN command has two sequential writing modes—OUTPUT for creating a new file, and APPEND for writing to the end of an existing file. We'll discuss each of these modes in turn.

Creating a new file

The following statement creates the file *SAMPLE.NUM* on disk *B*, and prepares to write data values to it:

```
OPEN "B:SAMPLE.NUM" FOR OUTPUT AS #1
```

As a result of this statement, the new—and currently empty—file *SAMPLE.NUM* will be opened and assigned a file number of *1*. You can subsequently use the WRITE# statement or the PRINT# statement to send data values to the file.

If a specified file already exists when you open it in the OUTPUT mode, the file's contents will be lost. In its place, QuickBASIC will open a new empty file and prepare to write new data to the file. In some cases, a program is designed intentionally to replace an old version of a file with a completely new version; such a program can use OPEN both to erase the old file and to create the new one.

A more careful approach, however, is to retain the old version of a file as a backup copy before creating a new version. One way to accomplish this is to use the NAME command to rename the existing file, and then use OPEN to create the new one. The NAME command has the following general format:

```
NAME "oldName" AS "newName"
```

For example, in the following sequence the current version of the *SAMPLE.NUM* file is renamed *SAMPLE.BAK* before a new version of the file is created:

```
NAME "B:SAMPLE.NUM" AS "SAMPLE.BAK"
OPEN "B:SAMPLE.NUM" FOR OUTPUT AS #1
```

Use the NAME command cautiously: It produces runtime errors in several different situations. For example, an error will occur if:

- The file represented by *oldName* does not exist.

- The file represented by *newName* already exists.

- The file represented by *oldName* is open.

Normally you'll want to set up an error trap to handle one or more of these potential errors when you use the NAME command.

Appending data to an existing file

In some cases a program may need to append new data to an existing file. To accomplish this, QuickBASIC supplies the second writing mode, APPEND. For example, the following statement opens the existing file named *SAMPLE.NUM* and prepares to append data values to the end of the file:

```
OPEN "B:SAMPLE.NUM" FOR APPEND AS #1
```

This command saves all the data that is stored in *SAMPLE.NUM*. A subsequent write operation will store additional data at the end of the file.

If *SAMPLE.NUM* does not exist at the time this statement is executed, QuickBASIC creates a new file and prepares to write data to it. In this one special case, the QuickBASIC APPEND mode is the same as the OUTPUT mode.

In summary, the distinction between the two writing modes is obviously very important:

- The OUTPUT mode creates a new file and prepares to write data to the file. If the file already exists, its current contents will be destroyed.

- The APPEND mode opens an existing file and prepares to append data to the file. If the specified file does not exist, APPEND creates it.

When a file is open in either of the two writing modes, you can use the WRITE# or PRINT# commands to send data values to the file. Let's explore the differences between these two commands.

The WRITE# statement

A WRITE# statement sends one or more values to the file. The general form of WRITE# is:

```
WRITE #fileNumber, dataList
```

The list of data values can be expressed as constant values, variables, or expressions. For example, the following command sends two strings and two numbers to file #1:

```
WRITE #1, studentName$, idNumber%, "English 101", score / 100
```

WRITE# automatically performs two important formatting tasks on the data values sent to a file. Specifically, WRITE# encloses string values in quotation marks in the file and supplies commas as *delimiters* between values sent to the file.

A delimiter is a special ASCII character that separates one data value from the next in a sequential file. Here are the delimiters that QuickBASIC recognizes:

- The comma character

- The carriage return/line feed combination (ASCII codes 13 and 10, respectively)

In addition, a space character (or a string of multiple spaces) can serve as a valid delimiter between two numeric values.

One advantage of the WRITE# statement is that it takes care of supplying delimiters correctly where they are needed. For example, consider this sequence:

```
string1$ = "first line": value1% = 1
string2$ = "second line": value2% = 2
OPEN "B:SAMPLE.NUM" FOR OUTPUT AS #1
WRITE #1, string1$, value1
WRITE #1, string2$, value2
CLOSE #1
```

The two WRITE# statements send two lines of values to the file. Each line consists of a string value and an integer. This is what the file will look like:

```
"first line",1
"second line",2
```

As you can see, the string values are enclosed in quotes and there is a comma between the two values contained in each line. In addition, each WRITE# statement sends a carriage return/line feed combination after the final data value in a line.

The quotation marks around string values can prove particularly important when a program writes lines of text to a file. For example, the *Survey* program stores the questions and multiple-choice answers of a survey in a sequential file. Sometimes one of these lines of text will contain a comma. However, in this case the comma is simply one of the characters in a string value, not to be considered a delimiter between string values. To prevent QuickBASIC from reading the comma as a delimiter, the entire string must be enclosed in quotes. As we'll see when we examine the *Survey* program, the easiest way to accomplish this is via the WRITE# statement.

The PRINT# statement

The PRINT# statement also sends values to a data file. Its general form is similar to the WRITE# statement:

```
PRINT #fileNumber, dataList
```

The elements in the *dataList* can be separated by semicolons or commas in the syntax of the PRINT# command. If you use semicolons, the data values will be stored side by side in the file; if you use commas, each successive element will be stored at the beginning of the next 14-space tab zone.

Unlike the WRITE# statement, PRINT# does not automatically send a comma delimiter to the file between each data value, nor does it enclose strings within quotation marks. If a file requires either of these elements, you must supply them explicitly in a PRINT# statement. For example, consider the following statements:

```
string1$ = "A": string2$ = "B": string3$ = "C"
PRINT #1, string1$; ","; string2$; ","; string3$
```

This statement sends three string values to a file, with two commas as delimiters between the values. The strings are not enclosed in quotes. Here is the resulting line of data in the file:

```
A,B,C
```

Examples in the *Survey* program will give us the opportunity to compare and contrast the use of PRINT# and WRITE#.

The next section presents a few miscellaneous notes about other features and commands you may want to know about as you use sequential files.

Other commands and features for sequential files

In addition to the format we have already examined, an abbreviated form of the OPEN command is also available. For example, these three commands open a file named *SAMPLE.NUM* as file #1 for reading, writing, and appending, respectively:

```
OPEN "I", 1, "SAMPLE.NUM"
OPEN "O", 1, "SAMPLE.NUM"
OPEN "A", 1, "SAMPLE.NUM"
```

You might encounter this form in programs written in an older version of BASIC, so you should learn to recognize it. However, the longer form is easier to understand, and therefore preferable.

The OPEN statement also includes an optional LEN clause, which specifies the size of the *buffer* that QuickBASIC establishes for each open data file. A buffer is an area in memory that is set aside for storing data on its way to or from a file. If you omit the LEN clause in the OPEN statement when opening a sequential file, the default size of this buffer is 512 bytes. Increasing the size can sometimes result in faster reading and writing processes for sequential files. For example, the following statement establishes a buffer size of one kilobyte:

```
OPEN surFile$ FOR INPUT AS #1 LEN=1024
```

The LEN clause is more important for opening random-access files, in which case the clause specifies the record length of the file. See Chapter 7 for more information.

In addition, the QuickBASIC OPEN statement has *access* and *lock* clauses to control file operations that take place in a multiuser networked environment. Chapter 7 presents a brief discussion of this subject; for greater detail, consult the QuickBASIC documentation.

We should note that QuickBASIC has two less commonly used input commands, designed for reading sequential files. The LINE INPUT# command reads an entire line of a file, up to a carriage return/line feed sequence, regardless of other delimiter characters or quotation marks that can be located within the line. The command takes the following format:

```
LINE INPUT #fileNumber, stringVariable
```

For example, the following command reads one line from file #1 and stores the contents of the line in the string variable *first$*:

```
LINE INPUT #1, first$
```

The LINE INPUT# command is illustrated in the *List* program, presented in Chapter 4.

In contrast, the INPUT$ function reads a specified number of characters from a sequential file. The function has the following form:

```
INPUT$(numCharacters, fileNumber)
```

The first argument, *numCharacters,* is an integer value specifying the number of characters the function will read from the file. For example, the following statement reads one character from file #1 and displays the character's ASCII code number:

```
PRINT ASC(INPUT$(1,1))
```

Now that we've discussed the tools available for handling sequential files, let's begin exploring the features of the *Survey* program.

USING THE *SURVEY* PROGRAM

Figure 6-1 shows the recurring menu for the *Survey* program. As you can see, the program offers four main options. Here is a summary of what the options do:

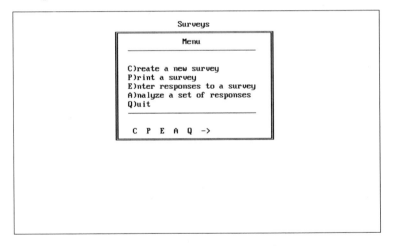

Figure 6-1. *The* Survey *program's main menu.*

- *Create a new survey.* This option presents a series of input screens on which you can enter questions and multiple-choice answers for a new survey. The program saves the questionnaire on disk for you, in a sequential data file. You can create as many surveys as you want and store each under its own name on disk.

- *Print a survey.* This option begins by eliciting the filename of a survey that you want to print. The program then opens the file and prints the survey in a questionnaire form that you can copy and distribute to participants.

- *Enter responses to a survey.* This option displays input screens to record the responses that you have received from participants in a survey. You can enter answers from as many questionnaires as you have received. The program saves these responses together in a data file.

- *Analyze a set of responses.* This option examines the responses you have received from a questionnaire. For each question, the program computes the percentage of all those surveyed who answered in a certain way. The Analyze option produces a printed report incorporating these percentages with a copy of the questionnaire.

Let's examine each of these options in detail. As we go through the options, we will develop and analyze a sample questionnaire: a customer-satisfaction survey for an imaginary small business named *Sam's Friendly Auto Repair.*

The Create option

The Create option starts out by displaying a set of instructions for generating a new survey, as shown in Figure 6-2.

```
Create a new survey.
------ - --- -------

Each question may be from one to four
lines long, and you may supply from two
to ten responses per question.

To complete a question or a group
of responses, press the <Enter> key
when you see the new input prompt.

Enter the filename for this survey:
(The extension .SUR will automatically
be added to the filename.)

      ->
```

Figure 6-2. *Instructions for the Create option.*

In short, each question in the survey can contain from one to four lines of text, followed by as many as ten multiple-choice answers. At the end of these instructions, the *Survey* program elicits a filename for storing the new survey. For Sam's Friendly Auto Repair we'll use the filename *CARSHOP*.

Next, the program requests a descriptive title for the survey:

```
Enter a title for this survey:
 ->
```

We'll use the title *Sam's Friendly Auto Repair* for our sample survey. This title will ultimately appear at the top of each printed questionnaire.

After supplying a filename and a title, you are ready to begin entering the questions of the survey. The program conducts a carefully controlled input dialog for eliciting the questions and the corresponding answers. First you'll see a prompt for each line of the question. You type a line and then press the Enter key. For example:

```
                Question # 1

Line #1: How did you first hear about Sam's Friendly
Line #2: Auto Repair Shop?
Line #3:
```

While the program allows up to four lines of text for the question, you can stop after one, two, or three lines if your question is complete. To do so, press the Enter key when you see the next line prompt.

To prompt you for the multiple-choice answers, the program supplies uppercase letters, potentially from *A* to *J*, to represent each response. You supply a short answer for each letter and then press the Enter key; for example:

```
            Responses to Question # 1

A: From a friend.
B: In our newspaper advertisement.
C: From our radio commercial.
D: In the phone book.
E: By passing the shop on the street.
F: Other.
G:

            Another question? (Y or N)->
```

After you have entered one response, the program displays a prompt for the next one. To stop at fewer than ten multiple-choice responses, press the Enter key when you see the new response prompt. (The program requires at least two responses for each question.)

When you create a new survey, the *Survey* program generates three different disk files to store information about your survey. Let's look at these files before we continue with the other options of the program.

Files for a new survey

The initial three files that the program creates have extension names of *SUR* (for "survey"), *ALT* (for "alternate") and *NUM* (for "number"). For example, the *CARSHOP* questionnaire will be represented by the following files:

```
CARSHOP.SUR
CARSHOP.ALT
CARSHOP.NUM
```

The primary file in this example, containing the complete text of the questionnaire, is *CARSHOP.SUR*. This file stores each question line and each response in sequential order. The lines of text are enclosed in quotation marks in the file. Let's look at the complete *CARSHOP.SUR* file that we'll generate for our sample survey. The file contains six questions in all, each followed by an assortment of possible responses:

```
"How did you first hear about Sam's Friendly"
"Auto Repair Shop?"
"From a friend."
"In our newspaper advertisement."
"From our radio commercial."
"In the phone book."
"By passing the shop on the street."
"Other."
"Including the latest visit, how many times"
"have you brought your current car to be serviced"
"at Sam's Auto Repair?"
"Once"
"Twice"
"Three to five times"
"Six times or more"
```

```
"Every service up to now"
"What impressed you most favorably about your most "
"recent car service at Sam's?"
"The fast service and prompt delivery."
"The thorough explanation of what needed to be done."
"The courteous attendants."
"The reasonable price for the service."
"All of the above."
"Was there anything you were not happy about in"
"your recent car service at Sam's?"
"The time taken for the repair."
"The attitude of the attendants."
"The explanation of the service."
"The price."
"None of the above."
"What was the reason you brought your car in "
"for your most recent service at Sam's Friendly"
"Auto Repair Shop?"
"Routine service."
"A problem that you couldn't identify yourself."
"A specific repair that you knew had to be done."
"A follow-up on an inadequate previous service."
"The first 7500-mile check-up for a new car."
"Would you recommend Sam's Friendly Auto Repair"
"Shop to a friend?"
"Yes"
"No"
```

To read this file correctly, the program needs a way to find out the number of lines in each question and the number of corresponding multiple-choice answers. As we have seen, both these numbers can vary from question to question: The question can be from one to four lines long, and there can be from two to ten responses.

The *ALT* file supplies the dimensions of the questionnaire. Here is the *CARSHOP.ALT* that corresponds to the *CARSHOP* survey:

```
"How did you fir"
2
6
"Including the l"
3
5
"What impressed "
2
5
```

```
"Was there anyth"
2
5
"What was the re"
3
5
"Would you recom"
2
2
```

You can see that the file gives three items of information describing each question in the survey:

1. The first *15* characters of the question

2. The number of lines in the question (from *1* to *4*)

3. The number of multiple-choice answers (from *2* to *10*)

For example, look at the description of the survey's first question. The two numerical values in this description (*2* and *6*) instruct the program to read the first survey question as follows: The first two lines in *CARSHOP.SUR* are the lines of the question, and the next six lines are the responses for the question. We'll see exactly how *Survey* uses this information as we progress through the program. We'll also find out why the *ALT* file includes a short excerpt from the beginning of the question text.

The *Survey* program creates a third short file to describe the questionnaire. The *NUM* file contains only two items of information:

1. The title of the survey

2. The total number of questions in the survey

For example, here is *CARSHOP.NUM,* which describes a survey containing six questions:

```
"Sam's Friendly Auto Repair"
6
```

Conveniently, the program does not create this little file until you have completed the input process for the new survey. Because you may not know in advance exactly how many questions you are going to put into a survey, the program simply counts them as you go along and records the number in the *NUM* file when you are finished. This way you are not required to commit to a fixed number of questions before beginning the input process.

Each of the subsequent program options uses all or some of the three files produced during the Create option. In addition, we'll see that the final option, *Analyze a set of responses*, creates a fourth file for the survey application.

The Print option

To print a working copy of any survey stored on disk, you choose the Print a survey option. Print begins by giving you the opportunity to specify the disk or directory where you want to search for survey files. You can enter a drive or directory specification, or you can press the Enter key to use the current directory:

```
Print a Survey
----- - ------


Where do you want to search for survey files?
(Press <Enter> to search the current directory.)->
```

In response, the program shows you a listing of all the *SUR* files stored in the directory you have specified; for example:

```
Here is the directory of *.SUR:

----------------------------------------------------------------
C:\QB4
CARSHOP .SUR      SERVICE .SUR      VOTERS  .SUR      PRODUCT .SUR
CUSTOMER.SUR      OUTCOME .SUR
 12017664 Bytes free
----------------------------------------------------------------

Which one do you want to work with?
```

To open a survey file, all you have to do is enter the base name of the file in response to the program's next question; for example:

```
Which one do you want to work with? CARSHOP
```

If you should mistype the filename—producing a name that does not exist on the disk—the program displays an error message and ultimately returns you to the main menu:

```
Which one do you want to work with? CARSHP


*** This file is not available. ***

Press the spacebar to continue.
```

By the way, the program makes an attempt at this point to open all three of the survey files we have discussed: *SUR, ALT,* and *NUM.* If any of the files is missing from your disk, the program won't be able to work with the survey and will therefore display the file error message.

However, if the files are opened successfully, the program is ready to read them and produce a printed survey form. To give you a chance to prepare your printer for the operation, the program pauses and displays the following message on the screen:

```
Press the spacebar
when your printer is
ready to operate.
```

When you press the spacebar, the program begins reading the survey files and sends each question to the printer. Figure 6-3 shows the customer-satisfaction survey for Sam's Friendly Auto Repair. Notice that the program prints a pair of square brackets at the left of each response. To answer a question, the participant should simply place an *X* within one of these pairs of brackets.

```
             Survey: Sam's Friendly Auto Repair


1 - How did you first hear about Sam's Friendly
        Auto Repair Shop?

        [ ]  A: From a friend.
        [ ]  B: In our newspaper advertisement.
        [ ]  C: From our radio commercial.
        [ ]  D: In the phone book.
        [ ]  E: By passing the shop on the street.
        [ ]  F: Other.


2 - Including the latest visit, how many times
        have you brought your current car to be serviced
        at Sam's Auto Repair?

        [ ]  A: Once
        [ ]  B: Twice
        [ ]  C: Three to five times
        [ ]  D: Six times or more
        [ ]  E: Every service up to now
```

Figure 6-3. *The printed CARSHOP survey.*   *(continued)*

Figure 6-3. *continued*

```
3 - What impressed you most favorably about your most
        recent car service at Sam's?

        [ ]  A: The fast service and prompt delivery.
        [ ]  B: The thorough explanation of what needed to be done.
        [ ]  C: The courteous attendants.
        [ ]  D: The reasonable price for the service.
        [ ]  E: All of the above.


4 - Was there anything you were not happy about in
        your recent car service at Sam's?

        [ ]  A: The time taken for the repair.
        [ ]  B: The attitude of the attendants.
        [ ]  C: The explanation of the service.
        [ ]  D: The price.
        [ ]  E: None of the above.


5 - What was the reason you brought your car in
        for your most recent service at Sam's Friendly
        Auto Repair Shop?

        [ ]  A: Routine service.
        [ ]  B: A problem that you couldn't identify yourself.
        [ ]  C: A specific repair that you knew had to be done.
        [ ]  D: A follow-up on an inadequate previous service.
        [ ]  E: The first 7500-mile check-up for a new car.


6 - Would you recommend Sam's Friendly Auto Repair
        Shop to a friend?

        [ ]  A: Yes
        [ ]  B: No
```

Now imagine that you have produced a survey like the one for Sam's Friendly Auto Repair and you have begun receiving completed questionnaires back from your customers. No matter how many responses you receive for a survey—dozens, hundreds, or even thousands—you will want an efficient way to record all the answers in one place and to tally the results. The Enter and Analyze options of the *Survey* program provide these operations.

The Enter option

A programmer must think carefully about designing an input process that can involve large amounts of data. For example, the process for entering survey responses should be simple and efficient, allowing a good typist to store a large amount of data in as short a time as possible. The screen prompts for this process should display just enough information to identify a question and to elicit an appropriate single-letter response. Furthermore, the program should require only one keystroke for each answer and should ignore alphabetic case in the input response. Finally, the program should recognize and reject inappropriate responses and alert the typist with an audible signal.

As we will see, all these features are built into the input dialog that the Enter responses to a survey option conducts. When you select this option, the program begins by asking you to enter the name of the directory in which you want to search for survey files. The program displays the directory and then asks you to indicate which survey you want to work with. (From one activity to the next, the program never assumes that you want to continue with the same survey that you have just finished working with. Each menu option gives you the chance to select a new survey application from those that you have created and stored on disk.)

To make sure you have chosen the correct file, the program displays the descriptive survey title on the screen before beginning the input process; for example:

```
Survey title: Sam's Friendly Auto Repair

Is this the correct survey? (Y or N)->
```

If you answer affirmatively, the input begins. For each question, the program displays the question number, along with a short "teaser" quotation from the text of the question. (The program reads this excerpt from the *ALT* file.) Then, below the text, the program shows the appropriate responses. For example, here is one complete set of responses to the questions in Sam's survey:

```
1 - How did you fir...
        A B C D E F-> C
2 - Including the 1...
      A B C D E-> E
```

```
3 - What impressed ...
      A B C D E-> D
4 - Was there anyth...
      A B C D E-> E
5 - What was the re...
      A B C D E-> A
6 - Would you recom...
      A B-> A
```

To answer a question, you press a single letter key. The program records the response and moves immediately to the next question. Notice that the prompt shows the exact sequence of appropriate letters for each question: Question *1* has six possible responses (*A* through *F*); Question *2* has five (*A* through *E*); and so on. If you enter a letter that is not in the correct set, the program sounds a beep from the computer's speaker.

After going though all the questions for a questionnaire, the program asks if there is to be another round:

```
Another (Y or N) ->
```

Again, only a single keystroke response is necessary: *Y* or *N*. Depending on your answer, the program either starts again with a new input dialog or returns you to the main menu. As you enter questionnaire responses, the Enter option creates a fourth data file to be associated with a survey. This file has an extension name of *RES* (for "responses"). For example, here is a selection of responses for Sam's customer-satisfaction survey, stored in the file *CARSHOP.RES*:

```
B, C, A, D, E, A
D, E, A, B, C, A
A, B, C, D, E, A
A, D, A, B, C, A
D, E, E, A, C, B
D, D, A, C, D, A
D, A, B, C, D, A
B, C, D, A, C, A
D, D, A, B, E, A
C, C, B, D, A, B
A, C, D, E, A, A
F, D, B, C, A, A
D, D, A, B, C, A
A, C, C, B, E, A
D, C, C, B, E, A
```

For each completed questionnaire received for a survey, the *RES* file contains one line of responses. Each line of the file contains six one-letter entries, separated by commas, representing one participant's responses to the six questions of the survey.

The *RES* file can grow to be the largest sequential data file of the four files that the program produces. Each time you select the Enter option, the program prepares to append new lines of data to the file. In this way, you can enter new questionnaire responses over a period of time, as long as you continue receiving them.

Finally, the Analyze a set of responses option goes through the *RES* file and tallies the responses for a question.

The Analyze option

When you select the Analyze option, the *Survey* program again asks you to supply the location and the filename for the survey you want to work with. As in the Examine option, the program opens the various files and displays the name of the survey. The output of the Analyze option is a printed report that supplies the tallied responses. Accordingly, the program pauses for you to prepare your printer and begins the report when you press the spacebar to indicate that you are ready.

Figure 6-4 shows a sample report for Sam's Friendly Auto Repair. You can see that the output is similar to the original questionnaire form, except for two new details. Beneath the title line, the report shows the number of questionnaires that have been recorded up to now. This figure represents the total number of lines the program has read from the *CARSHOP.RES* file.

```
            Survey: Sam's Friendly Auto Repair
               243 Survey Responses Received


 1 - How did you first hear about Sam's Friendly
        Auto Repair Shop?

        30%    A: From a friend.
        15%    B: In our newspaper advertisement.
         6%    C: From our radio commercial.
        44%    D: In the phone book.
         0%    E: By passing the shop on the street.
         5%    F: Other.
```

Figure 6-4. *The* CARSHOP *Analyze option.*   *(continued)*

Figure 6-4. *continued*

```
2 - Including the latest visit, how many times
        have you brought your current car to be serviced
        at Sam's Auto Repair?

    10%    A: Once
     5%    B: Twice
    49%    C: Three to five times
    25%    D: Six times or more
    11%    E: Every service up to now


3 - What impressed you most favorably about your most
        recent car service at Sam's?

    35%    A: The fast service and prompt delivery.
    20%    B: The thorough explanation of what needed to be done.
    25%    C: The courteous attendants.
    11%    D: The reasonable price for the service.
    10%    E: All of the above.


4 - Was there anything you were not happy about in
        your recent car service at Sam's?

    15%    A: The time taken for the repair.
    30%    B: The attitude of the attendants.
    15%    C: The explanation of the service.
    25%    D: The price.
    16%    E: None of the above.


5 - What was the reason you brought your car in
        for your most recent service at Sam's Friendly
        Auto Repair Shop?

    21%    A: Routine service.
     5%    B: A problem that you couldn't identify yourself.
    30%    C: A specific repair that you knew had to be done.
    10%    D: A follow-up on an inadequate previous service.
    35%    E: The first 7500-mile check-up for a new car.
```

(continued)

Figure 6-4. *continued*

```
6 - Would you recommend Sam's Friendly Auto Repair
        Shop to a friend?

        61%    A: Yes
        39%    B: No
```

Then, beneath each question, the program supplies the percentage of participants who chose a response. For a question, these percentages will add up to 100% (or approximately so, because the program rounds them to the nearest integer). This is the end result of the program, supplying you with the data you need to judge the results of the survey.

Of course, you might want to expand the scope of the *Survey* program to generate more sophisticated statistical analyses of the response data. We'll discuss some possibilities at the end of this chapter. For now, keep in mind that all the raw data from questionnaire responses is available in the *RES* file; you can write routines that work with this data in any way you want.

In summary, the *Survey* program creates four different sequential-access data files for each survey that you generate. These files are identified by their extension names:

- A *SUR* file stores the text of the questionnaire.

- An *ALT* file specifies the length of each question and the number of responses; it also supplies a teaser excerpt from the question for use in the Enter option.

- A *NUM* file gives the title of the survey and the number of questions in the survey.

- A *RES* file stores the responses from the survey. Each time you choose the Enter option, the program appends additional data to the *RES* file.

As we turn now to the listing of the *Survey* program, we'll concentrate on the creation and handling of these four essential files.

INSIDE THE *SURVEY* PROGRAM

The complete program listing appears in Figure 6-5, beginning on page 262. The various definitions and declarations appear at the top of the program listing, followed by the main program section, the error-handling section, and the functions and subprograms listed in alphabetic order. Throughout the program discussion you'll see references to functions and subprograms—these are labeled along the left and right margins of the listing with tabs bearing the function or subprogram name.

The definitions and declarations section

As usual, the first part of the program listing contains a diverse collection of definitions and declarations. First, the program establishes a small set of global constants, along with one user-defined type. The symbolic constants include the logical values *true%* and *false%*. In addition, a value named *tabPos%* sets the screen position that the program uses for the left margin of text:

```
CONST tabPos% = 15
```

The user-defined type *altFileType* handles information that the program will eventually read from *ALT* files. This type has three elements, corresponding to the three fields of information stored in an *ALT* file—the teaser string, the number of question lines, and the number of responses:

```
TYPE altFileType
    teaser AS STRING * 15
    questionLines AS INTEGER
    responseOptions AS INTEGER
END TYPE
```

We'll see exactly how this type is used later in the program.

Next comes the list of DECLARE statements, identifying the program's procedures and their parameters. Following these declarations, a DIM statement sets up a small string array for the program's menu options:

```
DIM mainMenu$(5)
```

A COMMON SHARED statement then establishes a very small group of global variables, several of which are used in error-trapping routines.

Finally, a series of DATA statements contain the text of the menu options. We'll encounter all these variables and data values as we continue examining the program.

The main program section

The main program section begins by storing the menu options in the *mainMenu$()* array. A READ statement reads each option in turn from the DATA statements:

```
FOR i% = 1 TO 5
    READ mainMenu$(i%)
NEXT i%
```

As we'll see, the program sends this array as an argument to the *Menu%* function.

The most important structure of the main program section is the DO...UNTIL loop that controls the action of the recurring menu. Each iteration of the loop performs the following three steps:

1. Display the menu on the screen.

2. Accept the user's menu choice.

3. Call one of the four major subprograms to carry out the choice.

Inside the loop, a SELECT CASE statement efficiently processes each menu choice:

```
SELECT CASE Menu%(mainMenu$())
CASE 1
    Create
CASE 2
    PrSurvey
CASE 3
    Responses
CASE 4
    Analyze
CASE 5
    done% = true%
END SELECT
```

You'll recall from Chapter 2 that the *Menu%* function displays the menu on the screen and returns an integer representing the user's choice. In the *Survey* program, the user's menu choice comes back as an integer from *1* to *5*. Given a value of *1*, *2*, *3*, or *4*, the SELECT CASE statement calls one of the four main subprograms: *Create,* to generate a new survey; *PrSurvey,* to print a working copy of a questionnaire; *Responses,* to record answers received from the survey; or *Analyze,* to prepare and print a report from the survey responses. A value of 5 terminates the DO...UNTIL loop and the program execution.

Notice the three error routines listed in the error-handling section: *MissingFile, NoSurveysFound, and PrinterError.* As we'll see, these routines are designed to handle various problems that can arise during execution of the program. In the sections ahead we'll look at each of the program's major subprograms in turn.

The *Create* subprogram

When the user selects the first menu option, the *Create* subprogram prepares to generate the three disk files that the program requires for storing and describing a new survey. *Create* conducts the input dialog eliciting data and text values to store in these files.

The procedure begins by calling the *Explain* subprogram to display instructions for the input procedure. Then *Create* elicits a filename for the new survey:

```
INPUT " -> ", fileName$
```

If the user enters a filename that includes an extension (despite instructions to the contrary), *Create* must eliminate the extension:

```
dotPos% = INSTR(fileName$, ".")
IF dotPos% <> 0 THEN fileName$ = LEFT$(fileName$, dotPos% - 1)
```

The INSTR function looks for a period (".") in the filename. If one exists, the LEFT$ function isolates the base of the filename (that is, all the characters before the period), and an assignment statement stores them back in the original string variable, *fileName$.*

Next the procedure creates filenames (with identifying extensions) for the three sequential data files:

```
surFile$ = fileName$ + ".SUR"
altFile$ = fileName$ + ".ALT"
numFile$ = fileName$ + ".NUM"
```

Given these three names, the following statements create the new files and open them for writing:

```
OPEN surFile$ FOR OUTPUT AS #1
OPEN altFile$ FOR OUTPUT AS #2
OPEN numFile$ FOR OUTPUT AS #3
```

The *Create* subprogram next calls three input routines to elicit data for these newly opened files. First, *GetTitle* is called once to receive the survey title. Then, within a DO...UNTIL loop, *GetQuest* and *GetResp* are called repeatedly to accept the lines of text for a survey question and the corresponding responses. These routines write the data to the open files. Let's examine these operations.

Eliciting survey text: *GetTitle, GetQuest,* and *GetResp*

All three of the routines use the LINE INPUT statement to accept lines of text from the keyboard. For example, here is how the *GetTitle* subprogram receives the title text:

```
LINE INPUT " -> "; title$
```

If the user enters a line of text that contains a comma, the INPUT statement would read the comma as a delimiter between two input values. In contrast, the LINE INPUT statement considers the comma to be part of the input text value. Thanks to LINE INPUT, then, the user has the freedom to punctuate lines of text in any appropriate manner.

After accepting the title string from the keyboard, the *GetTitle* routine writes the value to file #3, the *NUM* file:

```
WRITE #3, title$
```

Recall that the WRITE# statement encloses a text value in quotation marks in the file. Once again the program is allowing for punctuation within the line of text.

To elicit the text of the questions and answers, *Create* calls the *GetQuest* and *GetResp* subprograms from within a loop. The loop continues the input dialog as long as the user wants to enter additional survey questions. At the bottom of the loop, a call to the *YesNo%* function determines whether the program will elicit text for another question. Given an affirmative response to the prompt *Another question?*, *YesNo%* returns a value of true, and the looping continues.

The loop counts the number of questions that the user enters and stores the count in the integer variable *questions%*. The final action in the *Create* subprogram is to write the value of *questions%* to the *NUM* file and then close the file:

```
WRITE #3, questions%
CLOSE #3
```

For each question that the user enters, the *GetQuest* and *GetResp* subprograms write values to both the *SUR* and the *ALT* files. Within a DO…UNTIL loop, *GetQuest* accepts each line of the question and stores the line in the *SUR* file:

```
LINE INPUT ": "; questionText$
    [other program lines]
WRITE #1, questionText$
```

GetQuest uses the counter variable *lineNumber%* to keep track of the number of lines that the user has entered for a question. After receiving the first line, the routine stores the teaser text in the *ALT* file, which is currently open as file #2:

```
IF lineNumber% = 1 THEN
    sample$ = LEFT$(questionText$, 15)
    WRITE #2, sample$
END IF
```

Then, when the user has entered all the lines of text that make up the question, *GetQuest* stores the number of lines in the *ALT* file:

```
WRITE #2, lineNumber%
```

Similarly, the *GetResp* subprogram elicits each response line, stores the line in the *SUR* file and keeps track of the number of responses:

```
LINE INPUT ": "; responseText$
    [other program lines]
WRITE #1, responseText$
responseNumber% = responseNumber% + 1
```

When all the responses have been entered, the routine stores the value of *responseNumber%* in the *ALT* file:

```
WRITE #2, responseNumber%
```

Back in the *Create* subprogram, the following CLOSE statement closes the *SUR* and *ALT* files after the input dialog:

```
CLOSE #1, #2
```

This ends the process of generating a survey. The original three survey files—*SUR*, *ALT*, and *NUM*—are now stored safely on disk, ready for the other operations that the program offers.

The *PrSurvey* subprogram

PrSurvey prints a copy of a questionnaire form and calls two other important procedures: *OpenFiles,* to open the three files describing a survey; and *DoPrint,* to perform the actual printing process. Both of these two subprograms are used elsewhere in the *Survey* program, and are therefore designed to adjust their respective tasks appropriately to the situation at hand.

Opening the survey files: The *OpenFiles%* function

A call to the *OpenFiles%* function takes an argument of *true%* or *false%.* Given an argument of *false%, OpenFiles%* opens the original three survey files, *SUR, ALT,* and *NUM,* for reading. With an argument of *true%, OpenFiles%* also opens the response file, *RES.* The function returns a logical value indicating whether or not the survey files have been successfully opened. This value controls the subsequent action inside the *PrSurvey* procedure:

```
IF OpenFiles%(false%) THEN
```

OpenFiles% stores its incoming logical argument in the parameter variable *all%.* The function begins by eliciting a directory name from the user, then stores the name in the string variable *dirPath$.* Then the FILES command displays a directory of *SUR* files on the screen:

```
ON ERROR GOTO NoSurveysFound
FILES dirPath$ + "*.SUR"
ON ERROR GOTO 0
```

FILES would normally result in a runtime error if no *SUR* files were found in the specified directory. To prevent an interruption of execution, the program instead sends control to the error routine located at *NoSurveysFound* if this error occurs. Looking back at the error-handling section, you'll see that this routine sets the value of the global variable *surveysFound%* to *false%.*

The *OpenFiles%* function continues its action only if *surveysFound%* is true:

```
IF surveysFound% THEN
```

If so, the first task is to elicit a filename from the user:

```
INPUT "Which one do you want to work with"; fileName$
```

OpenFiles% combines the base filename with each of the four extension names, creating four different names. Then the routine makes an attempt to open the appropriate files:

```
ON ERROR GOTO MissingFile
OPEN surFile$ FOR INPUT AS #1
OPEN altFile$ FOR INPUT AS #2
OPEN numFile$ FOR INPUT AS #3
IF all% THEN OPEN resFile$ FOR INPUT AS #4
ON ERROR GOTO 0
```

Depending on the value of *all%*, this code opens either three or four files for reading.

This second ON ERROR GOTO statement sets up an error trap that will be activated if any or all the files are missing. In this event, control of the program branches to the error routine labeled *MissingFile*, also shown in the error-handling section:

```
MissingFile:
    okFile% = false%
RESUME NEXT
```

The global variable *okFile%* is initialized to *true%* before the *OpenFiles%* function tries to open any files. If the value of *okFile%* has been switched to *false%* after the attempt, the condition indicates that the *MissingFile* error routine has been executed. In this case, *OpenFiles%* displays an error message, closes any files that may have been opened and returns control to the calling subprogram:

```
IF NOT okFile% THEN
    PRINT : PRINT
    PRINT "*** This file is not available. ***"
    CLOSE
```

On the other hand, if *OpenFiles%* locates and opens all the necessary files, *PrSurvey* can begin the work of printing the questionnaire. *OpenFiles%* returns a value of true if both *surveysFound%* and *okFile%* are true: *OpenFiles% = surveysFound% AND okFile%*. *PrSurvey* uses this logical value to decide whether or not to proceed. Assuming the survey files have been opened successfully, *PrSurvey* reads two items of information from the *NUM* file: the title of the survey (*title$*) and the number of questions in the survey (*questions%*). Then the routine closes the file:

```
IF OpenFiles%(false%) THEN
    INPUT #3, title$, questions%
    CLOSE #3
```

PrSurvey then calls the *DoPrint* procedure to print the question-naire. A call to *DoPrint* requires three arguments: the title of the current survey, the number of responses received from the survey, and an integer array containing the tallied responses. Because *PrSurvey* calls *DoPrint* simply to print a blank questionnaire, the routine sets up a dummy array to send as the third parameter:

```
REDIM dummyArray%(questions%, 0)
DoPrint title$, 0, dummyArray%()
```

In this case, the second argument value, *0*, instructs *DoPrint* to print a questionnaire form. In another context, we'll see that an integer value greater than *0* results in a survey analysis report.

Printing the survey: The *DoPrint* subprogram

The *DoPrint* subprogram receives its three arguments in the parameter variables *surveyName$*, *surveysReceived%*, and *surveyArray%()*. The routine starts out with a call to the *ReadyPrint* procedure. This routine creates a pause in the flow of the program, giving the user time to prepare the printer for the upcoming operation.

When the user presses the spacebar, *DoPrint* prepares the title strings and attempts to print the title of the survey:

```
ON ERROR GOTO PrinterError
LPRINT TAB(titlePos1%); title1$
ON ERROR GOTO 0
```

The LPRINT command sends information to the printer device that MS-DOS identifies as LPT1. This command can result in a runtime error if the printer is off line, so the *Survey* program contains an error-trapping routine to handle this possibility. The routine is labeled *PrinterError* and is located near the top of the program listing in the error-handling section.

If a printer error occurs, *PrinterError* assigns a value of *true%* to the global variable *printerOff%* and displays an error message on the screen. Subsequently an EXIT SUB statement terminates the execution of the *DoPrint* routine:

```
IF printerOff% THEN EXIT SUB
```

EXIT SUB is not a particularly elegant way to end a procedure; its use is normally not recommended in carefully structured programs. But in this special case, where the program is reacting to a trapped runtime error, EXIT SUB is perhaps the most convenient way to send control out of the routine.

Assuming the printer is switched on, however, *DoPrint* continues its job. A FOR...NEXT loop controls the printing of each question in the survey:

```
FOR i% = 1 TO numQuestions%
```

To print a question, *DoPrint* must read information from both the *ALT* file and the *SUR* file. Here is a summary of the necessary steps:

1. From the *ALT* file (file #2), find out the number of lines in the current question (*questionLines%*).

2. Read *questionLines%* lines from the *SUR* file (file #1) and send each line to the printer.

3. From the *ALT* file again, find out the number of responses for the current question (*numChoices%*).

4. Read *numChoices%* lines from the *SUR* file and send each response to the printer.

Let's look briefly at the details of these steps. Recall that the *ALT* file contains three items of information for each question:

- A 15-character text excerpt from the first line of the question

- The number of lines in the question (*questionLines%*)

- The number of multiple-choice responses for the question (*numChoices%*)

Although the *DoPrint* subprogram only requires the second and third items, the routine must read all three items in order. This is the nature of a sequential file. The following INPUT# statements read the teaser text value and the value for *questionLines%*:

```
INPUT #2, garbage$
INPUT #2, questionLines%
```

As you can see, the text value is stored in a string variable named *garbage$* to indicate that the value is of no use to this routine.

Given *questionLines%*, the number of lines in the current question, the following nested FOR...NEXT loop reads the correct number of lines from the *SUR* file and sends each line to the printer:

```
FOR j% = 1 TO questionLines%
    INPUT #1, questionText$
    IF j% > 1 THEN LPRINT SPACE$(10);
    LPRINT questionText$
    NEXT j%
```

A similar process occurs for reading and printing the responses. The program reads the number of responses, *numChoices%* from the *ALT* file; then a second nested FOR…NEXT loop reads each response from the *SUR* file and sends it to the printer. When the entire survey has been printed, control goes back to the *PrSurvey* subprogram, which closes the *SUR* and *ALT* files:

```
CLOSE #1, #2
```

We'll be looking again at the *DoPrint* routine later, when we discuss the *Analyze* subprogram.

The *Responses* subprogram

The *Responses* subprogram conducts the input dialog for questionnaire responses and appends each group of responses to the *RES* file. To elicit a filename, the routine starts out with a call to the *OpenFiles%* function. Assuming the program successfully opens the survey files (*OpenFiles%* returns a value of true), *Responses* reads the survey title and the number of questions from the *NUM* file:

```
IF OpenFiles%(false%) THEN
    INPUT #3, title$, questions%
```

Then, to record the information stored in the *ALT* file, the routine sets up a dynamic array of records, *altInfo()*:

```
REDIM altInfo(questions%) AS altFileType
```

A FOR…NEXT loop reads the entire *ALT* file into this array and then the routine closes all files:

```
FOR i% = 1 TO questions%
    INPUT #2, altInfo(i%).teaser
    INPUT #2, altInfo(i%).questionLines
    INPUT #2, altInfo(i%).responseOptions
NEXT i%
CLOSE
```

Unlike *DoPrint,* the *Responses* procedure may need to use the *ALT* file data repeatedly, in many successive input dialogs. This is why *Responses* saves the data in the *altInfo()* array.

Responses next displays the survey title on the screen and asks the user to confirm that the correct files have been selected. If the answer is affirmative, the *Responses* subprogram opens the *RES* file in the

APPEND mode as file #1. The name of this file is stored in the global variable *resfile$*:

```
OPEN resFile$ FOR APPEND AS #1
```

Remember that this statement creates the response file if the file does not yet exist, or opens it for an append operation if it does exist.

Now the *Responses* subprogram is ready to start the input dialog. The routine uses the information in the *altInfo()* array to guide the input process. For each question in the survey, the routine must perform these tasks:

1. Display the teaser string (that is, the 15-character excerpt from the question text).

2. Display the correct sequence of single-letter responses as an input prompt.

3. Get one character of input from the keyboard and make sure the input is one of the valid letter responses for the question.

Responses begins this process by displaying the question number along with the teaser element of the *altInfo()* array:

```
PRINT TAB(tabPos%); i%; "- "; altInfo(i%).teaser$; "..."
```

Then, a special input function named *GetLetter$* displays the input prompt and elicits the answer:

```
ans$ = GetLetter$(altInfo(i%).responseOptions)
```

GetLetter$* is designed to accept a valid single-letter response from the keyboard. The function's integer argument value tells *GetLetter$ how many possible responses there are for a question. For example, if the function receives an argument of 5, it displays the following input prompt on the screen:

```
A B C D E->
```

If the user presses any of these five letter keys, the function returns the character as the input answer. (*GetLetter$* rejects any invalid input characters and beeps to alert the typist of the error.)

The *Responses* subprogram stores the result of *GetLetter$* in the variable *ans$*. One by one, each value of *ans$* is stored in the *RES* file (currently open as file #1):

```
PRINT #1, ans$;
```

After each entry in the file (except for the final entry in a line), the program stores a comma as a delimiter:

```
IF i% <> questions% THEN PRINT #1, ", ";
```

Then, at the end of each line in the file, the program sends a carriage return/line feed combination:

```
PRINT #1,
```

As you'll recall, the data in the *RES* file is stored in a table format. The WRITE# statement would be a much less convenient tool for producing this particular result.

When a *RES* file exists for a survey, the *Analyze* subprogram can produce its printed report, supplying a statistical description of the answers received. Let's look at this final routine in the program.

The *Analyze* subprogram

Given a set of open survey files, *Analyze* has two major tasks to perform:

1. For each multiple-choice answer to each question in the survey, tally the total number of participants who selected the answer.

2. Print a survey report in which these tallies are converted to percentages.

This process requires information from all four of the survey files: *SUR* (the text of the questions and answers), *ALT* (the dimensions of the file), *NUM* (the survey title and the number of questions in the file), and *RES* (the recorded responses to the survey). To open all these files at once, the subprogram calls the *OpenFiles%* function:

```
IF OpenFiles%(true%) THEN
```

Recall that an argument of *true%* instructs *OpenFiles%* to open all four survey files, including the *RES* file. The function then returns a value of *true%* if all four files have been successfully opened.

Like the *Responses* routine before it, *Analyze* displays the survey title on the screen and gives the user the opportunity to confirm the file selection. When this is done, *Analyze* sets up a two-dimensional array of integers as a table for tallying the responses:

```
REDIM responseArray%(questions%, 10)
```

The first dimension of *responseArray%()* is the number of questions in the current survey. The second dimension is fixed at 10, the maximum number of responses for any question.

In preparation for the tallying process, *Analyze* creates two other important variables. The integer variable *totalResponses%* will be used to count the total number of questionnaires that are recorded in the *RES* file; this variable is initialized to *0*:

```
totalResponses% = 0
```

A string variable named *range$* receives the range of single-letter responses that the program can expect to find in the *RES* file:

```
range$ = "ABCDEFGHIJ"
```

Ultimately the program will have to convert each letter response, *answer$* into a number from *1* to *10*. Using *range$* and the INSTR function, this is an easy task:

```
ansCode% = INSTR(range$, answer$)
```

For example, if *answer$* contains the letter *D*, this statement will assign a corresponding value of *4* to the integer variable *ansCode%*.

A DO...WHILE loop reads the *RES* file (currently opened as file #4) from beginning to end:

```
DO WHILE NOT EOF(4)
```

Inside this WHILE loop, a nested FOR...NEXT loop reads the answer to each question and performs the necessary letter-to-integer conversion:

```
FOR i% = 1 TO questions%
    INPUT #4, answer$
    ansCode% = INSTR(range$, answer$)
```

The integer *ansCode%* now represents the number of the answer that was selected on the current questionnaire. The following statement increments the corresponding element of the *responseArray%()* table to tally the answer:

```
responseArray%(i%, ansCode%) = responseArray%(i%, ansCode%) + 1
```

After reading an entire line of answers, the subprogram increments the value of *totalResponses%*, the total number of questionnaires received:

```
totalResponses% = totalResponses% + 1
```

Finally, to print the survey report, *Analyze* calls the *DoPrint* subprogram:

```
DoPrint title$, totalResponses%, responseArray%()
```

The three arguments represent the title of the survey, the total number of questionnaires received from the survey, and the table of tallied responses.

As we have seen, the *DoPrint* routine receives the number of questionnaires in the parameter variable *surveysReceived%*, and the table of responses in the array *surveyArray%()*. If *surveysReceived%* is greater than *0*, *DoPrint* displays a message at the top of the report, giving the total number of questionnaires received. Then, before sending each line of answer text to the printer, *DoPrint* converts the corresponding element of the *surveyArray%()* table to a percentage of the total number of questionnaires and prints the value:

```
IF surveysReceived% > 0 THEN
    percent% = CINT((surveyArray%(i%, j%) / surveysReceived%) * 100)
    RSET percentSpace$ = STR(percent%) + "%"
    LPRINT TAB(8); percentSpace$;
```

This is the key to creating the statistical survey report.

Conclusion

We have seen that sequential files are designed to be read item by item from the first value in the file to the last. QuickBASIC supplies a versatile set of commands and functions for performing sequential file input and output operations.

An application program that works with a particular set of data or text values might be designed to create more than one sequential file on disk to describe the data set. QuickBASIC allows a program to open multiple files at once. During a performance, each open file is identified by a file number, and is associated with a memory buffer that temporarily stores data going to and from the file.

The programmer's job is to devise a data-file system that conveniently stores and adequately describes the data set for a particular application. For example, we have seen that the *Survey* program creates four different data files for each survey it generates. We can describe the purposes of these files in the following general terms.

- Storing the text of the survey
- Describing the length of each question
- Describing the length of the survey
- Storing data generated from the survey

Together these four files give the *Survey* program all the information it needs to manage the various survey operations efficiently.

If you are interested in pursuing additional programming projects with the *Survey* application, here are a few suggestions:

1. Create a routine that expands the analysis of responses received from a survey. Specifically, write a subprogram that isolates all those participants who answered a specified question in the same way. Then, within this subgroup of participants, analyze the results of other questions. For example, in the customer-satisfaction survey for Sam's Friendly Auto Repair, we might like to look at the group of customers who came in for routine service (answer *A* of question *5*), and find out how this group first heard about Sam's shop (question *1*).

2. Go one step further with the analysis: Write a routine that looks for participants who answered two or more specified questions in a certain way and examine the characteristics of this subgroup. For example, imagine a survey aimed at characterizing consumers of a particular business software program. We might want to focus on all those participants who are in a certain age group and income level.

3. Think of ways to improve the presentation of the statistical report produced by the Analyze option. One idea is to rearrange the response lines beneath each question in the order of the percentages, from the highest to the lowest. For example, take a look at the following lines to see how the first question from Sam's survey might appear.

```
1 - How did you first hear about Sam's Friendly
    Auto Repair Shop?

45%   D: In the phone book.
30%   A: From a friend.
15%   B: In our newspaper advertisement.
 5%   C: From our radio commercial.
 5%   F: Other.
 0%   E: By passing the shop on the street.
```

To do this you'll need to include a sort routine in the *Survey* program. You can use any one of the three sort procedures included in this book: the QuickSort (Chapter 4), the bubble sort (Chapter 5), or the Shell sort (Chapter 7).

THE *SURVEY* PROGRAM

```
'    SURVEY.BAS
'    The Survey program supplies a number of operations that are useful
'        for a company or organization that conducts surveys or opinion
'        polls. Using the program, you can create a survey consisting
'        of multiple-choice questions. The program will print the survey,
'        conduct an input dialog for recording responses from the survey,
'        and then analyze the resulting file of responses. (The Survey
'        program is written for QuickBASIC 4.0 and 4.5.)

'    ---- Definitions and declarations section.

CONST false% = 0, true% = NOT false%
CONST tabPos% = 15

TYPE altFileType
    teaser AS STRING * 15
    questionLines AS INTEGER
    responseOptions AS INTEGER
END TYPE

DECLARE FUNCTION GetLetter$ (upto%)
DECLARE FUNCTION Menu% (choices$())
DECLARE FUNCTION OpenFiles% (all%)
DECLARE FUNCTION YesNo% (prompt$)
DECLARE SUB Analyze ()
DECLARE SUB Create ()
```

Declarations

Figure 6-5. *The* Survey *program.*

(continued)

Figure 6-5. *continued*

```
DECLARE SUB DisplayMenuBox (choiceList$(), leftCoord%, prompt$, ok$)
DECLARE SUB DoPrint (surveyName$, surveysReceived%, surveyArray%())
DECLARE SUB Explain ()
DECLARE SUB Frame (left%, right%, top%, bottom%)
DECLARE SUB GetQuest ()
DECLARE SUB GetResp ()
DECLARE SUB GetTitle ()
DECLARE SUB Pause ()
DECLARE SUB PrSurvey ()
DECLARE SUB ReadyPrint ()
DECLARE SUB Responses ()

DIM mainMenu$(5)
COMMON SHARED resFile$, okFile%, surveysFound%, printerOff%

DATA create a new survey
DATA print a survey
DATA enter responses to a survey
DATA analyze a set of responses
DATA quit

'    ---- Main program section.

CLS

FOR i% = 1 TO 5
    READ mainMenu$(i%)
NEXT i%

'    ---- Display the recurring menu and accept the user's menu choice.
'         Call the appropriate subprogram in response.

done% = false%

DO
    LOCATE 2, 37: PRINT "Surveys"
    SELECT CASE Menu%(mainMenu$())

    CASE 1
        Create

    CASE 2
        PrSurvey
```

Main program

(continued)

Figure 6-5. *continued*

```
      CASE 3
          Responses

      CASE 4
          Analyze

      CASE ELSE
          done% = true%

      END SELECT
LOOP UNTIL done%

END
```

Error handling

```
'    ---- Error-handling section.

'    ---- MissingFile and NoSurveysFound are designed to handle
'         potential file-handling errors from the OpenFiles% function.

MissingFile:
    okFile% = false%
RESUME NEXT

NoSurveysFound:
    surveysFound% = false%
    PRINT
    PRINT "    *** No surveys found in this directory."
    PRINT
RESUME NEXT

'    ---- PrinterError takes over from the DoPrint subprogram in the event
'         that the printer is turned off or disconnected at the beginning
'         of the routine.

PrinterError:
    printerOff% = true%
    PRINT : PRINT
    PRINT TAB(tabPos%); "*** Printer is not in operation."
    PRINT
    PRINT TAB(tabPos%);
    Pause
RESUME NEXT
```

(continued)

Figure 6-5. *continued*

```
SUB Analyze STATIC                                                          Analyze

'   The Analyze subprogram examines a set of survey responses
'       and determines the selection percentages for each
'       individual answer. Analyze supplies a printed survey
'       form that includes these percentages.

    PRINT : PRINT : PRINT
    PRINT "Analyze the Responses to a Survey"
    PRINT "------- --- --------- -- - ------"
    PRINT : PRINT

'   ---- OpenFiles% opens the target files. Sending an argument
'        of true also opens the name.RES file, which contains
'        the set of responses.

    IF OpenFiles%(true%) THEN
        INPUT #3, title$, questions%
        CLOSE #3

'   ---- Confirm that the user has opened the correct file.

        PRINT : PRINT : PRINT
        PRINT TAB(tabPos%); "Survey title: "; title$
        PRINT
        PRINT TAB(tabPos%);

        IF YesNo("Is this the correct survey?") THEN
            PRINT
            range$ = "ABCDEFGHIJ"
            REDIM responseArray%(questions%, 10)
            totalResponses% = 0

'   ---- Analyze the response data. Go through the entire response
'        file, and tally the occurrences of each response. Store
'        the tally in the array responses%().

            DO WHILE NOT EOF(4)
            FOR i% = 1 TO questions%
                INPUT #4, answer$
                ansCode% = INSTR(range$, answer$)
                responseArray%(i%, ansCode%) = responseArray%(i%, ansCode%) + 1
```

(continued)

Figure 6-5. *continued*

```
                NEXT i%
                totalResponses% = totalResponses% + 1
                LOOP

    '    ---- DoPrint prints the survey form.

                DoPrint title$, totalResponses%, responseArray%()

            END IF
        END IF
        CLS
        CLOSE

    END SUB

    SUB Create STATIC

    '    The Create subprogram conducts the input dialog for a new set of
    '        survey questions. The subprogram creates three different files:
    '
    '        name.SUR    contains the questions
    '        name.ALT    describes the dimensions of the survey
    '        name.NUM    contains the name of the survey and
    '                    the number of questions

    '    ---- Explain the input rules and elicit a filename.

        Explain
        DO
            PRINT TAB(tabPos% + 5); : INPUT " -> ", fileName$
        LOOP UNTIL fileName$ <> ""

    '    ---- Isolate the base of the filename.

        dotPos% = INSTR(fileName$, ".")
        IF dotPos% <> 0 THEN fileName$ = LEFT$(fileName$, dotPos% - 1)

        surFile$ = fileName$ + ".SUR"
        altFile$ = fileName$ + ".ALT"
        numFile$ = fileName$ + ".NUM"
```

Create

(continued)

Figure 6-5. *continued*

```
    OPEN surFile$ FOR OUTPUT AS #1
    OPEN altFile$ FOR OUTPUT AS #2
    OPEN numFile$ FOR OUTPUT AS #3

    CLS
    GetTitle
    questions% = 1

'   ---- Elicit the questions and answers.

    DO
        PRINT TAB(tabPos%); "Question #"; questions%
        PRINT
        GetQuest

        PRINT : PRINT
        PRINT TAB(tabPos%); "Responses to Question #"; questions%
        PRINT
        GetResp

        PRINT
        PRINT TAB(tabPos%);
        continue% = YesNo("Another question?")
        IF continue% THEN questions% = questions% + 1
        CLS
    LOOP UNTIL NOT continue%

    CLOSE #1, #2
    WRITE #3, questions%
    CLOSE #3

END SUB

SUB DisplayMenuBox (choiceList$(), leftCoord%, prompt$, ok$)

'   The DisplayMenuBox subprogram displays the menu choices on the
'       screen, and prepares the prompt string and validation string.
'       This subprogram is called from the Menu% function.

'   ---- Find the number of choices (numChoices%); initialize variables.
```

DisplayMenuBox

(continued)

Figure 6-5. *continued*

```
    numChoices% = UBOUND(choiceList$)
    prompt$ = " "
    ok$ = ""
    longChoice% = 0

'   ---- Prepare the prompt string (prompt$) and the string of
'        legal input characters (ok$). Also, find the length of
'        the longest choice string (longChoice%).

    FOR i% = 1 TO numChoices%
        first$ = UCASE$(LEFT$(choiceList$(i%), 1))
        ok$ = ok$ + first$
        prompt$ = prompt$ + first$ + "  "
        longTemp% = LEN(choiceList$(i%))
        IF longTemp% > longChoice% THEN longChoice% = longTemp%
    NEXT i%

    longChoice% = longChoice% + 1
    prompt$ = prompt$ + "-> "

'   ---- Test to see if the prompt string is longer than longChoice%.

    IF LEN(prompt$) >= longChoice% THEN longChoice% = LEN(prompt$) + 1

'   ---- Given longChoice% and numChoices%, determine the dimensions of
'        the menu frame. Draw the frame with the Frame subprogram.

    leftCoord% = 37 - longChoice% \ 2
    rightCoord% = 80 - leftCoord%
    topCoord% = 3
    bottomCoord% = 10 + numChoices%
    Frame leftCoord%, rightCoord%, topCoord%, bottomCoord%

'   ---- Display the menu choices. The first letter of each choice is
'        displayed in uppercase, followed by a parenthesis character.

    FOR i% = 1 TO numChoices%
        LOCATE 6 + i%, leftCoord% + 3
        PRINT UCASE$(LEFT$(choiceList$(i%), 1)) + ")" + MID$(choiceList$(i%), 2)
    NEXT i%
```

(continued)

Figure 6-5. *continued*

```
    LOCATE 4, 38: PRINT "Menu"
    line$ = STRING$(longChoice%, 196)
    LOCATE 5, leftCoord% + 3: PRINT line$
    LOCATE 7 + numChoices%, leftCoord% + 3: PRINT line$

'   ---- Print the input prompt.

    LOCATE 9 + numChoices%, leftCoord% + 3: PRINT prompt$;

END SUB

SUB DoPrint (surveyName$, surveysReceived%, surveyArray%()) STATIC                    DoPrint

'   The DoPrint subprogram prints the survey in two different formats:
'       a blank survey sheet for a customer to fill in, or a survey
'       sheet that contains the calculated percentages from a group
'       of completed surveys. A call to DoPrint takes three arguments:
'       surveyName$ (the title of the survey), surveysReceived%
'       (the number of survey responses received), and surveyArray%
'       (the array of tallied survey responses). If surveysReceived%
'       is 0, DoPrint prints a blank survey sheet.

    percentSpace$ = SPACE$(4)
    ReadyPrint

    title1$ = "Survey: " + surveyName$
    titlePos1% = (80 - LEN(title1$)) / 2
    title2$ = STR$(surveysReceived%) + " Survey Responses Received"
    titlePos2% = (79 - LEN(title2$)) / 2
    printerOff% = false%
    ON ERROR GOTO PrinterError
    LPRINT TAB(titlePos1%); title1$
    ON ERROR GOTO 0
    IF printerOff% THEN EXIT SUB

    IF surveysReceived% > 0 THEN
        LPRINT TAB(titlePos2%); title2$
    ELSE
        LPRINT
    END IF
    LPRINT
    numQuestions% = UBOUND(surveyArray%, 1)
    FOR i% = 1 TO numQuestions%
```

(continued)

Figure 6-5. *continued*

```
'    ---- Print the lines of the question.

         INPUT #2, garbage$
         INPUT #2, questionLines%
         LPRINT i%; "- ";
         FOR j% = 1 TO questionLines%
             INPUT #1, questionText$
             IF j% > 1 THEN LPRINT SPACE$(10);
             LPRINT questionText$
         NEXT j%
         LPRINT


'    ---- Print the responses.

         INPUT #2, numChoices%
         FOR j% = 1 TO numChoices%
             IF surveysReceived% > 0 THEN
                 percent% = CINT((surveyArray%(i%, j%) / surveysReceived%) * 100)
                 RSET percentSpace$ = STR$(percent%) + "%"
                 LPRINT TAB(8); percentSpace$;
             ELSE
                 LPRINT TAB(10); "[ ]";
             END IF
             INPUT #1, choiceText$
             LPRINT TAB(15); CHR$(64 + j%);
             LPRINT ": "; choiceText$
         NEXT j%
         LPRINT : LPRINT
     NEXT i%

END SUB

SUB Explain STATIC

'    The Explain subprogram displays messages on the screen
'        describing the input process for a new survey.

     PRINT : PRINT : PRINT
     PRINT TAB(tabPos%); "Create a new survey."
     PRINT TAB(tabPos%); "------ - --- -------"
     PRINT
     PRINT TAB(tabPos%); "Each question may be from one to four"
     PRINT TAB(tabPos%); "lines long, and you may supply from two"
```

Explain

(continued)

270

Figure 6-5. *continued*

```
    PRINT TAB(tabPos%); "to ten responses per question."
    PRINT

    PRINT TAB(tabPos%); "To complete a question or a group"
    PRINT TAB(tabPos%); "of responses, press the <Enter> key"
    PRINT TAB(tabPos%); "when you see the new input prompt."
    PRINT

    PRINT TAB(tabPos%); "Enter the filename for this survey:"
    PRINT TAB(tabPos%); "(The extension .SUR will automatically"
    PRINT TAB(tabPos%); "be added to the filename.)"
    PRINT

END SUB

SUB Frame (left%, right%, top%, bottom%) STATIC

'   The Frame subprogram draws a rectangular double-line frame on
'       the screen, using "text-graphics" characters from the
'       IBM Extended ASCII character set.

'   ---- Draw the four corners.

    LOCATE top%, left%: PRINT CHR$(201)
    LOCATE top%, right%: PRINT CHR$(187)
    LOCATE bottom%, left%: PRINT CHR$(200);
    LOCATE bottom%, right%: PRINT CHR$(188);

'   ---- Draw the vertical lines.

    FOR vert% = top% + 1 TO bottom% - 1
        LOCATE vert%, left%: PRINT CHR$(186);
        LOCATE vert%, right%: PRINT CHR$(186);
    NEXT vert%

'   ---- Draw the horizontal lines.

    horiz% = right% - left% - 1
    hline$ = STRING$(horiz%, 205)
    LOCATE top%, left% + 1: PRINT hline$
    LOCATE bottom%, left% + 1: PRINT hline$;

END SUB
```

Frame

(continued)

Figure 6-5. *continued*

GetLetter$

```
FUNCTION GetLetter$ (upto%)

'   The GetLetter$ function elicits a single letter (from A to J)
'       for each response of a given question. This function is called
'       by the Responses subprogram, which conducts the input dialog
'       for the "E)nter responses" option.

'   ---- Create the prompt string and the string of legal characters
'       for a given question.

    prompt$ = ""
    legal$ = ""
    FOR i% = 1 TO upto%
        prompt$ = prompt$ + CHR$(64 + i%) + " "
        legal$ = legal$ + CHR$(64 + i%)
    NEXT i%

    PRINT prompt$; "-> ";

'   ---- Elicit the response. The computer beeps if the user enters
'       an invalid response.

    DO
        ans$ = UCASE$(INKEY$)
        ansPos% = INSTR(legal$, ans$)
        IF ansPos% = 0 THEN BEEP
    LOOP UNTIL ans$ <> "" AND ansPos% <> 0

    PRINT ans$
    GetLetter$ = ans$

END FUNCTION
```

GetQuest

```
SUB GetQuest STATIC

'   The GetQuest subprogram elicits a survey question. The question
'       may be from one to four lines long.

    questionText$ = " "
    lineNumber% = 1
    DO
        PRINT "Line #"; LTRIM$(STR$(lineNumber%));
```

(continued)

Figure 6-5. *continued*

```
'     ---- The LINE INPUT command allows the user to enter text that
'          includes commas.

      LINE INPUT ": "; questionText$

'     ---- Store each line of the question in the SUR file, currently
'          open as file #1. Store the first 15 characters of each
'          question in the ALT file, currently open as file #2.

      IF questionText$ <> "" THEN
          WRITE #1, questionText$
          IF lineNumber% = 1 THEN
              sample$ = LEFT$(questionText$, 15)
              WRITE #2, sample$
          END IF
          lineNumber% = lineNumber% + 1

'     ---- Force the user to enter at least one nonblank line for the question.

      ELSEIF lineNumber% = 1 THEN
          questionText$ = " "
      END IF

   LOOP UNTIL questionText$ = "" OR lineNumber% > 4

'     ---- Record the number of lines in the question in the name.ALT file.

   lineNumber% = lineNumber% - 1
   WRITE #2, lineNumber%

END SUB

SUB GetResp STATIC
```

GetResp

```
'   The GetResp subprogram elicits a set of possible responses for a
'        given multiple-choice question. Each question may include up
'        to 10 responses.

   responseText$ = " ": responseNumber% = 1
   DO
       PRINT TAB(10); CHR$(64 + responseNumber%);
       LINE INPUT ": "; responseText$
```

(continued)

Figure 6-5. *continued*

```
'    ---- Save the responses in the SUR file, currently open as file #1.

     IF responseText$ <> "" THEN
        WRITE #1, responseText$
        responseNumber% = responseNumber% + 1

'    ---- Each question must have at least two responses.

     ELSEIF responseNumber% = 1 OR responseNumber% = 2 THEN
        responseText$ = " "
     END IF
  LOOP UNTIL responseText$ = "" OR responseNumber% > 10

'    ---- Save the number of responses in the ALT file, currently
'         open as file #2.

  responseNumber% = responseNumber% - 1
  WRITE #2, responseNumber%

END SUB

SUB GetTitle STATIC

'  The GetTitle subprogram elicits a title for the survey.

  PRINT : PRINT : PRINT
  PRINT TAB(tabPos%); "Enter a title for this survey:"

'    ---- Do not accept an empty string for the title.

  DO
     PRINT TAB(tabPos%);
     LINE INPUT " -> "; title$
  LOOP UNTIL title$ <> ""

'    ---- Store the title string in the NUM file, currently
'         open as file #3.

  WRITE #3, title$

  CLS

END SUB
```

`GetTitle`

(continued)

Figure 6-5. *continued*

```
FUNCTION Menu% (choices$()) STATIC                                           Menu%

'    The Menu% function displays a menu on the screen and elicits
'        a menu choice from the user. Menu% receives a string array
'        (choices$()) containing the menu choices, and returns an
'        integer indicating the user's selection from among those choices.

    listLength% = UBOUND(choices$)
    DisplayMenuBox choices$(), leftMargin%, promptStr$, okStr$

'    ---- Get a menu choice. Validate and verify the choice.

    controlKeys$ = CHR$(13) + CHR$(27)
    DO
        LOCATE , , 1
        charPos% = 0
        DO
            answer$ = UCASE$(INKEY$)
            IF answer$ <> "" THEN
                charPos% = INSTR(okStr$, answer$)
                IF charPos% = 0 THEN BEEP
            END IF
        LOOP UNTIL charPos% > 0

        PRINT answer$
        LOCATE 11 + listLength%, 23, 0
        PRINT "<Enter> to confirm; <Esc> to redo."
        inChoice% = charPos%

        charPos% = 0
        DO
            answer$ = INKEY$
            IF answer$ <> "" THEN
                charPos% = INSTR(controlKeys$, answer$)
                IF charPos% = 0 THEN BEEP
            END IF
        LOOP UNTIL charPos% > 0

        IF charPos% = 1 THEN
            done% = true%
            CLS
```

(continued)

Figure 6-5. *continued*

```
        ELSE
            done% = false%
            LOCATE 11 + listLength%, 23: PRINT SPACE$(35)
            LOCATE 9 + listLength%, leftMargin% + 3 + LEN(promptStr$): PRINT " ";
            LOCATE , POS(0) - 1:
        END IF
    LOOP UNTIL done%

    Menu% = inChoice%

END FUNCTION
```

OpenFiles%

```
FUNCTION OpenFiles% (all%) STATIC

'   The OpenFiles% function begins by displaying the names of the
'       survey files stored in the requested drive and directory or
'       the current directory. Then it elicits the name of a file and
'       tries to open the file. If the attempt is unsuccessful, the
'       function displays an error message and returns a value of false;
'       if successful, OpenFiles% returns a value of true. The logical
'       argument all% determines whether the function will open all four
'       files (SUR, ALT, NUM, and RES) or only the first three.

    PRINT "Where do you want to search for survey files?"
    INPUT "(Press <Enter> to search the current directory.) -> ", dirPath$
    PRINT
    PRINT "Here is the directory of "; UCASE$(dirPath$); "*.SUR:"
    PRINT
    PRINT STRING$(65, "-")
    surveysFound% = true%
    ON ERROR GOTO NoSurveysFound
    FILES dirPath$ + "*.SUR"
    ON ERROR GOTO 0
    PRINT STRING$(65, "-")
    PRINT

    IF surveysFound% THEN
        INPUT "Which one do you want to work with"; fileName$
        fileName$ = dirPath$ + fileName$

        dotPos% = INSTR(fileName$, ".")
        IF dotPos% <> 0 THEN fileName$ = LEFT$(fileName$, dotPos% - 1)
```

(continued)

Figure 6-5. *continued*

```
          surFile$ = fileName$ + ".SUR"
          altFile$ = fileName$ + ".ALT"
          numFile$ = fileName$ + ".NUM"
          resFile$ = fileName$ + ".RES"
          okFile% = true%

'   ---- The error trap sets okFile% to false if the files
'         cannot be found.

          ON ERROR GOTO MissingFile
          OPEN surFile$ FOR INPUT AS #1
          OPEN altFile$ FOR INPUT AS #2
          OPEN numFile$ FOR INPUT AS #3
          IF all% THEN OPEN resFile$ FOR INPUT AS #4
          ON ERROR GOTO 0

          IF NOT okFile% THEN
              PRINT : PRINT
              PRINT "*** This file is not available. ***"
              CLOSE
              PRINT
              Pause
          END IF
          CLS
      ELSE
          PRINT
          Pause
          CLS
      END IF
      OpenFiles% = surveysFound% AND okFile%

END FUNCTION

SUB Pause

    The Pause subprogram pauses until the user presses the spacebar.

    PRINT "Press the spacebar to continue.";
    DO
        ch$ = INKEY$
    LOOP UNTIL ch$ = " "

END SUB
```

(continued)

Figure 6-5. *continued*

PrSurvey

```
SUB PrSurvey

'   The PrSurvey subprogram controls the process of printing a survey.

    PRINT : PRINT : PRINT
    PRINT "Print a Survey"
    PRINT "----- - ------"
    PRINT : PRINT


'   ---- OpenFiles elicits the target filename and opens the
'        necessary files.

    IF OpenFiles%(false%) THEN

'   ---- Get the title of the survey and the number of questions in the
'        survey from the name.NUM file, currently open as file #3.

        INPUT #3, title$, questions%
        CLOSE #3
        REDIM dummyArray%(questions%, 0)

'   ---- DoPrint prints the survey.

        DoPrint title$, 0, dummyArray%()

    END IF

    CLOSE #1, #2
    CLS

END SUB
```

ReadyPrint

```
SUB ReadyPrint STATIC

'   The ReadyPrint subprogram creates a pause in the action while the
'        user prepares the printer. Program execution continues when
'        the user presses the spacebar.

    PRINT : PRINT : PRINT

    PRINT TAB(tabPos%); "Press the spacebar"
    PRINT TAB(tabPos%); "when your printer is"
    PRINT TAB(tabPos%); "ready to operate.";
```

(continued)

Figure 6-5. *continued*

```
    DO
        ch$ = INKEY$
    LOOP UNTIL ch$ = " "

END SUB

SUB Responses STATIC

'   The Responses subprogram conducts the input dialog for the
'       "E)nter responses to a survey" option.

    PRINT : PRINT : PRINT
    PRINT "Enter Responses to a Survey"
    PRINT "----- --------- -- - ------"
    PRINT : PRINT

'   ---- OpenFiles elicits a filename and opens the appropriate files.

    IF OpenFiles%(false%) THEN

'   ---- Get the title from the NUM file and read information from
'        the ALT file.

        INPUT #3, title$, questions%
        REDIM altInfo(questions%) AS altFileType
        FOR i% = 1 TO questions%
            INPUT #2, altInfo(i%).teaser
            INPUT #2, altInfo(i%).questionLines
            INPUT #2, altInfo(i%).responseOptions
        NEXT i%
        CLOSE

'   ---- Make sure this is the file the user wants.

        PRINT : PRINT : PRINT
        PRINT TAB(tabPos%); "Survey title: "; title$
        PRINT
        PRINT TAB(tabPos%);

        IF YesNo("Is this the correct survey?") THEN
            CLS
```

(continued)

Figure 6-5. *continued*

```
'    ---- Store the responses in the name.RES file.

            OPEN resFile$ FOR APPEND AS #1
            DO
                FOR i% = 1 TO questions%
                    PRINT TAB(tabPos%); i%; "- "; altInfo(i%).teaser$; "..."
                    PRINT TAB(tabPos% + 7);
                    ans$ = GetLetter$(altInfo(i%).responseOptions)
                    PRINT #1, ans$;
                    IF i% <> questions% THEN PRINT #1, ", ";
                    PRINT
                NEXT i%

                PRINT #1,
                PRINT
                continue% = YesNo("Another?")
                CLS
            LOOP UNTIL NOT continue%
        ELSE
            CLS
        END IF
    END IF
    CLOSE

END SUB
```

` YesNo% `

```
FUNCTION YesNo% (prompt$)

'   The YesNo% function asks a yes-or-no question and returns
'       a Boolean value indicating the user's response: true meaning
'       yes or false meaning no.

'   ---- Display the question prompt and initialize variables.

    PRINT prompt$; " (Y or N) -> ";
    ans$ = ""
    charPos% = 0

'   ---- Get a single-letter response.

    DO
        LOCATE , , 1
        ans$ = UCASE$(INKEY$)
```

(continued)

Figure 6-5. *continued*

```
      IF ans$ <> "" THEN
          charPos% = INSTR("YN", ans$)
          IF charPos% = 0 THEN BEEP
      END IF
   LOOP UNTIL charPos% > 0

   PRINT ans$

'   ---- Convert the response into a Boolean value.

   YesNo% = (ans$ = "Y")

END FUNCTION
```

CHAPTER **7**

Random-Access Data Files: The *Employee* Program

To continue our discussion of disk-based data files, we now turn our attention to QuickBASIC's built-in facilities for handling *random-access files*. In this chapter we'll see why the random-access file is ideal for database applications that require direct access to individual records of information stored on disk. After reviewing QuickBASIC's random-access file procedures, we'll explore efficient solutions for all the essential database operations: reading records from a file, adding new records, and revising the information stored in existing records. We'll also discuss the new features introduced in QuickBASIC Version 4.0 that make all these operations much simpler than they have ever been before.

Database management is one of the most important general applications for personal computers. Storing structured information on disk and gaining direct access to individual parts of that information are essential activities in business, scientific, and technological fields, and even in personal life. QuickBASIC provides a good programming environment in which to develop customized database applications. The random-access file commands—combined with a few important tools like sorting and searching routines—give QuickBASIC a facility for a broad range of database management tasks.

As an exercise with these language elements, this chapter presents a sample program that builds and maintains a typical database of employee records. Like most database applications, the *Employee* program offers specific features that help the user develop the database and gain access to the information it contains about individual employees. For example, this menu-driven program provides easy steps for accomplishing all of the following:

- Entering new employee records into the database

- Locating a particular employee record by name and displaying it on the screen

- Revising specific information stored in a record

- Marking records for deletion when employees depart

- Printing tables of employee records in a specified order

As you can infer from this list of activities, a *record* is the main organizational unit of a database. In the case of the employee database, each record contains all the relevant information about one employee. Records, in turn, are organized into *fields* of information. For example, the *Employee* program requests several items of information about each new employee: name, social security number, date hired, department, job title, and salary. These items become the fields of an employee record.

A random-access file has some important general characteristics that conform to the requirements of database applications. First, records have a fixed length in a random-access file. Given the specifications of a particular application, a database program supplies an explicit structure for dividing the records of the file into fields of information. Thanks to the fixed-length record structure of a random-access file, records can be read from or written to the file in any order.

At the beginning of this chapter we'll review the commands and functions that create and handle random-access files. These language features allow a program to:

- Open a random-access file and define an operating record structure (OPEN and TYPE)

- Determine the current length of an open file (LOF)

- Read a record from any location in the file (GET#)

- Store a new record at the end of the file or write a revised record at a particular location in the file (PUT#)

- Close a file when the program is finished working with it (CLOSE)

Significantly, QuickBASIC's new user-defined data type is now the most efficient medium for expressing the record structure of a random-access file. We first discussed this compound data structure and the TYPE statement that defines it in Chapter 4. In this chapter we'll see exactly how this structure is supported in QuickBASIC's newly enhanced random-access file procedures.

Along with all these commands and functions, we will build some special routines in this chapter to manage an *index* for the employee database. These routines include a sorting procedure to keep the index alphabetized and a search function to look for particular entries in the sorted index. Through this index, the program can locate any employee record in the database, regardless of the order in which the records are stored.

Before we turn to the *Employee* program, let's review QuickBASIC commands and functions that work with random-access files.

RANDOM-ACCESS FILE HANDLING IN QUICKBASIC

Unlike sequential files, random-access files can be opened for both reading and writing at once. Whether you want to read records from a file, store records in the file, or perform both operations in the same program, the process of opening the file is the same. We'll begin by looking at the syntax of the OPEN statement for random-access files.

The OPEN statement

The OPEN statement takes the following format for opening a random-access file and specifying the file's record length:

```
OPEN "fileName" FOR RANDOM AS #fileNumber LEN = recordLength
```

The filename can be any string value that follows the MS-DOS rules for filenames: a base name of up to eight characters and an optional extension name of up to three characters. You can also precede the filename with drive and path designations.

Because QuickBASIC allows you to open more than one file at a time during execution of a program, a file number is necessary to identify an open file. After OPEN, subsequent program statements will refer to the file by its number. For example, we'll see that GET# and PUT# both work with a particular file that is identified by number.

Finally, you use the LEN clause of the OPEN statement to indicate the record length of the file you are opening. The length is specified in characters (or bytes). As we will see, this number should be equal to the sum of all the field lengths in the file's record structure. If you omit the LEN clause, the default record length is 128 characters.

Here is an example of the OPEN statement, taken from the *Employee* program:

```
OPEN "EMP.DAT" FOR RANDOM AS #1 LEN = LEN(openRecord)
```

This statement opens a random-access file named *EMP.DAT* and assigns it a file number of *1*. In this case, *openRecord* is a record variable that the program has set up to define the structure of the file. We will discuss the role of record variables a little later in this chapter. For now, notice that QuickBASIC's built-in LEN function supplies the total fixed length of all elements in this compound user-defined structure. This new use of the LEN function is available in QuickBASIC 4.0 and 4.5.

EMP.DAT may or may not already exist on disk at the time this OPEN statement is executed. If the file exists, QuickBASIC gets ready to read from it or write to it. If the file does not exist, QuickBASIC creates it, though the file remains empty until you begin writing records into it. As a result of the OPEN statement, QuickBASIC sets aside an area in the computer's memory for storing records of data that are on their way to or from the file. This memory area is called a *buffer*.

As we saw in Chapter 6 and as we can see in the following example, the OPEN statement has a second form, shorter and somewhat more cryptic than the first.

```
OPEN "R", 1, "EMP.DAT", LEN(openRecord)
```

The result of this statement is the same as the first example: The statement opens *EMP.DAT* as a random-access file, with a file number of *1* and a record length equal to the length of the *openRecord* structure. While this shortened form may save you a few keystrokes as you type your program, the first form is clearer and more readable.

One final note about the OPEN statement: QuickBASIC supports file sharing in a *multiuser environment,* such as a network in which two or more computers share a storage device. We'll discuss this option briefly in the next section.

Random-access files in a multiuser environment

If you are writing a database management program for a network environment, you will have to plan for the possibility that more than one user will try to access the same database at once. Unless a program carefully controls this situation, a number of mishaps could occur. For example, one user might be reading a record while another user is writing new data to the same record. In this case, the first user would not be aware that the data on the screen is no longer current. A different problem would come up if two users tried simultaneously to write new data to a record: The validity of the resulting record would be open to question.

QuickBASIC offers two ways to control multiple use of a database. For control at the file level, the OPEN statement has optional *access* and *lock* clauses. The *access* clause specifies whether the current use of the file is for reading, writing, or both. The *lock* clause places restrictions on other uses of the file. For example, the following statement opens the random-access *EMP.DAT* file for reading and at the same time disallows any writing to the file by other users:

```
OPEN "EMP.DAT" FOR RANDOM ACCESS READ LOCK WRITE AS #1
```

For control at the record level, QuickBASIC has the LOCK and UNLOCK statements. The LOCK statement restricts the use of a range of records in a database. The statement's general format is:

```
LOCK #fileNumber, firstRecord TO lastRecord
```

You can also use LOCK to protect one record at a time. For example, the following statement prevents other users from accessing record 12 in file #1 while the program is working with the record:

```
LOCK #1, 12
```

After the current user has completed an operation on record 12, the following statement makes the record available again to others:

```
UNLOCK #1, 12
```

These features are only available in a version of MS-DOS that supports networking (specifically, MS-DOS 3.1 or higher). See the QuickBASIC documentation for further details.

Next we'll see how to use record variables and the TYPE statement to define the structure of a random-access file.

Record structures: The TYPE statement

In previous chapters we have discussed several examples of QuickBASIC's new user-defined type. Specifically, we've seen that the record variable is a convenient compound data structure for handling groups of related values in almost any kind of application. Now we will explore the use of record variables to express the structure of a random-access file.

In Chapter 4, we used the TYPE statement to define the *elements* of a user-defined type. To review briefly, here is the general syntax of the TYPE statement:

```
TYPE userTypeName
    elementName1 AS type
    elementName2 AS type
    elementName3 AS type
    [additional type declarations]
END TYPE
```

The *type* specification for each element can be one of the following reserved words: INTEGER, LONG, SINGLE, DOUBLE, or STRING. Only fixed-length strings are allowed as elements.

Given a particular user-defined type, several statements are available in QuickBASIC to establish record variables belonging to the type. These statements include DIM, REDIM, COMMON, STATIC, and SHARED. For example, the general format for defining a record variable with the DIM statement is:

```
DIM recordName AS userTypeName
```

A record variable can store one data value in each of its elements. The notation for referring to a record element includes both the record variable name and the element name as defined in the original TYPE statement. The two names are separated by a period, as you can see in the general form of the notation:

```
recordName.elementName
```

The purpose of a user-defined type in a database application is to divide the fixed-length record of a random-access file into named fields. For example, here is the record type used for records in the *Employee* program:

```
TYPE empType
    lastName AS STRING * 16
    firstName AS STRING * 10
    ss AS STRING * 11
    hireDate AS STRING * 10
    dept AS STRING * 15
    position AS STRING * 15
    salary AS SINGLE
    salType AS STRING * 1
    depDate AS STRING * 10
END TYPE
```

As you can see, this definition specifies nine different fields, including eight fixed-length strings and one single-precision numeric value. The following DIM statement defines a record variable, *empRec*, as belonging to this type:

```
DIM empRec AS empType
```

In QuickBASIC 4.0 and 4.5, the random-access file commands can use such a variable to refer to the structure of a file.

Previous versions of QuickBASIC offered only the FIELD statement for defining a random-access file's record structure. For compatibility, FIELD is still available in QuickBASIC, but its use is no longer recommended now that user-defined types are available. The FIELD statement establishes a special set of field variables that correspond to a particular structure. If you have worked with random-access files in one of the earlier versions of QuickBASIC, you'll recall having to perform a number of inconvenient operations and conversions in order to work with these field variables.

Specifically, the variables defined in a FIELD statement must always be strings. Working with numeric values in these field variables requires a set of special built-in functions—MKI$, MKL$, MKS$, and MKD$ to produce fixed-length numeric formats; and CVI, CVL, CVS, and CVD to convert these formats back into numbers. Furthermore, values must be assigned to FIELD variables via one of two particular commands—LSET or RSET—in order to maintain the structure of the file.

These special measures are no longer necessary in QuickBASIC. User-defined types and record variables provide a number of distinct advantages over the old FIELD approach. Specifically, the elements of a record variable can belong to any of the elementary data types available in QuickBASIC. Using a record variable, you can write both strings and numeric values directly to a random-access file. In the case of a numeric field, QuickBASIC produces by default the appropriate fixed-length format for storing the value in the file, without the use of any special conversion functions. Finally, you can use standard assignment statements to store values in a record variable; LSET and RSET are not required.

In the sections ahead we'll find that QuickBASIC's GET# and PUT# commands can work directly with record variables to read and write the records of a random-access file. First we'll examine the process of reading a record.

Reading a record from a random-access file

The GET# statement takes the following syntax:

```
GET #fileNumber, recordNumber, variableName
```

The *fileNumber* argument must match the number you originally assigned to the file in the corresponding OPEN statement. The *recordNumber* argument is an integer identifying the position of the record that you want to read from the file. Finally, the *variableName* argument is a predefined record variable in which QuickBASIC will store the fields of the record as a result of the read operation.

After a GET# statement, you can access the field data directly from the elements of the specified record variable. For example, the following statements use a record variable conforming to the *empType* structure defined in the previous section:

```
DIM empRec AS empType
GET #1, 12, empRec
PRINT empRec.lastName, empRec.firstName
```

The GET# statement in this code reads record 12 from the file that is opened as file #1 and stores the data in the record variable named *empRec*. Then the PRINT statement displays two fields of the record on the screen.

Notice how the record variable is used in each step of this reading process:

1. The DIM statement creates the variable and specifies its user-defined type.

2. The GET# statement reads a record into the variable from the file.

3. The program accesses field values directly from the named elements of the record variable.

We'll see further examples of these steps when we examine the *Employee* program.

Determining the length of a random-access file

If a GET# statement attempts to read a record number that is greater than the number of records actually stored in the file, the result will be unpredictable. To avoid this situation, a program often needs a way of determining the number of records stored in a random-access file. QuickBASIC's built-in LOF ("length of file") function is a convenient tool for this purpose.

LOF returns the length, in bytes, of an open file. Dividing this value by the record length yields the number of records in the file. LOF takes one numeric argument, a file number:

```
LOF(fileNumber)
```

For example, consider the following statement:

```
totEmps% = LOF(1) / LEN(empRec)
```

The expression on the right side of the equal sign determines the number of records in file *1*. As you can see, the built-in LEN function supplies the length of the file's record structure. The statement assigns the result to the variable *totEmps%* ("total employees").

If you know how many records are in a random-access file, you can write simple loops to process the records. For example, the following FOR...NEXT loop reads each record in turn from the beginning to the end of the open file, using the calculated value of *totEmps%* to express the range of the loop:

```
FOR i% = 1 TO totEmps%
    GET #1, i%, empRec
    DisplayRec empRec
NEXT i%
```

After reading a record into the variable *empRec*, the loop sends the record to a procedure named *DisplayRec* for further processing. We'll see code similar to this example in the *Employee* program.

In summary, here are the steps for reading records from a random-access file:

1. Create a record variable to represent the file's structure (TYPE and DIM).

2. Open the file and specify a record length that is the same size as the designated record variable (OPEN and LEN).

3. (Optional) Determine the current number of records in the file (LOF).

4. Read a specific record from the file into the record variable (GET#).

5. Use the named elements of the record variable to access particular field values from the file.

QuickBASIC allows you to supply more than one field structure for a random-access file in order to read record values in different ways. For example, imagine a subprogram that needs to read only the first two fields of the employee database, *lastName* and *firstName,* and to print a table of these two fields. The following additional user-defined type accommodates the needs of this particular subprogram:

```
TYPE altType
    fullName AS STRING * 26
    garbage AS STRING * 66
END TYPE
```

The length of the *fullName* element is equal to the sum of the lengths of the first two fields in the employee database. Thus *fullName* contains two items of information: the employee's last name and first name. The *garbage* element is designed to store the remaining characters of a record, which will remain unused in this particular application.

Given this second record structure, the program can create a record variable for an alternate reading of individual records from the file. For example, the following lines create such a variable and use it to display employee names on the screen.

```
DIM altRecord AS altType
OPEN "EMP.DAT" FOR RANDOM AS #1 LEN = LEN(altRecord)
numRecords% = LOF(1) / LEN(altRecord)

FOR i% = 1 TO numRecords%
    GET #1, i%, altRecord
    PRINT altRecord.fullName
NEXT i%

CLOSE #1
```

Keep in mind that this second record structure can coexist with the first. Different parts of the program can use the particular record structure that suits the requirements at hand.

To write records to a random-access file, we use the PUT# command and employ a record variable as the medium for storing the outgoing records. We'll discuss this process in the next section.

Writing a record to a random-access file

The PUT# statement writes a record from a variable to an open random-access file. PUT# takes the following syntax:

```
PUT #fileNumber, recordNumber, variableName
```

As in the GET# statement, the *fileNumber* refers to the number originally assigned to the file by the corresponding OPEN statement. The *recordNumber* parameter is an integer identifying the location where the record will be written. Finally, the *variableName* is the variable containing the record that will be written to the file.

QuickBASIC does not require that every record element receive a value before the record is written to its file. Blank fields will be written to the file as strings of spaces. For example, the following sequence assigns values to four elements of the record variable *empRecord* and then writes the information as the tenth record of the file:

```
DIM empRecord AS empType
OPEN "EMP.DAT" FOR RANDOM AS #1 LEN = LEN(empRecord)
empRecord.lastName = "Smith"
empRecord.firstName = "Robin"
empRecord.hireDate = DATE$
empRecord.position = "Office Mgr"
PUT#1, 10, empRecord
```

In summary, these are the steps for writing a record to an open random-access file:

1. Create a record variable with elements representing the fields of the file (TYPE and DIM).

2. Assign values to the designated elements of the record variable.

3. Write the record to a specific location in the file (PUT#).

You can use this process either to write a completely new record to a file or to revise the contents of a record currently stored in the file. We'll see examples of both procedures in the *Employee* program.

The CLOSE command closes an open file. As we saw in Chapter 6, the command has several different formats. For example, the following statement closes file #1:

```
CLOSE #1
```

When this file has been closed, the program can use the number one to open another file. The file number is associated with a file only as long as the file is open.

The following CLOSE command closes two files, #1 and #3:

```
CLOSE #1, #3
```

Finally, this simplest form closes all open files:

```
CLOSE
```

We've seen how to use the commands and functions designed for handling random-access files in QuickBASIC. Now let's turn our attention to the *Employee* program. We'll begin by examining how the program runs.

A SAMPLE RUN OF THE *EMPLOYEE* PROGRAM

The *Employee* program's recurring menu appears in Figure 7-1. This menu offers four options that deal with individual records in the database and one option that works with the entire database:

- The *Examine an employee's record* option displays a record on the computer screen.

- The *Add a new employee* option conducts an input dialog to request field information for a new employee record. When the dialog is complete, the program writes the record to the file.

- The *Change an employee's record* option allows you to change certain fields of information in an employee's record. Specifically, you can enter new values for the employee's department, job title, and salary.

- The *Record a departure* option modifies the record of an employee who is leaving the company. The departure is recorded in a special way that we will discuss later, but the record is not physically deleted from the file.

- The *Print a list of employees* option prints a table of employee records arranged in alphabetic order. According to your instructions, the program can either include or omit the records of employees who have left the firm.

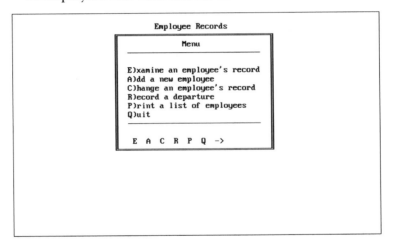

Figure 7-1. *The main menu for the* Employee *program.*

Because the menu reappears on the screen after each individual operation, you can work with as many employee records as you want during a session. The final option in the menu is *Quit*, which ends the program. The *Employee* program carefully completes all required file operations before ending execution.

The data files maintained by the program

Employee creates and maintains two different files on disk. The database is stored in a random-access file named *EMP.DAT*. Each time you add a new record to the database or revise the contents of a record, *Employee* writes the information to this database file. By default, the records in this file are stored in chronological order; that is, each new record that you add to the database is placed at the end of the file.

In addition, *Employee* creates an index file, stored in a sequential file named *EMP.NDX*. During execution of the program, you will see no explicit evidence that this index file exists, but the program would not be able to locate employee records without it. The file contains two items of information for each employee:

1. The employee's name

2. The employee's record-number location in the database

At the beginning of execution, the program reads this index into the computer's memory. While *Employee* is running, the program keeps the index sorted in alphabetic order by the name entries. Each time you add a new record to the database, the program adds the new employee's name and record number to the index and then re-sorts the index. Finally, at the end of execution, the program stores the current index on disk again, where it will be found at the beginning of the next execution.

When you request an option that deals with a record stored in the database, the *Employee* program's first step is to ask you for the employee's name. The program then searches for this name in the alphabetized index. Assuming the name is in the index, the program gets the employee's record number from the index and then reads that record from the database file. This all occurs so quickly that you will not be aware that a search process is taking place.

In short, an employee's name is the key to locating a record in the database. For this reason, the program begins by asking you for a name whenever you choose any of the first four options in the menu.

The *Examine* option

The following is a sample of the dialog that takes place when you choose the *Examine* option.

```
Enter the employee's name:
----- --- ---------- -----


Last name    --> Moltry
First name   --> Robert
```

In response to this input, the program looks for employee *Robert Moltry* in the index to the database, finds the employee's record number, reads the corresponding record from the database, and displays it on the screen for you to examine. Figure 7-2 shows how the record might appear.

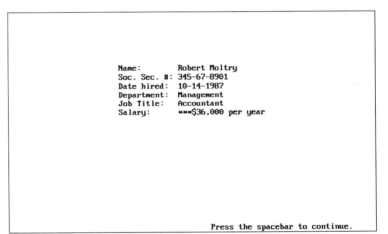

Figure 7-2. *Displaying an employee record.*

If you enter an employee name that does not exist in the index, the *Employee* program displays an appropriate error message:

```
Enter the employee's name:
----- --- ---------- -----


Last name    --> Moltry
First name   --> Richard

This name is not in the employee file.
```

After this message is displayed, the menu reappears on the screen, and you can select the *Examine* option again and try a new name.

The *Add* option

When you select the *Add* option, the *Employee* program requests all the necessary field information for a new employee's record. Here is an example of this dialog:

```
Enter information for new employee
----- ----------- --- --- --------


Last name    --> Breuner
First name   --> Patricia
Soc. Sec. #  --> 765-43-2109
Department   --> Sales
Position     --> Salesperson
Salary       --> 1500
H)ourly,
M)onthly, or
A)nnually    --> M
```

Interestingly, the program asks for only seven items of information, even though we know that the record structure contains nine fields. The two extra fields are dates: the date hired and the date of departure from the firm. By default, the program stores the current system date as the date hired. The date of departure is, of course, left blank until an employee leaves the firm.

Notice how the program asks for the employee's salary. First you enter the salary amount, then the program requests the period of time for which this salary is paid. In response to this prompt you press one of three keys: *H, M,* or *A,* for *hourly, monthly,* or *annually.* When the program later displays a record on the screen, this field is combined with the salary in display lines such as the following:

```
Salary:      ***$11.50 per hour
Salary:      ***$1,750 per month
Salary:      ***$32,000 per year
```

When you have entered all the fields of information that the *Add* option asks you for, the following confirmation question appears on the screen:

```
Save this record? (Y or N) ->
```

This feature gives you the opportunity to examine the field information that you have entered and make sure everything is correct. Press *Y* to confirm that the record should be saved, or if you made a mistake in the input process, press *N* to abandon the record. In the latter case, the program will not write the record to the database file.

The *Add* option cannot allow you to enter a new record under an employee name that already exists in the file. The program's indexing system relies on having distinct names for every employee. For this reason, the program searches through the index as soon as you enter an employee's name in the *Add* option dialog. If the name is found, the program displays this message on the screen:

```
This name is already in the employee file.
```

In the unusual event that two employees have the same first and last names, you would have to create a distinction: For example, include a middle initial, or abbreviate one of the first names.

The *Change* option

The *Change* option begins by asking for the name of the employee whose record you want to revise. Upon locating the employee's record, the program displays a secondary menu on the screen as shown in Figure 7-3. This menu serves two purposes: It displays current information from the employee's file and it allows you to select the field or fields that you want to change. You can enter new values for the employee's department, job title, or salary. In each case, the program conducts a short dialog to accept the new field value or values.

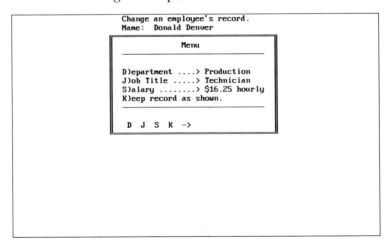

Figure 7-3. *The display for the* Change an employee's record *option.*

For example, if you select the *Salary* option, here is a sample of the ensuing dialog:

```
New Salary      --> 16.25
H)ourly, M)onthly, A)nnually  --> H
```

After you complete this dialog, the *Change* menu reappears on the screen, displaying the new information that you have just entered. When you have made all the necessary changes in the record, you must select the last option in the *Change* menu to save the changes on disk:

```
K)eep record as shown.
```

In response, the *Employee* program will write the new version of the record—with any changes you have made—to the database file.

The *Record* option

The *Record* option modifies a departing employee's record in two ways:

1. The word "DEPARTED" is stored in the department field of the record.

2. The current date is stored in the departure date field.

As always, the procedure first asks you for the employee's name. Then the program displays the employee's record on the screen so that you can be sure that you are modifying the correct record.

Here is an example of the display for a departing employee:

```
Name:        Arthur Hines
Soc. Sec. #: 901-23-4567
Date hired:  04-09-1984
Department:  Personnel
Job Title:   Personnel Mgr.
Salary:      ***$37,500 per year


Is this the employee who is leaving? (Y or N) -> Y

*** The departure has been recorded. ***
```

The program asks you to confirm that the correct employee record has been located for the departure operation. If you respond affirmatively, the program modifies the record, stores the change on disk, and informs you that it is doing so. However, if you answer by pressing *N*, the program takes no action on the record. The following message appears on the screen:

```
No change in this employee's status.
```

The subsequent record display for an employee who has left the company is different from the usual display. For example, here is a display produced by the *Examine* option for a former employee:

```
Name:        Arthur Hines
Soc. Sec. #: 901-23-4567
Date hired:  04-09-1984
Department:  Personnel
Job Title:   Personnel Mgr.
Salary:      ***$37,500 per year

*** No longer an employee ***

Date left:   12-05-1987
```

Notice that the departure date appears at the bottom of the display.

The *Print* option

The *Print* option sends a table of employee records to the printer. The program arranges the table in alphabetic order. When you select this option, the program first asks you the following question:

```
Do you want to include
former employees
in the printed list? (Y or N) ->
```

Depending on your answer, the program prints the entire database or prints only the records for employees who still work for the firm.

Before printing the table, the program gives you a chance to turn on your printer and make sure the paper is positioned properly. This message appears on the screen:

```
Press the spacebar
when the printer is ready.
```

As soon as you press the spacebar, printing begins. Figure 7-4 on the next page shows an example of a printed employee table, including both current employees and former employees. Notice that the program places a double asterisk to the left of the record of any former employee.

```
      Last Name        First      Soc.Sec.#  Job Title      Current Salary
      ---------        -----      ---------  ---------      --------------


      Atkins           Jacqueline 234-56-7890 Vice President  ***$38,000 /yr
      Bradford         Alice       876-54-3210 Artist          ***$13.25 /hr
      Breuner          Patricia    765-43-2109 Salesperson     ***$1,500 /mo
      Carlson          Emmy        890-12-3456 Staff Attorney  ***$45,000 /yr
      Denver           Donald      567-89-0123 Technician      ***$16.25 /hr
   ** Hines            Arthur      901-23-4567 Personnel Mgr   ***$37,500 /yr
   ** Holt             Douglas     543-21-0987 Sales Assistant ***$11.50 /hr
      Jackson          Jaime       876-54-3210 Sales Mgr       ***$2,100 /mo
      Kelly            Lynne       765-43-2109 Advertising Mgr ***$28,000 /yr
      Larson           Richard     678-90-1234 Artist          ***$14.50 /hr
      Manley           Jacqueline  888-99-1111 Editor          ***$37,000 /yr
      Moltry           Robert      345-67-8901 Accountant      ***$36,000 /yr
   ** Oliver           Michael     789-01-2345 Secretary       ****$8.75 /hr
      Quinn            Paris       654-32-1098 Secretary       ***$1,350 /mo
      Wilson           Terry       987-65-4321 Clerk           ****$8.25 /hr
      Young            Sara        123-45-6789 President       ***$45,000 /yr
   ** Zim              Patricia    456-78-9012 Office Manager  ***$1,950 /mo


   ** Former employee.
```

Figure 7-4. *The printed employee table.*

We turn next to the listing of the *Employee* program to examine the various techniques that the program uses for managing the database. This program is a simple example of a database application; however, the techniques illustrated here will also work effectively in programs that perform more sophisticated database operations and deal with more complex record structures.

INSIDE THE *EMPLOYEE* PROGRAM

The complete *Employee* program listing appears in Figure 7-5, which begins on page 318. The various declarations and definitions required by the program appear at the top of the program listing, followed by the main program section, and the functions and subprograms in alphabetic order. Throughout the program discussion you'll see references to functions and subprograms—these are labeled along the right and left margins of the listing with tabs bearing the function or subprogram name. As we examine the listing, we'll concentrate on two aspects of database programming:

1. Using QuickBASIC's random-access file commands

2. Developing a technique for indexing the database

The definitions and declarations section

The first page of the program listing defines a variety of important types, values, and variables. Here is a summary of the definitions and declarations section:

- The CONST statements establish three symbolic constants for the program: the logical values *true%* and *false%* and the integer *tabPos%*, which represents the left-margin position of the program's screen displays.

- Two TYPE statements set up the user-defined types that the program uses. As we have already seen, the first of these is *empType*, the record structure for the main employee file. The second is *indexType*, a structure for the index file. This structure contains two elements representing employee record numbers and names, respectively:

```
TYPE indexType
    empNumber AS INTEGER
    empName AS STRING * 26
END TYPE
```

- The list of DECLARE statements identifies the names and parameters of the program's procedures.

- A DIM statement creates two structures: a record variable, *empRec*, for use in the main program section; and a string array, *empMenu$()*, for storing the menu options.

- A COMMON SHARED statement establishes two global variables: *totEmps%*, which will indicate the total number of records stored in the employee file at any moment; and *index()*, an array of *indexType* records for handling the program's index structure.

- Finally, a group of DATA statements contains the actual text of the menu options.

303

We'll see how all these values and structures are used as we begin exploring the program.

The main program section

The program's main controlling section begins with a FOR...NEXT loop that reads the menu choices into the *empMenu$()* array. Then the program calls the *OpenFile* subprogram to open both the employee database file and the index file. Let's look briefly at this routine.

Opening the *Employee* file and its index

The *OpenFile* routine begins with a DIM statement that creates a record variable named *openRecord*. This local variable will represent the employee record structure during the process of opening the file. (We'll find that each major routine in the *Employee* program creates its own local record variable for handling employee records.)

An OPEN command subsequently opens *EMP.DAT* as a random-access file, assigning the file the number *1* and establishing its record length:

```
DIM openRecord AS empType
OPEN "EMP.DAT" FOR RANDOM AS #1 LEN = LEN(openRecord)
```

As we've seen, the built-in LOF function determines the length of the newly opened file. Dividing this value by the record length supplies the number of records currently in the file:

```
totEmps% = LOF(1) / LEN(openRecord)
```

This is the initial value assigned to the global variable *totEmps%*.

Finally, assuming the database file is not empty, *OpenFile* next calls the *OpenIndex* subprogram to open *EMP.NDX*, the index file:

```
IF totEmps% <> 0 THEN OpenIndex
```

The first task of the *OpenIndex* routine is to establish the initial dimension of the *index()* array. The array will contain one element for every employee record in the file:

```
REDIM index(totEmps%) AS indexType
```

Next, the routine opens the index file. The following OPEN statement prepares to read *EMP.NDX* as a sequential file:

```
OPEN "EMP.NDX" FOR INPUT AS #2
```

Notice that the index receives the file number 2, because there are now two open files. Within a FOR...NEXT loop, an INPUT# statement reads each entry of the index file into the record elements of the *index()* array:

```
FOR i% = 1 TO totEmps%
    INPUT #2, index(i%).empNumber, index(i%).empName
NEXT i%
```

Because the index will be held in memory now until the end of execution, the disk file can be closed:

```
CLOSE #2
```

Back in the main program section, the stage is now set for execution to begin. Let's examine the program's main control structure.

Controlling the program

Within a DO...UNTIL loop, the program calls the *Menu* function repeatedly to display the main menu and to elicit the user's menu choices:

```
DO
    LOCATE 2, 32: PRINT "Employee Records"
    SELECT CASE Menu(empMenu$())
```

For each menu choice that the user supplies, a SELECT CASE structure selects the appropriate subprogram call: *Examine*, to display an individual employee record; *Add*, to add a new record to the file; *Change*, to modify the contents of a record; *Departure*, to record the departure of an employee; and *PrintEmps*, to print a table of records. In all cases except for *Add*, a nested IF statement prevents a subroutine call if *totEmps%* is zero—that is, if the employee database is still empty. For example, here is the call to the *PrintEmps* routine:

```
IF totEmps% <> 0 THEN PrintEmps
```

In effect, only the *Add* option is available until the database contains at least one record.

When the user selects the *Quit* option to terminate execution, the CASE ELSE clause calls the *CloseFiles* routine to close the database files. Finally, to stop the iterations of the DO...UNTIL loop, the program switches the value of the logical variable *done%* to *true%*.

```
CASE ELSE
    CloseFiles
    done% = true%

END SELECT

LOOP UNTIL done%
```

We'll look at each of the program's major subprograms in turn, starting with *Add*.

The *Add* subprogram

As we work through the activities of the *Add* subprogram—and the various other routines that it calls—we'll be able to develop a complete picture of the *Employee* program's indexing system. Specifically, we'll discover exactly how the program builds the database index and how individual entries that go into the index are formatted. We'll also see how the program uses the sorting and searching routines to manage the index.

The routine begins by creating a local record variable named *addRecord* to store the fields of the new employee record. Then the procedure displays a title on the screen and immediately makes a call to the *GetName* subprogram. All the major subprograms in the *Employee* program call *GetName*. The routine is responsible for asking for information for the name fields in the record that is to be added to the database (or, in other contexts, in the record that is to be examined or revised). *GetName* then searches through the database index to see if the name exists in the file. Let's look at the routine.

Eliciting an employee name — The *GetName* subprogram

A call to *GetName* takes three variable arguments, which are always passed by reference. *GetName* subsequently uses its three parameter variables, *empRecord*, *recNo%*, and *target$*, to pass information back to the calling subprogram:

```
SUB GetName (empRecord AS empType, recNo%, target$) STATIC
```

The record variable *empRecord* stores the current employee record. The integer value *recNo%* indicates whether or not the name is in the file:

- A value of *0* indicates that the name is not in the file.

- An integer value greater than *0* is the actual record number of the name.

The string value *target$* is the employee name, specially formatted for the index file. To produce this value, *GetName* begins by asking for the employee's last name and first name and storing the input values in the variables *lastTemp$* and *firstTemp$,* respectively:

```
PRINT TAB(tabPos%); : INPUT "Last name   --> ", lastTemp$
PRINT TAB(tabPos%); : INPUT "First name   --> ", firstTemp$
```

The resulting index entry is a concatenation of these two values with all spaces removed and all letters converted to uppercase. *GetName* uses the program's *RemSpace$* function and QuickBASIC's built-in UCASE$ function to achieve this standardized index format:

```
target$ = UCASE$(RemSpace$(lastTemp$ + firstTemp$))
```

The *RemSpace$* function simply removes all spaces from the string that it receives as an argument.

Let's see what kind of string results from this process. Imagine that the user has entered the following two name fields in response to the input prompts:

```
Last name   --> La Monte
First name   --> Joseph
```

Concatenating these two strings, removing the space, and capitalizing the letters produces the following string:

```
LAMONTEJOSEPH
```

Given the employee name *Joseph La Monte,* this is the standardized string entry that the *GetName* subprogram will search for in the database index. With the string stored in the variable *target$,* the following call to the *Search%* function performs the search:

```
recNo% = Search%(target$)
```

The *Search%* function searches through the *index()* array for the string stored in *target$.* If the string is found, *Search%* returns the corresponding record number from the index element *empNumber.* If the string is not found, the function returns a value of *0.* Let's see how this search is performed.

The *Search%* function

Search% receives the target search string in the variable *whatText$:*

```
FUNCTION Search% (whatText$) STATIC
```

307

Keep in mind that the program always sorts the *index()* array by the employee names. This is the key to the success of the search function.

Search% performs what is known as a *binary search* operation. The function begins by initializing some important variables— *begin%* and *ending%* are markers for the *index()* array, and *located%* is a logical value that will be switched to true when the target record is located:

```
begin% = 1
ending% = totEmps%
located% = false%
```

The routine begins the search process by comparing the target string with the name string located in the middle of the index. This comparison determines if the target name will ultimately be found in the first half or the last half of the list. Then *Search%* compares the name with the string in the middle of the appropriate half. This process continues within a DO...WHILE loop, focusing on a quarter of the list, an eighth of the list, a sixteenth of the list, and so on until the name is located or until the program determines that the name is not in the index.

Inside the DO...WHILE loop, the values *begin%* and *ending%* are constantly adjusted, allowing the routine to focus on progressively smaller portions of the list. The comparisons continue until the target value is found (and the variable *located%* becomes true) or until the value of *ending%* is smaller than the value of *begin%*, meaning that the target value is not in the list:

```
DO WHILE begin% <= ending% AND NOT located%
```

If the target string is located, the routine assigns the corresponding record number to the variable *getNum%*:

```
indexName$ = RTRIM$(index(middle%).empName)
IF whatText$ = indexName$ THEN
    located% = true%
    getNum% = index(middle%).empNumber
```

At the end of the routine, this value is returned as the result of the function:

```
Search% = getNum%
```

As we have seen, the *GetName* procedure stores this return value in the variable *recNo%*.

Eliciting field values

Back in the *Add* subprogram, the variable *inFile%* receives the value of *recNo%*. In the following passage, *Add* uses *inFile%* as a logical variable to determine the next action:

```
IF inFile% THEN
    PRINT
    PRINT TAB(tabPos%) "This name is already in the employee file."
ELSE
    [elicit the rest of the information for the new employee]
```

In other words, if *inFile%* is any number other than *0*—meaning that the input name was located in the database index—the *Add* sub-program will go no further. *Add* cannot allow duplicate names to go into the employee database.

However, if *inFile%* contains a value of *0*, *Add* continues on to ask for information to fill the remaining fields of data for the new employee record. The routine places a series of prompts on the screen and stores the input values in the appropriate elements of the *addRecord* variable. For example, here are the input statements for the social security number, the department name, and the employee's position:

```
PRINT TAB(tabPos%);
INPUT "Soc. Sec. # --> ", addRecord.ss
PRINT TAB(tabPos%);
INPUT "Department  --> ", addRecord.dept
PRINT TAB(tabPos%);
INPUT "Position    --> ", addRecord.position
```

To request values for the salary and the salary type, *Add* employs two special input functions. The *GetSal!* function accepts a valid numeric value for the salary. The *GetSalType$* function accepts one of three letters from the keyboard: *H* for an hourly salary, *M* for a monthly salary, or *A* for an annual salary. The *Add* routine stores these two values in the appropriate record elements:

```
addRecord.salary = GetSal!
addRecord.salType = GetSalType$
```

The program uses the built-in DATE$ function to read the current date from the system calendar. This date is assigned to the *hireDate* element:

```
addRecord.hireDate = DATE$
```

Finally, with all the field values in place for this record, the *Add* subprogram is ready to write the record to the database file. Before doing so, however, the subprogram calls the *YesNo%* function to request confirmation for the operation:

```
IF YesNo("Save this record?") THEN
```

YesNo% requests a yes-or-no response to the question string it receives as an argument. If the user confirms that the record should be saved, *Add* increments the number of records in the database by *1*:

```
totEmps% = totEmps% + 1
```

Then the current record is written to the end of the database file:

```
PUT#1, totEmps%, addRecord
```

As you can see, the current value of *totEmps%* becomes the record number for the new record.

Two tasks remain. The program has to add an entry to the index for this new record and then re-sort the index. These tasks are performed by the *Reindex* subprogram. In a call to the routine, *Add* sends the formatted string value that was originally prepared by the *GetName* subprogram (for example, *"LAMONTEJOSEPH"*). This value is stored in the argument variable *newName$*:

```
Reindex newName$
```

In the next section we'll see how *Reindex* accomplishes its job.

The *Reindex* subprogram

The *Reindex* subprogram proceeds through the following steps:

1. It makes a temporary copy of the *index()* array in an array of *indexType* records called *tempIndex()*.

2. It uses the REDIM statement to establish the new dimension of the *index()* array. (The array will be one element longer than before.)

3. It transfers the temporary copy of the index back into the newly dimensioned *index()* array.

4. It stores the index entry for the new record at the end of the *index()* array.

5. It sorts the index.

The *Reindex* routine must make a temporary copy of the index at the beginning of this process because the original *index()* array will lose all its values when it is redimensioned by the REDIM statement.

The length of the temporary array is established at the beginning of the *Reindex* routine. The global variable *totEmps%* has already been incremented in the *Add* subprogram to represent the new length of the database. The length of the temporary array will be set at one element less than this value:

```
oldTot% = totEmps% - 1
REDIM tempIndex(oldTot%) AS indexType
```

A FOR...NEXT loop copies the index into the temporary array:

```
FOR i% = 1 TO oldTot%
    tempIndex(i%) = index(i%)
NEXT i%
```

Notice that the assignment statement inside this loop copies entire records from *index()* into *tempIndex()*.

Next the actual *index()* array is redimensioned to a length that is one element longer than its previous length to accommodate the new record entry.

```
REDIM index(totEmps%) AS indexType
```

After this statement, all the *empNumber* elements of *index()* will contain values of *0* and all the *empName* elements will be null. Another FOR...NEXT loop copies the index back into this array from the temporary array:

```
FOR i% = 1 TO oldTot%
    index(i%) = tempIndex(i%)
NEXT i%
```

The final element of the *index()* array will be an index entry for the new record. The *empNumber* element receives the record number represented by *totEmps%*:

```
index(totEmps%).empNumber = totEmps%
```

The *empName* element receives the formatted employee name entry that is currently stored in the string parameter variable *empName$*:

```
index(totEmps%).empName = empName$
```

Finally, a call to the *Sort* subprogram rearranges the index in alphabetic order by the employee names. The *Employee* program's *Sort* routine implements a Shell sort. Thanks to this routine, the reindexing process does not slow down the program even if the employee database grows to several thousand records. Let's look briefly at how the Shell sort works.

The Shell sort

This sorting algorithm is named after its developer, Donald Shell. The routine begins by comparing pairs of records that are located relatively far from each other in the array and swapping any pair that is out of order. When all the pairs at one interval are in order, the interval is reduced for the next round of comparisons. This process continues, progressively reducing the interval for each successive round of comparisons. By the time the routine is finally ready to compare consecutive values in the list, the array is nearly sorted.

The *Sort* routine works with index records stored in the *index()* array. The length of this array is given by the global variable *totEmps%*:

```
length% = totEmps%
```

Sort uses the variable *jump%* to represent the interval between pairs of records. A trio of nested loops performs the sort. The inner FOR...NEXT loop compares each pair of records at a *jump%* interval and uses QuickBASIC's SWAP command to switch them if they are out of order:

```
IF index(upper%).empName > index(lower%).empName THEN
    SWAP index(upper%), index(lower%)
```

Notice that the *empName* element is the sorting key.

A middle DO...UNTIL loop repeats these comparisons until all the pairs of records at an interval are in order. The outer DO...WHILE loop carries the process through progressively smaller *jump%* intervals until the final round compares consecutive records in the array.

Now that we've seen how the *Employee* application's indexing system works, let's look at the remaining procedures in the program.

The *Examine* subprogram

Examine is a relatively simple subprogram that displays a record on the screen. It begins by calling *GetName* to elicit the employee name for the desired record:

```
GetName examineRecord, number%, searchName$
```

As we have seen, *GetName* passes back a value of *0* to *number%* if the record is not found in the index. In this case, *Examine* displays an appropriate error message:

```
IF number% = 0 THEN
    PRINT
    PRINT TAB(tabPos%); "This name is not in the employee file."
```

If the record is located, *Examine* reads the entire record from the database file and stores it in the record variable *examineRecord*:

```
ELSE
    CLS
    GET #1, number%, examineRecord
```

After the GET# statement, the program can access the field values from the elements of the *examineRecord* variable. For example, here is how the employee's name is displayed:

```
PRINT TAB(tabPos%) "Name:        ";
PRINT RTRIM$(examineRecord.firstName); " "; examineRecord.lastName
```

Notice the use of the RTRIM$ function to remove the spaces from the end of the *firstName* element. This is necessary because QuickBASIC automatically "pads" fixed-string values with spaces to fill out the defined width of the string.

The *Examine* subprogram uses a SELECT CASE structure to display the salary and the salary type. The structure contains three different PRINT USING commands:

```
SELECT CASE examineRecord.salType
CASE "H"
    PRINT USING "**$###.## per hour"; examineRecord.salary
CASE "M"
    PRINT USING "**$#,#### per month"; examineRecord.salary
CASE ELSE
    PRINT USING "**$#,##### per year"; examineRecord.salary
END SELECT
```

The *Examine* subprogram ends with a special passage that deals with former employees. We've seen that the *Record* option stores the word "DEPARTED" in the record of an employee who leaves the firm. If *Examine* finds this value, the routine displays an appropriate message along with the date of departure.

```
IF LEFT$(examineRecord.dept, 8) = "DEPARTED" THEN
    PRINT
    PRINT TAB(tabPos%) "*** No longer an employee ***"
    PRINT
    PRINT TAB(tabPos%) "Date left:   "; examineRecord.depDate
END IF
```

The *Change* subprogram

The *Change* subprogram is responsible for displaying the secondary menu, which elicits changes for three fields of an employee record: the department, job title, and salary fields.

Like *Add* and *Examine* before it, the *Change* subprogram calls *GetName* to accept the name for the target record. If the name is located, *Change* begins building menu-option strings in the array *chMenu$()*. The first three elements of this array receive prompt strings that include the current values of the three relevant fields. When the menu array is ready, the *Menu%* function is called within a SELECT CASE structure to display the menu on the screen and to process the user's menu choice:

```
SELECT CASE Menu%(chMenu$())
```

The subsequent action depends upon the user's response. The SELECT CASE structure conducts an appropriate input dialog for eliciting each new field value. Thanks to a controlling DO...UNTIL loop, the menu reappears on the screen after each input dialog until the user chooses the fourth option, *Keep record as shown*. When all changes are complete, the *Change* subprogram writes the revised record back to its original location in the database file:

```
PUT #1, num%, changeRecord
```

The *Departure* subprogram

The *Departure* routine is responsible for altering the record of a departing employee. This routine begins by creating the local record variable *departRecord* to store the target employee record. Then the procedure displays the target record on the screen and asks the user to confirm that the record shown is in fact that of the departing employee. The *Departure* subprogram economically calls on the *Examine* routine to display the record:

```
Examine departRecord, which%
```

Examine passes back the target record number in the variable *which%*.

If the user confirms that this is the correct record, the routine stores the word "DEPARTED" in the department field and the current system date in the departure date field:

```
IF YesNo%("Is this the employee who is leaving?") THEN
    departRecord.dept = "DEPARTED"
    departRecord.depDate = DATE$
```

Departure is the only routine in the program that assigns a value to the *depDate* field. (Other routines leave the field blank.) The procedure's next task is to write the revised record back to its original location in the database file:

```
PUT #1, which%, departRecord
```

You will notice that main action of the *Departure* subprogram is structured within a pair of nested IF...THEN...ELSE loops. The outer loop checks to see if the target record already represents a former employee. The inner loop gives the user the opportunity to cancel the record revision.

The *PrintEmps* subprogram

PrintEmps prints a table of records from the employee database. The subprogram starts out by asking the user whether or not former employees should be included in the table. The *YesNo%* function gets the answer to this question and the routine stores the logical result of this function in the variable *former%*:

```
former% = YesNo%(prompt$)
```

A DO...UNTIL loop then creates a pause in the action until the user presses the spacebar:

```
DO
    pr$ = INKEY$
LOOP UNTIL pr$ = " "
```

This gives the user the chance to prepare the printer for the output.

PrintEmps then issues a series of LPRINT statements to send lines of information to the printer, starting with the headings for the table. The records are printed within a FOR...NEXT loop. At the beginning of each loop iteration, a GET# statement reads one record from the database file into this routine's local record variable, *printRecord*.

```
FOR i% = 1 TO totEmps%
    GET #1, index(i%).empNumber, printRecord
```

This loop takes the record numbers one by one from the *empNumber* element of the *index()* array. Because the records are in alphabetic order in the index, the resulting table will also be in alphabetic order.

To determine whether or not to print a record, the program looks to see if the record represents a former employee. The employee's status is stored in the logical variable *gone%*:

```
gone% = (LEFT$(printRecord.dept, 8) = "DEPARTED")
```

The variables *gone%* and *former%* determine whether or not a record will be printed:

```
IF gone% IMP former% THEN
```

This IF statement uses the logical operator IMP to decide on the outcome. If *gone%* is true (meaning that this is a former employee) and *former%* is false (meaning that the user does not want to include former employees in the table), then the IMP expression will result in a value of false. In this case, the record will not be printed. All other logical combinations of *gone%* and *former%* will result in a value of true and the record will be printed.

At the very end of the program's execution, the *CloseFiles* subprogram closes the database file and saves the current index. We'll look at this routine next.

The *CloseFiles* subprogram

CloseFiles begins by closing the database file, which is file #1:

```
CLOSE #1
```

Then, assuming the database file contains at least one record, the routine opens the sequential file *EMP.NDX*, preparing to write the new version of the index to it:

```
OPEN "EMP.NDX" FOR OUTPUT AS #1
```

As a result of this statement, any previous disk version of *EMP.NDX* will be lost. A FOR...NEXT loop writes the current index to the file from the record elements stored in the *index()* array:

```
FOR i% = 1 TO totEmps%
    WRITE #1, index(i%).empNumber, RTRIM$(index(i%).empName)
NEXT i%
```

Finally, the routine closes the index file:

```
CLOSE #1
```

The next execution of the program will find an index file that correctly describes the records stored in the database.

Conclusion

QuickBASIC's random-access file commands provide efficient techniques for building and managing a database file. These commands allow you to open a random-access file, establish its record structure, read records from the file, write new records to the end of the file, and revise records that are currently stored in the file. Teamed with a small library of essential subprograms like *Sort* and *Search*, these commands provide the necessary resources for creating complete database applications.

If you would like to continue working with the *Employee* program, here are a few suggestions for programming exercises:

1. Write an error-handling routine that will take over if the program cannot locate the index file, *EMP.NDX*. (Sometimes computer users inadvertently erase important files. This error routine would restore the use of the database in the case of a lost index.) The routine should open the database file (*EMP.DAT*) and read each record in the file. As the routine progresses through the database, it should store the names and numbers in the *index()* array. After sorting the new index, the *Employee* program can resume as usual.

2. Devise a subprogram that will weed out former employees from the database. One possible approach is to divide *EMP.DAT* into two files: *EMPFORM.DAT* to store records of former employees and *EMPCUR.DAT* to store records of current employees. When the process is complete, the original *EMP.DAT* can be deleted (or renamed as a backup file, *EMP.BAK*), and *EMPCUR.DAT* should be renamed as *EMP.DAT*. You might also develop a separate set of subprograms to give the user access to the database of former employees.

3. Create other indexes to access records in the file. For example, one index might arrange the records by department and by employee names within each department. Each element in the

string array of the index should contain a concatenation of the department name first and then an employee name. Using such an index, the program could produce a table in which employees are listed by department.

4. Write a utility program designed to expand the field structure of the database. For example, such a utility might add fields for the employee's birth date and family status. To implement the new database structure, the utility should begin by creating an entirely new database with the necessary record length and field structure. Then, opening the new database and *EMP.DAT* simultaneously, the program should copy current field information from each record of *EMP.DAT* to the new database. Finally, the process should include an input dialog to elicit the new field values for each employee.

THE *EMPLOYEE* PROGRAM

```
'     EMPLOYEE.BAS
'     The Employee program manages a database of information about
'         a company's employees. The program keeps two files on disk:
'         EMP.DAT is the database itself (a random-access file), and
'         EMP.NDX is an index into the database (a sequential file).
'         (The Employee program is written for QuickBASIC 4.0. and 4.5.)

'     ---- Definitions and declarations section.

CONST false% = 0, true% = NOT false%
CONST tabPos% = 25

TYPE empType
    lastName AS STRING * 16
    firstName AS STRING * 10
    ss AS STRING * 11
    hireDate AS STRING * 10
    dept AS STRING * 15
    position AS STRING * 15
    salary AS SINGLE
    salType AS STRING * 1
    depDate  AS STRING * 10
END TYPE
```

Figure 7-5. *The* Employee *program.*   *(continued)*

Figure 7-5. *continued*

```
TYPE indexType
    empNumber AS INTEGER
    empName AS STRING * 26
END TYPE

DECLARE FUNCTION GetSal! ()
DECLARE FUNCTION GetSalType$ ()
DECLARE FUNCTION Menu% (choices$())
DECLARE FUNCTION RemSpace$ (entry$)
DECLARE FUNCTION Search% (whatText$)
DECLARE FUNCTION YesNo% (prompt$)
DECLARE SUB Add ()
DECLARE SUB Change ()
DECLARE SUB CloseFiles ()
DECLARE SUB Departure ()
DECLARE SUB DisplayMenuBox (choiceList$(), leftCoord%, prompt$, ok$)
DECLARE SUB Examine (examineRecord AS empType, number%)
DECLARE SUB Frame (left%, right%, totabPos%, bottom%)
DECLARE SUB GetName (empRecord AS empType, recNo%, target$)
DECLARE SUB OpenFile ()
DECLARE SUB OpenIndex ()
DECLARE SUB Pause ()
DECLARE SUB PrintEmps ()
DECLARE SUB Reindex (empName$)
DECLARE SUB Sort ()

DIM empRec AS empType, empMenu$(6)

COMMON SHARED totEmps%, index() AS indexType

DATA examine an employee's record
DATA add a new employee
DATA change an employee's record
DATA record a departure
DATA print a list of employees
DATA quit

'    ---- Main program section.

CLS
LOCATE , , 1
```

`Main program`

(continued)

Figure 7-5. *continued*

```
FOR i% = 1 TO 6
    READ empMenu$(i%)
NEXT i%

OpenFile

'   ---- Display the main menu on the screen and call an appropriate
'        subprogram to respond to each menu choice.

done% = false%
DO
    LOCATE 2, 32: PRINT "Employee Records"

    SELECT CASE Menu%(empMenu$())

    CASE 1
        IF totEmps% <> 0 THEN
            Examine empRec, dummy%
            Pause
        END IF

    CASE 2
        Add

    CASE 3
        IF totEmps% <> 0 THEN Change

    CASE 4
        IF totEmps% <> 0 THEN Departure

    CASE 5
        IF totEmps% <> 0 THEN PrintEmps

    CASE ELSE
        CloseFiles
        done% = true%

    END SELECT

LOOP UNTIL done%

END
```

(continued)

Figure 7-5. *continued*

```
SUB Add STATIC                                                         Add

'   The Add subprogram controls the process of adding a
'       new employee to the database.

    DIM addRecord AS empType

    PRINT : PRINT : PRINT : PRINT
    PRINT TAB(tabPos%); "Enter information for new employee"
    PRINT TAB(tabPos%); "----- ----------- --- --- --------"

'   ---- GetName elicits the name of the employee.

    GetName addRecord, inFile%, newName$

'   ---- Do not allow duplicates of the same name.

    IF inFile% THEN
        PRINT
        PRINT TAB(tabPos%); "This name is already in the employee file."
    ELSE

'   ---- Elicit the rest of the information for the new employee.

        PRINT TAB(tabPos%);
        INPUT "Soc. Sec. # --> ", addRecord.ss
        PRINT TAB(tabPos%);
        INPUT "Department  --> ", addRecord.dept
        PRINT TAB(tabPos%);
        INPUT "Position    --> ", addRecord.position
        PRINT TAB(tabPos%);
        addRecord.salary = GetSal!
        PRINT TAB(tabPos%); "H)ourly,"
        PRINT TAB(tabPos%); "M)onthly, or"
        PRINT TAB(tabPos%); "A)nnually   --> ";
        addRecord.salType = GetSalType$
        addRecord.hireDate = DATE$

        PRINT
        PRINT TAB(tabPos%);
```

(continued)

Figure 7-5. *continued*

```
'    ---- Allow the user to abandon the new record for any reason
'         (for example, if an input error has occurred). Otherwise,
'         save the record in the employee file.

      IF YesNo%("Save this record?") THEN
          totEmps% = totEmps% + 1
          PUT #1, totEmps%, addRecord
          Reindex newName$
      END IF
   END IF

   Pause

END SUB

SUB Change

'  The Change subprogram elicits revisions for an employee record.

   DIM changeRecord AS empType, chMenu$(4)

   deptStr$ = "Department ....> "
   jobStr$ = "Job Title .....> "
   salStr$ = "Salary ........> "
   chMenu$(4) = "Keep record as shown."
   PRINT : PRINT : PRINT : PRINT
   PRINT TAB(tabPos%); "Enter the employee's name:"
   PRINT TAB(tabPos%); "----- --- ---------- -----"
   GetName changeRecord, num%, dummy$
   IF num% = 0 THEN
       PRINT
       PRINT TAB(tabPos%); "This name is not in the employee file."
       Pause
   ELSE
       CLS
       GET #1, num%, changeRecord
       changeChoice% = 0
       DO
           PRINT TAB(tabPos%); "Change an employee's record."
           PRINT TAB(tabPos%); "Name: ";
           PRINT RTRIM$(changeRecord.firstName); " "; changeRecord.lastName
           chMenu$(1) = deptStr$ + RTRIM$(changeRecord.dept)
           chMenu$(2) = jobStr$ + RTRIM$(changeRecord.position)
```

Change

(continued)

Figure 7-5. *continued*

```
        SELECT CASE changeRecord.salType

        CASE "H"
            sal$ = " hourly"

        CASE "M"
            sal$ = " monthly"

        CASE ELSE
            sal$ = " annually"

        END SELECT
        sal$ = "$" + LTRIM$(STR$(changeRecord.salary)) + sal$
        chMenu$(3) = salStr$ + sal$
        done% = false%
        SELECT CASE Menu%(chMenu$())

        CASE 1
            PRINT : PRINT : PRINT : PRINT : PRINT TAB(tabPos%);
            INPUT "New department --> ", changeRecord.dept

        CASE 2
            PRINT : PRINT : PRINT : PRINT : PRINT TAB(tabPos%);
            INPUT "New job title --> ", changeRecord.position

        CASE 3
            PRINT : PRINT : PRINT : PRINT : PRINT TAB(tabPos%); "New ";
            changeRecord.salary = GetSal!
            PRINT TAB(tabPos%);
            PRINT "H)ourly, M)onthly, A)nnually --> ";
            changeRecord.salType = GetSalType$
            Pause

        CASE ELSE
            done% = true%

        END SELECT
        CLS
    LOOP UNTIL done%
    PUT #1, num%, changeRecord
    END IF

END SUB
```

(continued)

Figure 7-5. *continued*

CloseFiles

```
SUB CloseFiles STATIC

'   The CloseFiles subprogram closes the database file and
'       saves the current updated index in the file EMP.NDX.

    CLOSE #1

    IF totEmps% > 0 THEN
        OPEN "EMP.NDX" FOR OUTPUT AS #1

        FOR i% = 1 TO totEmps%
            WRITE #1, index(i%).empNumber, RTRIM$(index(i%).empName)
        NEXT i%

        CLOSE #1
    END IF

END SUB
```

Departure

```
SUB Departure STATIC

'   The Departure subprogram revises an employee record to indicate
'       that the employee has left the firm. Specifically, the word
'       "DEPARTED" is stored in the departRecord.dept field, and the
'       depDate field receives the current date.

    DIM departRecord AS empType

    Examine departRecord, which%
    PRINT : PRINT : PRINT TAB(tabPos%);

    IF which% > 0 THEN
        IF LEFT$(departRecord.dept, 8) <> "DEPARTED" THEN
            IF YesNo%("Is this the employee who is leaving?") THEN
                departRecord.dept = "DEPARTED"
                departRecord.depDate = DATE$
                PRINT
                PRINT TAB(tabPos%); "*** The departure has been recorded. ***"
                PUT #1, which%, departRecord
            ELSE
                PRINT
                PRINT TAB(tabPos%); "No change in this employee's status."
            END IF
```

(continued)

Figure 7-5. *continued*

```
        ELSE
            PRINT
            PRINT TAB(tabPos%); "This employee has already left."
        END IF
    END IF

    Pause

END SUB

SUB DisplayMenuBox (choiceList$(), leftCoord%, prompt$, ok$)

'   The DisplayMenuBox subprogram displays the menu choices on the
'       screen and prepares the prompt string and validation string.
'       This routine is called from the Menu% function.

'   ---- Find the number of choices (numChoices%); initialize variables.

    numChoices% = UBOUND(choiceList$)
    prompt$ = " "
    ok$ = ""
    longChoice% = 0

'   ---- Prepare the prompt string (prompt$) and the string of
'       legal input characters (ok$). Also, find the length of
'       the longest choice string (longChoice%).

    FOR i% = 1 TO numChoices%
        first$ = UCASE$(LEFT$(choiceList$(i%), 1))
        ok$ = ok$ + first$
        prompt$ = prompt$ + first$ + "  "
        longTemp% = LEN(choiceList$(i%))
        IF longTemp% > longChoice% THEN longChoice% = longTemp%
    NEXT i%

    longChoice% = longChoice% + 1
    prompt$ = prompt$ + "-> "

'   ---- Test to see if the prompt string is longer than longChoice%.

    IF LEN(prompt$) >= longChoice% THEN longChoice% = LEN(prompt$) + 1
```

(continued)

DisplayMenuBox

Figure 7-5. *continued*

```
'   ---- Given longChoice% and numChoices%, determine the dimensions
'        of the menu frame. Draw the frame, calling on the Frame
'        subprogram.

    leftCoord% = 37 - longChoice% \ 2
    rightCoord% = 80 - leftCoord%
    topCoord% = 3
    bottomCoord% = 10 + numChoices%
    Frame leftCoord%, rightCoord%, topCoord%, bottomCoord%

'   ---- Display the menu choices. The first letter of each choice is
'        displayed in uppercase, followed by a parenthesis character.

    FOR i% = 1 TO numChoices%
        LOCATE 6 + i%, leftCoord% + 3
        PRINT UCASE$(LEFT$(choiceList$(i%), 1)) + ")" + MID$(choiceList$(i%), 2)
    NEXT i%

    LOCATE 4, 38: PRINT "Menu"
    line$ = STRING$(longChoice%, 196)
    LOCATE 5, leftCoord% + 3: PRINT line$
    LOCATE 7 + numChoices%, leftCoord% + 3: PRINT line$

'   ---- Print the input prompt.

    LOCATE 9 + numChoices%, leftCoord% + 3: PRINT prompt$;

END SUB

SUB Examine (examineRecord AS empType, number%) STATIC

'   The Examine subprogram displays a specified employee record
'        on the screen.

    PRINT : PRINT : PRINT : PRINT
    PRINT TAB(tabPos%); "Enter the employee's name:"
    PRINT TAB(tabPos%); "----- --- ---------- -----"
    GetName examineRecord, number%, searchName$
    IF number% = 0 THEN
        PRINT
        PRINT TAB(tabPos%); "This name is not in the employee file."
```

Examine

(continued)

Figure 7-5. *continued*

```
    ELSE
        CLS
        GET #1, number%, examineRecord
        PRINT : PRINT : PRINT
        PRINT : PRINT : PRINT
        PRINT TAB(tabPos%); "Name:          ";
        PRINT RTRIM$(examineRecord.firstName); " "; examineRecord.lastName
        PRINT TAB(tabPos%); "Soc. Sec. #: "; examineRecord.ss
        PRINT TAB(tabPos%); "Date hired: "; examineRecord.hireDate

        IF LEFT$(examineRecord.dept, 8) <> "DEPARTED" THEN
            PRINT TAB(tabPos%); "Department: "; examineRecord.dept
        END IF

        PRINT TAB(tabPos%); "Job Title:   "; examineRecord.position
        PRINT TAB(tabPos%); "Salary:      ";

        SELECT CASE examineRecord.salType
        CASE "H"
            PRINT USING "**$###.## per hour"; examineRecord.salary
        CASE "M"
            PRINT USING "**$#,#### per month"; examineRecord.salary
        CASE ELSE
            PRINT USING "**$#,##### per year"; examineRecord.salary
        END SELECT

'   ---- If the employee no longer works for the firm,
'        supply an extra note in the record display.

        IF LEFT$(examineRecord.dept, 8) = "DEPARTED" THEN
            PRINT
            PRINT TAB(tabPos%); "*** No longer an employee ***"
            PRINT
            PRINT TAB(tabPos%); "Date left:   "; examineRecord.depDate
        END IF
    END IF

END SUB

SUB Frame (left%, right%, top%, bottom%) STATIC

'   The Frame subprogram draws a rectangular double-line frame on
'        the screen, using "text-graphics" characters from the
'        IBM Extended ASCII character set.
```

Frame

(continued)

Figure 7-5. *continued*

```
'    ---- Draw the four corners.

     LOCATE top%, left%: PRINT CHR$(201)
     LOCATE top%, right%: PRINT CHR$(187)
     LOCATE bottom%, left%: PRINT CHR$(200);
     LOCATE bottom%, right%: PRINT CHR$(188);


'    ---- Draw the vertical lines.

     FOR vert% = top% + 1 TO bottom% - 1
         LOCATE vert%, left%: PRINT CHR$(186);
         LOCATE vert%, right%: PRINT CHR$(186);
     NEXT vert%


'    ---- Draw the horizontal lines.

     horiz% = right% - left% - 1
     hline$ = STRING$(horiz%, 205)
     LOCATE top%, left% + 1: PRINT hline$
     LOCATE bottom%, left% + 1: PRINT hline$;

END SUB

SUB GetName (empRecord AS empType, recNo%, target$) STATIC

'    The GetName subprogram elicits the name of the employee
'        that the program will subsequently search for in
'        the database. GetName passes two scalar values back
'        to the caller: recNo% is the record number (or 0, if the
'        record was not found); and target$ is the indexed
'        employee name. In addition, GetName passes back an
'        empRecord structure containing the first name and last
'        name record elements that the user has entered.

     PRINT : PRINT
     PRINT TAB(tabPos%); : INPUT "Last name    --> ", lastTemp$
     PRINT TAB(tabPos%); : INPUT "First name   --> ", firstTemp$
     target$ = UCASE$(RemSpace$(lastTemp$ + firstTemp$))

     IF totEmps% <> 0 THEN
         recNo% = Search%(target$)
     END IF
```

GetName

(continued)

Figure 7-5. *continued*

```
        empRecord.lastName = lastTemp$
        empRecord.firstName = firstTemp$

END SUB

FUNCTION GetSal!

'   The GetSal! function elicits a numeric input value for the current
'       employee's salary. GetSal! initially stores the input value in
'       a string variable and only accepts the value if it can be
'       successfully converted to a nonzero number.

    currentX% = POS(0)
    currentY% = CSRLIN

    DO
        INPUT "Salary        --> ", sal$
        sal = VAL(sal$)
        IF sal = 0 THEN
            LOCATE currentY%, currentX%
            PRINT SPACE$(LEN(sal$) + 16)
            LOCATE currentY%, currentX%
        END IF
    LOOP UNTIL sal > 0

    GetSal! = sal

END FUNCTION

FUNCTION GetSalType$

'   The GetSalType$ function accepts a single-letter keystroke
'       indicating the term of the current employee's salary:
'       hourly (H), monthly (M), or annual (A). The function
'       rejects any invalid keystrokes.

    DO
        LOCATE , , 1
        salaryType$ = UCASE$(INKEY$)
        IF INSTR("HMA", salaryType$) = 0 THEN
            BEEP
            salaryType$ = ""
```

GetSal!

GetSalType$

(continued)

PART II: LANGUAGE TOPICS AND SAMPLE PROGRAMS

Figure 7-5. *continued*

```
        END IF
    LOOP UNTIL LEN(salaryType$) > 0

    PRINT salaryType$

    GetSalType$ = salaryType$

END FUNCTION

FUNCTION Menu% (choices$()) STATIC

'   The Menu% function displays a menu on the screen and
'       elicits a menu choice from the user. Menu% receives a
'       string array (choices$) containing the menu choices
'       and returns an integer indicating the user's
'       selection from among those choices.

    listLength% = UBOUND(choices$)
    DisplayMenuBox choices$(), leftMargin%, promptStr$, okStr$

'   ---- Get a menu choice. Validate and verify the choice.

    controlKeys$ = CHR$(13) + CHR$(27)
    DO
        LOCATE , , 1
        charPos% = 0
        DO
            answer$ = UCASE$(INKEY$)
            IF answer$ <> "" THEN
                charPos% = INSTR(okStr$, answer$)
                IF charPos% = 0 THEN BEEP
            END IF
        LOOP UNTIL charPos% > 0

        PRINT answer$
        LOCATE 11 + listLength%, 23, 0
        PRINT "<Enter> to confirm; <Esc> to redo."
        inChoice% = charPos%

        charPos% = 0
        DO
            answer$ = INKEY$
```

Menu%

(continued)

Figure 7-5. *continued*

```
            IF answer$ <> "" THEN
                charPos% = INSTR(controlKeys$, answer$)
                IF charPos% = 0 THEN BEEP
            END IF
        LOOP UNTIL charPos% > 0

        IF charPos% = 1 THEN
            done% = true%
            CLS
        ELSE
            done% = false%
            LOCATE 11 + listLength%, 23: PRINT SPACE$(35)
            LOCATE 9 + listLength%, leftMargin% + 3 + LEN(promptStr$)
            PRINT " ";
            LOCATE , POS(0) - 1:
        END IF
    LOOP UNTIL done%

    Menu% = inChoice%

END FUNCTION

SUB OpenFile STATIC                                              OpenFile

'   The OpenFile subprogram opens the main database file and establishes
'       its field variables. Note that these variables are declared
'       global in the COMMON SHARED statement at the top of the program.

    DIM openRecord AS empType

    OPEN "EMP.DAT" FOR RANDOM AS #1 LEN = LEN(openRecord)

'   ---- Use the LOF function to calculate the number of records in
'       the employee file.

    totEmps% = LOF(1) / LEN(openRecord)

'   ---- Assuming the database file is not empty, open the index file next.

    IF totEmps% <> 0 THEN OpenIndex

END SUB
```

(continued)

Figure 7-5. *continued*

OpenIndex

```
SUB OpenIndex STATIC

    '   The OpenIndex subprogram opens the index file, named EMP.NDX,
    '       and reads the contents of the file into the index() array.
    '       The record variables empNumber and empName had the
    '       respective employee record numbers and employee names.

    '   ---- Since the size of the index will change each time an
    '       employee is added to the file, use the REDIM statement
    '       to set the current dimension of the index() array.

    REDIM index(totEmps%) AS indexType

    OPEN "EMP.NDX" FOR INPUT AS #2

    FOR i% = 1 TO totEmps%
        INPUT #2, index(i%).empNumber, index(i%).empName
    NEXT i%

    '   ---- Until the end of the current program performance,
    '       the index will be held in memory. Close the index file
    '       for the moment.

    CLOSE #2

END SUB
```

Pause

```
SUB Pause STATIC

    '   The Pause subprogram creates a pause in the action of the program,
    '       so that the user can examine a screenful of information.
    '       The user presses a key to continue the program.

    LOCATE 25, 45, 1
    PRINT "Press the spacebar to continue.";

    DO
        ch$ = INKEY$
    LOOP UNTIL ch$ = " "

    CLS

END SUB
```

(continued)

Figure 7-5. *continued*

```
SUB PrintEmps STATIC                                                    PrintEmps

'   The PrintEmps subprogram prints a table of employees.
'      The subprogram offers the user the option of printing
'      or omitting former employees.

    DIM printRecord AS empType

    PRINT : PRINT : PRINT
    PRINT TAB(tabPos%); "Do you want to include"
    PRINT TAB(tabPos%); "former employees "
    prompt$ = "in the printed list?"
    PRINT TAB(tabPos%);
    former% = YesNo%(prompt$)

    PRINT
    PRINT TAB(tabPos%); "Press the spacebar "
    PRINT TAB(tabPos%); "when the printer is ready. ";

    DO
        pr$ = INKEY$
    LOOP UNTIL pr$ = " "

    LPRINT "   Last Name         First      Soc.Sec.#   Job Title";
    LPRINT "       Current Salary"
    LPRINT "   ---------         -----      ---------   ----------";
    LPRINT "          --------------"
    LPRINT

    FOR i% = 1 TO totEmps%
        GET #1, index(i%).empNumber, printRecord
        gone% = (LEFT$(printRecord.dept, 8) = "DEPARTED")

        IF gone% IMP former% THEN
            IF gone% THEN
                LPRINT "** ";
            ELSE
                LPRINT "   ";
            END IF

            LPRINT printRecord.lastName; " "; printRecord.firstName; " ";
            LPRINT printRecord.ss; " "; printRecord.position;
```

(continued)

Figure 7-5. *continued*

```
                IF printRecord.salType = "H" THEN
                    LPRINT USING " **$###.## /hr"; printRecord.salary
                ELSEIF printRecord.salType = "M" THEN
                    LPRINT USING " **$#.#### /mo"; printRecord.salary
                ELSE
                    LPRINT USING " **$#.##### /yr"; printRecord.salary
                END IF
            END IF
        NEXT i%


        IF former% THEN
            LPRINT : LPRINT : LPRINT
            LPRINT "** Former employee."
        END IF

        Pause

    END SUB


    SUB Reindex (empName$) STATIC

    '   The Reindex subprogram rebuilds the index after each new
    '       employee is added to the database.

    '   ---- Begin by copying the current index into a temporary
    '           index array.

        IF totEmps% > 1 THEN
            oldTot% = totEmps% - 1
            REDIM tempIndex(oldTot%) AS indexType

            FOR i% = 1 TO oldTot%
                tempIndex(i%) = index(i%)
            NEXT i%
        END IF


    '   ---- Now redimension the index() array to the new required
    '           length. (This process also erases all data from the
    '           array, which is why the program has to make a temporary
    '           copy first.)
```

Reindex

(continued)

Figure 7-5. *continued*

```
    REDIM index(totEmps%) AS indexType

'   ---- Finally, copy the index entries back into the index()
'        array, and also store the new entry at the end of the
'        index.

    IF totEmps% > 1 THEN
        FOR i% = 1 TO oldTot%
            index(i%) = tempIndex(i%)
        NEXT i%
    END IF

    index(totEmps%).empNumber = totEmps%
    index(totEmps%).empName = empName$

'   ---- Re-sort the rebuilt index.

    Sort

END SUB

FUNCTION RemSpace$ (entry$)

'   The RemSpace$ function removes all spaces from the string it
'        receives as an argument. RemSpace$ is used to create the
'        name entries for the index and to prepare field items for
'        display on the screen.

    entry$ = LTRIM$(RTRIM$(entry$))
    temp$ = ""
    FOR i% = 1 TO LEN(entry$)
        oneChar$ = MID$(entry$, i%, 1)
        IF oneChar$ <> " " THEN
            temp$ = temp$ + oneChar$
        END IF
    NEXT i%

    RemSpace$ = temp$

END FUNCTION
```

RemSpace$

(continued)

Figure 7-5. *continued*

```
                  FUNCTION Search% (whatText$) STATIC
Search%

                  '   The Search% function performs a binary search operation.
                  '       Specifically, the routine searches for a target text
                  '       value (whatText$) in the empName element of the index() array.
                  '       If the value is located, Search% returns the corresponding
                  '       integer from the empNumber element of the index() array.
                  '       If the value is not located, Search% returns a value of zero.

                      begin% = 1
                      ending% = totEmps%
                      located% = false%
                      getNum% = 0

                      DO WHILE begin% <= ending% AND NOT located%
                          middle% = (begin% + ending%) \ 2
                          indexName$ = RTRIM$(index(middle%).empName)
                          IF whatText$ = indexName$ THEN
                              located% = true%
                              getNum% = index(middle%).empNumber
                          ELSEIF whatText$ > indexName$ THEN
                              begin% = middle% + 1
                          ELSE
                              ending% = middle% - 1
                          END IF
                      LOOP

                      Search% = getNum%

                  END FUNCTION

Sort              SUB Sort STATIC

                  '   The Sort subprogram rearranges the index() array, using the
                  '       empName element of the index() record structure as
                  '       the key to the sort. This subprogram implements the
                  '       Shell sort algorithm.

                      length% = totEmps%
                      jump% = 1
                      DO WHILE jump% <= length%
                          jump% = jump% * 2
                      LOOP
```

(continued)

Figure 7-5. *continued*

```
    DO WHILE jump% > 1
        jump% = (jump% - 1) \ 2
        DO
            finished% = true%
            FOR upper% = 1 TO length% - jump%
                lower% = upper% + jump%
                IF index(upper%).empName > index(lower%).empName THEN
                    SWAP index(upper%), index(lower%)
                    finished% = false%
                END IF
            NEXT upper%
        LOOP UNTIL finished%
    LOOP

END SUB

FUNCTION YesNo% (prompt$)                                              YesNo%

'   The YesNo% function asks a yes-or-no question and returns
'       a logical value indicating the user's response:
'       true meaning yes or false meaning no.

'   ---- Display the question prompt and initialize variables.

    PRINT prompt$; " (Y or N) -> ";
    ans$ = ""
    charPos% = 0

'   ---- Get a single-letter response.

    DO
        LOCATE , , 1
        ans$ = UCASE$(INKEY$)
        IF ans$ <> "" THEN
            charPos% = INSTR("YN", ans$)
            IF charPos% = 0 THEN BEEP
        END IF
    LOOP UNTIL charPos% > 0
    PRINT ans$

'   ---- Convert the response into a logical value.

    YesNo% = (ans$ = "Y")

END FUNCTION
```

Graphics: The *QuickChart* Program

Microsoft QuickBASIC has a rich vocabulary of graphics commands that are versatile and powerful, yet easy to use. Using these commands, a program can create an infinite variety of screen images by combining geometric shapes such as points, lines, rectangles, circles, arcs, and wedges. One useful application for these graphics elements is the production of business charts. In this chapter we'll review QuickBASIC's graphics capabilities and study an example of a complete charting program that converts tables of numbers into a variety of business charts.

In business presentations, tables of numbers tend to be dry, static, and easy to ignore. Charts, on the other hand, are dramatic and attractive—and they command attention. A well-designed chart provides a clear and simple picture of numeric data. The goal of a chart is to communicate facts and ideas that would be difficult to grasp from an equivalent table of numbers. A chart can highlight a variety of meaningful characteristics, including:

- Major statistical trends
- Consistencies and disparities in the data
- Relationships of individual data elements to the whole
- Numeric high points and low points

QuickBASIC provides a good software environment for developing general-purpose charting tools. The program that we'll examine in this chapter, called *QuickChart*, produces three kinds of charts on the computer screen: column charts, line charts, and pie charts. This menu-driven program has the ability to read tables of data for the charts either directly from the keyboard or from specially formatted data files stored on disk. Furthermore, *QuickChart* provides a variety of opportunities for transferring the program's screen displays to the printer, thus producing paper copies of the charts.

Before we begin studying QuickBASIC's graphics commands, let's preview the features of this program.

A FIRST LOOK AT THE *QUICKCHART* PROGRAM

To illustrate the capabilities of the *QuickChart* program, we'll examine some charts that give different views of the same table of numeric data. Specifically, we'll work with data representing the annual net incomes of four small neighborhood grocery stores. Let's imagine that the stores' owner has compiled the income records for a five-year period as follows:

	Store A	Store B	Store C	Store D
1983	34,500	42,750	67,900	75,000
1984	42,000	45,000	75,000	88,000
1985	48,000	53,000	82,000	95,000
1986	53,000	49,000	91,000	107,000
1987	62,000	45,000	99,000	99,000

After entering this data into the *QuickChart* program, the owner can experiment with a variety of chart formats, including the charts appearing in Figures 8-1, 8-2, and 8-3 (on page 342).

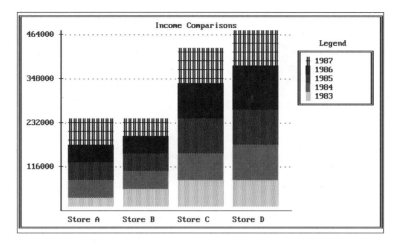

Figure 8-1. *A stacked column chart.*

A stacked column chart (Figure 8-1) compares the income levels of the four stores. Each column in this chart represents the total income of one store during the five-year period. The patterned divisions inside a column represent individual years of income. For example, you can see at a glance that stores *A* and *B* have earned approximately the same total income over the period, even though store *A* had an improved performance during 1987. Stores *C* and *D* earned about twice as much as the first two stores, but store *D* was the top earner for the five-year period.

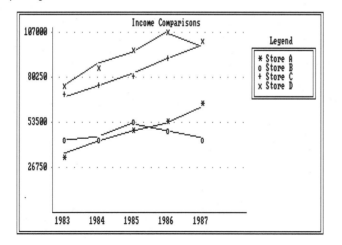

Figure 8-2. *A line chart.*

A line chart (Figure 8-2 on page 341) gives a clearer picture of each store's progress during the five years. For example, the chart shows that stores *A* and *C* both experienced consistent growth during the period, while the earnings of stores *B* and *D* fell at the end of the period. By the way, this line chart plots income as a function of time, an operation that requires a row-to-column transposition of the original data table. An important option in the *QuickChart* program makes such transpositions simple to accomplish.

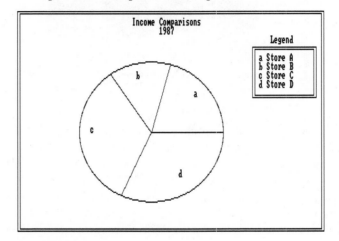

Figure 8-3. *A pie chart.*

Finally, a pie chart (Figure 8-3) focuses on a single year in the five-year period, 1987. The whole pie represents the combined annual income for all four stores, and each wedge in the chart represents one store's contribution to the total. Store *C* has the biggest wedge, and store *B* has the smallest.

Many intricately planned procedures contribute to the creation of these charts. For example, the *QuickChart* program contains special-purpose routines that translate each data value into an individual element of a particular chart type. Other routines produce supporting features such as axes, labels, and legends. In accomplishing these tasks, the program employs a variety of techniques for displaying graphics on the screen. Let's discuss these techniques.

GRAPHICS IN QUICKBASIC

QuickBASIC supports two distinct approaches for producing graphics images on different kinds of display hardware:

- For graphics on a text-only screen, QuickBASIC provides access to the special *text-graphics* characters in the IBM Extended Character Set. (We have worked with some of these characters in previous chapters—for example, the *Twenty-one* program and the *Frame* routine.)

- For graphics on any of the graphics display hardware configurations, QuickBASIC supplies a variety of medium-resolution and high-resolution graphics commands.

In the sections ahead we'll review each of these approaches.

Text graphics

As we have seen, the ASCII code assigns a numeric code value to each character that the computer can display on the screen. The first half of the ASCII code—with code numbers ranging from *0* to *127*—is nearly standard. It includes the letters of the alphabet (uppercase and lowercase), the digits (from *0* to *9*), the punctuation characters, and a few control characters that represent keyboard operations.

The second half of the code—from *128* to *255*—is not standard at all. On IBM personal computers and compatibles, these code numbers are named the IBM Extended Character Set and represent a variety of useful characters, including letters from foreign alphabets, special mathematical and technical symbols, and—what interests us primarily in this chapter—several dozen graphics characters.

Here is a program that displays the Extended Character Set:

```
CLS
rowPos% = 0
colPos% = 1

FOR i% = 127 TO 254
    rowPos% = rowPos% + 1
    LOCATE rowPos%, colPos%
    PRINT i%; " "; CHR$(i%)
    IF rowPos% = 16 THEN
        rowPos% = 0
        colPos% = colPos% + 10
    END IF
NEXT i%
```

In this program, the CHR$ function receives a particular code number as its argument and returns the corresponding ASCII character. The LOCATE command places the screen cursor at a specified row and column position, and the PRINT command displays the character. Figure 8-4 shows the resulting screen.

127	⌂	143	Å	159	ƒ	175	»	191	┐	207	╧	223	▀	239	∩
128	Ç	144	É	160	á	176	░	192	└	208	╨	224	α	240	≡
129	ü	145	æ	161	í	177	▒	193	┴	209	╤	225	ß	241	±
130	é	146	Æ	162	ó	178	▓	194	┬	210	╥	226	Γ	242	≥
131	â	147	ô	163	ú	179	│	195	├	211	╙	227	π	243	≤
132	ä	148	ö	164	ñ	180	┤	196	─	212	╘	228	Σ	244	⌠
133	à	149	ò	165	Ñ	181	╡	197	┼	213	╒	229	σ	245	⌡
134	å	150	û	166	ª	182	╢	198	╞	214	╓	230	µ	246	÷
135	ç	151	ù	167	º	183	╖	199	╟	215	╫	231	τ	247	≈
136	ê	152	ÿ	168	¿	184	╕	200	╚	216	╪	232	Φ	248	°
137	ë	153	Ö	169	⌐	185	╣	201	╔	217	┘	233	Θ	249	·
138	è	154	Ü	170	¬	186	║	202	╩	218	┌	234	Ω	250	·
139	ï	155	¢	171	½	187	╗	203	╦	219	█	235	δ	251	√
140	î	156	£	172	¼	188	╝	204	╠	220	▄	236	∞	252	ⁿ
141	ì	157	¥	173	¡	189	╜	205	═	221	▌	237	φ	253	²
142	Ä	158	₧	174	«	190	╛	206	╬	222	▐	238	ε	254	■

Press any key to continue

Figure 8-4. *The IBM Extended Character Set.*

Given an appropriate selection of characters, a charting program can use the same QuickBASIC procedures—LOCATE, PRINT, and CHR$—to build a stacked column chart on a text-only display screen. A number of the text-graphics characters are ideal for this task.

For example, the *QuickChart* program uses five ASCII characters to build the column chart that appears in Figure 8-1 on page 341. The ASCII characters 176, 177, 178, and 219 supply graduated shades of light and dark blocks, and character 215 is a vertical double-line character with a horizontal cross line. Each character takes up one space on the screen. Carefully juxtaposing many such characters, the *QuickChart* program creates the illusion of high-resolution graphics in any text or graphics display mode.

In the right circumstances you can even create printed copies of a display such as the column chart. If you have a dot-matrix or laser printer along with a graphics display device, you can use two MS-DOS commands—GRAPHICS and GRAFTABL—to prepare your system for "dumping" such displays directly to the printer.

The GRAPHICS command instructs the computer to print screen dumps in a graphics mode rather than a text mode. In addition, GRAFTABL (available in MS-DOS 3.0 and later) loads the upper-ASCII characters into memory for use in graphics display modes. When you have run these two commands, you can press the Shift-PrtSc key combination to print a column chart such as the one in Figure 8-1. In fact, you can use this same approach to print any of the charts produced by the *QuickChart* program. (See the MS-DOS documentation for more information about the GRAPHICS and GRAFTABL commands.)

Unfortunately, this printing technique is not possible if your computer system has a text-only display device or a daisy-wheel printer. Consequently a good charting program should offer alternative *text charts* that can be printed with any hardware configuration. The programming approach for building such a chart is essentially the same as for the text-graphics versions, but the characters for the chart must be selected exclusively from the visible characters in the first half of the ASCII code.

For example, the *QuickChart* program produces printable column charts such as the one shown in Figure 8-5. This version, which uses letters of the alphabet rather than text-graphics characters, is undeniably less attractive than the original; but it can be dumped to any printing device, including a daisy-wheel printer.

```
+--------------------------------------------------------------------+
:                          Income Comparisons                        :
: 464000 +-------------------------------EEEEEEEEEE---                :
:        :                               EEEEEEEEEE        Legend     :
:        :                    EEEEEEEEEE  EEEEEEEEEE   +-----------+  :
:        :                    EEEEEEEEEE  EEEEEEEEEE   : E 1987    :  :
:        :                    EEEEEEEEEE  DDDDDDDDDD   : D 1986    :  :
: 348000 +-------------------EEEEEEEEEE--DDDDDDDDDD---  : C 1985    :  :
:        :                    DDDDDDDDDD  DDDDDDDDDD   : B 1984    :  :
:        :                    DDDDDDDDDD  DDDDDDDDDD   : A 1983    :  :
:        :                    DDDDDDDDDD  DDDDDDDDDD   +-----------+  :
:        :                    DDDDDDDDDD  CCCCCCCCCC                  :
: 232000 +-EEEEEEEEEE--EEEEEEEEEE--CCCCCCCCCC--CCCCCCCCCC---          :
:        : EEEEEEEEEE  EEEEEEEEEE  CCCCCCCCCC  CCCCCCCCCC            :
:        : EEEEEEEEEE  DDDDDDDDDD  CCCCCCCCCC  CCCCCCCCCC            :
:        : DDDDDDDDDD  DDDDDDDDDD  CCCCCCCCCC  BBBBBBBBBB            :
:        : DDDDDDDDDD  CCCCCCCCCC  BBBBBBBBBB  BBBBBBBBBB            :
: 116000 +-CCCCCCCCCC--CCCCCCCCCC--BBBBBBBBBB--BBBBBBBBBB---          :
:        : CCCCCCCCCC  BBBBBBBBBB  BBBBBBBBBB  BBBBBBBBBB            :
:        : BBBBBBBBBB  BBBBBBBBBB  AAAAAAAAAA  AAAAAAAAAA            :
:        : BBBBBBBBBB  AAAAAAAAAA  AAAAAAAAAA  AAAAAAAAAA            :
:        : AAAAAAAAAA  AAAAAAAAAA  AAAAAAAAAA  AAAAAAAAAA            :
:        +-----------------------------------------------            :
:          Store A     Store B     Store C     Store D               :
+--------------------------------------------------------------------+
```

Figure 8-5. *A column chart displayed with text-graphics characters.*

When we examine the listing of the *QuickChart* program, we'll see exactly how the program produces the versions of the column chart. But for now, let's survey the QuickBASIC graphics commands that are available for graphics display systems.

The graphics commands

Many different graphics display adapter boards and color/graphics monitors are available for IBM personal computers and compatibles. For example, an IBM system might include any of the following adapters: the Color Graphics Adapter (CGA); the Enhanced Graphics Adapter (EGA); the Video Graphics Array (VGA); or the Multicolor Graphics Array (MCGA). Adapters such as these, when combined with appropriate monitors, offer various graphics *modes*. Each mode has its own range of screen resolutions and colors.

We usually describe the resolution of a particular graphics mode in terms of *pixels* (*picture elements*). A pixel is the smallest screen element that a program can control in a certain mode. Each mode offers a specific number of horizontal pixel positions across the screen and vertical pixel positions down the screen. QuickBASIC's SCREEN command selects one of the display modes available under a hardware configuration. We'll examine this command in the next section.

The SCREEN command

The simplest form of SCREEN is:

```
SCREEN mode
```

The *mode* parameter is an integer representing the display mode. The default display mode is SCREEN 0, the text-only mode. In a system that has a monochrome monitor and a text-only display card, this is the only mode available.

Other modes yield graphics screens with various resolutions and color ranges. The table at the top of the next page provides a summary of the *mode* options. For more information about graphics modes and the SCREEN command, see the QuickBASIC documentation.

Screen Mode	Hardware Required	Resolution
SCREEN 0	Any display adapter	80 columns by 25 rows
SCREEN 1	CGA, EGA, VGA, or MCGA	320 pixels by 200 pixels
SCREEN 2	CGA, EGA, VGA, or MCGA	640 pixels by 200 pixels
SCREEN 3*	Hercules	720 pixels by 348 pixels
SCREEN 4†	Olivetti	640 pixels by 400 pixels
SCREEN 7	EGA or VGA	320 pixels by 200 pixels
SCREEN 8	EGA or VGA	640 pixels by 200 pixels
SCREEN 9	EGA or VGA	640 pixels by 350 pixels
SCREEN 10	EGA or VGA	640 pixels by 350 pixels
SCREEN 11	VGA or MCGA	640 pixels by 480 pixels
SCREEN 12	VGA	640 pixels by 480 pixels
SCREEN 13	VGA or MCGA	320 pixels by 200 pixels

*Available in QuickBASIC 4.0 and later
†Available in QuickBASIC 4.5

Each pixel in a mode has a *screen address,* which we represent as:

(x, y)

The horizontal coordinate of the address is x and the vertical coordinate is y. By default, the upper-left corner of the screen is the beginning of the coordinate system, with an address of *(0, 0)*. For example, here are the four corner coordinates of SCREEN 2:

upper-left	upper-right
(0, 0)	(639, 0)
lower-left	lower-right
(0, 199)	(639, 199)

Because SCREEN 2 offers the highest resolution (640 by 200) that is universally available for all graphics boards, the *QuickChart* program uses this mode for drawing charts.

Like all the graphics screens, the SCREEN 2 mode allows either graphics display or text display. For text display at specific locations on the graphics screen, a program can use the LOCATE command to position the cursor before printing a character. For creating graphics shapes, QuickBASIC includes commands such as PSET, LINE, and CIRCLE. These commands offer a number of interesting options, which we'll explore in the following sections.

The PSET command

PSET illuminates a single pixel at a specified screen address. The simplest form of the command is:

```
PSET(x, y)
```

For example, the following command illuminates a pixel located approximately at the center of the SCREEN 2 mode graphics screen:

```
PSET(319, 99)
```

Even though PSET works with individual pixels, a program can also use PSET to draw shapes by plotting many pixels at varying screen addresses. For example, the following FOR...NEXT loop draws a horizontal line:

```
FOR i% = 200 TO 400
    PSET(i%, 99)
NEXT i%
```

However, QuickBASIC supplies simpler techniques for drawing regular shapes such as lines and rectangles, as we will discuss in the next section.

The LINE command

The basic form of the LINE command is:

```
LINE (x1, y1)-(x2, y2)
```

The result is a line drawn from the first coordinate address (*x1, y1*) to the second (*x2, y2*). An alternate form is:

```
LINE -(x, y)
```

In this case, QuickBASIC draws a line from the last point drawn on the screen to the address (*x, y*). We'll see that the *QuickChart* program uses this form to draw each segment of a line chart as the program loops through the data set.

An additional feature used by *QuickChart* is the *box* option of the LINE command. The following command draws a box on the screen, using the addresses (*x1, y1*) and (*x2, y2*) as opposite corners of the box:

```
LINE (x1, y1)-(x2, y2), , B
```

In this example, two commas separate the addresses from the *B* option. The second comma represents a missing optional argument, *color*, which normally specifies the color in which the line or box will be drawn. The *QuickChart* program does not use the *color* argument.

LINE takes yet another argument, called the *style* option:

```
LINE (x1, y1)-(x2, y2), , , style
```

Normally LINE draws solid lines across the screen. But with the *style* option, the command produces dotted lines or broken lines instead. This option requires an integer value representing a 16-digit binary number. LINE reads this number as a pattern for plotting the line; specifically, the LINE command plots a point for each binary digit of *1*, but plots no point for a digit of *0*. The resulting line consists of repeated segments that match the pattern of the *style* value.

We usually express the *style* option as a hexadecimal value. The prefix &H denotes a hexadecimal number in QuickBASIC. Here is an example from the *QuickChart* program:

```
FOR y% = 20 TO 140 STEP 40
    LINE (72, y%)-(479, y%), , , &H8000
NEXT y%
```

This loop draws four horizontal lines across the width of a line chart. (The lines mark heights that represent values on the vertical axis.) The hexadecimal number &H8000 is equivalent to the following binary number:

```
1000000000000000
```

Look back at Figure 8-2 on page 341, and you will see the dotted lines that this *style* pattern produces.

By the way, a graphics command can use both *absolute* and *relative* addressing modes. As in all the examples up to this point, an absolute address refers directly to a specific (*x, y*) position on the screen. In contrast, a relative address represents horizontal and vertical offsets from the last point that was referenced on the screen. The reserved word STEP designates a relative address, in this general format:

```
STEP(x, y)
```

For example, the following command draws a diagonal line with an ending point that is 20 pixels to the right and 30 pixels down from its starting point:

```
LINE (20, 20)-STEP(20, 30)
```

Alternatively, the following command uses two absolute addresses to draw the same line:

```
LINE (20, 20)-(40, 50)
```

The CIRCLE command

In its simplest form, the CIRCLE command takes the following syntax:

```
CIRCLE (x, y), r
```

This command draws a circle of radius *r*, with its center at (*x, y*).

Because *QuickChart* represents data values as proportional wedges of a circle, the program uses a somewhat more detailed form of the CIRCLE command:

```
CIRCLE (x, y), r, , start, end
```

In this syntax, the *start* and *end* arguments are angles expressed in *radians;* they represent the starting angle and ending angle of a wedge. (Again, notice the missing *color* argument, represented by the two commas after the radius value.)

Radian values of 0 to 2π are equivalent to angles of 0 to 360 degrees. For example, $\pi/2$ is the same as 90 degrees; π is 180 degrees; and so on. In the CIRCLE command, angles are measured from a line that extends horizontally to the right from the center of the circle.

To make the CIRCLE command draw the radius sides of a wedge (not just the arc), *start* and *end* must be expressed as negative numbers. For example, the following sequence draws the 45-degree wedge from 0 to $\pi/4$:

```
SCREEN 2
pi = 3.141592
CIRCLE (279, 110), 150, , -.00001, -pi/4
```

(To start a wedge at an angle of 0, the *start* argument must supply a very small negative number.) Each wedge in a pie chart is drawn by one execution of the CIRCLE command. Look back at Figure 8-3 on page 342 for an example.

While the PSET, LINE, and CIRCLE commands are easy to use in themselves, the characteristics of the screen's coordinate system can sometimes complicate the task of drawing a particular shape on the screen. QuickBASIC supplies two commands, VIEW and WINDOW, to simplify references to screen addresses. Used together, these two commands alter the coordinate system for addresses on a graphics screen, yielding a new system that matches the requirements of a task. We'll look at these commands in the next section.

The VIEW and WINDOW commands

The VIEW command identifies a rectangular portion of the graphics screen as a *viewport,* or work area. Here is the basic syntax of the command:

```
VIEW (x1, y1)-(x2, y2)
```

The two addresses in the command provide opposite corners of the rectangle that becomes the work area: (*x1, y1*) represents the upper-left corner, and (*x2, y2*) represents the lower-right corner. Within this work area, the WINDOW command assigns a new coordinate system:

```
WINDOW (x1, y1)-(x2, y2)
```

Inside the work area defined by VIEW, the WINDOW coordinate pair of (*x1, y1*) becomes the address of the lower-left corner, and (*x2, y2*) becomes the address of the upper-right corner.

For example, consider the following statements:

```
VIEW (80, 20)-(480, 180)
WINDOW (0, 0)-(50, 20)
```

The VIEW command in this sequence establishes a 400-pixel by 160-pixel rectangle as the work area. The WINDOW command then assigns a new coordinate system to this rectangle. Here are the corner coordinates of the work area after the WINDOW command:

upper-left	upper-right
(0, 20)	(50, 20)
lower-left	lower-right
(0, 0)	(50, 0)

As you can see, the *origin (0, 0)* of the new coordinate system is located at the lower-left corner of the work area. Given this new system, the following LINE commands produce, in effect, a vertical y-axis, a horizontal x-axis, and a diagonal line inside the quadrant represented by the work area:

```
LINE (0, 0)-(0, 20)      ' A vertical line
LINE (0, 0)-(50, 0)      ' A horizontal line
LINE (10, 4)-(40, 15)    ' A diagonal line
```

The significance of VIEW and WINDOW is clear: Using these two commands, a charting program can avoid all the messy arithmetic that would otherwise be necessary to convert the default SCREEN 2 coordinate system into appropriate addresses for a chart area.

QuickBASIC supplies several other graphics commands that you can read about in Microsoft's documentation for the product. These include the DRAW command for producing irregular graphics shapes and the COLOR and PALETTE commands for selecting colors. However, the six commands that we have discussed—SCREEN, PSET, LINE, CIRCLE, VIEW, and WINDOW—are the tools that the *QuickChart* program requires for producing its graphics screens. Let's turn back to the program now and examine its features in greater detail.

USING THE *QUICKCHART* PROGRAM

To present its various charting options, *QuickChart* displays a recurring main menu on the screen. The specific hardware configuration of your computer system determines the number of options that this menu offers. If you have a graphics adapter board installed inside your computer and an appropriate color display device attached to it, you can work with all three of the program's chart types. But if your display adapter board is designed to display only text characters on a monochrome monitor, you are limited to column charts.

Accordingly, the *QuickChart* program begins execution by checking the hardware environment in which it is running. Figure 8-6 shows

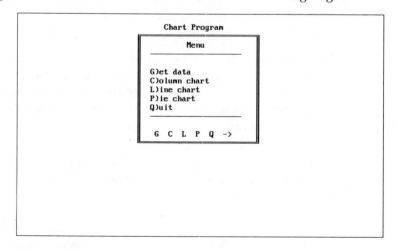

Figure 8-6. *The main menu for systems with graphics display hardware.*

the menu that the program presents if you are working on a system with graphics display hardware. On a text-only system, however, this menu does not offer the Line chart or Pie chart options.

The main menu's Get data option displays a second menu, shown in Figure 8-7. Get data is normally the first option you select when you run *QuickChart*, because the program cannot create a chart until you give it a set of data to work with. (An attempt to invoke one of the chart options before the program has read any data results in no action.) The second menu offers a variety of choices for entering data into the program. Let's examine these options before we look at the main menu.

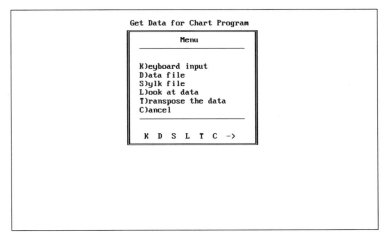

Figure 8-7. *The Get data menu.*

The Get data menu

One way to supply new data to the *QuickChart* program is to select the Keyboard input option and then enter the data directly from the keyboard. The program conducts an input dialog to accept your data. After you have entered an entire table of data, the program gives you the option of saving the table on disk as a data file. Thanks to this feature, you never have to key in the same data table twice. You can specify any disk location and filename you want to store the data.

The program can work with any number of different data tables, but only one table stays in memory at a time. When the program reads a new table, any previous data is lost. Fortunately, the *Data file* option reads a previously created data file back into memory so that the program can work with it again. When you select this option, the *QuickChart* program asks you for the name of the file you want to read and then reads the file into memory. The data file must conform to the format that *QuickChart* recognizes. In other words, it must be either a file that the program has created or a similarly formatted file that you have created in another editing environment.

Alternatively, the Sylk file option in the Get data menu reads data files conforming to a completely different format. SYLK, which stands for *Symbolic Link,* is a Microsoft data-file format designed for sharing data among different application programs. For example, you can create a table of data on a Microsoft Multiplan worksheet, instruct Multiplan to save the worksheet in the SYLK file format, and then run the *QuickChart* program to create charts from the data.

The fourth option in the Get data menu, Look at data, lets you examine the data table that is currently in memory. No matter which method you use to read the data into the program, this option displays the data on the screen in table form.

Finally, the Transpose the data option reorganizes the shape of the current data table. The previous data rows become columns in the new table, and columns become rows. As we discussed earlier, this important operation lets you control the way the program organizes a chart created from the data table. We'll see another example of the transpose operation later in the chapter.

To escape from the Get data menu without performing any of its first five options, choose Cancel. This returns you immediately to the program's main menu.

When you have given the program a table of data to work with, you can choose chart options from the main menu.

The main menu options

The main menu comes back onto the screen after each activity you perform. Using this recurring menu, you can produce as many charts as you want for a data table. Alternatively, you can choose the Get data option at any time to read a new data table into the program.

The Column chart and Line chart options immediately display the specified chart, which is derived from the data table that is currently stored in memory. The Pie chart option requires you to select a single column of data from which the program subsequently creates the pie chart. To stop the program, you select the Quit option. (Any data that you have not saved as a data file up to that point will subsequently be lost.)

In addition to the program's two menus, *QuickChart* conducts a number of input dialogs to get information for the charts. In the next section we'll see examples of these input dialogs and examine the charts that result from the input.

A sample run of the *QuickChart* program

For this sample run, let's work with a table of sales data. Imagine that the following table represents the number of policies that a particular insurance agent has sold over a five-year period:

Insurance Policies Sold					
	1983	*1984*	*1985*	*1986*	*1987*
Life	34	58	62	75	41
Home	14	29	42	45	78
Auto	40	75	89	95	92
Other	49	62	75	89	117

Each column in the table contains the sales figures for a year. The rows of the table show the sales for four kinds of insurance policies.

To enter this data table into memory, run the *QuickChart* program and select the Get data option from the main menu. From the Get data menu, choose the Keyboard input option. In response, the program initiates an input dialog designed to accept the data from the keyboard. Here is part of the ensuing dialog:

```
How many rows of data? (no more than 10) ==> 4
How many data values in each row? (no more than 10) ==> 5

Title of graph? Insurance Policies Sold

    Category names:
                column 1 ==> 1983
                column 2 ==> 1984
                column 3 ==> 1985
                column 4 ==> 1986
                column 5 ==> 1987
```

```
Series name for row 1 ==> Life
   Numeric data values:
                        1983 ==> 34
                        1984 ==> 58
                        1985 ==> 62
                        1986 ==> 75
                        1987 ==> 41

Series name for row 2 ==> Home
   Numeric data values:
                        1983 ==> 14
                        1984 ==> _
```

The first information the program needs to know is the size of the data table—that is, the number of rows and columns of numeric data in the table, not counting any labels. The maximum table size that the program allows is 10 rows by 10 columns, for a total of 100 data values. The insurance table has four rows and five columns of data, so you enter these two values in response to the program's first two questions.

Next, the program asks for a title for the table. This title will appear at the top of each chart that you produce from the table. Enter *Insurance Policies Sold* as the title.

In the dialog that follows, the program introduces two terms that describe the dimensions of a data table. The columns of a table are called *categories* and the rows are called *series*. The headings at the top of the columns are thus category names, and the row labels are series names. We'll see in a moment how categories and series translate into the elements of a chart.

The program next asks for a complete set of category names, one for each column of the table. In the insurance table, the category names are the five years from 1983 through 1987. Subsequently the program prompts you for each data series in turn: first a series name, and then each numeric value in a row. The program conveniently displays the corresponding category name as a prompt for each data value.

By the way, the current version of the program works only with positive numbers. If you try to enter a negative number, the program displays an error message and then waits for a new entry:

```
Redo. (Positive numbers only.) ==>
```

After you enter the entire data table, the program offers you a chance to save the table on disk as a data file:

```
Enter a filename for storing this data.
(Or press Enter if you do not want to save data.) ==>
```

In response to this prompt, you can enter a filename along with an optional disk or path specification. If you enter a filename, the program saves the data on disk. If you just press Enter, the program retains the table in memory, but does not save it on disk. (This is the only opportunity that the program offers to save the file.)

When the insurance table is in memory, you can perform the program's charting functions. Figures 8-8, 8-9 (on the next page), and 8-10 (on the next page) show a column chart, a line chart, and a pie chart derived from the data. Let's consider how the program creates these charts from the insurance data table.

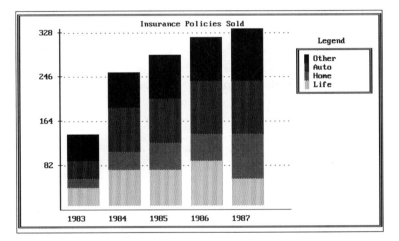

Figure 8-8. *A column chart based on the Insurance Policies Sold table.*

In a column chart, each different display pattern represents a row of data. The column names of the data table become the category labels along the horizontal axis of the chart. The row labels become the series labels in the chart's legend. Because the program creates stacked column charts, the height of each column represents the total of all the numeric values in a column of the data table.

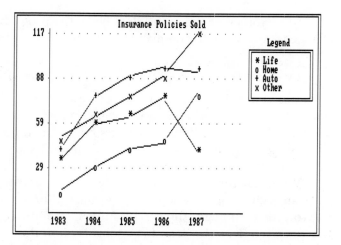

Figure 8-9. *A line chart based on the Insurance Policies Sold table.*

In a line chart, each row of data becomes one line in the chart. The point markers along each line represent the data values in a row of data. The column names of the data table become category labels along the chart's horizontal axis, and the row names become series labels in the legend. The numbers along the vertical axis and the dotted value lines that extend horizontally from these numbers provide a scale for determining the value represented by each data point.

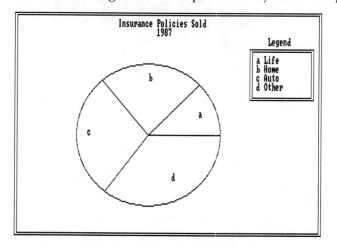

Figure 8-10. *A pie chart based on the 1987 column of the Insurance Policies Sold table.*

Column charts and line charts represent entire tables of data. In contrast, a pie chart represents only one column of values. Before drawing a pie chart, the *QuickChart* program asks you which column to use for the chart. For example, here is the dialog that requests this information for the Insurance Policies Sold table:

```
Select a column of data for the pie chart:

    1. 1983
    2. 1984
    3. 1985
    4. 1986
    5. 1987


    1 to  5 ==>
```

The program lists the column names of the data table and asks you to select a target column of data. For example, if you enter *5* to select the fifth data column, you will see a pie chart like the one shown in Figure 8-10. The column's category name becomes the subtitle on the pie chart and the series names appear as the labels in the chart's legend. The program identifies the wedges of the chart with lowercase letters, matching each wedge with a label displayed in the legend.

The *QuickChart* program never varies its method of translating the rows and columns of the data into the elements of a chart. The arrangement of the data thus determines how the charts will appear. To produce a different set of charts, you must transpose the row-column orientation of the data table.

For example, imagine that you want to create a pie chart representing all the life insurance sold over the five-year period. You want each wedge in the chart to represent one year of sales. To achieve this effect, select the Get data option from the main menu and then the Transpose the data option from the Get data menu. The revised table contains five rows of data representing the five years of sales and four columns representing the four kinds of insurance. Figure 8-11 on the next page shows how the Look at data option (from the Get data menu) displays the newly arranged table.

The data of the table is the same as before; only the row-column orientation is new. Figure 8-12 on the next page shows the pie chart that *QuickChart* produces for the first column in this table.

```
Insurance Policies Sold
          Life            Home           Auto           Other
1983      34              14             40             49
1984      58              29             75             62
1985      62              42             89             75
1986      75              45             95             89
1987      41              78             92             117

Press the spacebar to continue.
```

Figure 8-11. *The transposed Insurance Policies Sold table displayed by the Look at data option.*

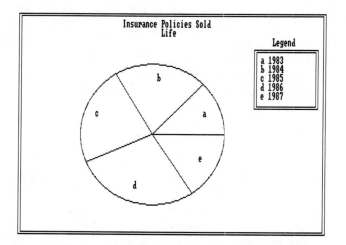

Figure 8-12. *A pie chart based on the Life column of the transposed Insurance Policies Sold table.*

So far we've seen only the first of the three methods available for entering data into the program—manual data entry from the keyboard. In the other two methods, you direct the program to read a data file. As we've discussed, the program can read two different data-file formats: files that the program has created or SYLK files. Let's look at these options.

Reading *QuickChart* data files

The Data file option from the Get data menu conducts the following dialog:

```
Enter the name of the file you want to read.
(Include the base name and the extension,
along with the drive designation if necessary.)
==> Policies


Reading data file...

Press the spacebar to continue.
```

After you specify a file, the program locates the file and reads it into memory. When the main menu reappears, you can use any of the chart options to format the data.

The file for the Insurance Policies Sold table is an example of the format that *QuickChart* produces.

```
4,5
Insurance Policies Sold, 1983, 1984, 1985, 1986, 1987
Life,   34,   58,   62,   75,   41
Home,   14,   29,   42,   45,   78
Auto,   40,   75,   89,   95,   92
Other,  49,   62,   75,   89,   117
```

The format is simple. Here is a summary of its elements:

- The first line in the file contains two integers separated by a comma. The first integer is the number of rows; the second integer is the number of columns.

- The second line contains the title of the table, followed by the column headings. Again, values are separated by commas.

- Subsequent lines represent rows of data. Each line begins with the row label, followed by the numeric data values belonging to the row.

If you prefer, you can use a text editor or a word processor to create a data file in this format. The only stipulation is that you must save your file as an ASCII text file without any special word-processing control characters. For example, you might use the QuickBASIC editor to enter (or edit) and save a data file with the Text option selected. As long as you follow the required format, the *QuickChart* program can read your file.

Reading SYLK files

An alternative approach for supplying data to the *QuickChart* program is to start with a Microsoft Multiplan worksheet and to save the worksheet as a SYLK file. *QuickChart* imposes some simple requirements on the format of the source worksheet:

- Cell R1C1 must contain the title of the table (for example, *Insurance Policies Sold*).

- Row 1 must contain the column headings (for example, *1983, 1984, 1985*, and so on).

- Column 1 must contain the row labels (for example, *Life, Home, Auto*, and *Other*).

- The numeric data values must appear in the rectangular range of cells immediately below the column headings and to the right of the row labels.

- The worksheet may contain no negative values.

- The worksheet may contain no more than 10 columns or 10 rows of data values.

Assuming that you start with a worksheet that meets the requirements listed above, here are the steps for creating a SYLK file from Multiplan:

1. Choose the Transfer Options command.

2. Select the Symbolic option so that the subsequent save operation will result in a SYLK file.

3. Choose the Transfer Save command.

In *QuickChart*'s Get data menu, the Sylk file option directs the program to read a SYLK file and to store the resulting data table in memory. We'll discuss SYLK files in more detail later in this chapter.

Before attempting to read the numeric values stored in a data file or in a SYLK file, *QuickChart* performs validation checks to make sure the file conforms to the expected format. If the file does not conform, the program displays an error message, then returns you to the main menu.

Now that we've looked at the various options available in *QuickChart*, let's examine the program listing.

INSIDE THE *QUICKCHART* PROGRAM

The complete program listing appears in Figure 8-14, beginning on page 388. The various declarations and definitions required by the program appear at the top of the listing, followed by the main program section, the error-handling section, and the functions and subprograms in alphabetic order. Throughout the program discussion you'll see references to functions and subprograms—these are labeled along the right and left margins of the listing with tabs bearing the function or subprogram name. We'll begin our discussion with the declarations and definitions section and the main program section; then we'll look at each of the program's major charting procedures.

The declarations and definitions section

The first part of the program listing declares symbolic constants, user-defined types, and global variables. It also contains a list of DECLARE statements and a small group of DATA statements.

Like all the programs in this book, *QuickChart* defines the logical values *true%* and *false%* as symbolic constants. In addition, the constant *maxVals%* sets the maximum number of values allowed in a row or column of a data table:

```
CONST false% = 0, true% = NOT false%, maxVals% = 10
```

If you want the program to work with larger data tables, you can adjust the value of *maxVals%* accordingly.

Four additional constants, declared at the top of the program, are integer codes that represent the various chart types:

```
CONST columns% = 1, printColumns% = 2, lines% = 3, pies% = 4
```

These constants are all global.

A user-defined type named *chartType* contains string elements that represent each chart type:

```
TYPE chartType
    columns AS STRING * 1
    printColumns AS STRING * 1
    lines AS STRING * 1
    pies AS STRING * 1
END TYPE
```

The program subsequently defines an array belonging to this type:

```
DIM SHARED chartChars(maxVals%) AS chartType
```

The *chartChars()* array is a convenient structure for storing the display characters that the program uses in each chart type. A procedure named *Initialize* reads individual characters into this array from the DATA statements.

A second user-defined type, *infoType*, has four single-precision elements representing statistical values that the program calculates for each new data table:

```
TYPE infoType
    largestValue AS SINGLE
    largestColumn AS SINGLE
    scaleFactor AS SINGLE
    columnFactor AS SINGLE
END TYPE
```

Given this type, the program declares a global record variable named *tableInfo* to store the statistical values.

The DECLARE statements list the names and parameters of the program's 32 procedures. Then a pair of COMMON SHARED statements declares a small group of important global variables. The string array *dataTable$()* is the structure that stores the program's current data table, and the variables *tableRows%* and *tableColumns%* give the dimensions of the table. As we have seen, *tableInfo* is a record that stores statistical information about the current table.

The logical values *okData%, noFile%,* and *grafTablExists%* represent conditions that can affect the program's execution, and *file$* is the name of a data file that the user wants to read. We'll see how the program uses all these variables and constants as we look at the charting procedures.

The main program section

Before displaying the first menu on the screen, the main program section has to test the display hardware to find out if it can display graphics. You'll recall that the main menu contains five options for a system equipped with graphics hardware, but only three for a system equipped with text-only hardware. To determine which type is available, the main program calls the *ScreenTest* subprogram. Let's see how this important procedure works.

Testing the display hardware

The purpose of *ScreenTest* is to assign one of two values to the variable *menuOptions%*—*5* if the computer can display graphics or *3* if the computer can display only text. The main program begins by assigning the variable a value of *5*:

```
menuOptions% = 5
```

To test the display hardware, *ScreenTest* issues a pair of graphics commands that can be performed only on a graphics screen:

```
SCREEN 2
PSET(0, 0)
```

If the display adapter is a text-only device, QuickBASIC normally responds to these commands by terminating the program and supplying an error message. Anticipating this event, the *ScreenTest* subprogram encloses the SCREEN and PSET commands inside an error trap:

```
ON ERROR GOTO IfMono
    SCREEN 2
    PSET(0, 0)
ON ERROR GOTO 0
```

If the graphics statements result in an error, QuickBASIC branches to the error-handling routine located at the label *IfMono* in the error-handling section. *IfMono* assigns *menuOptions%* a new value of *3*, indicating that the program is running on a text-only display device. Then the RESUME NEXT statement returns control of the program to the line following the command that caused the error:

```
IfMono:
    menuOptions% = 3
RESUME NEXT
```

In the *ScreenTest* subprogram, execution continues at the ON ERROR GOTO 0 statement, which simply restores QuickBASIC's normal run-time error checking.

ScreenTest has an additional task to perform if the program is running on a graphics display system. The procedure attempts to load the IBM Extended Character Set (ASCII 128–255) into memory so that the program can display column charts in the SCREEN 2 display mode.

The MS-DOS GRAFTABL command installs these characters; accordingly, *ScreenTest* begins by searching for GRAFTABL.COM on the disk:

```
grafTablExists% = true%
ON ERROR GOTO NoGrafTablFile
    FILES "GRAFTABL.COM"
ON ERROR GOTO 0
```

If the FILES command results in an error—meaning that GRAFTABL.COM cannot be found on disk—the error routine at *NoGrafTablFile* switches the logical variable *grafTablExists%* to *false%*. But if the variable is still *true%* after this passage, the program uses a SHELL statement to exit to MS-DOS and execute the GRAFTABL command:

```
IF grafTablExists% THEN SHELL "GRAFTABL"
```

Thanks to this procedure, *QuickChart* can display column charts in the SCREEN 2 mode, allowing you to dump the charts directly to an appropriate printer. In summary, if you want to print screen dumps of the charts produced by this program, prepare your system as follows:

1. Be sure that the GRAFTABL.COM command is available on disk where *QuickChart* can find it.

2. Execute the GRAPHICS command from MS-DOS before you run *QuickChart*.

The final statement in *ScreenTest* is a SCREEN 0 command, which restores the text display mode. After executing *ScreenTest,* the main program uses the *menuOptions%* variable to establish the correct size of the first menu array, *mainMenu$()*:

```
DIM mainMenu$(menuOptions%), dataMenu$(6)
```

The second menu array, *dataMenu$,* always contains six menu options, regardless of the display hardware.

A call to the *AssignMenus* procedure reads the menu option strings into these two arrays:

```
AssignMenus menuOptions%, mainMenu$(), dataMenu$()
```

AssignMenus contains a sequence of READ statements. These statements read strings into *mainMenu$()* and *dataMenu$()* from the first two DATA lines shown in the definitions and declarations section.

Next, the main program calls the *Initialize* subprogram to assign special display characters to the array of records named *chartChars()*. Let's see how the program stores values in this array.

The *Initialize* subprogram

Initialize contains three FOR...NEXT loops. Each FOR...NEXT loop works with the characters for one or two of the chart types. For example, the first loop stores the column chart characters in the *chartChars()* array:

```
FOR i% = 1 TO maxVals%
    READ temp%
    chartChars(i%).columns = CHR$(temp%)
NEXT i%
```

This loop reads code numbers from the following DATA line:

```
DATA 176, 177, 178, 219, 215, 222, 237, 179, 232, 181
```

Each iteration of the loop reads one of these codes into the variable *temp%*. The subsequent assignment statement uses CHR$ to convert *temp%* to a character in the IBM Extended Character Set and stores the character in the *columns* element of the corresponding record.

A similar process reads characters into the *lines* elements of the array. These elements are used to identify the data points of a line chart. Finally, a single FOR...NEXT loop stores the uppercase letters *A* through *J* in the *printColumns* elements (used to create the printable column chart) and lowercase *a* through *j* in the *pies* elements (used for identifying the wedges of a pie chart).

```
FOR i% = 1 TO maxVals%
    chartChars(i%).printColumns = CHR$(64 + i%)
    chartChars(i%).pies = CHR$(96 + i%)
NEXT i%
```

The letters of the uppercase alphabet have ASCII codes starting at 65, and the lowercase alphabet begins at ASCII code 97.

When these initial tasks are completed, the program is ready to display the main menu on the screen. A DO...UNTIL loop performs the recurring menu action, and a pair of nested SELECT CASE structures processes the menu choices. Let's see how these structures control the action of the program.

Controlling the program

The main menu appears on the screen after each charting activity is completed. To display this menu, the program calls the *Menu%* function inside the DO…UNTIL loop:

```
DO
    LOCATE 2, 33: PRINT "Chart Program"
    choice% = Menu%(mainMenu$())
```

Menu% displays the main menu on the screen and returns an integer representing the user's menu selection. The program stores this integer in the variable *choice%*. The DO…UNTIL loop repeatedly displays the main menu on the screen until the user selects the last option, Quit. The number of this option is the same as the value of *menuOptions%*— *3* for a text-only adapter or *5* for a graphics adapter.

For each iteration of the loop, the program's action depends on the value of *choice%*. If *choice%* equals *1*, the user has selected the Get data option. In response, the program displays the second menu, which offers the user another choice:

```
SELECT CASE choice%

CASE 1
    LOCATE 2, 27: PRINT "Get Data for Chart Program"
    dataChoice% = Menu%(dataMenu$())
```

Again, the *Menu%* function returns an integer representing the user's choice. This integer is stored in the variable *dataChoice%*. Another SELECT CASE structure then calls the appropriate procedure:

```
SELECT CASE dataChoice%
CASE 1
    InData
CASE 2, 3
    ReadFile dataChoice%
CASE 4
    IF okData% THEN DataLook
CASE 5
    IF okData% THEN TransposeTable
CASE ELSE
END SELECT
```

The *InData* procedure conducts the input dialog to read a data table from the keyboard. *ReadFile* controls the process of reading either a data file or a SYLK file. *DataLook* displays the data on the screen in table form. The *TransposeData* subprogram transposes the dimensions of the current data table.

A main menu selection that is greater than *1* and less than *menuOptions%* is a request for one of the chart options. In this case, the program must check the value of the global logical variable *okData%* before processing the menu choice; for example:

```
CASE 2
    IF okData% THEN
```

The subprograms that are responsible for reading a data table (either from the keyboard or from a disk file) assign a value of *true%* to *okData%* if the input process is successful and if a data table is available in memory. Only then can the program go ahead with a charting procedure—first calling *Analysis* (to compute scale factors from the data) and then calling one of the charting routines, *ColumnChart*, *LineChart*, or *PieChart*.

As always, the main program section gives us a broad outline of the program's activities. Now let's examine *QuickChart's* major procedures, starting with the data input routines.

Eliciting a data table from the keyboard: The *InData* subprogram

For keyboard entry and data-file input alike, the program's first task is to determine the size of the table and to redimension *dataTable$()*, the array that stores the data. Although each different input procedure has its own approach to accomplishing this task, the *dataTable$()* array is always organized in the same way.

- The element *dataTable$(0, 0)* stores the title of the data table.

- The elements represented by *dataTable$(i%, 0)*—where *i%* ranges from *1* up to and including the number of rows in the data table—contain the row labels.

- The elements represented by *dataTable$(0, j%)*—where *j%* ranges from *1* up to and including the number of columns in the data table—contain the column headings.

- The elements represented by *dataTable$(i%, j%)*—where *i%* ranges from *1* up to and including the number of rows and *j%* ranges from *1* up to and including the number of columns—contain the numeric data values.

For both convenience and economy, the program uses a single array to store both string data and numeric data. The "zeroth" elements of *dataTable$()* store labels and the title, and the remainder of the array stores the numbers. The program converts numeric values into their string equivalents for storage in *dataTable$()*. When the program needs to work with the actual numeric values, it simply converts these strings back into numbers.

The *InData* subprogram controls the input process for keyboard data entry. *InData* calls three other procedures in turn: *GetSize*, to ask for the size of the table; *GetTable*, to prompt for the data values; and *SaveData*, to store the table in a data file if the user so requests. We'll look briefly at each of these three routines.

The *GetSize* subprogram

GetSize uses a pair of INPUT statements to elicit values for the global variables *tableRows%* and *tableColumns%*, representing the dimensions of the data table. To ensure that both of these variables contain valid values (from *1* through *maxVals%*), *GetSize* employs two DO...UNTIL loops that can repeat each part of the input dialog until the dimensions are within the specified size. For example, here is the loop for the *tableRows%* value:

```
DO
     PRINT "How many rows of data? ";
     PRINT "(no more than"; STR$(maxVals%);
     INPUT ") ==> ", tableRows%
     ok% = tableRows% > 0 AND tableRows% <= maxVals%
LOOP UNTIL ok%
```

The logical variable *ok%* controls the looping. The logical expression at the bottom of the loop tests the validity of *tableRows%* and accordingly assigns a value of true or false to *ok%*. A similar loop elicits and validates the input number for *tableColumns%*.

When control returns to the *InData* subprogram, a REDIM statement establishes the current size of the *dataTable$()* array:

```
REDIM dataTable$(tableRows%, tableColumns%)
```

A subsequent call to the *GetTable* subprogram fills this array with data.

The *GetTable* subprogram

GetTable's job is organized into several different loops. First, a single FOR...NEXT loop elicits the category names and stores them in the array elements represented by *dataTable$(0, j%)*, where *j%* ranges from *1* to *tableColumns%*. Then a group of nested loops moves through the rows one by one, eliciting a series name and a row of numbers:

```
FOR i% = 1 TO tableRows%
    PRINT "    Series name for row"; i%;
    INPUT "==> ", dataTable$(i%, 0)
    PRINT "        Numeric data values:"
    FOR j% = 1 TO tableColumns%
        PRINT TAB(27); dataTable$(0, j%);
        DO
            INPUT " ==> ", temp
            IF temp < 0 THEN
                PRINT "        Redo. ";
                PRINT "(Positive numbers only.) ";
            END IF
        LOOP UNTIL temp >= 0
        dataTable$(i%, j%) = STR$(temp)
    NEXT j%
    PRINT
NEXT i%
```

The loop counters *i%* and *j%* become the subscripts into the *dataTable$()* structure as the program stores each input value in the correct array element. The innermost DO...UNTIL loop makes sure that each data value is a positive number. Finally, the program uses the STR$ function to convert the numeric values into strings so that they can be stored in the *dataTable$()* array.

To complete the data input process, the last statement in the *InData* routine switches the value of the global variable *okData%* to *true%*. In effect, this variable informs the rest of the program that a table is available in memory.

371

Another one of *InData's* tasks is to ask for a filename for the data table. The program saves this name in the global variable *file$*. If the user supplies a filename, the *SaveData* subprogram performs the save operation, creating a sequential data file.

The *SaveData* subprogram

SaveData begins by opening the file for output:

```
OPEN file$ FOR OUTPUT AS #1
```

A WRITE# statement sends the values of *tableRows%* and *tableColumns%* to the file:

```
WRITE #1, tableRows%, tableColumns%
```

Then, inside a pair of nested FOR...NEXT loops, a PRINT# statement sends each array element to the file:

```
PRINT #1, dataTable$(i%, j%)
```

The *ReadFile* procedure reads data files created by *SaveData* or SYLK files created by an outside program such as Microsoft Multiplan. As we'll see in the next section, this procedure calls a variety of subprograms to accomplish each part of the reading task.

Reading a data file: The *ReadFile* subprogram

ReadFile asks the user for a filename and stores the name in the global variable *file$*. The following command opens the file for reading:

```
OPEN file$ FOR INPUT AS #1
```

If QuickBASIC cannot locate *file$* on disk, this statement causes a run-time error. To avoid interrupting execution, *ReadFile* sets up an error trap, sending control to the *IfNoFile* routine in the error-handling section if *file$* cannot be found:

```
ON ERROR GOTO IfNoFile
    OPEN file$ FOR INPUT AS #1
ON ERROR GOTO 0
```

IfNoFile displays an error message on the screen and assigns a value of *true%* to the logical variable *noFile%*. The *ReadFile* routine attempts no further action if *noFile%* is true. However, if the value of this variable remains false, *ReadFile* can assume that the data file has been opened successfully. The procedure next calls either *DataRead* to read a data file or *SylkRead* to read a SYLK file:

```
IF NOT noFile% THEN
    IF format% = 2 THEN
        DataRead
    ELSE
        SylkRead
    END IF
```

The *format%* parameter contains the same value as the *dataChoice%* variable from the main program section. This value indicates whether the user has requested a data file (*format%* equals *2*) or a SYLK file (*format%* equals *3*).

When the reading of the file is complete, *ReadFile* issues a CLOSE command to close the file. Let's look briefly at the routines that read files, *DataRead* and *SylkRead*.

The *DataRead* subprogram

DataRead begins by reading the first two values stored in the data file. These values specify the size of the table:

```
INPUT #1, tableRows%, tableColumns%
```

After validating these dimensions, *DataRead* issues a REDIM command to establish the new size of the *dataTable$()* array. Each value is then read into *dataTable$* from within a pair of nested FOR...NEXT loops:

```
REDIM dataTable$(tableRows%, tableColumns%)

FOR i% = 0 TO tableRows%
    FOR j% = 0 TO tableColumns%
        INPUT #1, dataTable$(i%, j%)
    NEXT j%
NEXT i%
```

Finally, *DataRead* assigns a value of *true%* to the global variable *okData%*.

The *SylkRead* subprogram

A Microsoft Multiplan SYLK file supplies extensive information about a worksheet's format, structure, data, and formulas. For example, Figure 8-13 on the following pages contains the SYLK file that Microsoft Multiplan Version 3.0 creates from a worksheet containing the insurance policy data table that we worked with earlier in this chapter.

```
ID;PMP
P;PNONE
P;Pm/d/yy
P;Pm/d
P;Pd-mmm-yy
P;Pd-mmm
P;Pmmm-yy
P;Ph:mm\ AM/PM
P;Ph:mm:ss\ AM/PM
P;Ph:mm
P;Ph:mm:ss
P;Pm/d/yy\ h:mm
F;DG0G10
F;W1 1 23
B;Y5;X6
C;Y1;X1;K"Insurance Policies Sold"
C;X2;K"1983"
F;FD0R
C;X3;K"1984"
F;FD0R
C;X4;K"1985"
F;FD0R
C;X5;K"1986"
F;FD0R
C;X6;K"1987"
F;FD0R
C;Y2;X1;K"Life"
F;FD0R
C;X2;K34
C;X3;K58
C;X4;K62
C;X5;K75
C;X6;K41
C;Y3;X1;K"Home"
F;FD0R
C;X2;K14
C;X3;K29
C;X4;K42
C;X5;K45
C;X6;K78
C;Y4;X1;K"Auto"
F;FD0R
```

Figure 8-13. *A Microsoft Multiplan 3.0 SYLK file containing the Insurance Policies Sold table.* *(continued)*

Figure 8-13. *continued*

```
C;X2;K40
C;X3;K75
C;X4;K89
C;X5;K95
C;X6;K92
C;Y5;X1;K"Other"
F;FDOR
C;X2;K49
C;X3;K62
C;X4;K75
C;X5;K89
C;X6;K117
W;N1;A1 1;C7 0 7
E
```

As you can see, a SYLK file consists of many one-line records. Each record begins with a letter that identifies the kind of information it contains. Programs that read SYLK files are not always interested in all this information. For this reason, the SYLK file format is designed to allow a program to pick and choose only the information it requires and ignore the rest.

The *QuickChart* program is interested in only four kinds of SYLK records:

- The *ID* record, which is always the first record in a SYLK file. (If *QuickChart* does not find this record, the program assumes that the current file is not really a SYLK file.)

- The *B* record, which supplies the number of rows and columns in the source worksheet. (Each SYLK file has one *B* record.)

- The *C* records, which supply data values from the cells of the source worksheet. (A SYLK file typically has many *C* records.)

- The *E* record, which always marks the end of a SYLK file.

These records are in turn divided up into fields, and the various field types are also identified by letters. Inside the one-line records, each field is separated from the next by a semicolon.

The *B* record contains a *Y* field, which supplies the number of rows in the worksheet, and an *X* field, which gives the number of columns. Here's an example:

```
B;Y5;X6
```

Each *C* record includes a *K* field, which stores the data value from the corresponding worksheet cell. String values are enclosed in quotes in the *K* field, as in this example:

```
C;Y1;X1;K"Insurance Policies Sold"
```

Numeric values follow directly after the *K*:

```
C;X2;K34
```

These are all the SYLK characteristics that the *SylkRead* subprogram needs to know. The routine begins by reading the first record of the file into a variable named *sylkst$* (for "SYLK string"):

```
INPUT #1, sylkst$
```

The reading continues only if this first string contains the appropriate SYLK file identification:

```
IF LEFT$(sylkst$, 4) = "ID;P" THEN
```

If the identification is correct, *SylkRead* calls two subprograms to continue the reading process: *GetDims* looks for the *B* record and reads the dimensions of the table from it; and *GetSylkValues* reads data values from all the subsequent *C* records.

The *GetDims* and *GetSylkValues* subprograms

Each of these routines uses a DO...UNTIL loop to read record after record, ignoring any records that do not contain relevant information. For example, *GetDims* uses the following loop to read the file line by line until it encounters the *B* record:

```
DO
    INPUT #1, sylkString$
LOOP UNTIL LEFT$(sylkString$, 1) = "B" OR EOF(1)
```

Reading fields of information from a SYLK line is a detailed task that requires the help of a variety of QuickBASIC's string-handling functions—including INSTR, MID$, LEN, VAL, and CHR$. Both *GetDims* and *GetSylkValues* contain interesting examples of these functions.

Like *InData* and *DataRead,* *SylkRead* assigns a value of true to the global variable *okData%* to indicate that a valid table of data has been stored in *dataTable$().* When *okData%* is true, the program is ready to draw charts from the available data. Before drawing a chart, however, the program calls the *Analysis* procedure to analyze the data table. We'll look at this important procedure next.

The *Analysis* subprogram

To draw charts to scale in the space available on the display screen, *QuickChart* needs to calculate a small set of statistical values from the data table. The *Analysis* subprogram computes these values and stores them in the global *tableInfo* record.

The program allocates 20 screen lines in which to display column charts or line charts. Given the current data table, the program has to figure out the range of numeric values that those 20 lines will represent. Furthermore, the program needs a scaling factor that will successfully translate each individual data value into the height (for a column chart) or the position (for a line chart) that will accurately represent the value within the chart area of 20 screen lines.

In a line chart, this scaling factor is based on the largest numeric value in the data table. The program proportions the 20 screen lines to represent values from *0* up to this largest number. In a column chart, the scaling factor is based on the largest column total in the data set. To determine this value, the program adds each column of data and identifies the largest total. In this case, the program proportions the 20 screen lines to represent values from *0* up to the largest column total.

To meet these program requirements, the *Analysis* subprogram calculates four values and stores them in the named elements of the *tableInfo* record:

- *largestValue* is the largest numeric value in the data table.

- *largestColumn* is the largest column total in the data table.

- *scaleFactor* is the scaling factor for line charts, calculated from *largestValue.*

- *columnFactor* is the scaling factor for column charts, calculated from *largestColumn.*

The *largestValue* and *largestColumn* elements are determined within a pair of nested FOR...NEXT loops. First, the routine initializes both elements to zero. Then the FOR...NEXT loops move column by column through the data table and row by row through each column, searching for the largest single value and the largest column total. The IF statement inside the inner loop compares each new data value with the current value of the *largestValue* element. Whenever a number is found that is greater than the current *largestValue*, that number becomes the new value of *largestValue*.

Also inside the inner loop, an assignment statement accumulates the total of a column in the variable *temp*. Each time the inner loop counts through an entire column, an IF statement (located just outside the inner loop) compares *temp* with the current value of the *largestColumn* element. A larger column total becomes the new value of *largestColumn*.

Finally, when the looping is complete, the following statements compute the two required scaling factors:

```
tableInfo.columnFactor = 20 / tableInfo.largestColumn
tableInfo.scaleFactor = 20 / tableInfo.largestValue
```

Because the charting area contains 20 lines, the program can multiply any individual data value by the *scaleFactor* element to find a screen position to represent a value in a line chart. Likewise, multiplying a value by the *columnFactor* element yields the correct height to represent that value in a column chart.

The routines that draw column charts and line charts rely on these scale factors. In the next section, we'll examine the *ColumnChart* procedure.

The *ColumnChart* subprogram

ColumnChart draws two different versions of the column chart—one containing graphics characters from the IBM Extended Character Set, and the other containing standard ASCII characters that can be printed with a daisy-wheel printer.

To build each version, *ColumnChart* calls two subprograms named *TextScreen* and *BuildColumnChart*. Each of these routines takes one logical argument. A value of false results in the graphics version:

```
TextScreen false%
BuildColumnChart false%
```

And a value of true produces the printable version:

```
TextScreen true%
BuildColumnChart true%
```

Let's examine these two routines.

The *TextScreen* subprogram

The *TextScreen* subprogram supplies all the screen elements except for the chart: It draws the axes, prints the numeric values along the vertical axis, prepares the legend, and draws a frame around the entire screen.

To perform all these tasks, the routine calls on several small procedures in turn. The *Legend* routine places the chart's legend and title on the screen. The *AxisValues* routine computes and displays the numbers along the value axis. (The program also uses these procedures to prepare screen elements for other chart types.)

Finally, *TextScreen* calls the *Frame* subprogram to draw a frame around the chart. *QuickChart* initially displays the following message in the outer frame of a chart:

```
Press the spacebar to continue.
```

This screen message simply tells the user how to return to the main menu. In a printed screen dump of a chart, however, the message is irrelevant. For this reason, all three major charting procedures erase the message—and redraw the entire frame around the chart—within five seconds after the chart first appears on the screen. To accomplish this, the program uses ON TIMER statements to call an event-trapping routine in the error-handling section named *ErasePauseMessage*. You'll find ON TIMER statements in the *ColumnChart, LineChart,* and *PieDraw* routines. We'll discuss the topic of event trapping in Chapter 9.

When *TextScreen* has completed its tasks, the screen is ready for *BuildColumnChart* to draw the stacked columns.

The *BuildColumnChart* subprogram

BuildColumnChart accomplishes its job within three nested FOR...NEXT loops. During the course of the looping, the program uses two variables, *currentX%* and *currentY%*, to keep track of the constantly changing screen addresses at which individual graphics characters will be displayed. (These addresses become the arguments of the LOCATE command.) The variable *currentX%* is the current horizontal screen address, which starts at 12 for the position of the leftmost column of the chart:

```
currentX% = 12
```

The current vertical screen address, *currentY%*, positions the base of each new chart column at the bottom of the chart area, row 22:

```
currentY% = 22
```

After each element of a column is displayed on the screen, the program decrements the vertical address by *1* to move *upward* by one character position on the screen:

```
currentY% = currentY% - 1
```

Another important value that the program calculates is *columnWidth%*, the number of characters in the width of each chart column. This value depends upon the number of columns to be drawn. Given that the designated chart area is 48 characters wide, here is the formula for determining the width of each column:

```
columnWidth% = 48 \ tableColumns% - 2
```

So, for example, if the data table has four columns of values, each column in the chart will be 10 characters wide. After each column is drawn, the program calculates the horizontal screen address of the next column as follows:

```
currentX% = currentX% + columnWidth% + 2
```

This formula leaves two spaces between each column in the chart.

Let's look at the action of the three nested loops in *BuildColumnChart*. The outer loop produces each chart column from left to right. It begins by displaying a category name as a label at the bottom of each chart column. The loop reads the category names from *dataTable$(0, j%)*:

```
FOR j% = 1 TO tableColumns%
    LOCATE 24, currentX%
    PRINT LEFT$(dataTable$(0, j%), columnWidth%);
```

If any category name is longer than the width of its corresponding column, the LEFT$ function supplies the first *columnWidth%* characters for display.

The middle FOR...NEXT loop draws the stacked sections of each column from bottom to top. The height in characters of each section is calculated from the *dataTable$()* value that the section is to represent.

Here is where the scaling factor *tableInfo.columnFactor* (computed by the *Analysis* subprogram) comes into play:

```
FOR i% = 1 TO tableRows%
    height% = CINT(tableInfo.columnFactor * VAL(dataTable$(i%, j%)))
```

The VAL function converts the selected *dataTable$()* value to a number, and the CINT function rounds the product of *tableInfo.columnFactor* and the value to the nearest integer.

Finally, the inner loop moves row by row up this calculated height and prints an appropriate width of chart characters—either graphics characters or standard characters—at each vertical position:

```
FOR h% = 1 TO height%
    LOCATE currentY%, currentX%
    IF NOT printChart% THEN
        PRINT STRING$(columnWidth%, chartChars(i%).columns);
    ELSE
        PRINT STRING$(columnWidth%, chartChars(i%).printColumns);
    END IF
```

The variable *printChart%* contains the logical value that *BuildColumnChart* receives as its argument. Depending on the value of this variable, the routine prints either the *columns* characters or the *printColumns* characters from the *chartChars* structure.

Next we'll see how *QuickChart* creates line charts.

The *LineChart* subprogram

The *LineChart* subprogram first switches into the SCREEN 2 display mode, then makes calls to two subprograms that do the rest of the work: *GraphScreen* prepares the axes, the legend, and the frame; and *BuildLineChart* draws the lines that represent the data. Let's look at these two routines.

Preparing the screen for the line chart: The *GraphScreen* subprogram

Like the *TextScreen* routine, *GraphScreen* calls *Legend* to display the text for the legend and *AxisValues* to display numeric values along the vertical axis. To produce the double-line frame around the perimeter of the screen, *GraphScreen* uses two simple LINE statements rather than calling the *Frame* procedure:

```
LINE (0, 2)-(639, 199), , B
LINE (5, 4)-(634, 197), , B
```

Before calling the *Legend* procedure, *GraphScreen* issues another pair of LINE statements that draw the legend box. The two statements illustrate the *relative* addressing mode in a graphics command:

```
LINE (490, 34)-STEP(133, tableRows% * 8 + 13), , B
LINE (495, 36)-STEP(123, tableRows% * 8 + 9), , B
```

In both of these statements, the first address is an absolute reference to the upper-left corner of the legend box, and the second address is a relative reference to the lower-right corner. The vertical coordinates of these relative addresses are calculated from the value of *tableRows%*. The *B* option produces a box on the screen.

The next two LINE statements draw the axes:

```
LINE (74, 16)-(74, 180)
LINE -(479, 180)
```

The first of these statements draws the vertical axis from the top down to the point that represents the *origin* of the graph *(0, 0)*. The second command draws the horizontal axis, starting from the origin (the last point referenced).

Finally, *GraphScreen* uses a FOR...NEXT loop to draw four dotted horizontal lines marking the positions of the values along the vertical axis. We've already discussed how the LINE command's *style* parameter produces dotted lines in this code:

```
LINE (72, y%)-(479, y%), , , &H8000
```

With all these background elements completed, the *BuildLineChart* routine takes control next to draw the chart.

Drawing the line chart: The *BuildLineChart* subprogram

The *BuildLineChart* routine begins by issuing VIEW and WINDOW statements to reorient the system of pixel addresses into an arrangement that is better suited to the task of drawing the lines. First, the VIEW command establishes the designated chart area:

```
VIEW (80, 20)-(479, 180)
```

Then, within this area, the WINDOW command sets a new system of pixel addresses, starting with *(0, 0)* at the lower-left corner of the chart area designated by the VIEW statement:

```
WINDOW (0, 0)-(50, INT(tableInfo.largestValue))
```

The vertical coordinate of the upper-right corner pixel is taken as *tableInfo.largestValue.* This is the largest numeric value in the data table, as determined by the *Analysis* subprogram. Given this new coordinate system, the program can plot the numeric values in *dataTable$()* directly as vertical addresses in the chart area; no further scale calculations are required.

The routine performs one more task before starting the chart. An assignment statement computes the number of spaces to put between each plotted point on the chart. The variable *between%* receives the value:

```
between% = 48 \ tableColumns%
```

Finally, a pair of nested FOR...NEXT loops draws the lines of the chart. The outer loop moves row by row through the data table and draws a line for each series of data. The initial task inside this loop is to plot the first data value of each row, using the PSET command:

```
FOR i% = 1 TO tableRows%
    PSET (2, VAL(dataTable$(i%, 1)))
```

The inner loop then draws line segments from the last plotted point to the point that represents each subsequent value in a row of data:

```
FOR j% = 2 TO tableColumns%
    LINE -(between% * (j% -1) + 2, VAL(dataTable$(i%, j%)))
```

The horizontal address coordinate is calculated from the value of *between%.* Thanks to the custom coordinate system established by VIEW and WINDOW, the program can express the vertical address coordinate simply as the data value.

BuildLineChart's last task is to supply text characters (from the *lines* elements of the *chartChars* array) to mark the data points. A pair of nested loops uses the LOCATE and PRINT commands to display the characters and the scaling factor *tableInfo.scaleFactor* to compute the vertical screen positions.

Finally, we turn to the last of the charting routines, the *PieChart* subprogram.

The *PieChart* subprogram

The *PieChart* subprogram begins by asking the user to select the target data column for creating the pie chart. The routine elicits a number from *1* up to and including the number of columns in the data table and stores the input value in the variable *pieColumn%*. *PieChart* then sends this value as an argument to two subsidiary procedures— *PieScreen*, which prepares the chart screen; and *PieDraw*, which draws the chart:

```
PieScreen pieColumn%
PieDraw pieColumn%
```

The *PieScreen* subprogram performs the usual preliminaries: switching the display into the SCREEN 2 graphics mode; drawing a frame around the perimeter of the screen; producing the legend; and displaying the title of the chart. Then *PieDraw* takes over to create the pie chart. Let's see how this routine works.

Drawing the pie: The *PieDraw* subprogram

PieDraw receives the data table column number in a parameter variable named *targetCol%*:

```
SUB PieDraw (targetCol%) STATIC
```

At the beginning of the routine, a FOR...NEXT loop totals up the values stored in the *targetCol%* column. The total is accumulated in a variable named *columnTotal*:

```
columnTotal = 0
FOR i% = 1 TO tableRows%
    columnTotal = columnTotal + VAL(dataTable$(i%, targetCol%))
NEXT i%
```

Next, *PieDraw* initializes a set of variables required for drawing the pie chart. The variables *centerX%* and *centerY%* represent center coordinates of the circle, and *radius%* represents the length of the circle's radius:

```
centerX% = 279
centerY% = 110
radius% = 150
```

The variable *start* receives the starting angle for the pie's first wedge. In principle this value should be *0* radians; but to meet the requirements of the CIRCLE command, *start* actually begins as a small negative number:

```
start = -.00001
```

Angles must be expressed as negative radian values for CIRCLE to draw the sides of the wedges.

Finally, the variable *piTimes2* receives the value of –2π, the angle that represents the entire circle:

```
piTimes2 = -3.141592 * 2
```

A single FOR...NEXT loop moves one by one through the data values in the target column and draws a wedge of the pie to represent each value. At the top of the loop the program calculates the absolute angle of the current wedge. This angle is assigned to the variable *portion*:

```
FOR i% = 1 TO tableRows%
    portion = (VAL(dataTable$(i%, targetCol%)) / columnTotal) * piTimes2
```

This calculation divides the current data value by the total of all the values and multiplies the result by *piTimes2*.

Inside the circle, the relative ending angle of the current wedge is normally the sum of *start* and *portion*. However, the final wedge should end at precisely *piTimes2*:

```
IF i% < tableRows% THEN
    wedge = start + portion
ELSE
    wedge = piTimes2
END IF
```

Given the relative starting and ending angles, *start* and *wedge*, the program is ready to draw the current wedge:

```
CIRCLE (centerX%, centerY%), radius%, , start, wedge
```

The next task is to position a text character (from the appropriate *pies* element of the *chartChars()* array) in the center of the wedge. This character will match one of the characters in the legend and thus identify the value that the wedge represents. Oddly enough, calculating the proper screen position for this character is one of the most difficult tasks in the entire program.

In effect, the program must define a second circumference around which to display the identification characters. The addresses for these text characters will appear as vertical and horizontal text screen coordinates in a LOCATE statement. In this context, the program cannot use the CIRCLE command. Instead, the routine uses the built-in SIN function to calculate the vertical text address coordinate, *rowLoc%,* and the built-in COS function to calculate the horizontal text address coordinate, *colLoc%:*

```
angle = -1 * (start + portion / 2)
rowLoc% = INT(-6 * SIN(angle) + 14.5)
colLoc% = INT(15 * COS(angle) + 35.5)
LOCATE rowLoc%, colLoc%
PRINT chartChars(i%).pies;
```

Finally, before attempting to draw the next wedge (in the next loop iteration) the program must assign a new value to the *start* variable:

```
start = wedge
```

In other words, the starting angle of the next wedge is the same as the ending angle of the previous wedge.

This completes our study of the three charting routines, *ColumnChart, LineChart,* and *PieChart.* Finally, let's look briefly at the *TransposeTable* procedure, the routine that transposes the shape of the data table.

The *TransposeTable* subprogram

To reorganize the data table, the *TransposeTable* subprogram must perform the following steps:

1. Make a copy of the current data table.

2. Exchange the current values of the row and column dimensions (*tableRows%* and *tableColumns%*) and redimension the *dataTable$()* array.

3. Copy the original data back into *dataTable$(),* exchanging rows for columns and columns for rows.

The routine begins by creating a dynamic array named *dataTemp$()* with the same dimensions as the current version of the *dataTable$()* array:

```
REDIM dataTemp$(tableRows%, tableColumns%)
```

Two nested FOR...NEXT loops copy *dataTable$()* into *dataTemp$().*

Next, a SWAP command exchanges the current dimensions of the table, and a REDIM statement redimensions the *dataTable$()* array:

```
SWAP tableRows%, tableColumns%
REDIM dataTable$(tableRows%, tableColumns%)
```

Finally, another pair of loops copies *dataTemp$()* back into *dataTable$()*:

```
FOR i% = 0 TO tableRows%
    FOR j% = 0 TO tableColumns%
        dataTable$(i%, j%) = dataTemp$(j%, i%)
    NEXT j%
NEXT i%
```

To copy rows to columns, the program simply reverses the dimension subscripts—assigning each element *(j%, i%)* of *dataTemp$()* to the corresponding *(i%, j%)* element in *dataTable$()*.

While *QuickChart* is running, the transpose operation occurs instantly when the user selects the Transpose the data option. Thanks to this option, the user can view an entirely new set of charts from the data table currently stored in memory.

Conclusion

If you would like to work further with the *QuickChart* program, here are a few suggestions for improvements:

1. Rework the column chart and line chart routines so that the program can handle negative numbers in the data table. The position of the horizontal category axis will have to be calculated in a manner that results in an appropriate scale for both negative and positive numbers.

2. Add routines to offer additional chart types: for example, a bar chart, producing horizontal bars to represent data values; and an *x-y* (or *scatter*) chart, in which ordered pairs of Cartesian coordinates are plotted against an x-axis and a y-axis.

3. Write procedures that allow the user to revise the data table—changing individual values or adding new rows and columns. These tasks should be as simple as possible, giving the user a reasonable alternative to reentering the entire table.

4. Add a sort routine so that the user can rearrange the data table. As keys for the sort, allow the user to select the row of category names, the column of series names, or any individual row or column of numeric data.

5. Add color to the charts in screen modes other than SCREEN 2. (Be careful not to compromise the quality of printed screen dumps as a result of adding color to the charts.)

THE *QUICKCHART* PROGRAM

```
'    QC.BAS
'    The QuickChart program draws column charts, line charts, and
'    pie charts. (QuickChart is written for QuickBASIC 4.0 and 4.5.)

'    ---- Definitions and declarations section.

CONST false% = 0, true% = NOT false%, maxVals% = 10
CONST columns% = 1, printColumns% = 2, lines% = 3, pies% = 4

TYPE chartType
    columns AS STRING * 1
    printColumns AS STRING * 1
    lines AS STRING * 1
    pies AS STRING * 1
END TYPE

TYPE infoType
    largestValue AS SINGLE
    largestColumn AS SINGLE
    scaleFactor AS SINGLE
    columnFactor AS SINGLE
END TYPE

DECLARE FUNCTION Menu% (choices$())
DECLARE FUNCTION YesNo% (prompt$)
DECLARE SUB Analysis ()
DECLARE SUB AssignMenus (options%, menu1$(), menu2$())
DECLARE SUB AxisValues (axisMax)
DECLARE SUB BuildColumnChart (printChart%)
DECLARE SUB BuildLineChart ()
DECLARE SUB ColumnChart ()
DECLARE SUB DataLook ()
DECLARE SUB DataRead ()
DECLARE SUB DisplayMenuBox (choiceList$(), leftCoord%, prompt$, ok$)
DECLARE SUB Frame (left%, right%, top%, bottom%)
DECLARE SUB GetDims ()
DECLARE SUB GetSize ()
DECLARE SUB GetSylkValues (goodFile%)
DECLARE SUB GetTable ()
DECLARE SUB GraphScreen ()
```

Figure 8-14. *The* QuickChart *program.*

(continued)

Figure 8-14. *continued*

```
DECLARE SUB InData ()
DECLARE SUB Initialize ()
DECLARE SUB Legend (chartCode%, backward%)
DECLARE SUB LineChart ()
DECLARE SUB Pause ()
DECLARE SUB PieChart ()
DECLARE SUB PieDraw (targetCol%)
DECLARE SUB PieScreen (whichCol%)
DECLARE SUB PrFrame (left%, right%, top%, bottom%)
DECLARE SUB ReadFile (format%)
DECLARE SUB SaveData ()
DECLARE SUB ScreenTest (options%)
DECLARE SUB SylkRead ()
DECLARE SUB TextScreen (printChart%)
DECLARE SUB TransposeTable ()

COMMON SHARED dataTable$(), tableRows%, tableColumns%, tableInfo AS infoType
COMMON SHARED okData%, noFile%, file$, grafTablExists%
DIM SHARED chartChars(maxVals%) AS chartType

'    ---- Menu choices and chart characters.

DATA get data, column chart, line chart, pie chart, quit, keyboard input
DATA data file, sylk file, look at data, transpose the data, cancel
DATA 176, 177, 178, 219, 215, 222, 237, 179, 232, 181
DATA *, o, +, x, v, @, #, z, -, =

'    ---- The main program section.

okData% = false%
menuOptions% = 5

ScreenTest menuOptions%
DIM mainMenu$(menuOptions%), dataMenu$(6)

AssignMenus menuOptions%, mainMenu$(), dataMenu$()
Initialize

'    ---- Display the menus, read the user's menu choices,
'         and take appropriate action.

CLS
```

Main program

(continued)

Figure 8-14. *continued*

```
DO
    LOCATE 2, 33: PRINT "Chart Program"
    choice% = Menu%(mainMenu$())

'   ---- The Get data submenu offers options for reading data.

    SELECT CASE choice%

    CASE 1
        LOCATE 2, 27: PRINT "Get Data for Chart Program"
        dataChoice% = Menu%(dataMenu$())

        SELECT CASE dataChoice%
        CASE 1
            InData
        CASE 2, 3
            ReadFile dataChoice%
        CASE 4
            IF okData% THEN DataLook
        CASE 5
            IF okData% THEN TransposeTable
        CASE ELSE
        END SELECT

'   ---- Once a valid set of data is available (okData% is true),
'        the charting options are available from the main menu.

    CASE 2
        IF okData% THEN
            IF menuOptions% > 3 AND grafTablExists% THEN SCREEN 2
            Analysis
            ColumnChart
            SCREEN 0
        END IF

    CASE 3
        IF okData% AND menuOptions% > 3 THEN
            Analysis
            LineChart
        END IF
```

(continued)

Figure 8-14. *continued*

```
    CASE 4
        IF okData% AND menuOptions% > 3 THEN
            Analysis
            PieChart
        END IF

    CASE ELSE

    END SELECT

LOOP UNTIL choice% = menuOptions%

END

'   ---- Error-handling section.

'   ---- The IfMono error routine sets menuOptions% to 3 if the system
'        has a text-only display adapter. (Called by the ScreenTest
'        subprogram.)

IfMono:
    menuOptions% = 3
RESUME NEXT

'   ---- The NoGrafTablFile error routine sets the logical variable
'        grafTablExists% to false% if the MS-DOS command GRAFTABL.COM
'        cannot be found. (Called by the ScreenTest subprogram.)

NoGrafTablFile:
    grafTablExists% = false%
RESUME NEXT

'   ---- The IfNoFile error routine displays an error message if
'        a requested file cannot be found. (Called by the ReadFile
'        subprogram.)

IfNoFile:
    PRINT "    "; UCASE$(file$); " does not exist."
    PRINT
    PRINT "    ";
```

Error handling

(continued)

Figure 8-14. *continued*

```
    Pause
    noFile% = true%
RESUME NEXT


'   ---- The ErasePauseMessage event-trapping routine erases the
'        message "Press the spacebar to continue." from a chart screen
'        display. (ON TIMER statements result in a call to this routine
'        five seconds after the program draws a chart.)

ErasePauseMessage:

    IF choice% = 4 THEN messageRow% = 25 ELSE messageRow% = 1
    LOCATE messageRow%, 47, 0

    SELECT CASE choice%

    CASE 2
        Frame 1, 80, 1, 25

    CASE 3, 4
        VIEW
        WINDOW
        PRINT SPACE$(33);
        LINE (0, 2)-(639, 199), , B
        LINE (5, 4)-(634, 197), , B

    CASE ELSE

    END SELECT

    TIMER OFF

RETURN

SUB Analysis STATIC

'   The Analysis subprogram examines the data set and computes
'       a set of statistical values required by the charting routines.
'       The values are saved in the following elements of the
'       global record structure named tableInfo:
```

Analysis

(continued)

Figure 8-14. *continued*

```
'           -- largestValue is the largest numeric value in the data set.
'           -- largestColumn is the largest column total.
'           -- scaleFactor is a scaling factor used for line charts.
'           -- columnFactor is a scaling factor used for column charts.

    tableInfo.largestValue = 0
    tableInfo.largestColumn = 0
    FOR j% = 1 TO tableColumns%
        temp = 0
        FOR i% = 1 TO tableRows%
            IF VAL(dataTable$(i%, j%)) > tableInfo.largestValue THEN
                tableInfo.largestValue = VAL(dataTable$(i%, j%))
            END IF
            temp = temp + VAL(dataTable$(i%, j%))
        NEXT i%
        IF temp > tableInfo.largestColumn THEN tableInfo.largestColumn = temp
    NEXT j%
    tableInfo.columnFactor = 20 / tableInfo.largestColumn
    tableInfo.scaleFactor = 20 / tableInfo.largestValue

END SUB

SUB AssignMenus (options%, menu1$(), menu2$()) STATIC
```

`AssignMenus`

```
'   The AssignMenus subprogram establishes the two sets of menu choices.
'       The number of choices in the main menu depends upon the
'       value of options%; this value is 3 for a text-only display adapter
'       or 5 for a graphics display adapter.

    IF options% = 3 THEN
        READ menu1$(1)
        READ menu1$(2)
        READ garbage$
        READ garbage$
        READ menu1$(3)
    ELSE
        FOR i% = 1 TO options%
            READ menu1$(i%)
        NEXT i%
    END IF
```

(continued)

Figure 8-14. *continued*

```
    FOR i% = 1 TO 6
        READ menu2$(i%)
    NEXT i%

END SUB
```

AxisValues

```
SUB AxisValues (axisMax) STATIC

'   The AxisValues subprogram displays an array of numbers along the
'       vertical value axis for column charts and line charts.
'       AxisValues has one parameter, axisMax, which contains the
'       largest numeric value represented on the chart.

    FOR i% = 1 TO 4
        LOCATE 23 - (i% * 5), 2
        IF axisMax > 9999999 THEN
            PRINT USING "##.#^^^^"; axisMax * (.25 * i%);
        ELSE
            PRINT USING "#######"; axisMax * (.25 * i%);
        END IF
    NEXT i%

END SUB
```

BuildColumnChart

```
SUB BuildColumnChart (printChart%) STATIC

'   The BuildColumnChart subprogram creates the "stacked" columns
'       of the chart and displays a category name below each column.

    columnWidth% = 48 \ tableColumns% - 2

    currentX% = 12
    FOR j% = 1 TO tableColumns%
        LOCATE 24, currentX%
        PRINT LEFT$(dataTable$(0, j%), columnWidth%);
        currentY% = 22
        FOR i% = 1 TO tableRows%
            height% = CINT(tableInfo.columnFactor * VAL(dataTable$(i%, j%)))
            FOR h% = 1 TO height%
                LOCATE currentY%, currentX%
```

(continued)

Figure 8-14. *continued*

```
                IF NOT printChart% THEN
                    PRINT STRING$(columnWidth%, chartChars(i%).columns);
                ELSE
                    PRINT STRING$(columnWidth%, chartChars(i%).printColumns);
                END IF
                currentY% = currentY% - 1
                IF currentY% < 3 THEN currentY% = 3
            NEXT h%
        NEXT i%
        currentX% = currentX% + columnWidth% + 2
    NEXT j%

END SUB

SUB BuildLineChart STATIC

'   The BuildLineChart subprogram draws the lines of a line chart and
'       marks the actual data points with character symbols.

'   ---- The VIEW and WINDOW commands establish a new coordinate system,
'       in this case vastly simplifying the use of the LINE command
'       for drawing the lines of the chart.

    VIEW (80, 20)-(479, 180)
    WINDOW (0, 0)-(50, INT(tableInfo.largestValue))
    between% = 48 \ tableColumns%

    FOR i% = 1 TO tableRows%
        PSET (2, VAL(dataTable$(i%, 1)))
        FOR j% = 2 TO tableColumns%
            LINE -(between% * (j% - 1) + 2, VAL(dataTable$(i%, j%)))
        NEXT j%
    NEXT i%

'   ---- Once the lines have been drawn, the line chart symbols
'       are displayed to represent the actual data points.
'       Since these are text symbols, LOCATE and PRINT are used to
'       display them, rather than any of the graphics commands.

    FOR j% = 1 TO tableColumns%
        LOCATE 24, 11 + (between% * (j% - 1))
```

BuildLineChart

(continued)

Figure 8-14. *continued*

```
            PRINT LEFT$(dataTable$(0, j%), between% - 2);
            FOR i% = 1 TO tableRows%
                yPos% = 23 - CINT(tableInfo.scaleFactor * VAL(dataTable$(i%, j%)))
                LOCATE yPos%, 13 + between% * (j% - 1)
                PRINT chartChars(i%).lines
            NEXT i%
        NEXT j%

    END SUB

    SUB ColumnChart STATIC

    '   The ColumnChart subprogram draws a column chart in two different
    '       versions. The first version uses "text-graphics" characters
    '       to produce a chart, and the second version uses uppercase
    '       letters to produce a chart that can be printed by any printer.

    '   ---- TextScreen and BuildColumnChart create the elements of the
    '        chart display. The call to each routine requires a logical
    '        argument: false% results in the first version of the
    '        graph; true% results in the printable version.

        TextScreen false%
        BuildColumnChart false%

        ON TIMER(5) GOSUB ErasePauseMessage
        TIMER ON
            LOCATE 1, 47
            Pause
        TIMER OFF

        PRINT : PRINT : PRINT
        CLS
        IF YesNo%("Do you want a printable version of this chart? ") THEN
            Pause
            CLS
            LOCATE , , 0
            TextScreen true%
            BuildColumnChart true%
            ch$ = "": WHILE ch$ = "": ch$ = INKEY$: WEND: CLS
        END IF
        CLS
    END SUB
```

ColumnChart

(continued)

Figure 8-14. *continued*

```
SUB DataLook STATIC

'   The DataLook subprogram displays the current data set (in the
'       dataTable$() array) on the screen. This is the fourth
'       option in the Get data submenu.

'   ---- Arrange to display four columns of the table at a time.

    startColumn% = 1
    IF tableColumns% <= 4 THEN
        endColumn% = tableColumns%
    ELSE
        endColumn% = 4
    END IF

    DO
        PRINT
        FOR i% = 0 TO tableRows%
            PRINT dataTable$(i%, 0);
            columnTab% = 16
            FOR j% = startColumn% TO endColumn%
                PRINT TAB(columnTab%); dataTable$(i%, j%);
                columnTab% = columnTab% + 15
            NEXT j%
            PRINT
        NEXT i%
        PRINT
        IF endColumn% < tableColumns% THEN PRINT "More data...    ";
        Pause

        startColumn% = startColumn% + 4
        IF endColumn% + 4 > tableColumns% THEN
            endColumn% = tableColumns%
        ELSE
            endColumn% = endColumn% + 4
        END IF

    LOOP UNTIL startColumn% > tableColumns%

END SUB
```

DataLook

(continued)

Figure 8-14. *continued*

DataRead

```
SUB DataRead STATIC

'   The DataRead subprogram reads a data file. The routine expects the
'       file to match the format of files created by the InData subprogram.

    PRINT "    Reading data file..."
    INPUT #1, tableRows%, tableColumns%

'   ---- The first two values must be integers in the range 1 to
'       maxVals%. If not, the program cannot use the file. (Note
'       that INPUT# assigns values of 0 to tableRows% and tableColumns%
'       if the first two values in the file are non-numeric. This might
'       happen if the user inadvertently requested the reading of
'       a SYLK file by this routine.)

    ok% = tableRows% > 0 AND tableRows% <= maxVals%
    ok% = ok% AND tableColumns% > 0 AND tableColumns% <= maxVals%

    IF ok% THEN

'   ---- If tableRows% and tableColumns% contain valid values, read the
'       rest of the data set into the dataTable$() array.

        REDIM dataTable$(tableRows%, tableColumns%)

        FOR i% = 0 TO tableRows%
            FOR j% = 0 TO tableColumns%
                INPUT #1, dataTable$(i%, j%)
            NEXT j%
        NEXT i%

        okData% = true%

'   ---- Otherwise, display an error message and set the global
'       variable okData% to a logical value of false.

    ELSE
        PRINT
        PRINT "    Cannot use this data file."
        okData% = false%
    END IF

END SUB
```

(continued)

Figure 8-14. *continued*

```
SUB DisplayMenuBox (choiceList$(), leftCoord%, prompt$, ok$)          DisplayMenuBox

'   The DisplayMenuBox subprogram displays the menu choices on the
'       screen and prepares the prompt string and validation string.
'       This routine is called from the Menu% function.

'   ---- Find the number of choices (numChoices%); initialize variables.

    numChoices% = UBOUND(choiceList$)
    prompt$ = " "
    ok$ = ""
    longChoice% = 0

'   ---- Prepare the prompt string (prompt$) and the string of
'       legal input characters (ok$). Also, find the length of
'       the longest choice string (longChoice%).

    FOR i% = 1 TO numChoices%
        first$ = UCASE$(LEFT$(choiceList$(i%), 1))
        ok$ = ok$ + first$
        prompt$ = prompt$ + first$ + "  "
        longTemp% = LEN(choiceList$(i%))
        IF longTemp% > longChoice% THEN longChoice% = longTemp%
    NEXT i%

    longChoice% = longChoice% + 1
    prompt$ = prompt$ + "-> "

'   ---- Test to see if the prompt string is longer than longChoice%.

    IF LEN(prompt$) >= longChoice% THEN longChoice% = LEN(prompt$) + 1

'   ---- Given longChoice% and numChoices%, determine the dimensions
'       of the menu frame. Draw the frame, calling on the Frame
'       subprogram.

    leftCoord% = 37 - longChoice% \ 2
    rightCoord% = 80 - leftCoord%
    topCoord% = 3
    bottomCoord% = 10 + numChoices%
    Frame leftCoord%, rightCoord%, topCoord%, bottomCoord%
```

(continued)

Figure 8-14. *continued*

```
'    ---- Display the menu choices. The first letter of each
'         choice is displayed in uppercase, followed by a
'         parenthesis character.

     FOR i% = 1 TO numChoices%
         LOCATE 6 + i%, leftCoord% + 3
         PRINT UCASE$(LEFT$(choiceList$(i%), 1)) + ")" + MID$(choiceList$(i%), 2)
     NEXT i%

     LOCATE 4, 38: PRINT "Menu"
     line$ = STRING$(longChoice%, 196)
     LOCATE 5, leftCoord% + 3: PRINT line$
     LOCATE 7 + numChoices%, leftCoord% + 3: PRINT line$

'    ---- Print the input prompt.

     LOCATE 9 + numChoices%, leftCoord% + 3: PRINT prompt$;

END SUB

SUB Frame (left%, right%, top%, bottom%) STATIC

'    The Frame subprogram draws a rectangular double-line frame on
'         the screen, using "text-graphics" characters from the
'         IBM Extended ASCII character set.

'    ---- Draw the four corners.

     LOCATE top%, left%: PRINT CHR$(201)
     LOCATE top%, right%: PRINT CHR$(187)
     LOCATE bottom%, left%: PRINT CHR$(200);
     LOCATE bottom%, right%: PRINT CHR$(188);

'    ---- Draw the vertical lines.

     FOR vert% = top% + 1 TO bottom% - 1
         LOCATE vert%, left%: PRINT CHR$(186);
         LOCATE vert%, right%: PRINT CHR$(186);
     NEXT vert%

'    ---- Draw the horizontal lines.
```

Frame

(continued)

Figure 8-14. *continued*

```
    horiz% = right% - left% - 1
    hline$ = STRING$(horiz%, 205)
    LOCATE top%, left% + 1: PRINT hline$
    LOCATE bottom%, left% + 1: PRINT hline$;

END SUB

SUB GetDims STATIC

'   The GetDims subprogram reads the "B" record of a SLYK file.
'       This record indicates the row and column dimensions of
'       the data set that is stored in the file.

'   ---- The routine ignores all records until the "B" record is read.

    DO
        INPUT #1, sylkString$
    LOOP UNTIL LEFT$(sylkString$, 1) = "B" OR EOF(1)

'   ---- In the event that the file does not contain a "B" record
'       (i.e., EOF is true at this point), the program must reject
'       the data set as unusable. Otherwise, the routine finds
'       values for tableRows% and tableColumns% in the "Y" and "X" fields,
'       respectively.

    IF NOT EOF(1) THEN
        yPos% = INSTR(sylkString$, "Y") + 1
        xPos% = INSTR(sylkString$, "X") + 1
        lengthY% = xPos% - yPos% - 2
        tableRows% = VAL(MID$(sylkString$, yPos%, lengthY%)) - 1
        tableColumns% = VAL(MID$(sylkString$, xPos%)) - 1
    ELSE
        tableRows% = 0
    END IF

END SUB

SUB GetSize STATIC

'   The GetSize subprogram finds out how many rows and columns
'       of numeric data the user wants to enter.
```

GetDims

GetSize

(continued)

Figure 8-14. *continued*

```
        DO
            PRINT "How many rows of data? ";
            PRINT "(no more than"; STR$(maxVals%);
            INPUT ") ==> ", tableRows%
            ok% = tableRows% > 0 AND tableRows% <= maxVals%
        LOOP UNTIL ok%

        DO
            PRINT "How many data values in each row? ";
            PRINT "(no more than"; STR$(maxVals%);
            INPUT ") ==> ", tableColumns%
            ok% = tableColumns% > 0 AND tableColumns% <= maxVals%
        LOOP UNTIL ok%

        PRINT

END SUB

SUB GetSylkValues (goodFile%) STATIC

    '   The GetSylkValues subprogram reads the data set from a SYLK file.
    '       The routine stores the data in the global array variable
    '       dataTable$(). In the event that the SYLK file does not contain
    '       all the necessary data to fill dataTable$(), the routine returns
    '       a logical value of false in the parameter goodFile%.

        goodFile% = true%

        count% = 0
        y% = 0
        x% = 0
        DO
            INPUT #1, sylkString$

    '   ---- The program reads only the "C" records; all others
    '           are irrelevant at this point.

            IF LEFT$(sylkString$, 1) = "C" THEN
                count% = count% + 1
                kPos% = INSTR(sylkString$, "K")
                sylkString$ = MID$(sylkString$, kPos% + 1)
                lengthString% = LEN(sylkString$)
```

GetSylkValues

(continued)

Figure 8-14. *continued*

```
'    ---- The "K" field (always the last field in the "C" record)
'         may contain a string value enclosed in double quotes or
'         a numeric value. For tableRows% > 0 and tableColumns% > 0,
'         all values should be numeric for the data set to be
'         accepted as valid.

            IF LEFT$(sylkString$, 1) = CHR$(34) THEN
                dataTable$(y%, x%) = MID$(sylkString$, 2, lengthString% - 2)
                IF y% > 0 AND x% > 0 THEN goodFile% = false%
            ELSE
                dataTable$(y%, x%) = sylkString$
            END IF
            x% = x% + 1
            IF x% > tableColumns% THEN
                x% = 0
                y% = y% + 1
            END IF
        END IF
    LOOP UNTIL sylkString$ = "E"

'    ---- If any of the "C" records did not contain "K" fields
'         (indicating that one or more worksheet cells were blank),
'         then some required data is missing; the data set must
'         therefore be rejected.

    IF count% <> (tableRows% + 1) * (tableColumns% + 1) THEN goodFile% = false%

END SUB


SUB GetTable STATIC
```

GetTable

```
'    The GetTable subprogram accepts the user's data from the
'         keyboard. It stores category names in row 0 and series
'         names in column 0.

    INPUT "Title of graph"; dataTable$(0, 0)
    PRINT
    PRINT "    Category names:"
    FOR j% = 1 TO tableColumns%
        PRINT TAB(20); "column"; j%;
        INPUT "==> ", dataTable$(0, j%)
    NEXT j%
```

(continued)

Figure 8-14. *continued*

```
         PRINT
         FOR i% = 1 TO tableRows%
             PRINT "     Series name for row"; i%;
             INPUT "==> ", dataTable$(i%, 0)
             PRINT "        Numeric data values:"
             FOR j% = 1 TO tableColumns%
                 PRINT TAB(27); dataTable$(0, j%);
                 DO
                     INPUT " ==> ", temp
                     IF temp < 0 THEN
                         PRINT "         Redo. ";
                         PRINT "(Positive numbers only.) ";
                     END IF
                 LOOP UNTIL temp >= 0
                 dataTable$(i%, j%) = STR$(temp)
             NEXT j%
             PRINT
         NEXT i%

     END SUB

     SUB GraphScreen STATIC

     '   The GraphScreen subprogram prepares the screen for the line chart by
     '       displaying the legend, drawing the axes, and placing a frame
     '       around the perimeter of the screen.

         LINE (0, 2)-(639, 199), , B
         LINE (5, 4)-(634, 197), , B

         LOCATE 4, 67: PRINT "Legend"
         LINE (490, 34)-STEP(133, tableRows% * 8 + 13), , B
         LINE (495, 36)-STEP(123, tableRows% * 8 + 9), , B
         Legend lines%, false%

         LINE (74, 16)-(74, 180)
         LINE -(479, 180)

         FOR y% = 20 TO 140 STEP 40
             LINE (72, y%)-(479, y%), , , &H8000
         NEXT y%
```

GraphScreen

(continued)

Figure 8-14. *continued*

```
      AxisValues tableInfo.largestValue

END SUB

SUB InData STATIC

'     The InData subprogram accepts a set of data from the keyboard
'         and saves the data in a disk file if the user requests.

'     ---- Find out the size of the data table.

      GetSize

'     ---- The dataTable$() array will hold the data.

      REDIM dataTable$(tableRows%, tableColumns%)

'     ---- Get the data.

      GetTable

'     ---- Store the data in a disk file if the user so requests.

      PRINT "Enter a filename for storing this data."
      INPUT "(Or press Enter if you do not wish to save data.) ==> ", file$
      file$ = LTRIM$(RTRIM$(file$))

      IF LEN(file$) <> 0 THEN
          SaveData
      END IF
      CLS

      okData% = true%

END SUB

SUB Initialize STATIC

'     The Initialize subprogram reads text characters for the
'         various chart types.

'     ---- Read the column chart characters.
```

InData

Initialize

(continued)

Figure 8-14. *continued*

```
        FOR i% = 1 TO maxVals%
            READ temp%
            chartChars(i%).columns = CHR$(temp%)
        NEXT i%


    '   ---- Read the line chart characters.


        FOR i% = 1 TO maxVals%
            READ chartChars(i%).lines
        NEXT i%


    '   ---- Create the arrays for the printable column chart
    '        and the pie chart.


        FOR i% = 1 TO maxVals%
            chartChars(i%).printColumns = CHR$(64 + i%)
            chartChars(i%).pies = CHR$(96 + i%)
        NEXT i%


    END SUB


    SUB Legend (chartCode%, backward%) STATIC


    '   The Legend subprogram creates the legend for all three chart
    '       types. Legend has two parameters: chartCode% indicates
    '       which type of chart is being created, and backward%
    '       (a logical value) indicates whether the legend strings
    '       should be displayed from bottom to top (true) or from
    '       top to bottom (false).


        FOR i% = 1 TO tableRows%
            IF backward% THEN
                LOCATE tableRows% + 6 - i%, 64
            ELSE
                LOCATE 5 + i%, 64
            END IF


            SELECT CASE chartCode%
            CASE columns%
                PRINT chartChars(i%).columns;
            CASE printColumns%
                PRINT chartChars(i%).printColumns;
```

Legend

(continued)

Figure 8-14. *continued*

```
        CASE lines%
            PRINT chartChars(i%).lines;
        CASE pies%
            PRINT chartChars(i%).pies;
        END SELECT

        PRINT " "; LEFT$(dataTable$(i%, 0), 11)
    NEXT i%

    titleLength% = LEN(dataTable$(0, 0))
    LOCATE 2, (80 - titleLength%) \ 2: PRINT dataTable$(0, 0);

END SUB

SUB LineChart STATIC
```

LineChart

```
'   The LineChart subprogram draws a line chart on a graphics screen
'       (SCREEN 2).

    SCREEN 2
    GraphScreen
    BuildLineChart

    ON TIMER(5) GOSUB ErasePauseMessage
    TIMER ON
        LOCATE 1, 47: PRINT " ";
        Pause
    TIMER OFF

    SCREEN 0

END SUB

FUNCTION Menu% (choices$()) STATIC
```

Menu%

```
'   The Menu% function displays a menu on the screen and elicits
'       a menu choice from the user. Menu% receives a string array
'       (choices$()) containing the menu choices and returns an
'       integer indicating the user's selection from among those choices.

    listLength% = UBOUND(choices$)
    DisplayMenuBox choices$(), leftMargin%, promptStr$, okStr$
```

(continued)

Figure 8-14. *continued*

```
'    ---- Get a menu choice. Validate and verify the choice.

    controlKeys$ = CHR$(13) + CHR$(27)
    DO
        LOCATE . , 1
        charPos% = 0
        DO
            answer$ = UCASE$(INKEY$)
            IF answer$ <> "" THEN
                charPos% = INSTR(okStr$, answer$)
                IF charPos% = 0 THEN BEEP
            END IF
        LOOP UNTIL charPos% > 0

        PRINT answer$
        LOCATE 11 + listLength%, 23, 0
        PRINT "<Enter> to confirm; <Esc> to redo."
        inChoice% = charPos%

        charPos% = 0
        DO
            answer$ = INKEY$
            IF answer$ <> "" THEN
                charPos% = INSTR(controlKeys$, answer$)
                IF charPos% = 0 THEN BEEP
            END IF
        LOOP UNTIL charPos% > 0

        IF charPos% = 1 THEN
            done% = true%
            CLS
        ELSE
            done% = false%
            LOCATE 11 + listLength%, 23: PRINT SPACE$(35)
            LOCATE 9 + listLength%, leftMargin% + 3 + LEN(promptStr$)
            PRINT " ";
            LOCATE , POS(0) - 1:
        END IF

    LOOP UNTIL done%
    Menu% = inChoice%

END FUNCTION
```

(continued)

Figure 8-14. *continued*

Pause

```
SUB Pause STATIC

'   The Pause subprogram simply creates a pause in the action
'       until the user presses a key at the keyboard. This routine
'       is used throughout the program to freeze the action while
'       the user examines a screenful of information.

    PRINT "Press the spacebar to continue.";

    DO
        ch$ = INKEY$
    LOOP UNTIL ch$ = " "
    CLS

END SUB
```

PieChart

```
SUB PieChart STATIC

'   The PieChart subprogram draws a pie chart from one selected
'       column of data.

'   ---- If the current data set (in the dataTable$() array) contains
'           more than one column, allow the user to select a column
'           for the pie chart.

    IF tableColumns% > 1 THEN
        PRINT : PRINT : PRINT
        PRINT "    Select a column of data for the pie chart:"
        PRINT
        FOR i% = 1 TO tableColumns%
            PRINT TAB(8); STR$(i%); ". "; dataTable$(0, i%)
        NEXT i%
        PRINT

        DO
            PRINT TAB(12); "1 to "; tableColumns%;
            INPUT "==> ", pieTemp$
            pieColumn% = VAL(pieTemp$)
        LOOP UNTIL pieColumn% >= 1 AND pieColumn% <= tableColumns%

    ELSE
        pieColumn% = 1
```

(continued)

Figure 8-14. *continued*

```
        END IF
        CLS

        PieScreen pieColumn%
        PieDraw pieColumn%

    END SUB

    SUB PieDraw (targetCol%) STATIC

    '   The PieDraw subprogram draws the pie chart.

    '   ---- Calculate columnTotal, the total of the column of numeric values.

        columnTotal = 0
        FOR i% = 1 TO tableRows%
            columnTotal = columnTotal + VAL(dataTable$(i%, targetCol%))
        NEXT i%

    '   ---- Assign constant values for the center coordinates, the
    '        radius, the starting point, and the value of 2 * pi.
    '        (Note that the variables start and piTimes2 receive negative
    '        values so that CIRCLE will draw the sides of each wedge.)

        centerX% = 279
        centerY% = 110
        radius% = 150
        start = -.00001
        piTimes2 = -3.141592 * 2

    '   ---- Use the CIRCLE command to draw the wedges of the pie
    '        chart, each wedge representing one of the values in
    '        the selected column.

        FOR i% = 1 TO tableRows%
            portion = (VAL(dataTable$(i%, targetCol%)) / columnTotal) * piTimes2
            IF i% < tableRows% THEN
                wedge = start + portion
            ELSE
                wedge = piTimes2
            END IF
            CIRCLE (centerX%, centerY%), radius%, , start, wedge
```

PieDraw

(continued)

Figure 8-14. *continued*

```
'    ---- Calculate the coordinates for positioning an identifying
'         symbol inside each wedge; display the symbol.

          angle = -1 * (start + portion / 2)
          rowLoc% = INT(-6 * SIN(angle) + 14.5)
          colLoc% = INT(15 * COS(angle) + 35.5)
          LOCATE rowLoc%, colLoc%
          PRINT chartChars(i%).pies;

          start = wedge
     NEXT i%

     ON TIMER(5) GOSUB ErasePauseMessage
     TIMER ON
          LOCATE 25, 47: PRINT " ";
          Pause
     TIMER OFF

     SCREEN 0

END SUB

SUB PieScreen (whichCol%) STATIC
```
PieScreen
```
'   The PieScreen subprogram prepares the pie chart screen by drawing
'        a frame, displaying the legend, and displaying the title and
'        subtitle of the chart.

     SCREEN 2

     LINE (0, 2)-(639, 199), , B
     LINE (5, 4)-(634, 197), , B

     LOCATE 4, 67: PRINT "Legend"
     LINE (490, 34)-STEP(133, tableRows% * 8 + 13), , B
     LINE (495, 36)-STEP(123, tableRows% * 8 + 9), , B
     Legend pies%, 0

     subTitleLength% = LEN(dataTable$(0, whichCol%))
     LOCATE 3, (80 - subTitleLength%) \ 2: PRINT dataTable$(0, whichCol%);

END SUB
```

(continued)

Figure 8-14. *continued*

PrFrame

```
SUB PrFrame (left%, right%, top%, bottom%) STATIC

    '   The PrFrame subprogram draws a rectangular frame on the
    '       screen, using printable ASCII characters.

    '   ---- Draw the four corners.

        LOCATE top%, left%: PRINT "+"
        LOCATE top%, right%: PRINT "+"
        LOCATE bottom%, left%: PRINT "+";
        LOCATE bottom%, right%: PRINT "+";

    '   ---- Draw the vertical lines.

        FOR vert% = top% + 1 TO bottom% - 1
            LOCATE vert%, left%: PRINT "¦";
            LOCATE vert%, right%: PRINT "¦";
        NEXT vert%

    '   ---- Draw the horizontal lines.

        horiz% = right% - left% - 1
        hline$ = STRING$(horiz%, "-")
        LOCATE top%, left% + 1: PRINT hline$
        LOCATE bottom%, left% + 1: PRINT hline$;

END SUB
```

ReadFile

```
SUB ReadFile (format%) STATIC

    '   The ReadFile subprogram elicits the name of a sequential
    '       data file or a SYLK file, checks to make sure the file
    '       exists, opens the file, and calls either DataRead or
    '       SylkRead to read the file.

        PRINT : PRINT : PRINT
        PRINT "    Enter the name of the file you want to read."
        PRINT "    (Include the base name and the extension,"
        PRINT "    along with the drive designation if necessary.)"

        DO
            INPUT "    ==> ", file$
            file$ = LTRIM$(RTRIM$(file$))
```

(continued)

Figure 8-14. *continued*

```
    LOOP UNTIL file$ <> ""

    PRINT : PRINT
    noFile% = false%

'   ---- Check to make sure the requested file exists.

    ON ERROR GOTO IfNoFile
        OPEN file$ FOR INPUT AS #1
    ON ERROR GOTO 0

'   ---- If it does, call the appropriate subprogram -- to read a
'        data file or a SYLK file. The value of format% depends upon
'        which menu choice the user has selected: 2 for a regular
'        data file and 3 for a SYLK file.

    IF NOT noFile% THEN
        IF format% = 2 THEN
            DataRead
        ELSE
            SylkRead
        END IF
        PRINT
        PRINT "    ";
        Pause
        CLOSE
    END IF

END SUB

SUB SaveData STATIC                                              SaveData

'   The SaveData subprogram saves a data set that has been entered
'        from the keyboard.

    OPEN file$ FOR OUTPUT AS #1
    WRITE #1, tableRows%, tableColumns%
    FOR i% = 0 TO tableRows%
        FOR j% = 0 TO tableColumns%
            PRINT #1, dataTable$(i%, j%);
            IF j% < tableColumns% THEN PRINT #1, ". ";
        NEXT j%                                          '
```

(continued)

Figure 8-14. *continued*

```
        PRINT #1,
        NEXT i%
        CLOSE

END SUB

SUB ScreenTest (options%) STATIC

    '   The ScreenTest subprogram determines if the display hardware
    '       supports graphics. The variable menuOptions% is the number of
    '       choices there will be in the main menu: 3 if this is a
    '       text-only adapter; 5 if this is a graphics adapter.

    '   ---- Try performing a graphics command in SCREEN 2. If an
    '       error results, this is a text-only adapter; if
    '       not, this is a graphics adapter. The IfMono routine
    '       sets menuOptions% to 3 if an error occurs.

    ON ERROR GOTO IfMono
        SCREEN 2
        PSET (0, 0)
    ON ERROR GOTO 0

    '   ---- If this is a graphics adapter, invoke the MS-DOS GRAFTABL
    '       command to load the IBM Extended Character Set (ASCII codes
    '       128-255) into memory.

    IF options% > 3 THEN
        grafTablExists% = true%
        ON ERROR GOTO NoGrafTablFile
            FILES "GRAFTABL.COM"
        ON ERROR GOTO 0
        IF grafTablExists% THEN SHELL "GRAFTABL"
    END IF

    SCREEN 0

END SUB
```

(continued)

Figure 8-14. *continued*

SylkRead

```
SUB SylkRead STATIC

'   The SylkRead subprogram reads a SYLK file. The routine first checks
'       to make sure that the file contains a usable data set and
'       then reads only the "K" fields in the "C" records. Other
'       records and fields are ignored.

    okData% = false%
    PRINT "    Reading SYLK file..."
    PRINT


'   ---- The first record should be the ID record. If not, the program
'       must assume that this is not a SYLK file.

    INPUT #1, sylkst$

    IF LEFT$(sylkst$, 4) = "ID;P" THEN
        GetDims
        ok% = tableRows% <= maxVals% AND tableRows% > 0
        ok% = ok% AND tableColumns% <= maxVals% AND tableColumns% > 0
        IF ok% THEN
            REDIM dataTable$(tableRows%, tableColumns%)
            GetSylkValues (ok%)
        END IF

        IF NOT ok% THEN
            PRINT "    This SYLK file does not match"
            PRINT "    the requirements of the program."
        ELSE
            okData% = true%
        END IF
    ELSE
        PRINT "    This is not a SYLK file."
    END IF

END SUB

SUB TextScreen (printChart%) STATIC
```

TextScreen

```
'   The TextScreen subprogram prepares the screen for the column chart:
'       It displays the legend, creates the axes, displays numeric
'       values along the value axis, and draws a frame around the
'       perimeter of the screen.
```

(continued)

Figure 8-14. *continued*

```
    LOCATE 4, 67: PRINT "Legend"
    IF NOT printChart% THEN
        Frame 1, 80, 1, 25
        Frame 62, 78, 5, tableRows% + 6
        Legend columns%, true%
        yAxis$ = CHR$(179)
        crossLine$ = CHR$(197) + STRING$(50, 250)
        xAxis$ = STRING$(50, 196)
        origin$ = CHR$(192)
    ELSE
        PrFrame 1, 80, 1, 25
        PrFrame 62, 78, 5, tableRows% + 6
        Legend printColumns%, true%
        yAxis$ = "|"
        crossLine$ = "+" + STRING$(50, "-")
        xAxis$ = STRING$(50, "-")
        origin$ = "+"
    END IF

'   ---- Draw the axes.

    LOCATE 23, 10: PRINT origin$
    LOCATE 23, 11: PRINT xAxis$

    FOR i% = 22 TO 3 STEP  1
        LOCATE i%, 10
        IF (i% + 2) MOD 5 = 0 THEN
            PRINT crossLine$
        ELSE
            PRINT yAxis$
        END IF
    NEXT i%

    AxisValues tableInfo.largestColumn

END SUB


SUB TransposeTable

'   The TransposeTable subprogram transposes the dimensions of
'       the data table, rows for columns and columns for rows.
```

TransposeTable

(continued)

Figure 8-14. *continued*

```
'    ---- Begin by making a temporary copy of the data table.

     REDIM dataTemp$(tableRows%, tableColumns%)
     FOR i% = 0 TO tableRows%
         FOR j% = 0 TO tableColumns%
             dataTemp$(i%, j%) = dataTable$(i%, j%)
         NEXT j%
     NEXT i%

'    ---- Swap the dimensions, redimension the dataTable$() array,
'         and copy back the data in the rearranged order.

     SWAP tableRows%, tableColumns%
     REDIM dataTable$(tableRows%, tableColumns%)
     FOR i% = 0 TO tableRows%
         FOR j% = 0 TO tableColumns%
             dataTable$(i%, j%) = dataTemp$(j%, i%)
         NEXT j%
     NEXT i%

END SUB

FUNCTION YesNo% (prompt$)
```

YesNo%

```
'    The YesNo% function asks a yes-or-no question and returns
'         a logical value indicating the user's response:
'         true means yes; false means no.

'    ---- Display the question prompt and initialize variables.

     PRINT prompt$; " (Y or N) -> ";
     ans$ = ""
     charPos% = 0

'    ---- Get a single-letter response.

     DO
         LOCATE , , 1
         ans$ = UCASE$(INKEY$)
         IF ans$ <> "" THEN
             charPos% = INSTR("YN", ans$)
             IF charPos% = 0 THEN BEEP
```

(continued)

Figure 8-14. *continued*

```
      END IF
   LOOP UNTIL charPos% > 0

   PRINT ans$

'    ---- Convert the response into a logical value.

   YesNo% = (ans$ = "Y")

END FUNCTION
```

CHAPTER 9

Event Trapping: The *Advanced Menu* Program

An *event trap* is a structure that interrupts a program's normal logical flow in response to a specific external event. QuickBASIC supplies event-trapping commands that can prepare a program for several categories of events, including:

- Serial-port communications
- Light pen or joystick activities
- Changes in the PLAY command's music buffer
- Elapsed time on the system clock
- Specially defined keystrokes

If a "trapped" event occurs, the program reacts by branching to an appropriate event-handling subroutine.

An event trap is similar in execution to an error trap. As we have discussed in previous chapters, an error trap prevents a program from terminating in the event of a runtime error. The ON ERROR GOTO statement puts the program on alert for the possibility of an error and causes a branch to an error-handling routine if an error occurs. Similarly, an event trap uses a special ON...GOSUB statement to identify the event-handling subroutine that will take control if a particular external event occurs.

In this brief chapter we'll discuss the techniques of event trapping. We'll focus on two particular event-trapping categories: elapsed-time trapping and keystroke trapping. Finally, we'll examine a program called *AdvMenu* ("Advanced Menu") as an illustration of event trapping.

The purpose of the *AdvMenu* program is to provide menu-driven access to all five of the major applications presented in previous chapters—*List, Twenty-one, Survey, Employee,* and *QuickChart.* In addition, the program contains a new version of *Menu%,* the function that we first discussed in Chapter 3. The new version, called *MenuPlus%,* has two features not available in the original function:

- *MenuPlus%* displays the date and the continually changing time on the screen immediately below the menu.

- *MenuPlus%* offers a help screen describing the menu options. (This screen appears when you press the F1 function key.)

The *AdvMenu* program uses event-trapping techniques to implement both of these new features. Before we look at this program, let's discuss QuickBASIC's event-trapping commands.

EVENT TRAPPING

To implement a successful event trap, you must incorporate several diverse elements into your program. These elements include:

- An event-handling subroutine

- An ON...GOSUB statement that identifies the event-handling subroutine

- An ON switch that activates the trap

- An OFF or STOP switch that deactivates the trap at the appropriate point in the program

We'll examine these elements in the following two sections.

Event-handling subroutines

An event-handling subroutine is designed to take control of the program if a specified external event occurs. You cannot code this routine as a subprogram or function: It must be a *subroutine*. QuickBASIC places subroutines in the module-level code of a program.

A BASICA-style subroutine is simply a sequence of statements beginning at a specified line number. In this scheme, a GOSUB statement sends control to the routine by number. For example, the following statement transfers control to the subroutine located at line 1000:

```
GOSUB 1000
```

A RETURN statement at the end of the subroutine transfers control back to the line following the GOSUB statement when the routine's execution is complete.

In QuickBASIC, line numbers are not required and are in fact inconsistent with structured programming style. Instead, you can use a *line label* to identify the beginning of a subroutine. A line label is a name containing up to 40 letters and digits. The label must begin with a letter and end with a colon. Here's the basic structure of a Quick-BASIC subroutine that uses a line label:

```
LineLabel:
     [the statements of the subroutine]
RETURN
```

In this structure, *LineLabel* marks the beginning of the subroutine in the program listing, and the RETURN statement marks the end of the routine. After execution of the subroutine, RETURN sends control of the program back to the location where the routine was called.

Except for implementing event traps, subroutines are not an ideal way to organize the tasks of a QuickBASIC program. As we have seen throughout this book, QuickBASIC's subprogram and function procedures result in a far superior program structure. Nonetheless, an event trap requires the use of a subroutine as an event-handling structure. We'll discuss the event-trapping commands in the next section.

Event-trapping commands

Along with the event-handling subroutine, you must include a variety of commands in your program to control the event trap. First, an ON...GOSUB statement establishes a particular event-handling routine for an anticipated event. This statement's syntax is:

```
ON event GOSUB LineLabel
```

The reserved word that identifies *event* in this ON...GOSUB statement can be COM, PEN, STRIG, PLAY, TIMER, or KEY. These words represent the six categories of event trapping available in QuickBASIC, as we'll see shortly.

After the ON...GOSUB statement, an ON switch activates the trap at an appropriate point in the program.

```
event ON
```

At the point where you no longer anticipate the external event, use an OFF switch to deactivate the trap:

```
event OFF
```

Alternatively, you can use a STOP switch to suspend the trap:

```
event STOP
```

As a result of a STOP switch, QuickBASIC records any relevant external event that occurs while the trap is suspended. A subsequent ON switch statement causes the program to react to the trapped event.

In the syntax of all these commands, one of the following *event* options identifies the event-trap category:

- COM(*port*) reacts when information is received at the specified serial port. The *port* argument can be *1* or *2*.

- PEN responds to light pen activity.

- STRIG(*trigger*) reacts when the specified joystick trigger is pressed.

- PLAY(*notes*) responds when the number of notes in the music buffer is less than *notes*.

- TIMER(*num*) executes the event-handling routine every *num* seconds.

- KEY(*keyCode*) responds when the user presses the key represented by *keyCode*.

AdvMenu uses two of these techniques—ON TIMER and ON KEY—to set up traps for the program's controlling menu. In the following sections, we'll examine these two categories of event trapping.

The ON TIMER command

ON TIMER is useful whenever you want a particular action to be repeated at timed intervals. For example, let's say you are designing a program that will change the screen display every five seconds. You might organize the program as follows:

```
ON TIMER(5) GOSUB ChangeScreen
TIMER ON
      [statements that will be executed
        while the trap is active]
TIMER OFF
      [other program lines]
END

ChangeScreen:
      [commands that change the screen]
RETURN
```

In this program, the ON TIMER(5) command identifies the event-handling subroutine located at the *ChangeScreen* label. TIMER ON activates the trap before the main activity of the program begins, and TIMER OFF deactivates the trap when the activity is over. While the trap is active, the program calls *ChangeScreen* every five seconds.

The ON KEY command

ON KEY traps a particular keystroke. Unlike the more commonly used commands for reading the keyboard—INPUT and INKEY$—a key trap only interrupts the current activity if the user presses a particular key.

The ON KEY statement uses code numbers to represent specific keys. These are the codes:

1 through 10	Function keys F1 through F10
11	The up-arrow key
12	The left-arrow key
13	The right-arrow key
14	The down-arrow key
15 through 25	User-defined key codes
30 and 31	Function keys F11 and F12 (on keyboards that have them)

See the *Microsoft QuickBASIC 4.0 BASIC Language Reference* or the QB Advisor in QuickBASIC 4.5 for more information about using these codes (especially the user-defined key codes from 15 through 25).

Imagine you are writing a program designed to respond in a particular way to the F10 function key. Your program might be organized as follows:

```
ON KEY(10) GOSUB FunctionTen
KEY(10) ON
    [statements that will be executed
       while the trap is active]
KEY(10) OFF
    [other program lines]
END

FunctionTen:
    [commands that respond to the F10 key press]
RETURN
```

In the program above, the ON KEY(10) command identifies the event-handling subroutine, located at the *FunctionTen* label. KEY(10) ON activates the trap before the main activity of the program begins, and KEY(10) OFF deactivates the trap when the activity is over. While the trap is active, the program calls the *FunctionTen* subroutine each time the user presses F10.

Now let's look at the *AdvMenu* program. First we'll see what the program does, and then we'll look inside the program to investigate its two event traps.

THE *ADVMENU* PROGRAM

AdvMenu illustrates a simple but effective way to combine diverse program applications under a single menu-driven interface. Figure 9-1 shows the program's menu. As you can see, the menu options include the five major applications developed in this book. (The sixth option terminates the program and returns you to MS-DOS.)

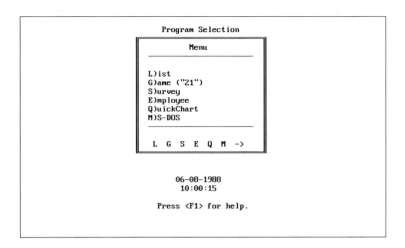

Figure 9-1. *The main menu for the* AdvMenu *program.*

When you select any of the first five options, the *AdvMenu* program uses the SHELL command to execute one of the following compiled program files:

LIST.EXE
21.EXE
SURVEY.EXE
EMPLOYEE.EXE
QC.EXE

To set up the program, you should store these five EXE files on disk along with the compiled version of *AdvMenu*. Choose QuickBASIC's Make EXE File command from the Run menu to create these files from the corresponding application programs. QuickBASIC's runtime module file, *BRUN45.EXE*, must also be available if you use the *EXE Requiring BRUN45.EXE* option to compile the five programs. If you compile the programs as stand-alone EXE files, *BRUN45.EXE* is not required.

If you look again at Figure 9-1, you can see the two new elements that the *AdvMenu* program incorporates into the menu screen. The time and the date appear below the menu box. (The program updates the time every second.) In addition, the following message appears near the bottom of the screen:

```
Press <F1> for help.
```

When you press F1, a help panel takes over the screen, succinctly describing the purpose of each application program. Figure 9-2 shows the help screen. Press the spacebar to return to the main menu. When you return from the help screen, the program displays the main menu exactly as it appeared before.

```
Program        Description
-------        -----------

List           Displays MS-DOS directories. (Send a
               parameter of /H to view a help screen.)

21             Plays the game of 21, or Blackjack.

Survey         Stores, prints, and tabulates results from
               survey questionnaires or opinion polls.

Employee       Maintains an employee database and allows
               searching, changing, deleting, and printing
               of database records. (Stores the database in
               EMP.DAT and the database index in EMP.NDX.)

QuickChart     Creates column charts, line charts, and pie
               charts. Data can be read from the keyboard
               or from data files (including SYLK files).

Press the spacebar to continue.
```

Figure 9-2. *The* AdvMenu *help screen.*

INSIDE THE *ADVMENU* PROGRAM

Now that we have seen some examples of *AdvMenu*, let's examine the program. The complete listing appears in Figure 9-3, which begins on page 430. The various declarations and definitions required by the program appear at the top of the listing, followed by the main program section, the event-handling section, and the function and four subprograms listed in alphabetic order. Throughout the program discussion you'll see references to the function and subprograms—these are labeled along the right and left margins of the listing with tabs bearing the function or subprogram name.

As we examine the listing, we'll concentrate on the following four sections:

- The main program section
- The event-handling section
- The *MenuPlus%* function
- The *Help* subprogram

The main program section

The main program section begins by storing the menu option strings in the string array *programMenu$()*. Then a DO...UNTIL loop takes control, displaying the menu on the screen and processing each menu selection. Inside the loop, the program calls the *MenuPlus%* function at the top of a SELECT CASE structure:

```
SELECT CASE MenuPlus%(programMenu$())
```

Each of the subsequent CASE blocks contains a SHELL statement that executes one of the compiled EXE programs. For example, here is the statement that executes the *Twenty-one* program:

```
SHELL "21"
```

By the way, if QuickBASIC cannot find the appropriate EXE file in the current directory or the command path, the SHELL statement results in an MS-DOS error message:

```
Bad command or file name
```

This error does not terminate the program, however. After the message appears on the screen, *AdvMenu* resumes its execution, once again calling the *MenuPlus%* function to display the main menu on the screen.

MenuPlus% and the event-handling subroutines

The new elements of *MenuPlus%* are the statements that establish the event traps. The function sets up two traps:

- A TIMER trap that branches to the *DisplayDateAndTime* subroutine and results in the date and time display below the menu box

- A KEY trap that branches to the *DisplayHelpScreen* subroutine and produces the help display whenever the user presses F1

Both traps are activated as soon as the menu appears on the screen. The following commands establish and activate the TIMER trap:

```
ON TIMER(1) GOSUB DisplayDateAndTime
TIMER ON
```

The argument of the TIMER command is *1*; thus the program calls *DisplayDateAndTime* once every second.

The *DisplayDateAndTime* subroutine starts out by recording the current cursor position on the text screen. The built-in POS function supplies the column position (from *1* through *80*) and the CSRLIN function gives the line number (from *1* through *25*):

```
xPos% = POS(0)
yPos% = CSRLIN
```

Next, the routine displays the date and the time on the screen:

```
LOCATE 19, 35
PRINT DATE$;
LOCATE 20, 36
PRINT TIME$;
```

Finally, *DisplayDateAndTime* restores the original cursor position and returns control to the *MenuPlus%* function:

```
        LOCATE yPos%, xPos%
RETURN
```

Back in *MenuPlus%*, the next commands establish and activate the KEY trap:

```
ON KEY(1) GOSUB DisplayHelpScreen
KEY(1) ON
```

In this case, the argument of the KEY command is a key code representing the F1 function key.

The *DisplayHelpScreen* subroutine begins by temporarily suspending the TIMER trap so that the date and time displays will not interfere with the help screen:

```
TIMER STOP
```

Then the routine clears the screen and calls the *Help* subprogram to produce the help panel:

```
CLS
Help
```

Help consists primarily of a sequence of PRINT statements that display the various program descriptions on the screen. *Help* also calls the *Frame* subprogram to display a frame around the help panel and the *Pause* subprogram to suspend the program's execution until the user presses the spacebar.

When *Help* has been executed, *DisplayHelpScreen* has to restore the original menu screen before relinquishing control. The subroutine calls the *DisplayMenuBox* subprogram to display the menu:

```
DisplayMenuBox programMenu$(), dummy%, promptStr$, okStr$
```

Then, if a menu selection is pending (*inChoice%* is not *0*), the subroutine also restores the option letter and the confirmation message:

```
IF inChoice% <> 0 THEN
    answer$ = MID$(okStr$, inChoice%, 1)
    PRINT answer$
    LOCATE 17, 23, 0
    PRINT "<Enter> to confirm; <Esc> to redo."
END IF
```

The variable *okStr$* contains the string of valid menu choices, and *inChoice%* is an integer representing the user's current selection.

Finally, *DisplayHelpScreen* reactivates the TIMER trap before sending control back to the *MenuPlus%* function:

```
    TIMER ON
RETURN
```

Both of the event traps remain active until the user exits from the program. Then, at the end of the *MenuPlus%* function, the following two commands deactivate the traps:

```
TIMER OFF
KEY(1) OFF
```

Conclusion

The *AdvMenu* program illustrates an interesting technique for collecting diverse program applications under one menu-driven interface system. Relying on the presence of compiled EXE program files on disk, the system is a simple but effective way to integrate a group of programs like the ones in this book. Furthermore, *AdvMenu* employs the ON TIMER and ON KEY error-trapping techniques to add useful features to the program's menu interface.

THE *ADVMENU* PROGRAM

```
'    ADVMENU.BAS
'    The Advanced Menu program supplies a menu-driven interface for running
'        all of the programs presented in this book, providing executable
'        versions of the programs are available in the current directory or
'        the command path. The program works with an advanced version of the
'        Menu function. (Advanced Menu is written for QuickBASIC 4.0 and 4.5.)

'    ---- Definitions and declarations section.

CONST false% = 0, true% = NOT false%

DECLARE FUNCTION MenuPlus% (choices$())
DECLARE SUB DisplayMenuBox (choiceList$(), leftCoord%, prompt$, ok$)
DECLARE SUB Frame (left%, right%, top%, bottom%)
DECLARE SUB Help ()
DECLARE SUB Pause ()

COMMON SHARED promptStr$, okStr$, inChoice%
DIM programMenu$(6)

DATA list, game ("21"), survey, employee, quickChart, MS-DOS

'    ---- Main program section.

FOR i% = 1 TO 6
    READ programMenu$(i%)
NEXT i%

done% = false%
DO
    CLS
    LOCATE 2, 32
    PRINT "Program Selection"
    LOCATE 22, 31
    PRINT "Press <F1> for help."

    SELECT CASE MenuPlus%(programMenu$())
```

Figure 9-3. *The* AdvMenu *program.*   *(continued)*

Figure 9-3. *continued*

```
    CASE 1
        CLS
        PRINT
        INPUT "Enter parameters for LIST (/H for help): ", listParams$
        SHELL "List " + listParams$
        LOCATE 25, 5
        Pause

    CASE 2
        SHELL "21"

    CASE 3
        SHELL "Survey"

    CASE 4
        SHELL "Employee"

    CASE 5
        SHELL "QC"

    CASE ELSE
        done% = true%

    END SELECT
    CLS
    inChoice% = 0
LOOP UNTIL done%

END

'   ---- Event-handling section.

'   ---- The DisplayDateAndTime routine displays the date and time
'        below the main menu. The MenuPlus% function calls this
'        routine every second to update the display.

DisplayDateAndTime:

'   ---- Begin by recording the current cursor position.

    xPos% = POS(0)
    yPos% = CSRLIN
```

Event handling

(continued)

Figure 9-3. *continued*

```
'    ---- Display the date and time below the menu.

    LOCATE 19, 35
    PRINT DATE$;
    LOCATE 20, 36
    PRINT TIME$;

'    ---- Restore the original cursor position.

    LOCATE yPos%, xPos%
RETURN

'    ---- The DisplayHelpScreen routine calls Help to display
'         a list of brief program descriptions. The MenuPlus%
'         function calls this routine whenever the user presses
'         the F1 function key.

DisplayHelpScreen:

'    ---- Temporarily turn off the TIMER trap, and display the help screen.

    TIMER STOP
    CLS
    Help

'    ---- When the user is finished with the help screen, restore
'         the main menu to its original status.

    LOCATE 2, 32
    PRINT "Program Selection"
    LOCATE 22, 31
    PRINT "Press <F1> for help."
    DisplayMenuBox programMenu$(), dummy%, promptStr$, okStr$

'    ---- If the user had pressed a menu selection before pressing
'         the F1 function key, display the selection and the appropriate
'         message below the menu box.

    IF inChoice% <> 0 THEN
        answer$ = MID$(okStr$, inChoice%, 1)
        PRINT answer$
        LOCATE 17, 23, 0
        PRINT "<Enter> to confirm; <Esc> to redo."
    END IF
```

(continued)

Figure 9-3. *continued*

```
'    ---- Turn the TIMER trap back on.

     TIMER ON
RETURN

SUB DisplayMenuBox (choiceList$(), leftCoord%, prompt$, ok$)

'    The DisplayMenuBox subprogram displays the menu choices on the
'         screen and prepares the prompt string and validation string.
'         This routine is called by the Menu% function.

'    ---- Find the number of choices (numChoices%); initialize variables.

     numChoices% = UBOUND(choiceList$)
     prompt$ = " "
     ok$ = ""
     longChoice% = 0

'    ---- Prepare the prompt string (prompt$) and the string of
'         legal input characters (ok$). Also, find the length of
'         the longest choice string (longChoice%).

     FOR i% = 1 TO numChoices%
         first$ = UCASE$(LEFT$(choiceList$(i%), 1))
         ok$ = ok$ + first$
         prompt$ = prompt$ + first$ + "  "
         longTemp% = LEN(choiceList$(i%))
         IF longTemp% > longChoice% THEN longChoice% = longTemp%
     NEXT i%

     longChoice% = longChoice% + 1
     prompt$ = prompt$ + "-> "

'    ---- Test to see if the prompt string is longer than longChoice%.

     IF LEN(prompt$) >= longChoice% THEN longChoice% = LEN(prompt$) + 1

'    ---- Given longChoice% and numChoices%, determine the dimensions
'         of the menu frame. Draw the frame, calling on the Frame
'         subprogram.
```

DisplayMenuBox

(continued)

Figure 9-3. *continued*

```
        leftCoord% = 37 - longChoice% \ 2
        rightCoord% = 80 - leftCoord%
        topCoord% = 3
        bottomCoord% = 10 + numChoices%
        Frame leftCoord%, rightCoord%, topCoord%, bottomCoord%

    '   ---- Display the menu choices. The first letter of each choice is
    '        displayed in uppercase, followed by a parenthesis character.

        FOR i% = 1 TO numChoices%
            LOCATE 6 + i%, leftCoord% + 3
            PRINT UCASE$(LEFT$(choiceList$(i%), 1)) + ")" + MID$(choiceList$(i%), 2)
        NEXT i%

        LOCATE 4, 38: PRINT "Menu"
        line$ = STRING$(longChoice%, 196)
        LOCATE 5, leftCoord% + 3: PRINT line$
        LOCATE 7 + numChoices%, leftCoord% + 3: PRINT line$

    '   ---- Print the input prompt.

        LOCATE 9 + numChoices%, leftCoord% + 3: PRINT prompt$;

END SUB

SUB Frame (left%, right%, top%, bottom%) STATIC

    '   The Frame subprogram draws a rectangular double-line frame on
    '        the screen, using "text-graphics" characters from the
    '        IBM Extended ASCII character set.

    '   ---- Draw the four corners.

        LOCATE top%, left%: PRINT CHR$(201)
        LOCATE top%, right%: PRINT CHR$(187)
        LOCATE bottom%, left%: PRINT CHR$(200);
        LOCATE bottom%, right%: PRINT CHR$(188);

    '   ---- Draw the vertical lines.

        FOR vert% = top% + 1 TO bottom% - 1
            LOCATE vert%, left%: PRINT CHR$(186);
            LOCATE vert%, right%: PRINT CHR$(186);
        NEXT vert%
```

`Frame`

(continued)

Figure 9-3. *continued*

```
'    ---- Draw the horizontal lines.

     horiz% = right% - left% - 1
     hline$ = STRING$(horiz%, 205)
     LOCATE top%, left% + 1: PRINT hline$
     LOCATE bottom%, left% + 1: PRINT hline$;

END SUB

SUB Help

'    The Help subprogram displays a list of brief program descriptions
'        on the screen.  This routine is called as a result of an ON KEY
'        error trap whenever the user presses the F1 function key.

     CLS
     PRINT
     PRINT "    Program"; TAB(20); "Description"
     PRINT "    -------"; TAB(20); "-----------"
     PRINT
     PRINT "    List";
     PRINT TAB(20); "Displays MS-DOS directories. (Send a"
     PRINT TAB(20); "parameter of /H to view a help screen.)"
     PRINT
     PRINT "    21";
     PRINT TAB(20); "Plays the game of 21, or Blackjack."
     PRINT
     PRINT "    Survey";
     PRINT TAB(20); "Stores, prints, and tabulates results from"
     PRINT TAB(20); "survey questionnaires or opinion polls."
     PRINT
     PRINT "    Employee";
     PRINT TAB(20); "Maintains an employee database and allows"
     PRINT TAB(20); "searching, changing, deleting, and printing"
     PRINT TAB(20); "of database records. (Stores the database in"
     PRINT TAB(20); "EMP.DAT and the database index in EMP.NDX.)"
     PRINT
     PRINT "    QuickChart";
     PRINT TAB(20); "Creates column charts, line charts, and pie"
     PRINT TAB(20); "charts. Data can be read from the keyboard"
     PRINT TAB(20); "or from data files (including SYLK files)."
     PRINT
```

Help

(continued)

Figure 9-3. *continued*

```
        Frame 1, 67, 1, 21
        PRINT
        PRINT "    ";
        Pause
        CLS

END SUB

FUNCTION MenuPlus% (choices$()) STATIC

'   The MenuPlus% function displays a menu on the screen and
'       elicits a menu choice from the user. MenuPlus% receives a
'       string array (choices$()) containing the menu choices
'       and returns an integer indicating the user's
'       selection from among those choices.

'    ---- This version of the routine illustrates event trapping.

        listLength% = UBOUND(choices$)
        DisplayMenuBox choices$(), leftMargin%, promptStr$, okStr$

'    ---- Get a menu choice. Validate and verify the choice.

        ON TIMER(1) GOSUB DisplayDateAndTime
        TIMER ON

        ON KEY(1) GOSUB DisplayHelpScreen
        KEY(1) ON

        controlKeys$ = CHR$(13) + CHR$(27)
        DO
            LOCATE , , 1
            charPos% = 0
            DO
                answer$ = UCASE$(INKEY$)
                IF answer$ <> "" THEN
                    charPos% = INSTR(okStr$, answer$)
                    IF charPos% = 0 THEN BEEP
                END IF
            LOOP UNTIL charPos% > 0
```

MenuPlus%

(continued)

Figure 9-3. *continued*

```
        PRINT answer$
        LOCATE 11 + listLength%, 23, 0
        PRINT "<Enter> to confirm; <Esc> to redo."
        inChoice% = charPos%

        charPos% = 0
        DO
            answer$ = INKEY$
            IF answer$ <> "" THEN
                charPos% = INSTR(controlKeys$, answer$)
                IF charPos% = 0 THEN BEEP
            END IF
        LOOP UNTIL charPos% > 0

        IF charPos% = 1 THEN
            done% = true%
            CLS
        ELSE
            done% = false%
            LOCATE 11 + listLength%, 23: PRINT SPACE$(35)
            LOCATE 9 + listLength%, leftMargin% + 3 + LEN(promptStr$)
            PRINT " ";
            LOCATE , POS(0) - 1
            inChoice% = 0
        END IF
    LOOP UNTIL done%

    MenuPlus% = inChoice%
    TIMER OFF
    KEY(1) OFF

END FUNCTION

SUB Pause

'   The Pause subprogram pauses until the user presses the spacebar.

    PRINT "Press the spacebar to continue.";
    DO
        ch$ = INKEY$
    LOOP UNTIL ch$ = " "

END SUB
```

Pause

INDEX

Special Characters

A

B

C

DOUGLAS HERGERT

A native Californian, Douglas Hergert received a bachelor's degree in English and French from Washington University, St. Louis, Missouri, in 1974. After graduation, he spent five years in the Peace Corps teaching English in Afghanistan and Senegal. Doug is the author of more than a dozen books, including **COMMAND PERFORMANCE: dBASE III PLUS, COMMAND PERFORMANCE: MICROSOFT EXCEL,** and **MICROSOFT EXCEL WITH MACROS,** all published by Microsoft Press.

OTHER TITLES FROM MICROSOFT® PRESS

MICROSOFT® QUICKBASIC PROGRAMMER'S TOOLBOX
An Essential Library of More Than 250 Functions, Routines, and Utilities for Supercharging QuickBASIC Programs
John Clark Craig

Multiply the power and speed of your Microsoft QuickBASIC programs. MICROSOFT QUICKBASIC PROGRAMMER'S TOOLBOX is an unrivaled collection of more than 250 helpful functions, subprograms, and utilities for both novices and professional programmers. The subprograms are easily referenced and address both common and unusual programming tasks: ANSI.SYS screen control, printer control, mouse interface routines, pop-up windows, fonts, graphics, editor routines, and more. Each function and subprogram is creative and practical, and each takes maximum advantage of Microsoft QuickBASIC's capabilities. This reference also contains a detailed section on interlanguage calling techniques, with examples.

512 pages, softcover $22.95   ISBN 1-55615-127-6

MICROSOFT® QUICKBASIC: PROGRAMMER'S QUICK REFERENCE
Kris Jamsa

Now you can have instant answers to all your Microsoft QuickBASIC questions! This handy guide puts essential information at your fingertips. Organized alphabetically for quick access, the guide covers every Microsoft QuickBASIC statement and function. Each entry contains a concise description of the statement or function, exact syntax and calling sequences, usage notes, and practical examples.

144 pages, softcover $6.95   ISBN 1-55615-204-3

ADVANCED MS-DOS® PROGRAMMING, 2nd ed.
The Microsoft® Guide for Assembly Language and C Programmers
Ray Duncan

Now completely updated with new data and programming advice, ADVANCED MS-DOS PROGRAMMING covers ROM BIOS for the IBM® PC, PC/AT,® PS/2,® and related peripherals including disk drives, video adapters, and pointing devices; MS-DOS through version 4; writing "well-behaved" *vs* "hardware-dependent" applications; version 4 of the Lotus®/Intel®/Microsoft Expanded Memory Specification; and compatibility considerations for OS/2. Ray Duncan, DOS authority and noted columnist, explores key programming topics including character devices, mass storage, memory allocation and management, and process management. In addition, a healthy assortment of updated assembly language and C listings range from programming samples to full-length utilities. The examples were developed using the Microsoft Macro Assembler version 5.1 and Microsoft C Compiler version 5.1. And the reference section, detailing each MS-DOS function and interrupt, is virtually a book within a book.

688 pages, softcover $24.95   ISBN 1-55615-157-8

THE MS-DOS® ENCYCLOPEDIA

General Editor: Ray Duncan
Foreword by Bill Gates

If you're a serious MS-DOS programmer, this is the ultimate reference. THE MS-DOS ENCYCLOPEDIA is an unmatched sourcebook for version-specific technical data, including annotations of more than 100 system function calls, each accompanied by C-callable assembly language routines. You'll find version-specific descriptions and usage information on each of the 90 MS-DOS user commands—the most comprehensive ever assembled. Articles cover debugging, TSRs, installable device drivers, writing applications for upward compatibility, and much more. THE MS-DOS ENCYCLOPEDIA contains hundreds of hands-on examples, thousands of lines of code, and an index to commands and topics. Covers MS-DOS through version 3.2, with a special section on version 3.3.

1600 pages, softcover $69.95   ISBN 1-55615-174-8

MS-DOS® FUNCTIONS: PROGRAMMER'S QUICK REFERENCE

Ray Duncan

This great quick reference is full of the kind of information every programmer —professional or casual—needs right at his or her fingertips. You'll find clearly organized data on each MS-DOS system service call (accessed via Interrupts 20H through 2FH) along with a list of the parameters it requires, the results it returns, version dependencies, and valuable programming notes. Duncan also includes special programming notes, uses, and warnings. Covers MS-DOS through version 4.

128 pages, softcover $5.95   ISBN 1-55615-128-4

MICROSOFT® QUICKC® PROGRAMMING
The Microsoft Guide to Using the QuickC Compiler

The Waite Group: Mitchell Waite, Stephen Prata, Bryan Costales, and Harry Henderson

The Waite Group, widely noted for its C expertise, teaches you how to master QuickC's built-in libraries; work creatively with strings, arrays, pointers, structures, and unions; manage file input and output; use the graphics modes and the built-in graphics library; debug your source code; and smoothly complete other essential QuickC programming tasks. A detailed overview of the language elements gets you started. And the scores of programming examples and tips show you how to manipulate QuickC's variable types, decision structures, functions, and pointers; how to program using the Graphics Library; how to port Pascal programs to QuickC; how to interface your QuickC programs with assembly language; how to use the powerful source-level debugger; and more. If you're new to C or familiar with Microsoft QuickBASIC or Pascal, MICROSOFT QUICKC PROGRAMMING is for you. If you're a seasoned programmer, you'll find solid, reliable information that's available nowhere else.

624 pages, softcover $19.95   ISBN 1-55615-048-2

MICROSOFT® QUICKC®: PROGRAMMER'S QUICK REFERENCE

Kris Jamsa

Whether you're new to Microsoft QuickC or a veteran, here's concise, handy information you'll want at your fingertips while you program. In addition to providing a brief overview of QuickC—its graphical user interface, program listings, compiler restrictions, and programs—Jamsa covers installing and starting up the QuickC programming environment, accessing QuickC help and the run-time library, debugging your programs, developing large libraries and programs in QuickC, and more. A final section includes a complete listing of QuickC compiler error messages.

176 pages, softcover $6.95   ISBN 1-55615-200-0

MICROSOFT® MOUSE PROGRAMMER'S REFERENCE

Microsoft Press and the Hardware Division of Microsoft Corporation

Currently attached to almost two million personal computers, the Microsoft Mouse is one of the world's most popular PC peripherals and an industry standard. Now a team of experts from Microsoft Press and the Hardware Division, Microsoft Corporation, has written an unprecedented guide that gives programmers all the information they need to add valuable mouse support to their programs. MICROSOFT MOUSE PROGRAMMER'S REFERENCE is both an essential reference to the mouse programming interface and a handbook for writing functional mouse menus. And this special package includes two 5.25-inch companion disks that contain MOUSE.LIB and EGA.LIB; sample mouse menus; and an extensive collection of programming examples in BASIC, Microsoft QuickBASIC, Microsoft QuickC,® Microsoft C, Pascal, Microsoft Macro Assembler, and FORTRAN.

336 pages, softcover with two 5.25-inch disks $29.95   ISBN 1-55615-191-8

THE *NEW* PETER NORTON PROGRAMMER'S GUIDE TO THE IBM® PC & PS/2®
The Ultimate Reference Guide to the Entire Family of IBM Personal Computers

Peter Norton and Richard Wilton

This revised and updated edition of the THE PETER NORTON PROGRAMMER'S GUIDE TO THE IBM PC will help intermediate and advanced programmers create effective, portable business and professional programs. Norton and Wilton give you practical advice on programming methods and techniques to create simple, clean programs that are portable among all current IBM machines. Updated material covers the 80286 and 80386 microprocessors; the enhanced keyboard, interrupts, device drivers, and video programming; the VGA and MCGA; the PS/2 ROM BIOS; programming in C, Microsoft QuickBASIC, and Turbo Pascal®; and more.

528 pages, softcover $22.95   ISBN 1-55615-131-4

The manuscript for this book was prepared and submitted to Microsoft Press in electronic form. Text files were processed and formatted using Microsoft Word.

Cover design by Greg Hickman
Interior text design by Darcie S. Furlan
Principal typography by Ruth Pettis
Principal production art by Peggy Herman

Text composition by Microsoft Press in Baskerville with display in Avant Garde Demi, using the Magna composition system and the Linotronic 300 laser imagesetter.